PLAC

ORIGINAL NARRATIVES
OF EARLY AMERICAN HISTORY

REPRODUCED UNDER THE AUSPICES OF THE
AMERICAN HISTORICAL ASSOCIATION

GENERAL EDITOR, J. FRANKLIN JAMESON, PH.D., LL.D., LITT.D.

DIRECTOR OF THE DEPARTMENT OF HISTORICAL RESEARCH IN THE
CARNEGIE INSTITUTION OF WASHINGTON

ORIGINAL NARRATIVES
OF EARLY AMERICAN HISTORY

BRADFORD'S HISTORY
OF PLYMOUTH PLANTATION,

1606—1646

EDITED BY

WILLIAM T. DAVIS

FORMERLY PRESIDENT OF THE PILGRIM SOCIETY

New York

BARNES & NOBLE, INC.

F
68
.B79
1964

CONTENTS

BRADFORD'S HISTORY OF PLYMOUTH PLANTATION

EDITED BY WILLIAM T. DAVIS

CONTENTS

BOOK 2

1620

1621

1622

1623

1624

CONTENTS

CONTENTS

1642

1643

1644

1645

1646

CONTENTS

NOTE

THE text followed in this edition of Bradford is that of the text-edition published by the Commonwealth of Massachusetts in 1898, which Mr. Davis assured me was unusually accurate. In all cases where doubt seemed warranted, comparison was made with the excellent facsimile mentioned in the editor's Introduction, and in a few cases with the original manuscript. But in some particulars a systematic departure has been made from the practice followed in the Massachusetts edition. That edition prints the symbols &, y^e, y^t and y^{ev}, and the contractions wth and w^{ch}, as they stand in the manuscript. In this edition I have followed what is believed to be a better practice, by giving to these manuscript marks the form which, we may presume, they would have borne in print if Bradford's manuscript had been printed in his lifetime; i. e., I have printed, for the above, the words *and*, *the*, *that*, *they*, *with* and *which*. Also, where the original places a short line over a letter, to indicate the omission of an *m* or an *n* directly following it, I have substituted the missing letter itself, as would commonly have been done in seventeenth-century printing; and have disregarded Bradford's underscoring or italicizing of words whenever it seemed to have no significance, or a significance other than that now conveyed by italics. Names of ships have been uniformly set in italics. Bradford's frequent use of parentheses in place of commas has not been followed.

The notes which Bradford appended to his text, often writing them on the margins of his pages, have been reproduced in the foot-notes of the present edition, but have been distinguished from the editor's notes by placing them in quotation-marks, and adding "Br." or some less abbreviated indication of their authorship. The notes which are attributed to Rev. Thomas Prince in this edition are notes which he wrote on the manuscript while it was in his posses-sion. Not all his notes have been repeated in these pages. The dates which are given in square brackets in the headlines of the pages may be understood to indicate years beginning on the

1

first of January, rather than, according to Bradford's custom, on the twenty-fifth of March.

To the note on p. 79 a reference might well be added to Mr. Reginald G. Marsden's article on the *Mayflower* in the *English Historical Review*, XIX 669–680, in which he essays to identify the famous *Mayflower* from among the many contemporary ships of that name, to show it to have been a ship of Harwich, and to trace its history from 1609 to 1626, when he supposes it to have been captured by Dunkirkers. To Mr. Davis the identification seemed "not proven;" the general editor would have been disposed to adopt it.

When this volume had nearly passed through the press, on December 3, 1907, its editor, Hon. William T. Davis, of Plymouth, died at the age of eighty-five. A native of Plymouth and a devoted and public-spirited citizen of that town, he had served for many years as vice-president and president of the Pilgrim Society, had edited the published records of the town, and had written, among other historical works, a *History of Plymouth* and a book of antiquarian research entitled *Ancient Landmarks of Plymouth*, both highly regarded. He was a man of high and genial character. Of this volume, his last work, he had finished his reading of the proof-sheets, except the very last pages, at the time of his death.

J. F. J.

INTRODUCTION

THE new liturgy adopted by the English Church at the time of the Reformation retained some features, to which, as relics of Romanism, a considerable body of the church refused to conform. They remained, however, within the fold of the church endeavoring to purify it from every taint of the old religion. These were called Puritans. Another body, under the pressure of persecution, were not long content with objections to a ritual, but resenting prelatical power abandoned the church and organized congregations of their own. These were called Separatists.

A biographical sketch of Governor Bradford must necessarily include a reference to the Separatist movement, with which he became early associated. Like an epidemic, which when checked in one locality breaks out in a far distant one, the seed of Separatism, when blasted in the ecclesiastical environment of London and its neighborhood, found a lodgment in more congenial soil in districts farther north. On or near the line of what was once called the great North Road were the town of Gainsborough in Lincolnshire and the villages of Austerfield and Bawtry in Yorkshire and Scrooby and Babworth in Nottinghamshire. Bawtry, the present railroad centre of these places, lies on the line of the Great Northern Railway, 151½ miles from London. It contains perhaps a population of about five hundred, but it is chiefly interesting as a convenient stopping-place for visitors to Austerfield, the birthplace of Governor Bradford, a mile or more away on the north, and to Scrooby, the birthplace of the Pilgrim Church, a mile or more away on the south. The student of Pilgrim history will recognize on its store-signs a number of names held by the families in Plymouth and its neighborhood to-day.

In the district including the places above mentioned, the two clergymen, especially distinguished in the early Separatist movement about the time of the close of Elizabeth's reign, and in the early years of King James, were Richard Clyfton and John Smyth, both of whom were Cambridge University men. Smyth appears to have been settled as a pastor of the established church in Lincoln until some time in 1605, when he began to minister to a non-conformist congregation in Gainsborough, from which place he went with his church to Amsterdam in 1606 or 1607.[1] His arrival in Gainsborough is thought by some writers to have been at an earlier period, and these writers have ventured to conjecture that some of those who later organized the Pilgrim Church in Scrooby were guided into the path leading to separatism by attending his ministrations. But after sifting all the evidence which researches up to the present date have disclosed, I have reached the conclusion that Smyth's church was in its origin contemporary with and not antecedent to the church at Scrooby.   With this conclusion, Rev. John Smyth and his church will have no further place in this narrative.

On the other hand, Rev. Richard Clyfton, who had been vicar at Marnham, became rector at Babworth as early as July 11, 1586,[2] when by his ministrations he prepared the way of many to organize the church in Scrooby, ten miles away on the north. Governor Bradford in his history calls him "a grave and reverend preacher, who by his pains and diligence had done much good, and under God had been the means of the conversion of many." He was born in Normanton, Derbyshire, and graduated at Cambridge, but the exact year in which he settled in Babworth is not known.   His assumption of the duties of pastor of the Pilgrim Church in Scrooby probably took place either in the latter part of 1606 or in the early part of 1607.   William Brewster, occupying the manor house

---

[1] See Edward Arber, *The Story of the Pilgrim Fathers* (London, 1897) pp. 48–54.   [2] See Arber, p. 52.

in that town, was the founder of the church, and holding the government office of master of the post in Scrooby from April 1, 1594, to September 30, 1607, it may be fairly conjectured that he could not have been an officer of the crown[1] many months after the organization of a proscribed church.

At this place in our narrative William Bradford enters the scene. His family, deriving its name from the Saxon Bradenford or Bradford, belonged to the yeoman class, and lived in Austerfield, a small town one mile or more from Bawtry, two miles or more from Scrooby, ten miles from Gainsborough, and ten miles from Babworth, and containing a farming population of about three hundred. Coats of arms have been held by Bradford families in Yorkshire and other counties, but there is no evidence that either of these families included the Austerfield Bradfords. In 1575 William Bradford and John Hanson of Austerfield were assessed to the subsidies. The former of these had three sons, Robert, Thomas and William, and died January 10, 1595. The last-named son married January 21, 1584, Alice, daughter of John Hanson, above mentioned, and was the father of William, the future Governor of the Plymouth Colony. William Bradford, the father, died July 15, 1591, leaving his son William, about two years of age, to the care of his uncles. Cotton Mather describes Austerfield at that time as an "obscure village, where the people were as unacquainted with the Bible as the Jews do seem to have been with part of it in the days of Josiah." After a long sickness, when about twelve years of age, young Bradford became much impressed by the Scriptures and by the preaching of Clyfton, to listen to which he was in the habit of walking to Babworth. The inevitable result was the question which he asked himself "whether it was not his duty to withdraw from the communion of the Parish Assemblies and engage with some Society of the Faithful that should keep close unto the written Word of God as the rule of their Worship." After reaching

[1] See Arber, p. 86.

a definite decision to abandon the church and faith of his family he answered their remonstrances by saying: "Were I like to endanger my life or consume my estate by any ungodly courses, your counsels to me were very seasonable. But you know that I have been diligent and provident in my Calling, and not only desirous to augment what I have, but also to enjoy it in your company, to part from which will be as great a cross as can befall me. Nevertheless, to keep a good conscience and walk in such a Way as God has prescribed in his Word, is a thing which I must prefer before you all, and above life itself. Wherefore, since it is for a good Cause that I am likely to suffer the disasters which you lay before me, you have no cause to be either angry with me or sorry for me. Yea, I am not only willing to part with everything that is dear to me in this world for this Cause, but I am also thankful that God hath given me a heart so to do, and will accept me so to suffer for him." Thus in the obscure town of Austerfield, three hundred years ago, the farmer boy spoke words which for all coming time will illustrate his character and illuminate his life. Among the nations of the earth what founder has sanctified his work with such words of godliness, self-sacrifice and duty?

Aside from family ties there was nothing in Austerfield to bind him to his native village. Its people had acquired little education, and its homes were lowly and unattractive. It has no features to-day of any interest to a stranger, except the house in which, according to a doubtful tradition, Bradford was born, and the small and unsightly St. Helen's chapel, a relic of days long before the Reformation, in which, as its register states, William Bradford was baptized by Rev. Henry Fletcher, March 19, 1589-1590.[1]

When it was decided by the Scrooby church to remove to

[1] It has been stated that the Bradford baptismal font was removed many years ago to the Retford church, but I learn from Rev. A. F. Ebworth, the rector of Retford, that this is not true. The font now in the Austerfield church is believed by Rev. Mr. Meredith, the present rector, to be the original Norman font which served at the baptism of Bradford.

Holland, Bradford, then about seventeen years of age, was ready to join them. It was necessary that the removal should be conducted as secretly as possible. A law passed March 23, 1593, requiring non-conformists to abjure the realm, had been repealed February 9, 1598, and the existing law forbade any one to go out of the kingdom without a royal license. Their destined port was Amsterdam, to which they were to proceed by the way of Boston in Lincolnshire. The passage to Boston was probably down the river Idle to Gainsborough, and thence by the River Witham to the seaboard. At that time the Idle was navigable as far up as Bawtry, and until the days of railroads freight was transported from Bawtry by the Idle and the Trent to the seaport of Hull. The attempt to reach Amsterdam was frustrated by the treachery of the captain of the transport engaged to receive the party at Boston, and after the dispersion of its members, and the imprisonment of some, all returned to their homes.

In the spring of 1608 another attempt was made to cross to Holland from the river Humber, near Grimsby, on a Dutch vessel engaged for the purpose. The Humber was reached by way of the Idle and the Trent, but after a portion of the party had gone on board, armed emissaries appeared on the shore and dispersed the remainder. The vessel sailed with those who had embarked, including Bradford, and after a narrow escape from wreck, reached Amsterdam in safety. At various times afterwards, those who were left behind reached Amsterdam, and before the close of the summer the whole congregation, including their pastors, Clyfton and Robinson, had reached that city. When the Privy Council was notified of the arrests, the persons arrested were soon released, the authorities doubtless believing it would be better to have them out of the kingdom than in. Bradford on his arrival in Holland was put under arrest for a time, but was soon released by the magistrates.

For reasons not necessary to explain in this narrative, the members of the Scrooby church, including Bradford, removed to Leyden in 1609, and made that place their home. According to Cotton Mather, it appears that while in Amsterdam Bradford was employed by a Frenchman in "the working of silks," and that about 1611, having come of age, he sold out his inheritance and converted it into money. While in Leyden he engaged in the business of making fustian, a kind of ribbed cloth like corduroy or velveteen, a business which Mather hints did not prove profitable. The records of the Stadhuis, or City Hall, in Leyden, show that the first publication of his bans of marriage was made on November 8, 1613, and that on November 30 William Bradford, fustian maker, a young man of Austerfield, in England, was married to Dorothy May of "Wizbuts."[1] Little besides the above is known of Bradford's career while in Leyden. To the older members of the church, John Carver, Robert Cushman and William Brewster, were intrusted the negotiations for their emigration to America, but it is evident that by study and industry, and the display of a trustworthy judgment, he was laying the foundation for the estimate in which he came to be held by the colonists. Mather says that at a later period "he attained unto a notable skill in language. The Dutch tongue was become almost as vernacular to him as the English. The French tongue he could also manage. The Latin and Greek he had mastered. But the Hebrew he most of all studied, because, he said, he would see with his own eyes the ancient oracles of God in their native beauty."

Nothing more is known concerning Bradford until after the arrival of the *Mayflower* in Cape Cod harbor on November 11, 1620. On that day an expedition was fitted out to explore the land, consisting of sixteen men under the command of Myles Standish, to whom were added as counsel William Bradford, Stephen Hopkins and Edward Tilley. The expedition returned on the 17th, reporting among other incidents

---

[1] Wisbech or Wisbeach, a municipal borough on the river Wen, in Cambridgeshire.

the entanglement of Bradford in an Indian deer-trap made with a noose attached to a bent tree.

On the 27th another expedition was fitted out under the command of Captain Jones of the *Mayflower*, of thirty or more whose names are not recorded, but which probably included Bradford. This expedition returned to the ship on the 29th and 30th, without results important to our narrative. On December 6 a third expedition was fitted away in the shallop with the determination to find, if possible, a suitable place for a permanent settlement. The following persons composed the shallop's party: Myles Standish, John Carver, William Bradford, Edward Winslow, John Tilley, Edward Tilley, John Howland, Richard Warren, Stephen Hopkins, Edward Doty, John Allerton, Thomas English, John Clark, mate, Robert Coppin, pilot, the master gunner and three sailors, eighteen in all. On the 8th, at a place now known as Eastham, they had an encounter with the Indians, and on the 11th landed at Plymouth, after spending Saturday the 9th and Sunday the 10th on Clarke's Island, at the entrance of Plymouth harbor. The landing at Plymouth on December 11, old style, was the historic landing.

On December 12th the expedition returned to the ship and learned the sad news of the death by drowning, December 7, of Dorothy the wife of Bradford. On the 16th the ship reached Plymouth harbor, where she remained until April 5, when she sailed for England. It is recorded that on "Thursday the 11th [of January] William Bradford being at work, for it was a fair day,[1] was vehemently taken with a grief and pain, and so shot to his huckle-bone it was doubted that he would have instantly died. He got cold in the former Discoveries, especially the last, and felt some pain in his ankles by times. But he grew a little better towards night, and in time, through God's

[1] The only positive information concerning the weather in Plymouth during the winter of 1620, is contained in a letter from Thomas White of Dorchester, in 1630, to a friend in England, which stated that a colony landed at Plymouth ten years before, when there was a foot of snow on the ground.

mercy in the use of means, recovered." On Friday the 19th, while Bradford lay sick in the rendezvous or common house, the building was burned, but he escaped without injury.

And now we have reached the threshold of Bradford's career, as governor of the Plymouth Colony. About the middle of April John Carver, who had been governor up to that time, died, and Bradford was chosen to succeed him. Winslow and Standish were comparatively recent members of the Pilgrim company, and Brewster was the elder, but Bradford had been a member of the church since the time of its organization in 1606, and his companions had discovered in him traits which suggested him at once as the man to take Carver's place.

Before Governor Carver died he had executed a treaty with Massasoit, the aim of which was to secure peace with the Indians, and one of the first acts of Bradford was to send a mission consisting of Winslow and Hopkins to the home of the great chief to more thoroughly confirm amicable relations between the natives and the colony. In September he sent ten men in the shallop to Massachusetts to examine what is now Boston harbor, and to trade with the Indians. In November it became necessary on the arrival of the *Fortune* with thirty-five passengers to provide for their comfort, and to arrange for a cargo of beaver skins and clapboards for her return voyage. A more important affair, however, was to be settled before the *Fortune* returned, which required tact and judgment. An unsatisfactory contract between Robert Cushman, the agent of the colonists, and the merchant adventurers in London had been drawn up before the *Mayflower* sailed from Southampton, which the colonists refused to sign, and the *Mayflower* sailed without its execution. Cushman came out in the *Fortune* to secure the necessary signatures of the colonists, and what is called a sermon delivered by him in the "common house" was clearly a speech to induce the colonists to close the contract. He was successful in his mission, and returned to England with the contract signed.

The winter and early spring of 1621 must be assigned as the period when Bradford first appeared as an author. In 1622 a book was printed in London entitled *A Relation or Journal of the Beginning and Proceedings of the English Plantation settled at Plymouth in New England*, commonly called "Mourt's Relation," the chief feature of which is a journal kept by William Bradford from the date of the departure of the *Mayflower* from old Plymouth on Wednesday, September 6, 1620, to Friday, March 23, on which day John Carver was chosen governor. The other contents of the book are a letter from John Robinson, written at the time of the departure of the *Mayflower* from England, four narratives of missions to Massasoit, to Nauset, to Nemasket and to Massachusetts; a letter from Edward Winslow, probably to George Morton, dated Plymouth in New England, December 11, 1621, and a statement by Robert Cushman on the lawfulness of moving out of England. It contains also a letter from R. G. to his much respected friend, Mr. J. P., dated Plymouth, in New England, and a notice to the reader, signed G. Mourt. The paging begins with the journal, and runs through seventy-two pages.

Inasmuch as Bradford was its chief author, I will attempt to clear up some of the mystery which has heretofore surrounded this interesting and valuable book. It has been assumed by former writers that the journal, the four narratives and the letter of Winslow were sent to England by the hand of Robert Cushman, who came out and returned in the *Fortune*, and were published by George Morton, who signed himself G. Mourt. I venture, however, to suggest that the journal of Bradford was sent to England by the *Mayflower*, which sailed on April 5, and not by the *Fortune*. This suggestion is strengthened by the probability that Bradford would wish to improve the first opportunity to send to friends in England an account of the voyage of the *Mayflower*, and of the incidents occurring since her arrival. Another conjecture naturally follows, that the narratives of the visits to Massasoit and to

Massachusetts, which bear internal evidence of having been written by Winslow, together with his letter, were sent to George Morton by the *Fortune*, while the Nauset and Nemasket narratives, written probably by Richard Gardiner and some other author, were sent to John Pierce, a friend of the Pilgrims, and later were delivered to Morton.

The assumption of Dr. Young, approved by Dr. Dexter and other writers, that the initials R. G. attached to the letter to J. P., were a misprint for R. C., and that Robert Cushman was the author, will not bear a close investigation. It is argued in its support that the author could not have been Richard Gardiner, who was the only *Mayflower* passenger with the initials R. G., because, first, he was an humble member of the colony who would not have referred to the other narratives in the book, including those of Bradford and Winslow, as "writ by the several actors themselves, after their plain and rude manner . . . better acquainted with planting than writing"; secondly, that his feeble interest in the colony is shown by the fact that he did not remain there long enough to share in the division of lands in the spring of 1624; and thirdly, that Bradford says in his history that Gardiner became a seaman, and died in England or at sea.

The answers to these arguments are, first, the presumption that there was no misprint; secondly, that Gardiner's place at the end of Bradford's list of passengers was naturally among those having no families, and not necessarily because he was among the less conspicuous, and further, that (as above suggested) the journal of Bradford had been sent by the *Mayflower*, while the narratives and letter written by Winslow were not those referred to by Gardiner, having been inclosed directly to George Morton, but were the narratives of himself and another of visits to Nauset and Nemasket; thirdly, that Gardiner did share in the division of lands in 1624, receiving one acre on the south side of the brook, and may have been a valued member of the colony five or six years, and that the fact that he became a seaman (not necessarily a mere sailor) does not prove his unfitness as a writer, and finally, the letter in question clearly shows that its author must have been one of the *Mayflower* passengers.[1]

It must be remembered that the *Fortune* was captured on her way home by a French man-of-war, and that the official complaints[2] against the outrages perpetrated by the master of the ship contained the specification "that he sent for all their letters; opened and kept what he pleased; especially, though he was much intreated to the contrary, a letter written by the Governor of our Colony in New England, containing a general relation of all matters there." This relation, written by Bradford as governor, was probably a continuation of that which, according to my theory, was sent by him, not yet governor, on the *Mayflower*. Its existence and loss confirm my theory, and lead to the further suggestion that some of the narratives sent to John Pierce, may have been also stolen.

[1] The letter of R. G. was as follows: "To his much respected friend Mr. J. P. Good friend: As we cannot but account it an extraordinary blessing of God in directing our course for these parts, after we came out of our native country, for that we had the happiness to be possessed of the comforts we receive by the benefit of one of the most pleasant, most healthful and most fruitful parts of the world, so must we acknowledge the same blessing to be multiplied upon our whole Company for that we obtained the honor to receive allowance and approbation of our free possession and enjoying thereof, under the authority of those thrice honored persons, the President and Council for the Affairs of New England; by whose bounty and grace in that behalf all of us are tied to dedicate our best service unto them, as those under His Majesty that we owe it unto, whose noble endeavors in these their actions the God of Heaven and earth multiply to his glory and their own eternal comforts.

"As for this poor *Relation*, I pray you to accept it, as being writ by the several actors themselves after their plain and rude manner. Therefore doubt nothing of the truth thereof. If it be defective in any thing, it is their ignorance that are better acquainted with planting than writing. If it satisfy those that are well affected to the business, it is all I care for. Sure I am the place we are in, and the hopes that are apparent cannot but suffice any that will not desire more then enough. Neither is there want of aught among us but company, to enjoy the blessings so plentifully bestowed upon the inhabitants that are here. While I was a writing this, I had almost forgot that I had but the recommendation of the *Relation* itself to your further consideration, and therefore I will end without saying more, save that I shall always rest, Yours in the way of Friendship,

R. G."

[2] See list of complaints in Arber, p. 507.

Of this valuable book only seven copies of the first edition are extant as far as I know, six of which are in the libraries of Harvard College, Yale College, the Lenox Library, the Library Company of Philadelphia, the Pilgrim Society of Plymouth, and the British Museum. The seventh is in a private library. The following entire or partial reprints of Mourt's Relation have been published. In 1624 an abstract was printed by John Smith in his *Generall Historie;* in 1625 it was published in a condensed form in the *Pilgrims* of Purchas, and in 1802 in the same form in the *Collections of the Massachusetts Historical Society*. The portion omitted by Purchas was printed in the above collections in 1822. In 1841 Rev. Dr. Alexander Young printed the whole work in a book entitled *Chronicles of the Pilgrim Fathers*. In 1848 Rev. George B. Cheever published the whole, and in 1865 Rev. Dr. Henry M. Dexter published a literal reprint. In 1897 Edward Arber published the entire book in London in his *Story of the Pilgrim Fathers*.

The above suggestion which I have ventured to make concerning a book which is the more valuable because it is the foundation stone of American literature, the first book written by permanent American citizens, is submitted to future writers on Pilgrim history for their reconsideration of the statements of Young and Dexter, and others, with some degree of confidence that it will be finally accepted as the only one which clears up the mystery which has heretofore surrounded the book.

William Bradford was chosen governor in 1621, and every year thereafter until 1657, except 1633, 1636 and 1644, when Edward Winslow was chosen, and 1634 and 1638, when Thomas Prence was chosen. To his faithful and judicious administration of affairs it cannot be doubted that the survival and permanent establishment of the Plymouth Colony were mainly due. On August 14, 1623, he married Alice, daughter of Alexander Carpenter and widow of Edward Southworth, who came in the *Anne* in July of that year. By his first wife he had a son, John, born in Leyden, who, coming over at some time later than 1620, lived at various times in Duxbury, Marshfield and Norwich, in which latter place he died childless in 1678. By his second wife he had William, born in 1624, who died in 1704, Mercy, born before 1627, who married Benjamin Vermayes, and Joseph, 1630, who died in 1715.

Governor Bradford owned at various times considerable tracts of land in Plymouth, among which may be mentioned a house and lot on the corner of Main Street and Town Square, and a house and lot near Stony Brook, in that part of Plymouth which was incorporated as Kingston, in 1726, in both of which he at various times made his home.

The *History of Plymouth Plantation* begun by Governor Bradford about the year 1630,[1] and coming down to 1648, has a value which it is impossible to exaggerate. Without it the history of the Plymouth Colony, now so complete, would have been, so far as its early years are concerned, involved in mystery. In a note written by him, found among papers in his pocket-book, he said soon after 1626 "it was God's marvellous Providence that we were able to wade through things as will better appear if God give me life and opportunity to handle them more particularly in another treatise more at large as I desire and purpose (if God permit) with many other things in a better order."

The manuscript had an eventful career.[2] According to an attestation attached to it by Samuel Bradford, dated March 20, 1705, it was given by the governor to his son William, who gave it to his son Major John Bradford, the father of Samuel. The manuscript bears also a memorandum made by Rev. Thomas Prince, dated June 4, 1728, stating that he borrowed it from Major John Bradford, and deposited it, together with

[1] See p. 28, *post.*

[2] See Justin Winsor, "Governor Bradford's Manuscript History of Plymouth Plantation and Its Transmission to Our Times," in the *Proceedings of the Massachusetts Historical Society.* XIX. 106–122.

Governor Bradford's letter-book, in the New England Library
in the tower of the Old South Church in Boston. When Prince
died in 1758 he gave his library to the church. While in the
possession of William, the son of the governor, the manuscript
was used by Nathaniel Morton in the preparation of the
New England's Memorial, published in 1669, and it is known
that later it was used by Prince in his *Chronological History
of New England*, by Hubbard in his *History of New England*,
and by Hutchinson in 1767 in his *History of Massachusetts
Bay*. It is not improbable that it was in Hutchinson's possession when, adhering to the crown, he left the country, and
that in some way before his death in Brompton, near London,
in June, 1780, it reached the Library of the Bishop of London
at Fulham, where it was discovered in 1855. Samuel Wilber-
force, Bishop of Oxford, published in 1844 a history of the
Protestant Episcopal Church in America, in the first edition of
which he referred to a manuscript history of the plantation of
Plymouth, which was recognized by John Wingate Thornton
of Boston, and Rev. J. S. Barry, the author of a history of
Massachusetts, as probably the long-lost history of Bradford.
A copy was at once secured by the Massachusetts Historical
Society, and ably edited by the late Charles Deane of Cam-
bridge, was published in their *Collections* in 1856.

Governor Bradford's letter-book and pocket-book were also
deposited in the New England Library in the tower of the Old
South Church. The former was found in Halifax after the
Revolution in a mutilated condition, and published in the
Collections of the Massachusetts Historical Society, first series,III.
27. The fragment of the letter-book which was recovered
begins with the 339th page, and contains about thirty letters
and original copies of one letter from Bradford to Robert
Cushman, two to Ferdinando Gorges, two to the Council for
New England, and three to the government of New Netherlands. The pocket-book, which was seen by Prince in 1736,
contained a register of deaths from that of Wm. Butten on

board the *Mayflower*, November 6, 1620, to the end of March, 1621. It is irretrievably lost.

The manuscript of the history, after a copy had been secured in 1855, reposed in the Fulham Library until 1897, when after several ineffectual attempts to recover it a renewed effort was made by a formal petition signed by Roger Wolcott, governor of Massachusetts, and others, and filed in the registry of the consistorial and episcopal court of London, by Thomas F. Bayard, the American Ambassador to the Court of St. James, requesting the delivery of the manuscript to the Commonwealth of Massachusetts. On April 12, 1897, a decree was issued, formally surrendering the manuscript to Mr. Bayard in behalf of the State, and its delivery to the governor of Massachusetts by Mr. Bayard was celebrated in a convention of the two houses of the legislature on May 26, 1897, where addresses were made by Senator George F. Hoar, who had been especially active in the recovery of the manuscript, by Mr. Bayard, and by Governor Roger Wolcott. The manuscript is now deposited in the Massachusetts State Library, protected by a fire-proof safe, and is daily exhibited under glass to visitors. A photographic fac-simile of the manuscript was printed in London in 1896, with an introduction by the late John A. Doyle. Besides the two above-mentioned republications the State of Massachusetts published it in 1898 in connection with a report of the proceedings incident to the delivery of the manuscript.

In the same volume with the history but forming no part of it, are eight pages of Hebrew roots and quotations with explanations in English, a reference to which, illustrating as they do the scholarly habits of the author, ought not to be omitted. By way of preface to these pages Bradford wrote,

"Though I am growne aged, yet I have had a longing desire, to see with my own eyes, something of that most ancient language, and holy tongue, in which the Law, and oracles of God were write; and in which God, and angels, spake to the holy patriarks, of old time; and what names were given to things, from the creation. And though I cannot attaine to much herein, yet I am refreshed, to have seen some glimpse hereof; (as Moses saw the Land of canan afarr of). My aime and desire is, to see how the words, and phrases lye in the holy texte; and to dicerne somewhat of the same for my owne contente."

Besides the literary productions of Governor Bradford above mentioned, he left some poetical lines referred to in his will, and others to be found in the Davis edition of Morton's *New England's Memorial*, p. 264, and in the *Collections of the Massachusetts Historical Society*, first series, III. 77, and third series, VII. 27. The lines contained in the former volume, about four hundred in number, written apparently after the death of John Cotton, which occurred in 1652, are interesting as throwing light on the condition of the Plymouth Colony thirty years after its settlement.

He also wrote a dialogue entitled, *A Dialogue or the Sum of a Conference between Some Young Men born in New England and Sundry Ancient Men that came out of Holland and Old England*, written in 1648, and printed for the first time in Dr. Young's *Chronicles of the Pilgrim Fathers* in 1841. In 1855 it was again published in full by the Congregational Board of Publication in a volume containing also Morton's *New England's Memorial*. It may be properly stated here that there is in the cabinet of the Pilgrim Society at Plymouth an original letter from Governor Bradford to Governor Winthrop, dated 1643–1644. Another of his letters, of 1623, recently discovered in the Public Record Office in London, is printed in the *American Historical Review*, VIII. 295–301.

It is unnecessary to refer to those incidents in Bradford's life which are fully described in his history, but such as need elucidation will be further treated in suitable annotations. Mather says in speaking of his death, "at length he fell into an indisposition of body which rendered him unhealthy for a whole winter [1656–1657], and as the Spring advanced his health yet more declined. . . . He died May 9th, 1657, in the

69th [or rather 68th] year of his age; lamented by all the Colonies of New England as a common Blessing and Father to them all."

He was probably buried on the Plymouth Burial Hill. There is a family tradition that his son William on his death-bed expressed a wish to be buried by the side of his father. In 1835 a modest marble obelisk was erected over his supposed grave adjoining the graves of his sons William and Joseph, and in excavating for its foundation relics of an ancient grave were found. It is not certain whether he died in his house on the corner of Main Street and Town Square in Plymouth, or in his house near Stony Brook in what is now Kingston, but the inventory[1] of his estate leads to the conclusion that his residence was in the latter place at the time of his death.[2]

WILLIAM T. DAVIS.

[1] While it is unnecessary to print the entire inventory of Governor Bradford's estate, a judicious selection from its contents will throw light on the personal life of the governor, and on the habits and customs of the Plymouth Colony. Among the articles mentioned are twelve chairs, three carpets, parts of an armor, seventeen sheets, seventy-nine napkins, ninety-odd pounds of pewter, seven porringers, four dozen trenchers, a cloth cloak, clothing including two suits with silver buttons, thirteen silver spoons, two silver beer-bowls, two silver wine-cups, and a case of six knives. There are no buckles, watch, carriage, looking-glass, forks, china or lamps. The value of the entire inventory was one thousand and five pounds and two shillings.

[2] For modern reading in Pilgrim history, the student may turn to J. A. Goodwin, *The Pilgrim Republic* (Boston, 1888), to Rev. John Brown, *The Pilgrim Fathers of New England* (London and New York, 1895), to Arber's book mentioned in previous footnotes, to Dr. Azel Ames's *The May-Flower and Her Log* (Boston, 1901), to Rev. Morton Dexter's *The England and Holland of the Pilgrims* (Boston, 1905), and to W. T. Davis's *Ancient Landmarks of Plymouth* (Boston, 1899).

HISTORY OF PLYMOUTH PLANTATION

HISTORY OF PLYMOUTH PLANTATION[1]

*And first of the occasion and indusments ther unto; the which
that I may truly unfould, I must begine at the very
roote and rise of the same. The which I shall endevor
to manefest in a plaine stile, with singuler regard
unto the simple trueth in all things, at least as near
as my slender judgmente can attaine the same.*

1. Chapter

I<small>T</small> is well knowne unto the godly and judicious, how ever
since the first breaking out of the lighte of the gospell in our
Honourable Nation of England, (which was the first of nations
whom the Lord adorned ther with, affter that grosse darknes
of popery which had covered and overspred the Christian
worled,) what warrs and opposissions ever since, Satan hath
raised, maintained, and continued against the Saincts, from
time to time, in one sorte or other. Some times by bloody
death and cruell torments; other whiles imprisonments,
banishments, and other hard usages; as being loath his kingdom should goe downe, the trueth prevaile, and the churches
of God reverte to their anciente puritie, and recover their
primative order, libertie, and bewtie. But when he could
not prevaile by these means, against the maine trueths of
the gospell, but that they began to take rootting in many
places, being watered with the blooud of the martires, and
blessed from heaven with a gracious encrease; He then begane

---

[1] The exact title which Bradford **gave** to his book, as may be seen from
the original first page, is "Of Plimoth Plantation." The manuscript sign
m̄, is intended for, and is properly represented in print by, *mm*, and in Bradford's text we shall print the name "Plimmoth." But it seems better to use,
for title-page and headings, the conventional title, *History of Plymouth Plantation*, by which the book is commonly known.

to take him to his anciente strategemes, used of old against the first Christians. That when by the bloody and barbarous persecutions of the Heathen Emperours, he could not stoppe and subuerte the course of the gospell, but that it speedily overspred with a wounderfull celeritie the then best known parts of the world, He then begane to sow errours, heresies, and wounderfull dissentions amongst the professours them selves, (working upon their pride and ambition, with other corrupte passions incidente to all mortall men, yea to the saints them selves in some measure,) by which wofull effects followed; as not only bitter contentions, and hartburnings, schismes, with other horrible confusions, but Satan tooke occasion and advantage therby to foyst in a number of vile ceremoneys, with many unproffitable cannons and decrees, which have since been as snares to many poore and peaceable souls even to this day. So as in the anciente times, the persecutions by the heathen and their Emperours, was not greater then of the Christians one against other; the Arians and other their complices against the orthodoxe and true Christians. As witneseth Socrates in his 2. booke. His words are these;[1] *The violence truly* (saith he) *was no less than that of ould practised towards the Christians when they were compelled and drawne to sacrifice to idoles; for many indured sundrie kinds of tormente, often rackings, and dismembering of their joynts; confiscating of ther goods; some bereaved of their native soyle; others departed this life under the hands of the tormentor; and some died in banishmente, and never saw ther cuntrie againe, etc.*

The like methode Satan hath seemed to hold in these later times, since the trueth begane to springe and spread after the great defection made by Antichrist, that man of sinne.

For to let pass the infinite examples in sundrie nations and severall places of the world, and instance in our owne, when as that old serpente could not prevaile by those firie

[1] "Lib. 2 Chap. 22." (Note by Bradford, referring to the *Church History* of Socrates Scholasticus.)

flames and other his cruell tragedies, which he by his instruments put in ure[1] every wher in the days of queene Mary and
before, he then begane an other kind of warre, and went more
closely to worke; not only to oppuggen,[2] but even to ruinate
and destroy the kingdom of Christ, by more secrete and subtile
means, by kindling the flames of contention and sowing the
seeds of discorde and bitter enmitie amongst the proffessors
and seeming reformed them selves. For when he could not
prevaile by the former means against the principall doctrins
of faith, he bente his force against the holy discipline and
outward regimente of the kingdom of Christ, by which those
holy doctrines should be conserved, and true pietie maintained
amongest the saints and people of God.

Mr. Foxe recordeth how that besids those worthy martires
and confessors which were burned in queene Marys days and
otherwise tormented,[3] *many (both students and others) fled
out of the land, to the number of 800. And became severall
congregations. At Wesell, Frankford, Bassill, Emden, Mark-
purge, Strausborugh,[4] and Geneva, etc.* Amongst whom (but
especialy those at Frankford) begane that bitter warr of contention and persecution aboute the ceremonies, and servise-
booke, and other popish and antichristian stuffe, the plague
of England to this day, which are like the highplases in Israell,
which the prophets cried out against, and were their ruine;
which the better parte sought, according to the puritie of the
gospell, to roote out and utterly to abandon. And the other
parte (under veiled pretences) for their ouwn ends and advanc-
ments, sought as stifly to continue, maintaine, and defend. As
appeareth by the discourse therof published in printe, An°:1575;
a booke that deserves better to be knowne and considered.[5]

---

[1] Use. [2] Oppugn, attack.

[3] "Acts and Mon: pag. 1587. editi: 2." (Note by Bradford.) The reference is to John Fox's *Acts and Monuments of the Christian Church*, commonly
called "Fox's Book of Martyrs." [4] Marburg, Strassburg.

[5] This book is entitled *A Brieff Discours off the Troubles begonne at Franck-
ford in Germany, anno Domini* 1554, printed in 1575, and probably written by
William Whittingham, afterward dean of Durham.

The one side laboured to have the right worship of God and discipline of Christ established in the church, according to the simplicitie of the gospell, without the mixture of mens inventions, and to have and to be ruled by the laws of Gods word, dispensed in those offices, and by those officers of Pastors, Teachers, and Elders, etc. according to the Scripturs.[1] The other partie, though under many colours and pretences, endevored to have the episcopall dignitie (affter the popish manner) with their large power and jurisdiction still retained; with all those courts, cannons, and ceremonies, togeather with all such livings, revenues, and subordinate officers, with other such means as formerly upheld their antichristian greatnes, and enabled them with lordly and tyranous power to persecute the poore servants of God. This contention was so great, as neither the honour of God, the commone persecution, nor the mediation of Mr. Calvin and other worthies of the Lord in those places, could prevaile with those thus episcopally minded, but they proceeded by all means to disturbe the peace of this poor persecuted church, even so farr as to charge (very unjustly, and ungodlily, yet prelatelike) some of their cheefe opposers, with rebellion and hightreason against the Emperour,[2] and other such crimes.

And this contention dyed not with queene Mary, nor was left beyonde the seas, but at her death these people returning into England under gracious queene Elizabeth, many of

[1] Authorities differ so much concerning pastors, teachers and elders in the Congregational churches that it is difficult to define their functions and duties. Indeed each church seems to have had rules of its own concerning them. According to the Cambridge Platform the pastor attended to exhortation; taught the word of God; prayed for the flock; administered the communion, and visited the sick. The teacher attended to the doctrine and was an assistant of the pastor. The duty of the elder was to call the church together, to prepare matters for church meetings, to act as moderator and guide and lead in church meetings, and in the absence of the pastor to preach. The church in Salem never had an elder, and Thomas Faunce, who died in 1745, was the last elder of the Plymouth church. After his death the office of elder was obsolete.

[2] The accusation was made at Frankfort in 1555 against John Knox, by some partisan of Richard Cox, in the course of the struggle between the two parties.

them being preferred to bishopricks and other promotions, according to their aimes and desires, that inveterate hatered against the holy discipline of Christ in his church hath continued to this day. In somuch that for fear it should preveile, all plotts and devices have been used to keepe it out, incensing the queene and state against it as dangerous for the common wealth; and that it was most needfull that the fundamentall poynts of Religion should be preached in those ignorante and superstitious times; and to winne the weake and ignorante, they might retaine diverse harmles ceremoneis; and though it were to be wished that diverse things were reformed, yet this was not a season for it. And many the like, to stop the mouthes of the more godly, to bring them over to yeeld to one ceremoney after another, and one corruption after another; by these wyles begyleing some and corrupting others till at length they begane to persecute all the zealous professors in the land (though they knew little what this discipline mente) both by word and deed, if they would not submitte to their ceremonies, and become slaves to them and their popish trash, which have no ground in the word of God, but are relikes of that man of sine. And the more the light of the gospell grew, the more they urged their subscriptions to these corruptions. So as (notwithstanding all their former pretences and fair colures) they whose eyes God had not justly blinded might easily see wherto these things tended. And to cast contempte the more upon the sincere servants of God, they opprobriously and most injuriously gave unto, and imposed upon them, that name of Puritans, which [it] is said the Novatians out of prid did assume and take unto themselves.[1] And lamentable it is to see the effects which have followed. Religion hath been disgraced, the godly greeved, afflicted, persecuted, and many exiled, sundrie have lost their lives in prisones and otherways. On

[1] "Eus: lib: 6. Chap. 42." (Note by Bradford, referring to the *Ecclesiastical History* of Eusebius of Cæsarea.)

the other hand, sin hath been countenanced, ignorance, profannes, and atheisme increased, and the papists encouraged
to hope againe for a day.

This made that holy man Mr. Perkins[1] crie out in his
exhortation to repentance, upon Zeph. 2. *Religion* (saith he)
hath been amongst us this 35. *years ; but the more it is published, the more it is contemned and reproached of many, etc.
Thus not prophanes nor wickednes, but Religion it selfe is a
byword, a moking-stock, and a matter of reproach ; so that in
England at this day the man or woman that begines to profes
Religion, and to serve God, must resolve with him selfe to sustaine
mocks and injueries even as though he lived amongst the enimies
of Religion.* And this commone experience hath confirmed
and made too apparente.

A late observation, as it were by the way, worthy to be Noted.[2]

Full litle did I thinke, that the downfall of the Bishops, with their
courts, cannons, and ceremonies, etc. had been so neare, when I first begane these scribled writings (which was aboute the year 1630, and so
peeced up at times of leasure afterward), or that I should have lived to
have seene or heard of the same; but it is the Lord's doing, and ought to
be marvelous in our eyes! Every plante which mine heavenly father hath
not planted (saith our Saviour) shall be rooted up. Mat: 15. 13.[3]   I
have snared the, and thou art taken, O Babell (Bishops), and thou wast
not aware; thou art found, and also caught, because thou hast striven
against the Lord. Jer. 50. 24.   But will they needs strive against the
truth, against the servants of God; what, and against the Lord him
selfe? Doe they provoke the Lord to anger? Are they stronger than
he? 1. Cor : 10. 22.   No, no, they have mete with their match.   Behold,
I come unto thee, O proud man, saith the Lord God of hosts; for thy
day is come, even the time that I will visite the.   Jer : 50. 31.   May
not the people of God now say (and these pore people among the rest),

[1] "Pag. 421." (Bradford, referring to William Perkins's sermon, *A Faithfull and Plaine Exposition upon the first two Verses of the 2. Chapter of Zephaniah,*
reprinted in his *Workes,* of which there are many editions. The passage quoted
occurs on p. 421 of the third volume of the edition of 1613.)

[2] A note of the author at this place, written subsequent to this portion of the
narrative, on the reverse of page 3 of his History.

[3] All these and subsequent passages are quoted from the Geneva version
of the Bible.

The Lord hath brought forth our righteousnes; come, let us declare in Sion the work of the Lord our God. Jer: 51. 10. Let all flesh be still before the Lord; for he is raised up out of his holy place. Zach : 2. 13.

In this case, these poore people may say (among the thousands of Israll), *When the Lord brougt againe the captivite of Zion, we were like them that dreame.* Psa : 126. 1. *The Lord hath done greate things for us, wherof we rejoyce.* v. 3. *They that sow in teares, shall reap in joye. They wente weeping, and carried precious seede, but they shall returne with joye, and bring their sheaves.* v. 5, 6.

Doe you not now see the fruits of your labours, O all yee servants of the Lord that have suffered for his truth, and have been faithfull witneses of the same, and yee litle handfull amongst the rest, the least amongest the thousands of Israll? You have not only had a seede time, but many of you have seene the joyefull harvest; should you not then rejoyse, yea, and againe rejoyce, and say Hallelu-iah, salvation, and glorie, and honour, and power, be to the Lord our God; for true and righteous are his judgments. Rev. 19. 1, 2.

But thou wilte aske what is the mater? What is done? Why, art thou a stranger in Israll, that thou shouldest not know what is done? Are not those Jebusites overcome that have vexed the people of Israll so long, even holding Jerusalem till Davids days, and been as thorns in their sids, so many ages; and now begane to scorne that any David should meadle with them; they begane to fortifie their tower, as that of the old Babelonians; but those proud Anakimes are throwne downe, and their glory laid in the dust. The tiranous bishops are ejected, their courts dissolved, their cannons forceless, their servise casheired, their ceremonies uselese and despised; their plots for popery prevented, and all their superstitions discarded and returned to Roome from whence they came, and the monuments of idolatrie rooted out of the land. And the proud and profane suporters, and cruell defenders of these (as bloody papists and wicked athists, and their malignante consorts) marvelously over throwne. And are not these greate things? Who can deney it?

But who hath done it? Who, even he that siteth on the white horse, who is caled faithfull, and true, and judgeth and fighteth righteously, Rev : 19. 11. whose garments are dipte in blood, and his name was caled the word of God, v. 13. for he shall rule them with a rode of iron; for it is he that treadeth the winepress of the feircenes and wrath of God almighty. And he hath upon his garmente, and upon his thigh, a name writen, The King of Kings, and Lord of Lords. v. 15, 16.   Hallelu-iah.

Anno Dom : 1646.

But that I may come more near my intendmente; when as by the travell and diligence of some godly and zealous preachers, and Gods blessing on their labours, as in other places of the land, so in the North parts, many became inlightened by the word of God, and had their ignorance and sins discovered unto them, and begane by his grace to reforme their lives, and make conscience of their wayes, the worke of God was no sooner manifest in them, but presently they were both scoffed and scorned by the prophane multitude, and the ministers urged with the yoak of subscription, or els must be silenced; and the poore people were so vexed with apparators, and pursuants,[1] and the comissarie courts, as truly their affliction was not smale; which, notwithstanding, they bore sundrie years with much patience, till they were occasioned (by the continuance and encrease of these troubls, and other means which the Lord raised up in those days) to see further into things by the light of the word of God.   How not only these base and beggerly ceremonies were unlawfull, but also that the lordly and tiranous power of the prelats ought not to be submitted unto; which thus, contrary to the freedome of the gospell, would load and burden mens consciences, and by their compulsive power make a prophane mixture of persons and things in the worship of God.   And that their offices and calings, courts and cannons, etc. were unlawfull and antichristian; being such as have no warrante in the word of God; but the same that were used in poperie, and still retained.   Of which a famous author thus writeth in his Dutch com[men]taries.[2]   At the coming of king James into England; *The new king* (saith he) *found their* [there] *established the reformed religion, according to the reformed religion of king Edward the* 6.   *Retaining, or keeping still the*

---

[1] Apparitors and pursuivants, officers of the ecclesiastical courts.

[2] "Em:meter:lib:25. fol. 119."   (Note by Bradford.)   The reference is to the Dutch history by Emanuel van Meteren, *Commentarien ofte Memorien van den Nederlandtschen Staet, Handel,* etc. (1610, etc.)   The passage quoted is on fol. 472 of the edition of 1652.

spirituall state of the Bishops, etc. after the ould maner, much varying and differing from the reformed churches in Scotland, France, and the Neatherlands, Embden, Geneva, etc. whose reformation is cut, or shapen much nerer the first Christian churches, as it was used in the Apostles times.[1]

So many therfore of these proffessors as saw the evill of these things, in thes parts, and whose harts the Lord had touched with heavenly zeale for his trueth, they shooke of this yoake of antichristian bondage, and as the Lords free people, joyned them selves (by a covenant of the Lord) into a church estate, in the felowship of the gospell, to walke in all his wayes, made known, or to be made known unto them, according to their best endeavours, whatsoever it should cost them, the Lord assisting them. And that it cost them something this ensewing historie will declare.

These people became 2. distincte bodys or churches,[2] and in regarde of distance of place did congregate severally; for they were of sundrie townes and vilages, some in Notingamshire, some of Lincollinshire, and some of Yorkshire, wher they border nearest togeather. In one of these churches (besids others of note) was Mr John Smith, a man of able gifts, and a good preacher, who afterwards was chosen their pastor. But these afterwards falling into some errours in the Low Countries, ther (for the most part) buried them selves, and their names.[3]

But in this other church (which must be the subjecte of

[1] "The reformed churches shapen much neerer the primitive patterne then England, for they cashered the Bishops with al their courts, cannons, and ceremoneis, at the first; and left them amongst the popish tr. . to c̄h wch they pertained." (Note by Bradford. The last word in the note is uncertain in the manuscript.)　　　[2] See the editor's Introduction.

[3] Rev. John Smyth, preacher to the city of Lincoln, became about 1606 a Separatist, and pastor of a Separatist church at Gainsborough. With it he migrated to Amsterdam in 1608. There, after various changes of doctrine and practice respecting baptism, the church divided in 1609. The majority, under Rev. Thomas Helwys, returned to England in 1613. Smyth died in Amsterdam in 1612. The minority of the church, his adherents, became absorbed among the Mennonites and other Dutch.

our discourse) besids other worthy men, was Mr. Richard Clifton,[1] a grave and reverend preacher, who by his paines and dilligens had done much good, and under God had ben a means of the conversion of many. And also that famous and worthy man Mr. John Robinson, who afterwards was their pastor for many years, till the Lord tooke him away by death. Also Mr. William Brewster[2] a reverent man, who afterwards was chosen an elder of the church and lived with them till old age.

But after these things they could not long continue in any peaceable condition, but were hunted and persecuted on every side, so as their former afflictions were but as flea-bitings in comparison of these which now came upon them. For some were taken and clapt up in prison, others had their houses besett and watcht night and day, and hardly escaped their hands; and the most were faine to flie and leave their howses and habitations, and the means of their livelehood. Yet these and many other sharper things which affterward befell them, were no other then they looked for, and therfore were the better prepared to bear them by the assistance of Gods grace and spirite. Yet seeing them selves thus molested, and that ther was no hope of their continuance ther, by a joynte consente they resolved to goe into the Low-Countries, wher they heard was freedome of Religion for all men; as also how sundrie from London, and other parts of the land, had been exiled and persecuted for the same cause, and were gone thither, and lived at Amsterdam, and in other places of the land. So affter they had continued togeither aboute a year, and kept their meetings every Saboth in one place or other, exercising the worship of God amongst them selves, notwithstanding all the dilligence and malice of their advers-

---

[1] Richard Clyfton was born in Normanton, Derbyshire. In 1586 he became rector of Babworth in Nottinghamshire. He afterwards became pastor of the Pilgrim church in Scrooby and went with the church to Amsterdam in 1608. He remained in Amsterdam when the church removed to Leyden, and died there May 20, 1616.   [2] See the Introduction.

saries, they seeing they could no longer continue in that
condition, they resolved to get over into Holland as they
could; which was in the year 1607. and 1608.; of which more
at large in the next chap.

2. Chap.

Of their departure into Holland and their troubls ther aboute,
with some of the many difficulties they found and
mete withall.[1]

An°. 1608.

BEING thus constrained to leave their native soyle and
countrie, their lands and livings, and all their freinds and
famillier acquaintance, it was much, and thought marvelous
by many. But to goe into a countrie they knew not (but
by hearsay), wher they must learne a new language, and get
their livings they knew not how, it being a dear place, and
subjecte to the misseries of warr,[2] it was by many thought
an adventure almost desperate, a case intolerable, and a
misserie worse then death. Espetially seeing they were not
aquainted with trads[3] nor traffique, (by which that countrie
doth subsiste,) but had only been used to a plaine countrie
life, and the inocente trade of husbandrey. But these things
did not dismay them (though they did some times trouble
them) for their desires were sett on the ways of God, and to
injoye his ordinances; but they rested on his providence, and
knew whom they had beleeved. Yet this was not all, for
though they could not stay, yet were they not suffered to goe,
but the ports and havens were shut against them,[4] so as

---

[1] See the Introduction.
[2] The war of Dutch independence, begun in 1567, continued till interrupted
by the truce of April, 1609.   [3] *I. e.*, handicrafts.
[4] The ports were not closed especially against the Pilgrims, but, under a
royal proclamation, emigrants to Virginia, their presumed destination, were for-
bidden to embark without a royal license.

they were faine to seeke secrete means of conveance, and
to bribe and fee the mariners, and give exterordinarie rates
for their passages. And yet were they often times betrayed
(many of them), and both they and their goods intercepted
and surprised, and therby put to great trouble and charge,
of which I will give an instance or tow, and omitte the
rest.

Ther was a large companie of them purposed to get passage at Boston in Lincoln-shire, and for that end had hired
a shipe wholy to them selves, and made agreement with
the maister to be ready at a certaine day, and take them and
their goods in, at a conveniente place, wher they accordingly
would all attende in readines. So after long waiting, and
large expences, though he kepte not day with them, yet he
came at length and tooke them in, in the night. But when
he had them and their goods abord, he betrayed them, haveing
before hand complotted with the serchers and other officers
so to doe; who tooke them, and put them into open boats,
and ther rifled and ransaked them, searching them to their
shirts for money, yea even the women furder then became
modestie; and then caried them back into the towne, and
made them a spectackle and wonder to the multitude, which
came flocking on all sids to behould them. Being thus first,
by the chatch-poule[1] officers, rifled, and stripte of their
money, books, and much other goods, they were presented to
the magestrates, and messengers sente to informe the lords
of the Counsell of them; and so they were commited to
ward. Indeed the magestrats used them courteously, and
shewed them what favour they could; but could not deliver
them, till order came from the Counsell-table. But the
issue was that after a months imprisonmente, the greatest
parte were dismiste, and sent to the places from whence they
came; but 7. of the principall[2] were still kept in prison, and
bound over to the Assises.

[1] Catchpole.   [2] William Brewster was one of them.

The nexte spring after, ther was another attempte made
by some of these and others, to get over at an other place.
And it so fell out, that they light of a Dutchman at Hull,
having a ship of his owne belonging to Zealand; they made
agreemente with him, and acquainted him with their condition, hoping to find more faithfullnes in him, then in the
former of their owne nation. He bad them not fear, for he
would doe well enough. He was by appointment to take
them in betweene Grimsbe and Hull, wher was a large commone
a good way distante from any towne. Now aganst the prefixed
time, the women and children, with the goods, were sent to
the place in a small barke, which they had hired for that end;
and the men were to meete them by land. But it so fell out,
that they were ther a day before the shipe came, and the sea
being rough, and the women very sicke, prevailed with the
seamen to put into a creeke hardby, wher they lay on ground
at lowwater. The nexte morning the shipe came, but they
were fast, and could not stir till aboute noone. In the mean
time, the shipe maister, perceiving how the matter was, sente
his boate to be getting the men abord whom he saw ready,
walking aboute the shore. But after the first boat full was
gott abord, and she was ready to goe for more, the m^{r}[1]
espied a greate company, both horse and foote, with bills,
and gunes, and other weapons; for the countrie was raised to
take them. The Dutch-man seeing that, swore his countries
oath, "sacremente," and having the wind faire, waiged his
Ancor, hoysed sayles, and away. But the poore men which
were gott abord,[2] were in great distress for their wives and
children, which they saw thus to be taken, and were left
destitute of their helps; and them selves also, not having a
cloath to shifte them with, more then they had on their
baks, and some scarce a peney aboute them, all they had
being abord the barke. It drew tears from their eyes,
and any thing they had they would have given to have

[1] Master.   [2] William Bradford was one of those on board the vessel.

been a shore againe; but all in vaine, ther was no remedy, they must thus sadly part. And afterward endured
a fearfull storme at sea, being 14. days or more before they
arived at their porte, in 7. wherof they neither saw son,
moone, nor stars, and were driven near the coast of Norway;
the mariners them selves often despairing of life; and once
with shriks and cries gave over all, as if the ship had been
foundred in the sea, and they sinking without recoverie.
But when mans hope and helpe wholy failed, the Lords power
and mercie appeared in ther recoverie; for the ship rose againe,
and gave the mariners courage againe to manage her. And
if modestie woud suffer me, I might declare with what fervente
prayres they cried unto the Lord in this great distres, (espetialy
some of them,) even without any great distraction, when the
water rane into their mouthes and ears; and the mariners
cried out, We sinke, we sinke; they cried (if not with mirake-
lous, yet with a great hight or degree of devine faith), Yet
Lord thou canst save, yet Lord thou canst save; with shuch
other expressions as I will forbeare. Upon which the ship
did not only recover, but shortly after the violence of the
storme begane to abate, and the Lord filed their afflicted minds
with shuch comforts as every one cannot understand, and in
the end brought them to their desired Haven, wher the people
came flockeing admiring their deliverance, the storme having ben so longe and sore, in which much hurt had been
don, as the masters freinds related unto him in their congrat-
tulations.

But to returne to the others wher we left. The rest of
the men that were in greatest danger, made shift to escape
away before the troope could surprise them; those only staying that best might, to be assistante unto the women. But
pitifull it was to see the heavie case of these poore women
in this distress; what weeping and crying on every side, some
for their husbands, that were caried away in the ship as is
before related; others not knowing what should become of

them, and their litle ones; others againe melted in teares, seeing their poore litle ones hanging aboute them, crying for feare, and quaking with could. Being thus aprehended, they were hurried from one place to another, and from one justice to another, till in the ende they knew not what to doe with them; for to imprison so many women and innocent children for no other cause (many of them) but that they must goe with their husbands, semed to be unreasonable and all would crie out of them; and to send them home againe was as difficult, for they aledged, as the trueth was, they had no homes to goe to, for they had either sould, or otherwise disposed of their houses and livings. To be shorte, after they had been thus turmolyed a good while, and conveyed from one constable to another, they were glad to be ridd of them in the end upon any termes; for all were wearied and tired with them. Though in the mean time they (poore soules) indured miserie enough; and thus in the end necessitie forste a way for them.

But that I be not tedious in these things, I will omitte the rest, though I might relate many other notable passages and troubles which they endured and underwente in these their wanderings and travells both at land and sea; but I hast to other things. Yet I may not omitte the fruite that came hearby, for by these so publick troubls, in so many eminente places, their cause became famouss, and occasioned many to looke into the same; and their godly cariage and Christian behaviour was such as left a deep impression in the minds of many. And though some few shrunk at these first conflicts and sharp beginings, (as it was no marvell,) yet many more came on with fresh courage, and greatly animated others. And in the end, notwithstanding all these stormes of opposstion, they all gatt over at length, some at one time and some at an other, and some in one place and some in an other, and mette togeather againe according to their desires, with no small rejoycing.

The 3. Chapter

Of their setling in Holand, and their maner of living, and enter-
tainmente ther.

BEING now come into the Low Countries, they saw many
goodly and fortified cities, strongly walled and garded with
troopes of armed men. Also they heard a strange and un-
couth language, and beheld the differente manners and cus-
tomes of the people, with their strange fashons and attires;
all so farre differing from that of their plaine countrie villages
(wherin they were bred, and had so longe lived) as it seemed
they were come into a new world. But these were not the
things they much looked on, or long tooke up their thoughts;
for they had other work in hand, and an other kind of warr
to wage and maintaine. For though they saw faire and
bewtifull cities, flowing with abundance of all sorts of welth
and riches, yet it was not longe before they saw the grimme
and grisly face of povertie coming upon them like an armed
man, with whom they must bukle and incounter, and from
whom they could not flye; but they were armed with faith
and patience against him, and all his encounters; and though
they were sometimes foyled, yet by Gods assistance they
prevailed and got the victorie.

Now when Mr. Robinson, Mr. Brewster, and other principall members were come over, (for they were of the last,
and stayed to help the weakest over before them,) such things
were thought on as were necessarie for their setling and best
ordering of the church affairs. And when they had lived
at Amsterdam aboute a year, Mr. Robinson, their pastor,
and some others of best discerning, seeing how Mr. John
Smith and his companie was allready fallen in to contention
with the church that was ther before them,[1] and no means

[1] A Separatist church, of which Francis Johnson was pastor and Henry
Ainsworth teacher, was already in Amsterdam when John Smith with his congregation arrived, and it was the contention between Smith and Johnson to which

they could use would doe any good to cure the same, and also
that the flames of contention were like to breake out in that
anciente church it selfe (as affterwards lamentably came
to pass); which things they prudently foreseeing, thought it
was best to remove, before they were any way engaged with
the same; though they well knew it would be much to the
prejudice of their outward estats, both at presente and in
licklyhood in the future; as indeed it proved to be.

Their remoovall to Leyden.

For these and some other reasons they removed to Leyden, a fair and bewtifull citie, and of a sweete situation, but
made more famous by the universitie wherwith it is adorned,
in which of late had been so many learned men.   But wanting
that traffike by sea which Amsterdam injoyes, it was not so
beneficiall for their outward means of living and estats.   But
being now hear pitchet they fell to such trads and imployments
as they best could;[1] valewing peace and their spirituall comforte above any other riches whatsoever.   And at lenght they
came to raise a competente and comforteable living, but with
hard and continuall labor.

Being thus setled (after many difficulties) they continued
many years in a comfortable condition, injoying much sweete

Bradford refers.   Francis Johnson, originally preacher to the Merchants of the
Staple in Middelburg, became in 1592 a Separatist, and minister of a Separatist
congregation in London.   He and its other leaders emigrated in 1597 to Amsterdam, and there, after many ecclesiastical disputes and vicissitudes, he died in 1618.

[1] William Brewster at first taught English to the students in the university
of Leyden, and afterwards engaged in publishing books proscribed in England,
among which were *Commentarii in Proverbia Salomonis* (1617), by Thomas
Cartwright with a preface by Polyander, Grevinchovius on the Arminian controversy (1617), *A Confutation of the Rhemists' Translation of the New Testament*
(1618) by Thomas Cartwright, a treatise in Latin *De Vera et Genuina Jesu
Christi Religione* (1618), and other works.   Those books published by him in
1617 have his imprint, but in consequence of efforts to suppress his work his
imprint was omitted in books printed at a later date.

William Bradford became a fustian-maker, Robert Cushman and William
White wool-carders, Samuel Fuller and Stephen Tracy silk-makers, John Jenney
a brewer, Edward Winslow a printer, and Degory Priest a hatter.

and delightefull societie and spirituall comforte togeather in the wayes of God, under the able ministrie, and prudente governmente of Mr. John Robinson, and Mr. William Brewster, who was an assistante unto him in the place of an Elder, unto which he was now called and chosen by the church. So as they grew in knowledge and other gifts and graces of the spirite of God, and lived togeather in peace, and love, and holines; and many came unto them from diverse parts of England, so as they grew a great congregation. And if at any time any differences arose, or offences broak out (as it cannot be, but some time ther will, even amongst the best of men) they were ever so mete with, and nipt in the head betims, or otherwise so well composed, as still love, peace, and communion was continued; or els the church purged of those that were incurable and incorrigible, when, after much patience used, no other means would serve, which seldom came to pass. Yea such was the mutuall love, and reciprocall respecte that this worthy man had to his flocke, and his flocke to him, that it might be said of them as it once was of that famouse Emperour Marcus Aurelious,[1] and the people of Rome, that it was hard to judge wheather he delighted more in haveing shuch a people, or they in haveing such a pastor. His love was greate towards them, and his care was all ways bente for their best good, both for soule and body; for besids his singuler abilities in devine things (wherin he excelled), he was also very able to give directions in civill affaires, and to foresee dangers and inconveniences; by which means he was very helpfull to their outward estats, and so was every way as a commone father unto them. And none did more offend him then those that were close and cleaving to them selves, and retired from the commone good; as also such as would be stiffe and riged in matters of outward order, and invey

[1] "Goulden booke, etc." (Note by Bradford.) The book to which he refers, known in its English translations as "The Golden Book of the Emperor Marcus Aurelius," was in reality a Spanish romance, written by Antonio de Guevara, bishop of Mondoñedo, and published in 1529.

against the evills of others, and yet be remisse in them selves, and not so carefull to express a vertuous conversation. They in like maner had ever a reverente regard unto him, and had him in precious estimation, as his worth and wisdom did deserve; and though they esteemed him highly whilst he lived and laboured amongst them, yet much more after his death,[1] when they came to feele the wante of his help, and saw (by woefull experience) what a treasure they had lost, to the greefe of their harts, and wounding of their sowls; yea such a loss as they saw could not be repaired; for it was as hard for them to find such another leader and feeder in all respects, as for the Taborits to find another Ziska.[2] And though they did not call themselves orphans, as the other did, after his death, yet they had cause as much to lamente, in another regard, their present condition, and after usage. But to returne; I know not but it may be spoken to the honour of God, and without prejudice to any, that such was the true pietie, the humble zeale, and fervent love, of this people (whilst they thus lived together) towards God and his waies, and the single hartednes and sinceir affection one towards another, that they came as near the primative patterne of the first churches, as any other church of these later times have done, according to their ranke and qualitie.

But seeing it is not my purpose to treat of the severall passages that befell this people whilst they thus lived in the Low Countries, (which might worthily require a large treatise of it selfe,) but to make way to shew the begining of this plantation, which is that I aime at; yet because some of their adversaries did, upon the rumore of their removall, cast out slanders against them, as if that state had been wearie of them, and had rather driven them out (as the heathen historians did faine of Moyses and the Isralits when they went out of

---

[1] John Robinson died in Leyden, March 1, 1624/5.

[2] John Ziska was the invincible leader of the Taborites or Hussites of Bohemia, in the fifteenth century.

Egipte), then that it was their owne free choyse and motion,
I will therfore mention a perticuler or too to shew the contrary
and the good acceptation they had in the place wher they
lived. And first though many of them weer poore, yet ther
was none so poore, but if they were known to be of that congregation, the Dutch (either bakers or others) would trust
them in any reasonable matter when they wanted money.
Because they had found by experience how carfull they were
to keep their word, and saw them so painfull and dilligente
in their callings; yea, they would strive to gett their custome,
and to imploy them above others, in their worke, for their
honestie and diligence.

Againe; the magistrats of the citie, aboute the time of their
coming away, or a litle before, in the publick place of justice,
gave this comendable testemoney of them, in the reproofe of
the Wallons,[1] who were of the French church in that citie.
These English, said they, have lived amongst us now this 12.
years, and yet we never had any sute or accusation came against
any of them; but your strifs and quarels are continuall, etc.
In these times allso were the great troubls raised by the Arminians,[2] who, as they greatly mollested the whole state, so
this citie in particuler, in which was the cheefe universitie; so
as ther were dayly and hote disputs in the schooles ther aboute;
and as the studients and other lerned were devided in their oppinions hearin, so were the 2. proffessors or devinitie readers
them selves; the one daly teaching for it, the other against it.
Which grew to that pass, that few of the discipls of the one

[1] The Walloons inhabited the Belgic border of France and spoke French.
Owing to persecution many of them who were Protestants moved into Holland.
Esther, the wife of Francis Cooke, was a Walloon, and so it is supposed was
William Mullens or Mollines, who came in the *Mayflower*, while Philip Delano
or De La Noye, who came in the *Fortune* in 1621, was "born of French parents."

[2] Jacobus Arminius, professor of theology in the University of Leyden from
1603 to his death in 1609, had taught a doctrine of grace opposed to the strictest
Calvinism. His successor, Simon Episcopius, and on the other side the other
divinity professor, Johannes Polyander, maintained the controversy with warmth.
Robinson's views were Calvinistic.

would hear the other teach. But Mr. Robinson, though he taught thrise a weeke him selfe, and write sundrie books,[1] besids his manyfould pains otherwise, yet he went constantly to hear ther readings, and heard the one as well as the other; by which means he was so well grounded in the controversie, and saw the force of all their arguments, and knew the shifts of the adversarie, and being him selfe very able, none was fitter to buckle with them then him selfe, as appered by sundrie disputs; so as he begane to be terrible to the Arminians; which made Episcopius (the Arminian professor) to put forth his best stringth, and set forth sundrie Theses, which by publick dispute he would defend against all men. Now Poliander the other proffessor, and the cheefe preachers of the citie, desired Mr. Robinson to dispute against him; but he was loath, being a stranger; yet the other did importune him, and tould him that such was the abilitie and nimblnes of the adversarie, that the truth would suffer if he did not help them. So as he condescended, and prepared him selfe against the time; and when the day came, the Lord did so help him to defend the truth and foyle this adversarie, as he put him to an apparent nonplus, in this great and publike audience. And the like he did a 2. or 3. time, upon such like occasions. The which as it caused many to praise God that the trueth had so famous victory, so it procured him much honour and respecte from those lerned men and others which loved the trueth. Yea, so farr were they from being weary of him and his people, or desiring their absence, as it was said by some, of no mean note, that were it not for giveing offence to the state of England, they would have preferd him otherwise if he would, and alowd them some pub-

---

[1] Robinson lived near the university. The following works written by him were published at the appended dates: *A Justification of Separation from the Church of England* (1610); *Apologia Brownistarum* (1619); *Defence of the Doctrine propounded by the Synode at Dort* (1624); *Essayes, or Observations Divine and Morall* (1625). Bradford's copy of the first named is still extant. A copy of the first edition of the last named, which is very rare, has been recently bought by the Pilgrim Society of Plymouth. Robinson's works in three volumes were reprinted in 1851.

like favour. Yea when ther was speech of their remoovall into
these parts, sundrie of note and eminencie of that nation would
have had them come under them, and for that end made them
large offers. Now though I might aledg many other perticulers
and examples of the like kinde, to shew the untruth and un-
licklyhode of this slander, yet these shall suffice, seeing it was
beleeved of few, being only raised by the malice of some, who
laboured their disgrace.

The 4. Chap.

Showing the reasons and causes of their remoovall.

AFTER they had lived in this citie about some 11. or 12.
years, (which is the more observable being the whole time of
that famose truce[1] between that state and the Spaniards,)
and sundrie of them were taken away by death, and many
others begane to be well striken in years, the grave mistris
Experience haveing taught them many things, those prudent
governours with sundrie of the sagest members begane both
deeply to apprehend their present dangers, and wisely to foresee the future, and thinke of timly remedy. In the agitation
of their thoughts, and much discours of things hear aboute, at
length they began to incline to this conclusion, of remoovall
to some other place. Not out of any newfanglednes, or other
such like giddie humor, by which men are oftentimes transported to their great hurt and danger, but for sundrie weightie
and solid reasons; some of the cheefe of which I will hear
breefly touch. And first, they saw and found by experience
the hardnes of the place and countrie to be such, as few in
comparison would come to them, and fewer that would bide
it out, and continew with them. For many that came to them,
and many more that desired to be with them, could not endure
that great labor and hard fare, with other inconveniences which
they underwent and were contented with. But though they

[1] This truce, signed April 9, 1609, was to expire in 1621.

loved their persons, approved their cause, and honoured their
sufferings, yet they left them as it weer weeping, as Orpah did
her mother in law Naomie, or as those Romans did Cato in
Utica, who desired to be excused and borne with, though they
could not all be Catoes. For many, though they desired to
injoye the ordinances of God in their puritie, and the libertie
of the gospell with them, yet, alass, they admitted of bondage,
with danger of conscience, rather than to indure these hardships; yea, some preferred and chose the prisons in England,
rather then this libertie in Holland, with these afflictions. But
it was thought that if a better and easier place of living could
be had, it would draw many, and take away these discourag-
ments. Yea, their pastor would often say, that many of those
who both wrote and preached now against them, if they were
in a place wher they might have libertie and live comfortably,
they would then practise as they did.

2$^{ly.}$ They saw that though the people generally bore all
these difficulties very cherfully, and with a resolute courage,
being in the best and strength of their years, yet old age began
to steale on many of them, (and their great and continuall
labours, with other crosses and sorrows, hastened it before the
time,) so as it was not only probably thought, but apparently
seen, that within a few years more they would be in danger to
scatter, by necessities pressing them, or sinke under their
burdens, or both. And therfore according to the devine
proverb, that a wise man seeth the plague when it cometh,
and hideth him selfe, Pro. 22. 3., so they like skillfull and
beaten[1] souldiers were fearfull either to be intrapped or surrounded by their enimies, so as they should neither be able to
fight nor flie; and therfor thought it better to dislodge betimes to some place of better advantage and less danger, if
any such could be found. Thirdly; as necessitie was a task-
master over them, so they were forced to be such, not only to
their servants, but in a sorte, to their dearest children; the

---

[1] *I. e.*, hardened, experienced.

which as it did not a litle wound the tender harts of many a
loving father and mother, so it produced likwise sundrie sad
and sorowful effects. For many of their children, that were
of best dispositions and gracious inclinations, haveing lernde
to bear the yoake in their youth, and willing to bear parte of
their parents burden, were, often times, so oppressed with
their hevie labours, that though their minds were free and
willing, yet their bodies bowed under the weight of the same,
and became decreped in their early youth; the vigor of nature
being consumed in the very budd as it were. But that which
was more lamentable, and of all sorowes most heavie to be
borne, was that many of their children, by these occasions,
and the great licentiousness of youth in that countrie, and the
manifold temptations of the place, were drawne away by evill
examples into extravagante and dangerous courses, getting the
raines off their neks, and departing from their parents. Some
became souldiers, others tooke upon them farr viages by sea,
and other some worse courses, tending to dissolutnes and the
danger of their soules, to the great greefe of their parents and
dishonour of God. So that they saw their posteritie would
be in danger to degenerate and be corrupted.

Lastly, (and which was not least), a great hope and inward zeall they had of laying some good foundation, or at
least to make some way therunto, for the propagating and
advancing the gospell of the kingdom of Christ in those remote parts of the world; yea, though they should be but even
as stepping-stones unto others for the performing of so great
a work.

These, and some other like reasons, moved them to undertake this resolution of their removall; the which they afterward prosecuted with so great difficulties, as by the sequell
will appeare.

The place they had thoughts on was some of those vast
and unpeopled countries of America, which are frutfull and
fitt for habitation, being devoyd of all civill inhabitants, wher

ther are only salvage and brutish men, which range up and
downe, litle otherwise then the wild beasts of the same.   This
proposition being made publike and coming to the scaning of
all, it raised many variable opinions amongst men, and caused
many fears and doubts amongst them selves.   Some, from
their reasons and hops conceived, laboured to stirr up and incourage the rest to undertake and prosecute the same; others,
againe, out of their fears, objected against it, and sought to
diverte from it, aledging many things, and those neither unreasonable nor unprobable; as that it was a great designe,
and subjecte to many unconceivable perills and dangers; as,
besids the casulties of the seas (which none can be freed from)
the length of the vioage was such, as the weake bodys of
women and other persons worne out with age and traville (as
many of them were) could never be able to endure.   And yet
if they should, the miseries of the land which they should be
exposed unto, would be to hard to be borne; and lickly, some
or all of them togeither, to consume and utterly to ruinate
them.   For ther they should be liable to famine, and nakednes, and the wante, in a maner, of all things.   The chang of
aire, diate, and drinking of water, would infecte their bodies
with sore sickneses, and greevous diseases.   And also those
which should escape or overcome these difficulties, should yett
be in continuall danger of the salvage people, who are cruell,
barbarous, and most trecherous, being most furious in their
rage, and merciles wher they overcome; not being contente
only to kill, and take away life, but delight to tormente men
in the most bloodie manner that may be; fleaing[1] some alive
with the shells of fishes, cutting of the members and joynts of
others by peesmeale, and broiling on the coles, eate the collops
of their flesh in their sight whilst they live; with other cruel-
ties horrible to be related.   And surely it could not be thought
but the very hearing of these things could not but move the
very bowels of men to grate within them, and make the weake

[1] Flaying.

to quake and tremble. It was furder objected, that it would require greater summes of money to furnish such a voiage, and to fitt them with necessaries, then their consumed estats would amounte too; and yett they must as well looke to be seconded with supplies,[1] as presently to be transported. Also many presidents of ill success, and lamentable misseries befalne others in the like designes, were easie to be found, and not forgotten to be aledged; besids their owne experience, in their former troubles and hardships in their removall into Holand, and how hard a thing it was for them to live in that strange place, though it was a neighbour countrie, and a civill and rich comone wealth.

It was answered, that all great and honourable actions are accompanied with great difficulties, and must be both enterprised and overcome with answerable courages. It was granted the dangers were great, but not desperate; the difficulties were many, but not invincible. For though their were many of them likly, yet they were not cartaine; it might be sundrie of the things feared might never befale; others by providente care and the use of good means, might in a great measure be prevented; and all of them, through the help of God, by fortitude and patience, might either be borne, or overcome. True it was, that such atempts were not to be made and undertaken without good ground and reason; not rashly or lightly as many have done for curiositie or hope of gaine, etc. But their condition was not ordinarie; their ends were good and honourable; their calling lawfull, and urgente; and therfore they might expecte the blessing of God in their proceding. Yea, though they should loose their lives in this action, yet might they have comforte in the same, and their endeavors would be honourable. They lived hear but as men in exile, and in a poore condition; and as great miseries might possibly befale them in this place, for the 12. years of truce were now [2] out, and ther was nothing but beating of

---

[1] *I. e.*, reinforcements.

[2] The truce between the Dutch and Spain would end in April, 1621.

drumes, and preparing for warr, the events wherof are allway uncertaine.   The Spaniard might prove as cruell as the salvages of America, and the famine and pestelence as sore hear as ther, and their libertie less to looke out for remedie.   After many other perticuler things answered and aledged on both sids, it was fully concluded by the major parte, to put this designe in execution, and to prosecute it by the best means they could.

The 5. Chap.

Shewing what means they used for preparation to this waightie vioag.

AND first after thir humble praiers unto God for his direction and assistance, and a generall conferrence held hear aboute, they consulted what perticuler place to pitch upon, and prepare for.   Some (and none of the meanest) had thoughts and were ernest for Guiana, or some of those fertill places in those hott climats; others were for some parts of Virginia, wher the English had all ready made enterance, and begining.   Those for Guiana aledged that the cuntrie was rich, frutfull, and blessed with a perpetuall spring, and a florishing greenes;[1] where vigorous nature brought forth all things in abundance and plentie without any great labour or art of man.   So as it must needs make the inhabitants rich, seing less provisions of clothing and other things would serve, then in more coulder and less frutfull countries must be had.   As also that the Spaniards (having much more then they could possess) had not yet planted there, nor any where very near the same.[2]   But to this it was answered, that out of question the countrie was both frutfull and pleasante, and might yeeld riches and main-

[1] Greenness.

[2] Though the contrary view was sometimes maintained at the time of the Venezuela-Guiana boundary controversy, it was shown in the report of the American commission (vol. I., pp. 37-56) that up to 1648, at least, Spain had no settlements on that coast, south of the Orinoco.   Several English attempts to settle in the region had been recently made.

tenance to the possessors, more easily then the other; yet, other things considered, it would not be so fitt for them. And first, that such hott countries are subject to greevuos diseases, and many noysome impediments, which other more temperate places are freer from, and would not so well agree with our English bodys. Againe, if they should ther live, and doe well, the jealous Spaniard would never suffer them long, but would displante or overthrow them, as he did the French in Florida,[1] who were seated furder from his richest countries; and the sooner because they should have none to protect them, and their owne strength would be too smale to resiste so potent an enemie, and so neare a neighbor.

On the other hand, for Virginia it was objected, that if they lived among the English which wear ther planted, or so near them as to be under their goverment, they should be in as great danger to be troubled and persecuted for the cause of religion, as if they lived in England, and it might be worse. And if they lived too farr of, they should neither have succour, nor defence from them.

But at length the conclusion was, to live as a distincte body by them selves, under the generall Goverment of Virginia; and by their freinds to sue to his majestie that he would be pleased to grant them freedome of Religion; and that this might be obtained, they wear putt in good hope by some great persons, of good ranke and qualitie, that were made their freinds. Whereupon 2. were chosen and sent in to England (at the charge of the rest) to sollicite this matter, who found the Virginia Company[2] very desirous to have them goe thither, and willing to grante them a patent, with as ample priviliges as they had, or could grant to any, and to give them the best furderance they could. And some of the cheefe of that com-

---

[1] The reference is to the destruction of the Huguenots at Port Royal by Menendez in 1565.

[2] On April 10, 1606, King James I. instituted two Virginia companies, of which the southern, or London Company, was authorized to make settlements on that part of the Atlantic coast extending from the 34th to the 41st degree of

pany douted not to obtaine their suite of the king for liberty in
Religion, and to have it confirmed under the kings broad
seale, according to their desires. But it prooved a harder peece
of worke then they tooke it for; for though many means were
used to bring it aboute, yet it could not be effected; for ther
were diverse of good worth laboured with the king to obtaine it,
(amongst whom was one of his cheefe secretaries,)[1] and some
other wrought with the archbishop[2] to give way therunto;
but it proved all in vaine. Yet thus farr they prevailed, in
sounding his majesties mind, that he would connive at them,
and not molest them, provided they carried them selves peacably. But to allow or tolerate them by his publick authoritie,
under his seale, they found it would not be. And this was all
the cheefe of the Virginia companie or any other of their best
freinds could doe in the case. Yet they perswaded them to
goe on, for they presumed they should not be troubled. And
with this answer the messengers returned, and signified what
diligence had bene used, and to what issue things were come.

But this made a dampe in the busines, and caused some
distraction, for many were afraid that if they should unsetle
them selves, and put of their estates, and goe upon these hopes,
it might prove dangerous, and but a sandie foundation. Yea,
it was thought they might better have presumed hear upon
without makeing any suite at all, then,[3] haveing made it, to
be thus rejected. But some of the cheefest thought other
wise, and that they might well proceede hereupon, and that
the kings majestie was willing enough to suffer them without
molestation, though for other reasons he would not confirme
it by any publick acte. And furdermore, if ther was no

north latitude, the northern company on that part between the 38th and the 45th.
The first patent or grant issued to the Pilgrims came from the southern company,
commonly now called the Virginia Company, but this was not used and another,
issued by the Council for New England, successor of the northern company,
was brought over in the *Fortune* in November, 1621.

[1] "Sr Robert Nanton." (Bradford.)
[2] George Abbot, archbishop of Canterbury 1611–1633.
[3] "Then" for "than."

securitie in this promise intimated, ther would be no great
certainty in a furder confirmation of the same; for if after
wards ther should be a purpose or desire to wrong them,
though they had a seale as broad as the house flore, it would
not serve the turne; for ther would be means enew found to
recall or reverse it. Seeing therfore the course was probable,
they must rest herein on Gods providence, as they had done
in other things.

Upon this resolution, other messengers were dispatched,
to end with the Virginia Company as well as they could. And
to procure a patent with as good and ample conditions as they
might by any good means obtaine. As also to treate and
conclude with such merchants and other freinds as had manifested their forwardnes to provoke too and adventure in this
vioage. For which end they had instructions given them
upon what conditions they should proceed with them, or els to
conclude nothing without further advice. And here it will be
requisite to inserte a letter or too that may give light to these
proceedings.

*A coppie of leter from Sr: Edwin Sands, directed to Mr. John Robinson
and Mr. William Brewster.*

After my hartie salutations. The agents of your congregation,
Robert Cushman[1] and John Carver,[2] have been in communication with

[1] Robert Cushman was born in England about 1580, but precisely when he
joined the Leyden church is not known. He was an active and efficient agent
of the church at various times in England and assented to a contract with the
merchant adventurers which was so unsatisfactory to the Pilgrim company that
they sailed without signing it. He came out in the *Fortune* in 1621, and delivered
in Plymouth an address commonly called a sermon, urging the colonists to close
the contract. After successfully accomplishing his mission he returned in the
Fortune, and died in England in 1625. He brought with him to Plymouth his son
Thomas, fourteen years of age, who was educated by Governor Bradford and
succeeded Brewster as the elder of the Plymouth church. Soon after his return
to England Robert Cushman published (1622) his "sermon," accompanied by a
vindication of the colonial enterprise and an appeal for a Christian mission to the
American Indians.

[2] Little is known of John Carver except that he was a deacon of the Leyden
church and one of the agents of the church to obtain if possible a charter from the
king, and to negotiate with the Virginia Company for a grant of lands, and with

diverse selecte gentlemen of his Majesties Counsell for Virginia; and by the writing of 7. Articles subscribed with your names,[1] have given them that good degree of satisfaction, which hath caried them on with a resolution to sett forward your desire in the best sorte that may be, for your owne and the publick good.   Divers perticulers wherof we leave to their faithfull reporte; having carried them selves heere with that good discretion, as is both to their owne and their credite from whence they came.[2] And wheras being to treate for a multitude of people, they have requested further time to conferr with them that are to be interested in this action, aboute the severall particularities which in the prosecution thereof will fall out considerable, it hath been very willingly assented too.   And so they doe now returne unto you.   If therfore it may please God so to directe your desires as that on your parts ther fall out no just impediments, I trust by the same direction it shall likewise appear, that on our parte, all forwardnes to set you forward shall be found in the best sorte which with reason may be expected.   And so I betake you with this designe (which I hope verily is the worke of God), to the gracious protection and blessing of the Highest.

London, Noṽbr: 12.

Anᵒ: 1617.

Your very loving freind

EDWIN SANDYS.[3]

the merchant adventurers of London for transportation and supplies for the colony.   The language of the letter dated July 27, 1620, which Robinson wrote to Carver, while the *Mayflower* lay at Southampton (p. 83, *post*) makes the conjecture plausible that Katherine, the wife of Carver, may have been Robinson's sister.   Carver was made governor of the *Mayflower* company and, after the compact was signed in the cabin of that ship after her arrival at Cape Cod harbor, he was confirmed in that office.   He was one of the eighteen who landed on Plymouth Rock December 11, O. S., and on April 1, 1621, he negotiated a treaty with Massasoit.   He died, probably of apoplexy, early in April.

[1] The manuscript of the Seven Articles, signed by Robinson and Brewster, is in the Public Record Office in London.   The articles, expressing the assent of the Leyden church to the Thirty-nine Articles of 1562, their desire to keep spiritual communion with the members of the Church of England, and their acknowledgment of the royal supremacy and of the authority of the bishops, may be found printed in the *History of Plymouth* by William T. Davis, p. 13, and in Goodwin's *Pilgrim Republic*, p. 41.

[2] *I. e.*, for their own credit and that of those from whom they came.

[3] Sir Edwin Sandys was the son of Edwin Sandys, archbishop of York, and was born in Worcester in 1561 and died in 1629.   He was a brother of Sir Samuel Sandys under whom William Brewster occupied Scrooby manor.   Sir Edwin Sandys wrote in 1599 a book entitled *A Relation of the State of Religion; and with what Hopes and Policies it hath beene framed and is maintained in the severall States of these western parts of the World*.   It was printed in London in 1605, and forthwith ordered by the High Commission to be burned.   It is

Their answer was as foloweth.

Righte Wor[pl]: [1]

Our humble duties remembred, in our owne, our messengers, and our churches name, with all thankfull acknowledgmente of your singuler love, expressing itselfe, as otherwise, so more spetially in your great care and earnest endeavor of our good in this weightie bussines aboute Virginia, which the less able we are to requite, we shall thinke our selves the more bound to commend in our prayers unto God for recompence; whom, as for the presente you rightly behould in our indeavors, so shall we not be wanting on our parts (the same God assisting us) to returne all answerable fruite, and respecte unto the labour of your love bestowed upon us. We have with the best speed and consideration withall that we could, sett downe our requests in writing, subscribed, as you willed, with the hands of the greatest parte of our congregation, and have sente the same unto the Counsell by our agente, and a deacon of our church, John Carver, unto whom we have also requested a gentleman of our company to adyone[2] him selfe; to the care and discretion of which two, we doe referr the prosecuting of the bussines. Now we perswade our selves Right Wor[pp:] that we need not provoke your godly and loving minde to any further or more tender care of us, since you have pleased so farr to interest us in your selfe, that, under God, above all persons and things in the world, we relye upon you, expecting the care of your love, counsell of your wisdome, and the help and countenance of your authority. Notwithstanding, for your encouragmente in the worke, so farr as probabilities may leade, we will not forbeare to mention these instances of indusmente.

1. We verily beleeve and trust the Lord is with us, unto whom and whose service we have given our selves in many trialls; and that he will graciously prosper our indeavours according to the simplicitie of our harts therin.

2[ly]. We are well weaned from the delicate milke of our mother countrie, and enured to the difficulties of a strange and hard land, which yet in a great parte we have by patience overcome.

3[ly]. The people are for the body of them, industrious, and frugall, we thinke we may safly say, as any company of people in the world.

4[ly]. We are knite togeather as a body in a most stricte and sacred

therefore rare. A copy is owned by the Pilgrim Society of Plymouth, which contains on its title-page two autographs of Rev. John Robinson. Sir Edwin Sandys had now become an eminent statesman and member of Parliament, of the "country party." From the time of his election as treasurer of the Virginia Company in April, 1619, he bore a leading part in its affairs.

[1] Worshipful.   [2] Adjoin.

bond and covenante of the Lord, of the violation [1] wherof we make great conscience, and by vertue wherof we doe hould our selves straitly tied to all care of each others good, and of the whole by every one and so mutually.

5. Lastly, it is not with us as with other men, whom small things can discourage, or small discontentments cause to wish them selves at home againe. We knowe our entertainmente in England, and in Holand; we shall much prejudice both our arts and means by removall; who, if we should be driven to returne, we should not hope to recover our present helps and comforts, neither indeed looke ever, for our selves, to attaine unto the like in any other place during our lives, which are now drawing towards their periods.

These motives we have been bould to tender unto you, which you in your wisdome may also imparte to any other our wor[pp]: freinds of the Counsell with you; of all whose godly dispossition and loving towards our despised persons, we are most glad, and shall not faile by all good means to continue and increase the same. We will not be further troublesome, but doe, with the renewed remembrance of our humble duties to your Wor[pp]: and (so farr as in modestie we may be bould) to any other of our wellwillers of the Counsell with you, we take our leaves, commiting your persons and counsels to the guidance and direction of the Almighty.

Yours much bounden in all duty,

Leyden, Desem: 15.   JOHN ROBINSON,
An°: 1617.   WILLIAM BREWSTER.

For further light in these proceedings see some other letters and notes as followeth.

[1] "O sacred bond, whilst inviollably preserved! how sweete and precious were the fruits that flowed from the same, but when this fidelity decayed, then their ruine approached. O that these anciente members had not dyed, or been dissipated, (if it had been the will of God) or els that this holy care and constante faithfullnes had still lived, and remained with those that survived, and were in times afterwards added unto them. But (alass) that subtill serpente hath slylie wound in himselfe under faire pretences of necessitie and the like, to untwiste these sacred bonds and tyes, and as it were insensibly by degrees to dissolve, or in a great measure to weaken, the same. I have been happy, in my first times, to see, and with much comforte to injoye, the blessed fruits of this sweete communion, but it is now a parte of my miserie in old age, to find and feele the decay and wante therof (in a great measure), and with greefe and sorrow of hart to lamente and bewaile the same. And for others warning and admonnition, and my owne humiliation, doe I hear note the same." (These reflections of Bradford were penned at a later period, on a reverse page of his History, at this place.)

The coppy of a letter sent to Sr. John Worssenham.[1]

Right Wor[pll]: with due acknowledgmente of our thankfullnse fcr your singular care and pains in the bussines of Virginia, for our, and, we hope, the commone good, we doe remember our humble dutys unto you, and have sent inclosed, as is required, a further explanation of our judgments in the 3. points specified by some of his majesties Hon[bl] Privie Counsell;[2] and though it be greevious unto us that such unjust insinuations are made against us, yet we are most glad of the occasion of making our just purgation unto so honourable personages. The declarations we have sent inclosed, the one more breefe and generall, which we thinke the fitter to be presented; the other something more large, and in which we express some smale accidentall differances, which if it seeme good unto you and other of our wor[pl] freinds, you may send in stead of the former. Our prayers unto God is, that your Wor[pp] may see the frute of your worthy endeaours, which on our parts we shall not faile to furder by all good means in us. And so praing that you would please with the convenientest speed that may be, to give us knowledge of the success of the bussines with his majesties Privie Counsell, and accordingly what your further pleasure is, either for our direction or furtherance in the same, so we rest

Your Wor[pp] in all duty,

Leyden, Jan: 27.   JOHN ROBINSON,
An°: 1617. old stile.[3]   WILLIAM BREWSTER.

The first breefe note was this.

Touching the Ecclesiasticall ministrie, namly of pastors for teaching, elders for ruling, and deacons for distributing the churches contribution, as allso for the too Sacrements, baptisme, and the Lords supper, we doe wholy and in all points agree with the French reformed churches, according to their publick confession of faith.[4]

The oath of Supremacie we shall willingly take if it be required of us, and that conveniente satisfaction be not given by our taking the oath of Alleagence.

JOHN ROB:
WILLIAM BREWSTER.

[1] Sir John Wolstenholme was one of the richest merchants in London, and a prominent member of the Virginia Company.

[2] The three points referred to are explained on the following page.

[3] Englishmen at that time began the year on March 25; so the date was 1618, according to the new style.

[4] The *Confessio Gallicana*, adopted by a French Reformed (or Huguenot) synod in 1559.

The 2. was this.

Touching the Ecclesiasticall ministrie, etc. as in the former, we agree in all things with the French reformed churches, according to their publick confession of faith; though some small differences be to be found in our practises, not at all in the substance of the things, but only in some accidentall circumstances.

1. As first, their ministers doe pray with their heads covered; ours uncovered.

2. We chose none for Governing Elders but such as are able to teach; which abilitie they doe not require.

3. Their elders and deacons are annuall, or at most for 2. or 3. years; ours perpetuall.

4. Our elders doe administer their office in admonitions and excommunications for publick scandals, publickly and before the congregation; theirs more privately, and in their consistories.

5. We doe administer baptisme only to such infants as wherof the one parente, at the least, is of some church, which some of ther churches doe not observe; though in it our practice accords with their publick confession and the judgmente of the most larned amongst them.

Other differences, worthy mentioning, we know none in these points. Then aboute the oath, as in the former.

Subscribed,   JOHN R.
                               W. B.

Part of another letter from him that delivered these.

London. Feb: 14.
    1617.[1]

Your letter to Sr. John Worstenholme I delivered allmost as soone as I had it, to his owne hands, and staid with him the opening and reading. Ther were 2. papers inclosed, he read them to him selfe, as also the letter, and in the reading he spake to me and said, Who shall make them? viz. the ministers; I answered his Wor[pp] that the power of making was in the church, to be ordained by the imposition of hands, by the fittest instruments they had. It must either be in the church or from the pope, and the pope is Antichrist. Ho! said Sr. John, what the pope houlds good, (as in the Trinitie,) that we doe well to assente too; but, said he, we will not enter into dispute now. And as for your letters he would not show them at any hand, least he should spoyle all. He expected you should have been of the archb[p] minde for the calling of ministers, but it seems you

---

[1] According to the new style the date was 1618.

differed.   I could have wished to have known the contents of your tow
inclosed, at which he stuck so much, espetially the larger.   I asked his
Wor^p what good news he had for me to write to morrow.   He tould me
very good news, for both the kings majestie and the bishops have consented.   He said he would goe to Mr. Chancelor, Sr. Fulk Grivell,[1]
as this day, and nexte weeke I should know more.   I mett Sr. Edw.
Sands on Wednesday night; he wished me to be at the Virginia Courte[2]
the nexte Wedensday, wher I purpose to be.   Thus loath to be troublsome at present, I hope to have somewhate nexte week of certentie
concerning you.   I committee you to the Lord.   Yours,

S. B.[3]

These things being long in agitation, and messengers
passing too and againe aboute them, after all their hopes they
were long delayed by many rubs that fell in the way; for at
the returne of these messengers into England they found things
farr otherwise then they expected.   For the Virginia Counsell
was now so disturbed with factions and quarrels amongst them
selves, as no bussines could well goe forward.   The which may
the better appear in one of the messengers letters as followeth.

To his loving freinds, etc.

I had thought long since to have write unto you, but could not effecte
that which I aimed at, neither can yet sett things as I wished; yet, notwithstanding, I doubt not but Mr. B.[4] hath writen to Mr. Robinson.
But I thinke my selfe bound also to doe something, least I be thought to
neglecte you.   The maine hinderance of our proceedings in the Virginia
bussines, is the dissentions and factions, as they terme it, amongst the
Counsell and Company of Virginia; which are such, as that ever since
we came up no busines could by them be dispatched.   The occasion of

---

[1] Sir Fulke Greville (Lord Brooke) was born in Warwickshire in 1554 and
studied at Cambridge.   He was knighted in 1597, was a member of Parliament
and in 1615 was made under-treasurer and chancellor of the exchequer.   In 1621
he became Baron Brooke and died in London in 1628.   He wrote a *Life of Sir
Philip Sidney*, his intimate friend, poems, two tragedies and other works.

[2] By Virginia court is meant the regular meeting of the Virginia Company,
occurring on February 18, 1617/8.

[3] S. B. were probably fictitious initials standing for Sabin Staresmore.   Prince
has a note upon this: "In Govr. Bradford's Collection of Letters, this letter is
more large, and subscribed Sabine Staresmore."   One of that name was a member
of a Separatist body in London, and afterward of Robinson's congregation in
Leyden.   [4] Brewster.

this trouble amongst them is, for that a while since Sr. Thomas Smith, repining at his many offices and troubls, wished the Company of Virginia to ease him of his office in being Treasurer and Gover^r. of the Virginia Company.[1] Whereupon the Company tooke occasion to dismisse him, and chose Sr. Edwin Sands Treasurer and Gover^r of the Company. He having 60. voyces, Sr. John Worstenholme 16. voices, and Alderman Johnsone 24. But Sr. Thomas Smith, when he saw some parte of his honour lost, was very angrie, and raised a faction to cavill and contend aboute the election, and sought to taxe Sr. Edwin with many things that might both disgrace him, and allso put him by his office of Governour. In which contentions they yet stick, and are not fit nor readie to intermedle in any bussines; and what issue things will come to we are not yet certaine. It is most like Sr. Edwin will carrie it away, and if he doe, things will goe well in Virginia; if otherwise, they will goe ill enough allways. We hope in some 2. or 3. Court days things will setle. Mean space I thinke to goe downe into Kente, and come up againe aboute 14. days, or 3. weeks hence; except either by these afforesaid contentions, or by the ille tidings from Virginia, we be wholy discouraged, of which tidings I am now to speake.

Captaine Argoll is come home this weeke (he upon notice of the intente of the Counsell, came away before Sr. Georg Yeardley[2] came ther, and so ther is no small dissention). But his tidings are ill, though his person be wellcome. He saith Mr. Blackwells[3] shipe came not ther till March, but going towards winter, they had still norwest winds, which carried them to the southward beyond their course. And the M^r of the ship and some 6. of the mariners dieing, it seemed they could not find the bay, till after long seeking and beating aboute. Mr. Blackwell is dead, and Mr. Maggner, the Captain; yea, ther are dead, he saith, 130. persons, one and other in that ship; it is said ther was in all an 180. persons in the ship, so as they were packed togeather like herings. They had amongst them the fluxe, and allso wante of fresh water; so as it is hear rather wondred

---

[1] Sir Thomas Smith's request may be seen, in the records of the Virginia Company for the transactions of this very meeting, in the fac-simile presented in *Early Narratives of Virginia*, p. 334, in this series. Smith had had the leading part in the Virginia Company from its beginning.

[2] Samuel Argall was the abductor of Pocahontas, the destroyer of Port Royal in 1613, and deputy governor of Virginia from 1617 to 1619. Sir George Yeardley, governor of Virginia 1619–1621 and 1626–1627.

[3] Francis Blackwell, one of the adherents of Rev. Francis Johnson in the "ancient church" at Amsterdam, seceded from him in 1618, became reconciled with the Anglican establishment, and sailed for Virginia with his followers, in September, 1618, in the *William and Thomas*.

at that so many are alive, then that so many are dead. The marchants hear say it was Mr. Blackwells faulte to pack so many in the ship; yea, and ther were great mutterings and repinings amongst them, and upbraiding of Mr. Blackwell, for his dealing and dispossing of them, when they saw how he had dispossed of them, and how he insulted over them. Yea, the streets at Gravsend[1] runge of their extreame quarrelings, crying out one of another, Thou hast brought me to this, and, I may thanke the for this. Heavie newes it is, and I would be glad to heare how farr it will discourage. I see none hear discouraged much, but rather desire to larne to beware by other mens harmes, and to amend that wherin they have failed. As we desire to serve one another in love, so take heed of being inthraled by any imperious persone, espetially if they be discerned to have an eye to them selves. It doth often trouble me to thinke that in this bussines we are all to learne and none to teach; but better so, then to depend upon such teachers as Mr. Blackwell was. Such a strategeme he once made for Mr. Johnson and his people at Emden,[2] which was their subversion. But though he ther clenlily (yet unhonstly) plucked his neck out of the collar, yet at last his foote is caught. Hear are no letters come, the ship captain Argole came in is yet in the west parts; all that we hear is but his report; it seemeth he came away secretly. The ship that Mr. Blackwell went in will be hear shortly. It is as Mr. Robinson once said; he thought we should hear no good of them.

Mr. B. is not well at this time; whether he will come back to you or goe into the north, I yet know not. For my selfe, I hope to see an end of this bussines ere I come, though I am sorie to be thus from you; if things had gone roundly forward, I should have been with you within these 14. days. I pray God directe us, and give us that spirite which is fitting for such a bussines. Thus having summarily pointed at things which Mr. Brewster (I thinke) hath more largely write of to Mr. Robinson, I leave you to the Lords protection.

Yours in all readines, etc.   London, May 8.
ROBART CUSHMAN.   An°: 1619.

A word or tow by way of digression touching this Mr. Blackwell; he was an elder of the church at Amsterdam, a

[1] Gravesend, at the mouth of the Thames, from which ships from London commonly "took their departure."

[2] Contention arose in the elder of the Separatist churches at Amsterdam, between the partisans of Rev. Francis Johnson and those of Rev. Henry Ainsworth. The burgomasters of the city awarded the meeting-house to the latter. The former then (1613) removed to Emden in East Friesland, and remained there three or four years.

man well known of most of them. He declined from the trueth
with Mr. Johnson and the rest, and went with him when they
parted assunder in that wofull maner, which brought so great
dishonour to God, scandall to the trueth, and outward ruine
to them selves in this world. But I hope, notwithstanding,
through the mercies of the Lord, their souls are now at rest
with him in the heavens, and that they are arrived in the
Haven of hapines; though some of their bodies were thus
buried in the terrable seas, and others sunke under the burthen
of bitter afflictions. He with some others had prepared for
to goe to Virginia. And he, with sundrie godly citizens, being
at a private meeting (I take it a fast) in London, being discovered, many of them were apprehended, wherof Mr. Blackwell was one; but he so glosed with the bp̃s,[1] and either dis-
sembled or flatly denied the trueth which formerly he had
maintained; and not only so, but very unworthily betrayed
and accused another godly man who had escaped, that so
he might slip his own neck out of the collar, and to obtaine
his owne freedome brought others into bonds. Wherupon
he so wone the bp̃s favour (but lost the Lord's) as he was not
only dismiste, but in open courte the archbishop gave him
great applause and his sollemne blessing to proseed in his
vioage. But if such events follow the bp̃s blessing, happie are
they that misse the same; it is much better to keepe a good
conscience and have the Lords blessing, whether in life or death.

But see how the man thus apprehended by Mr. Blackwells
means, writs to a freind of his.

Right dear freind and christian brother, Mr. Carver, I salute you and
yours in the Lord, etc. As for my owne presente condition, I doubt not
but you well understand it ere this by our brother Maistersone,[2] who should
have tasted of the same cupp, had his place of residence and his person

[1] Bishops.
[2] Richard Masterson was from Sandwich, England, and was a member of
the Leyden church. He married in Leyden in 1619 Mary Goodale of Leicester
and came to Plymouth in 1629, where he died in 1633. He was a deacon of the
Plymouth church.

been as well knowne as my selfe. Some what I have written to Mr.
Cushman how the matter still continues. I have petitioned twise to Mr.
Sherives, and once to my Lord Cooke,[1] and have used such reasons to
move them to pittie, that if they were not overruled by some others, I
suppose I should soone gaine my libertie; as that I was a yonge man
living by my credite, indebted to diverse in our citie, living at more then
ordinarie charges in a close and tedious prison; besids great rents abroad,
all my bussines lying still, my only servante lying lame in the countrie, my
wife being also great with child. And yet no answer till the lords of his
majesties Counsell gave consente. Howbeit, Mr. Blackwell, a man as
deepe in this action as I, was delivered at a cheaper rate, with a great deale
less adoe; yea, with an addition of the Archp̄: blessing. I am sorie for
Mr. Blackwels weaknes, I wish it may prove no worse. But yet he and
some others of them, before their going, were not sorie, but thought it was
for the best that I was nominated,[2] not because the Lord sanctifies evill
to good, but that the action was good, yea for the best. One reason I
well remember he used was, because this trouble would encrease the
Virginia plantation, in that now people begane to be more generally inclined to goe; and if he had not nomminated some such as I, he had not
bene free, being it was knowne that diverse citizens besids them selves
were ther. I expecte an answer shortly what they intende conscerning
me; I purpose to write to some others of you, by whom you shall know the
certaintie. Thus not haveing further at present to acquaint you withall,
commending myselfe to your prairs, I cease, and committe you and us all
to the Lord.

From my chamber in Wodstreete Compter.[3]

Your freind, and brother in bonds,

Sept.: 4. An°: 1618.   SABIN STARESMORE.

But thus much by the way, which may be of instruction
and good use.

But at last, after all these things, and their long attendance,
they had a patent granted them, and confirmed under the
Companies seale;[4] but these devissions and distractions had

---

[1] To the sheriffs of London and Middlesex, and to Sir Edward Coke, till
lately lord chief justice.   [2] I. e., informed against.

[3] Wood Street Compter (counter) was a prison in London.

[4] The records of the Virginia Company for May 26 and June 9, 1619, show
"one Mr. Wencop, commended to the Company by the [late] Earle of Lincolne,"
presenting his patent for confirmation on the former date; on the latter it was
ordered to be sealed.

shaken of many of ther pretended freinds, and disappointed
them of much of their hoped for and proffered means. By
the advise of some freinds this pattente was not taken in the
name of any of their owne, but in the name of Mr. John
Wincob (a religious gentleman then belonging to the Countess
of Lincoline), who intended to goe with them. But God so
disposed as he never went, nor they ever made use of this
patente,[1] which had cost them so much labour and charge,
as by the sequell will appeare. This patente being sente over
for them to veiw and consider, as also the passages aboute the
propossitions between them and such marchants and freinds as
should either goe or adventure with them, and espetially with
those[2] on whom they did cheefly depend for shipping and
means, whose proffers had been large, they were requested to
fitt and prepare them selves with all speed. A right emblime,
it may be, of the uncertine things of this world; that when men
have toyld them selves for them, they vanish into smoke.

The 6. Chap.

*Conscerning the agreements and artickles between them, ana
such marchants and others as adventured moneys; with
other things falling out aboute making their provissions.*

Upon the receite of these things by one of their messengers,
they had a sollemne meeting and a day of humilliation to
seeke the Lord for his direction; and their pastor tooke this
texte, 1 *Sam.* 23. 3, 4. *And David's men said unto him, see,
we be afraid hear in Judah, how much more if we come to Keilah
against the host of the Phillistines? Then David asked counsell
of the Lord againe*, etc. From which texte he taught many
things very aptly, and befitting ther present occasion and
condition, strengthing them against their fears and perplexities,
and incouraging them in the resolutions. After which they
concluded both what number and what persons should prepare

[1] It was undoubtedly surrendered afterward.
[2] "Mr. Tho: Weston, etc."   (Br.)

them selves to goe with the first; for all that were willing to have gone could not gett ready for their other affairs in so shorte a time; neither if all could have been ready, had ther been means to have transported them alltogeather. Those that staied being the greater number required the pastor to stay with them; and indeede for other reasons he could not then well goe, and so it was the more easilie yeelded unto. The other then desired the elder, Mr. Brewster, to goe with them, which was also condescended unto. It was also agreed on by mutuall consente and covenante, that those that went should be an absolute church of them selves, as well as those that staid; seing in such a dangrous vioage, and a removall to such a distance, it might come to pass they should (for the body of them) never meete againe in this world; yet with this proviso, that as any of the rest came over to them, or of the other returned upon occasion, they should be reputed as members without any further dismission or testimoniall. It was allso promised to those that wente first, by the body of the rest, that if the Lord gave them life, and means, and opportunitie, they would come to them as soone as they could.

Aboute this time, whilst they were perplexed with the proseedings of the Virginia Company, and the ill news from thence aboute Mr. Blackwell and his company, and making inquirey about the hiring and buying of shiping for their vioage, some Dutchmen made them faire offers aboute goeing with them.[1] Also one Mr. Thomas Weston,[2] a merchant of London, came to Leyden aboute the same time, (who was well aquainted with

[1] This seems to dispose of the statement of Morton in *New England's Memorial* that Captain Jones of the *Mayflower* was bribed by the Dutch to keep away from New Netherland.

[2] Thomas Weston, whose first dealings with the Pilgrims are here recounted, is referred to by Cushman as one of the "adventurers," but he probably left them before 1622. He sent several vessels to New England and came himself with a colony which afterwards settled at Wessagusset (Weymouth). He was charged with fraudulent transactions by Robert Gorges, who for a time was governor-general of New England, but saved from punishment by the intercession of Governor Bradford. He died in Bristol, England, not far from 1640.

some of them, and a furtherer of them in their former proseedings,) haveing much conferance with Mr. Robinson and
other of the cheefe of them, perswaded them to goe on (as it
seems) and not to medle with the Dutch, or too much to depend
on the Virginia Company; for if that failed, if they came to resolution, he and such marchants as were his friends (togeather
with their owne means) would sett them forth; and they
should make ready, and neither feare 'wante of shipping nor
money; for what they wanted should be provided. And, not
so much for him selfe as for the satisfing of such frends as he
should procure to adventure in this bussines, they were to
draw such articls of agreemente, and make such propossitions,
as might the better induce his freinds to venture. Upon which
(after the formere conclusion) articles were drawne and agreed
unto, and were showne unto him, and approved by him; and
afterwards by their messenger (Mr. John Carver) sent into
England, who, togeather with Robart Cushman, were to receive
the moneys and make provissione both for shiping and other
things for the vioage; with this charge, not to exseede their
commission, but to proseed according to the former articles.
Also some were chossen to doe the like for such things as were
to be prepared there; so those that weare to goe, prepared
them selves with all speed, and sould of their estats and (such
as were able) put in their moneys into the commone stock,
which was disposed by those appointed, for the making of
generall provissions. Aboute this time also they had heard,
both by Mr. Weston and others, that sundrie Hon[bl]: Lords
had obtained a large grante from the king, for the more northerly parts of that countrie, derived out of the Virginia patente,
and wholy secluded from their Govermente, and to be called by
another name, viz. New-England.[1] Unto which Mr. Weston, and

---

[1] The reference is, of course, to the famous patent of November 3, 1620, by
which forty noblemen and gentlemen were constituted the Council for New
England, with jurisdiction over the territory from 40° to 48° north latitude.
Though it did not pass the great seal till November, the warrant for its preparation
was issued in July.

the cheefe of them, begane to incline it was best for them to goe, as for other reasons, so cheefly for the hope of present profite to be made by the fishing that was found in that countrie.

But as in all bussineses the acting parte is most difficulte, espetially wher the worke of many agents must concurr, so it was found in this; for some of those that should have gone in England, fell of and would not goe; other marchants and freinds that had offered to adventure their moneys withdrew, and pretended many excuses. Some disliking they wente not to Guiana; others againe would adventure nothing excepte they wente to Virginia. Some againe (and those that were most relied on) fell in utter dislike with Virginia, and would doe nothing if they wente thither. In the midds of these distractions, they of Leyden, who had put of their estats, and laid out their moneys, were brought into a greate streight, fearing what issue these things would come too; but at length the generalitie was swaid to this latter opinion.

But now another difficultie arose, for Mr. Weston and some other that were for this course, either for their better advantage or rather for the drawing on of others, as they pretended, would have some of those conditions altered that were first agreed on at Leyden. To which the 2. agents sent from Leyden (or at least one of them who is most charged with it) did consente; seeing els that all was like to be dashte, and the opportunitie lost, and that they which had put of their estats and paid in their moneys were in hazard to be undon. They presumed to conclude with the marchants on those termes, in some things contrary to their order and commission, and without giving them notice of the same; yea, it was conceled least it should make any furder delay; which was the cause afterward of much trouble and contention.

It will be meete I here inserte these conditions, which are as foloweth.

An°: 1620. July 1.

1. The adventurers and planters doe agree, that every person that

goeth being aged 16. years and upward, be rated at 10*li.*, and ten pounds to be accounted a single share.

2. That he that goeth in person, and furnisheth him selfe out with 10*li.* either in money or other provissions, be accounted as haveing 20*li.* in stock, and in the devission shall receive a double share.

3. The persons transported and the adventurers shall continue their joynt stock and partnership togeather, the space of 7. years, (excepte some unexpected impedimente doe cause the whole company to agree otherwise,) during which time, all profits and benifits that are gott by trade, traffick, trucking, working, fishing, or any other means of any person or persons, remaine still in the commone stock untill the division.

4. That at their comming ther, they chose out such a number of fitt persons, as may furnish their ships and boats for fishing upon the sea; imploying the rest in their severall faculties upon the land; as building houses, tilling, and planting the ground, and makeing shuch commodities as shall be most usefull for the collonie.

5. That at the end of the 7. years, the capitall and profits, viz. the houses, lands, goods and chatles, be equally devided betwixte the adventurers, and planters; which done, every man shall be free from other of them of any debt or detrimente concerning this adventure.

6. Whosoever cometh to the colonie herafter, or putteth any into the stock, shall at the ende of the 7. years be alowed proportionably to the time of his so doing.

7. He that shall carie his wife and children, or servants, shall be alowed for everie person now aged 16. years and upward, a single share in the devision, or if he provid them necessaries, a duble share, or if they be between 10. year old and 16., then 2. of them to be reconed for a person, both in transportation and devision.

8. That such children as now goe, and are under the age of ten years, have noe other shar in the division, but 50. acers of unmanured land.

9. That such persons as die before the 7. years be expired, their executors to have their parte or sharr at the devision, proportionably to the time of their life in the collonie.

10. That all such persons as are of this collonie, are to have their meate, drink, apparell, and all provissions out of the common stock and goods of the said collonie.

The cheefe and principall differences betwene these and the former conditions, stood in those 2. points; that the houses, and lands improved, espetialy gardens and home lotts should remaine undevided wholy to the planters at the

7. years end. 2^ly, that they should have had 2. days in a weeke for their owne private imploymente, for the more comforte of them selves and their families, espetialy such as had families. But because letters are by some wise men counted the best parte of histories, I shall shew their greevances hereaboute by their owne letters, in which the passages of things will be more truly discerned.

A letter of Mr. Robinsons to John Carver.

June 14. 1620. N. Stile.[1]

My dear freind and brother, whom with yours I alwaise remember in my best affection, and whose wellfare I shall never cease to commend to God by my best and most earnest praires. You doe throwly understand by our generall letters the estate of things hear, which indeed is very pitifull; espetialy by wante of shiping, and not seeing means lickly, much less certaine, of having it provided; though withall ther be great want of money and means to doe needfull things. Mr. Pickering,[2] you know before this, will not defray a peny hear; though Robart Cushman presumed of I know not how many 100*li.* from him, and I know not whom. Yet it seems strange that we should be put to him to receive both his and his partners adventer, and yet Mr. Weston write unto him, that in regard of it, he hath drawne upon him a 100*li.* more. But ther is in this some misterie, as indeed it seems ther is in the whole course. Besids, wheras diverse are to pay in some parts of their moneys yet behinde, they refuse to doe it, till they see shiping provided, or a course taken for it. Neither doe I thinke is ther a man hear would pay any thing, if he had againe his money in his purse. You know right well we depended on Mr. Weston alone, and upon such means as he would procure for this commone bussines; and when we had in hand another course with the Dutchmen, broke it of at his motion, and upon the conditions by him shortly after propounded. He did this in his love I know, but things appeare not answerable from him hitherto. That he should have first have put in his moneys, is thought by many to have been but fitt, but that I can well excuse, he being a marchante and haveing use of it to his benefite; wheras others, if it had been in their hands, would have consumed it. But that he should not but have had either shipping ready before this time, or at

---

[1] On the back of the preceding page of manuscript Prince wrote these words: "June 14 N. S. is June 4 O. S. which is Lords Day and therefore here is doubtless a mistake."

[2] Edward Pickering was one of the merchant adventurers.

least certaine means, and course, and the same knowne to us for it, or
have taken other order otherwise, cannot in my conscience be excused.
I have heard that when he hath been moved in the bussines, he hath put
it of from him selfe, and referred it to the others; and would come to
Georg Morton,[1] and enquire news of him aboute things, as if he had scarce
been some accessarie unto it. Wether he hath failed of some helps from
others which he expected, and so be not well able to goe through with
things, or whether he hath feared least you should be ready too soone and
so encrease the charge of shiping above that is meete, or whether he have
thought by withhoulding to put us upon straits, thinking that therby Mr.
Brewer[2] and Mr. Pickering would be drawne by importunitie to doe more,
or what other misterie is in it, we know not; but sure we are that things
are not answerable to such an occasion. Mr. Weston maks himselfe
mery with our endeavors about buying a ship, but we have done nothing
in this but with good reason, as I am perswaded, nor yet that I know in
any thing els, save in those tow; the one, that we imployed Robart Cushman, who is known (though a good man, and of spetiall abilities in his kind
yet) most unfitt to deale for other men, by reason of his singularitie, and
too great indifferancie for any conditions, and for (to speak truly) that we
have had nothing from him but termes and presumptions. The other,
that we have so much relyed, by implicite faith as it were, upon general-
ities, without seeing the perticuler course and means for so waghtie an
affaire set down unto us. For shiping, Mr. Weston, it should seeme, is
set upon hireing, which yet I wish he may presently effecte; but I see litle
hope of help from hence if so it be. Of Mr. Brewer you know what to
expecte. I doe not thinke Mr. Pickering will ingage, excepte in the course
of buying, in former letters specified. Aboute the conditions, you have
our reasons for our judgments of what is agreed. And let this spetially
be borne in minde, that the greatest parte of the Collonie is like to be

[1] George Morton had been a merchant in the city of York and probably went
to Holland with the Pilgrim Church. He married in Leyden in 1612 a sister of
the second wife of Governor Bradford. "Mourt's *Relation*," written chiefly by
Bradford and Winslow, was published under his direction in 1622, prefaced by
him with an address to the reader signed "G. Mourt." He came over in the
Anne in 1623 with his wife and four children and died in 1624. His son Nathaniel,
born in Leyden in 1613, was secretary of the Plymouth Colony and author of
New England's Memorial, published in 1669.

[2] Thomas Brewer was a landed proprietor of Kent and one of the merchant
adventurers. He was a Separatist, a neighbor of Elder Brewster in Leyden,
and a sustaining partner in his printing business, which was carried on in Brewer's
garret. For the history of King James's persecution of him see Arber, *Story of
the Pilgrim Fathers*, pp. 195–247. He was imprisoned in England from 1626
to 1640, and died in the latter year.

imployed constantly, not upon dressing ther perticuler land and building houses, but upon fishing, trading, etc.   So as the land and house will be but a trifell for advantage to the adventurers, and yet the devission of it a great discouragmente to the planters, who would with singuler care make it comfortable with borowed houres from their sleep.   The same consideration of commone imploymente constantly by the most is a good reason not to have the 2. daies in a weeke denyed the few planters for private use, which yet is subordinate to commone good.   Consider also how much unfite that you and your liks must serve a new prentishipe of 7. years, and not a daies freedome from taske.   Send me word what persons are to goe, who of usefull faculties, and how many, and perticulerly of every thing.   I know you wante not a minde.   I am sorie you have not been at London all this while, but the provissions could not wante you. Time will suffer me to write no more; fare you and yours well allways in the Lord, in whom I rest.

Yours to use,

JOHN ROBINSON.

An other letter from sundrie of them at the same time.

To their loving freinds John Carver and Robart Cushman, these, etc.
Good bretheren, after salutations, etc.   We received diverse letters at the coming of Mr. Nash[1] and our pilott, which is a great incouragmente unto us, and for whom we hop after times will minister occasion of praising God; and indeed had you not sente him, many would have been ready to fainte and goe backe.   Partly in respecte of the new conditions which have bene taken up by you, which all men are against, and partly in regard of our owne inabillitie to doe any one of those many waightie bussineses you referr to us here.   For the former wherof, wheras Robart Cushman desirs reasons for our dislike, promising therupon to alter the same, or els saing we should thinke he hath no brains, we desire him to exercise them therin, refering him to our pastors former reasons, and them to the censure of the godly wise.   But our desires are that you will not entangle your selvs and us in any such unreasonable courses as those are, viz. that the marchants should have the halfe of mens houses and lands at the dividente; and that persons should be deprived of the 2. days in a weeke agreed upon, yea every momente of time for their owne perticuler; by reason wherof we cannot conceive why any should carie servants for their own help and comfort; for that we can require no more of them then all men one of another.   This we have only by relation from

---

[1] Thomas Nash was one of the Leyden church but nothing more is known of him.

Mr. Nash, and not from any writing of your owne, and therfore hope you have not proceeded farr in so great a thing without us.   But requiring you not to exseed the bounds of your commission, which was to proceed upon the things or conditions agred upon and expressed in writing (at your going over about it), we leave it, not without marveling, that your selfe, as you write, knowing how smale a thing troubleth our consultations, and how few, as you fear, understands the busnes aright, should trouble us with such matters as these are, etc.

Salute Mr. Weston from us, in whom we hope we are not deceived; we pray you make known our estate unto him, and if you thinke good shew him our letters, at least tell him that (under God) we much relie upon him and put our confidence in him; and, as your selves well know, that if he had not been an adventurer with us, we had not taken it in hand; presuming that if he had not seene means to accomplish it, he would not have begune it; so we hope in our extremitie he will so farr help us as our expectation be no way made frustrate concerning him.   Since therfore, good brethren, we have plainly opened the state of things with us in this matter, you will, etc.   Thus beseeching the Allmightie, who is allsufficiente to raise us out of this depth of dificulties, to assiste us herein; raising such means by his providence and fatherly care for us, his pore children and servants, as we may with comforte behould the hand of our God for good towards us in this our bussines, which we undertake in his name and fear, we take leave and remaine

Your perplexed, yet hopfull

June 10. New Stille,   bretheren,
An°: 1620.   S. F. E. W. W. B. J. A.[1]

A letter of Robart Cushmans to them.

Brethern, I understand by letters and passagess that have come to me, that ther are great discontents, and dislike of my proceedings amongst you.   Sorie I am to hear it, yet contente to beare it, as not doubting but that partly by writing, and more principally by word when we shall come togeather, I shall satisfie any reasonable man.   I have been perswaded by some, espetialy this bearer, to come and clear things unto you; but as things now stand I cannot be absente one day, excepte I should hazard all the viage.   Neither conceive I any great good would come of it.   Take then, brethern, this as a step to give you contente.   First, for your dislike of the alteration of one clause in the conditions, if you conceive it right,

[1] "In Gov. Bradford's Collection of Letters, these subscribers are thus wrote out at length: SAMUEL FULLER, WILLIAM BRADFORD, ISAAC ALLERTON, ED. WINSLOW."   (Note by Rev. Thomas Prince.)

ther can be no blame lye on me at all.   For the articles first brought over by John Carver were never seene of any of the adventurers hear, excepte Mr. Weston, neither did any of them like them because of that clause; nor Mr. Weston him selfe, after he had well considered it.   But as at the first ther was 500*li.* withdrawne by Sr. Georg Farrer and his brother upon that dislike, so all the rest would have withdrawne (Mr. Weston excepted) if we had not altered that clause.   Now whilst we at Leyden conclude upon points, as we did, we reckoned without our host, which was not my falte.   Besids, I shewed you by a letter the equitie of that condition, and our inconveniences, which might be sett against all Mr. Rob:[1] inconveniences, that without the alteration of that clause, we could neither have means to gett thither, nor supplie wherby to subsiste when we were ther.   Yet notwithstanding all those reasons, which were not mine, but other mens wiser then my selfe, without answer to any one of them, here cometh over many quirimonies,[2] and complaints against me, of lording it over my brethern, and making conditions fitter for theeves and bondslaves then honest men, and that of my owne head I did what I list.   And at last a paper of reasons, framed against that clause in the conditions, which as they were delivered me open, so my answer is open to you all.   And first, as they are no other but inconveniences, such as a man might frame 20. as great on the other side, and yet prove nor disprove nothing by them, so they misse and mistake both the very ground of the article and nature of the project.   For, first, it is said, that if ther had been no divission of houses and lands, it had been better for the poore. True, and that showeth the inequalitie of the condition; we should more respecte him that ventureth both his money and his person, then him that ventureth but his person only.

2.   Consider wheraboute we are, not giveing almes, but furnishing a store house; no one shall be porer then another for 7. years, and if any be rich, none can be pore.   At the least, we must not in such bussines crie, Pore, pore, mercie, mercie.   Charitie hath it[s] life in wraks, not in venturs; you are by this most in a hopefull pitie of makeing, therfore complaine not before you have need.

3.   This will hinder the building of good and faire houses, contrarie to the advise of pollitiks.[3]   A.   So we would have it; our purpose is to build for the presente such houses as, if need be, we may with litle greefe set a fire, and rune away by the lighte; our riches shall not be in pompe, but in strenght; if God send us riches, we will imploye them to provid more men, ships, munition, etc.   You may see it amongst the best polli-

---

[1] Robinson's.   [2] Querimonies, fault-findings.
[3] Writers upon political theory.

tiks, that a commonwele is readier to ebe then to flow, when once fine houses and gay cloaths come up.

4.   The Gove[t] [1] may prevente excess in building.   A. But if it be on all men beforehand resolved on, to build mean houses, the Gove[ts] laboure is spared.

5.   All men are not of one condition.   A. If by condition you mean wealth, you are mistaken; if you mean by condition, qualities, then I say he that is not contente his neighbour shall have as good a house, fare, means, etc. as him selfe, is not of a good qualitie.   2[ly]. Such retired persons, as have an eie only to them selves, are fitter to come wher catching is, then closing; and are fitter to live alone, then in any societie, either civill or religious.

6.   It will be of litle value, scarce worth 5*li*.   A. True, it may be not worth halfe 5*li*.   If then so smale a thing will content them, why strive we thus aboute it, and give them occasion to suspecte us to be worldly and covetous?   I will not say what I have heard since these complaints came first over.

7.   Our freinds with us that adventure mind not their owne profite, as did the old adventurers.   A. Then they are better then we, who for a litle matter of profite are readie to draw back, and it is more apparente brethern looke too it, that make profite your maine end; repente of this, els goe not least you be like Jonas to Tarshis.   2[ly]. Though some of them mind not their profite, yet others doe mind it; and why not as well as we? venturs are made by all sorts of men, and we must labour to give them all contente, if we can.

8.   It will break the course of communitie, as may be showed by many reasons.   A. That is but said, and I say againe, it will best foster comunion, as may be showed by many reasons.

9.   Great profite is like to be made by trucking, fishing, etc.   A. As it is better for them, so for us; for halfe is ours, besids our living still upon it, and if such profite in that way come, our labour shall be the less on the land, and our houses and lands must and will be of less value.

10.   Our hazard is greater then theirs.   A. True, but doe they put us upon it? doe they urge or egg us? hath not the motion and resolution been always in our selves? doe they any more then in seeing us resolute if we had means, help us to means upon equall termes and conditions? If we will not goe, they are content to keep their moneys.   Thus I have pointed at a way to loose those knots, which I hope you will consider seriously, and let me have no more stirre about them.

[1] Government.

Now furder, I hear a noise of slavish conditions by me made; but surly this is all that I have altered, and reasons I have sent you. If you mean it of the 2. days in a week for perticuler, as some insinuate, you are deceived; you may have 3. days in a week for me if you will. And when I have spoken to the adventurers of times of working, they have said they hope we are men of discretion and conscience, and so fitte to be trusted our selves with that. But indeed the ground of our proceedings at Leyden was mistaken, and so here is nothing but tottering every day, etc.

As for them of Amsterdam I had thought they would as soone have gone to Rome as with us; for our libertie is to them as ratts bane, and their riggour as bad to us as the Spanish Inquision. If any practise of mine discourage them, let them yet draw back; I will undertake they shall have their money againe presently paid hear. Or if the company thinke me to be the Jonas, let them cast me of before we goe; I shall be content to stay with good will, having but the cloaths on my back; only let us have quietnes, and no more of these clamors; full litle did I expecte these things which are now come to pass, etc.

Yours,   R. Cushman.

But whether this letter of his ever came to their hands at Leyden I well know not; I rather thinke it was staied by Mr. Carver and kept by him, forgiving offence. But this which follows was ther received; both which I thought pertenent to recite.

Another of his to the aforesaid, June 11. 1620.[1]

Salutations, etc. I received your le[tte]r yesterday, by John Turner,[2] with another the same day from Amsterdam by Mr. W. savouring of the place whenc it came. And indeed the many discouragements I find her, togeather with the demurrs and retirings ther, had made me to say, I would give up my accounts to John Carver, and at his comeing aquainte him fully with all courses, and so leave it quite, with only the pore cloaths on my back. But gathering up my selfe by further consideration, I resolved yet to make one triall more, and to aquainte Mr. Weston with the fainted state of our bussines; and though he hath been much discontented at some thing amongst us of late, which hath made him often say that

---

[1] "June 11. O. S. is Lord's day, and therefore 't is likely the Date of this Letter should be June 10, the same with the Date of the Letter following." (Note by Thomas Prince.)

[2] John Turner came with two sons in the *Mayflower*; all died in the first winter.

save for his promise, he would not meadle at all with the bussines any more, yet considering how farr we were plunged into maters, and how it stood both on our credits and undoing, at the last he gathered up him selfe a litle more, and coming to me 2. hours after, he tould me he would not yet leave it.   And so advising togeather we resolved to hire a ship, and have tooke liking of one till Monday, about 60. laste,[1] for a greater we cannot gett, excepte it be tow great; but a fine ship it is.   And seeing our neer freinds ther are so streite lased, we hope to assure her without troubling them any further; and if the ship fale too small, it fitteth well that such as stumble at strawes allready, may rest them ther a while, least worse blocks come in the way ere 7. years be ended.   If you had beaten this bussines so throuly a month agoe, and write to us as now you doe, we could thus have done much more conveniently.   But it is as it is; I hop our freinds ther, if they be quitted of the ship hire, will be indusced tʳ venture the more.   All that I now require is that salt and netts may ther be boughte, and for all the rest we will here provid it; yet if that will not be, let them but stand for it amonth or tow, and we will take order to pay it all.   Let Mr. Reinholds[2] tarie ther, and bring the ship to Southampton. We have hired another pilote here, one Mr. Clarke, who went last year to Virginia with a ship of kine.[3]

You shall here distinctly by John Turner, who I thinke shall come hence on Tewsday night.   I had thought to have come with him, to have answered to my complaints; but I shal lerne to pass litle for ther censurs; and if I had more minde to goe and dispute and expostulate with them, then I have care of this waightie bussines, I were like them who live by clamours and jangling.   But neither my mind nor my body is at libertie to doe much, for I am fettered with bussines, and had rather study to be quiet, then to make answer to their exceptions.   If men be set on it, let them beat the eair; I hope such as are my sinceire freinds will not thinke but I can give some reason of my actions.   But of your mistaking aboute the mater, and other things tending to this bussines, I shall nexte informe you more distinctly.   Mean space entreate our freinds not to be too bussie in answering matters, before they know them.   If I doe such things as

[1] Sixty last equals 120 tons.

[2] Reinholds was the captain of the *Speedwell*, the vessel which abandoned the voyage.

[3] This was John Clarke.   Rev. E. D. Neill has shown that a Captain Jones, whom he believed to be identical with the captain of the *Mayflower*, went to Virginia in 1619 in command of a vessel with kine, and that a man named John Clarke was employed by the Virginia Company to go with him.   But see *post*, p. 87, note 1.

I cannot give reasons for, it is like you have sett a foole aboute your bussines, and so turne the reproofe to your selves, and send an other, and let me come againe to my Combes.[1]   But setting a side my naturall infirmities, I refuse not to have my cause judged, both of God, and all indifferent men; and when we come togeather I shall give accounte of my actions hear.   The Lord, who judgeth justly without respect of persons, see into the equitie of my cause, and give us quiet, peaceable, and patient minds, in all these turmoiles, and sanctifie unto us all crosses whatsoever.   And so I take my leave of you all, in all love and affection.

I hope we shall gett all hear ready in 14. days.

Your pore brother,

June 11. 1620.   ROBART CUSHMAN.

Besids these things, ther fell out a differance amongs those 3. that received the moneys and made the provissions in England; for besids these tow formerly mentioned sent from Leyden for this end, viz. Mr. Carver and Robart Cushman, ther was one chosen in England to be joyned with them, to make the provisions for the vioage; his name was Mr. Martin,[2] he came from Billirike in Essexe, from which parts came sundrie others to goe with them, as also from London and other places; and therfore it was thought meete and conveniente by them in Holand that these strangers that were to goe with them, should apointe one thus to be joyned with them, not so much for any great need of their help, as to avoyd all susspition, or jelosie of any partiallitie.   And indeed their care for giving offence, both in this and other things afterward, turned to great inconvenience unto them, as in the sequell will apeare; but however it shewed their equall and honest minds.   The provissions were for the most parte made at Southhamton, contrarie to Mr. Westons and Robert Cushmans mind (whose counsells did most concure in all things).   A touch of which things I shall give in a letter of his to Mr. Carver, and more will appear afterward.

---

[1] The writer of this letter was a wool-carder in Leyden; by "combes" he meant the cards or combs used in his trade.

[2] Christopher Martin. of Billericay, came in the *Mayflower* and died January 6, 1620/1.

To his loving freind Mr. John Carver, these, etc.

Loving freind, I have received from you some letters, full of affection and complaints, and what it is you would have of me I know not; for your crieing out, Negligence, negligence, negligence, I marvell why so negligente a man was used in the bussines. Yet know you that all that I have power to doe hear, shall not be one hower behind, I warent you. You have reference to Mr. Weston to help us with money, more then his adventure; wher he protesteth but for his promise, he would not have done any thing. He saith we take a heady course, and is offended that our provissions are made so farr of; as also that he was not made aquainted with our quantitie of things; and saith that in now being in 3. places, so farr remote, we will, with going up and downe, and wrangling and expostulating, pass over the sommer before we will goe. And to speake the trueth, ther is fallen already amongst us a flatt schisme; and we are redier to goe to dispute, then to sett forwarde a voiage. I have received from Leyden since you wente 3. or 4. letters directed to you, though they only conscerne me. I will not trouble you with them. I always feared the event of the Amsterdamers striking in with us. I trow you must excommunicate me, or els you must goe without their companie, or we shall wante no quareling; but let them pass. We have reckoned, it should seeme, without our host; and, counting upon a 150. persons, ther cannot be founde above 1200*li.* and odd moneys of all the venturs you can reckone, besids some cloath, stockings, and shoes, which are not counted; so we shall come shorte at least 3. or 400*li.* I would have had some thing shortened at first of beare and other provissions in hope of other adventurs, and now we could have, both in Amsterd: and Kent, beere inough to serve our turne, but now we cannot accept it without prejudice. You fear we have begune to build and shall not be able to make an end; indeed, our courses were never established by counsell, we may therfore justly fear their standing. Yea, ther was a schisme amongst us 3. at the first. You wrote to Mr. Martin, to prevente the making of the provissions in Kente, which he did, and sett downe his resolution how much he would have of every thing, without respecte to any counsell or exception. Surely he that is in a societie and yet regards not counsell, may better be a king then a consorte. To be short, if ther be not some other dispossition setled unto then yet is, we that should be partners of humilitie and peace, shall be examples of jangling and insulting. Yet your money which you ther must have, we will get provided for you instantly. 500*li.* you say will serve; for the rest which hear and in Holand is to be used, we may goe scratch for it. For Mr. Crabe,[1] of whom you write, he hath promised

[1] "He was a minister." (Br.)

to goe with us, yet I tell you I shall not be without feare till I see him shipped, for he is much opposed, yet I hope he will not faile. Thinke the best of all, and bear with patience what is wanting, and the Lord guid us all.

Your loving freind,

London, June 10.   ROBART CUSHMAN.
    An°: 1620.

I have bene the larger in these things, and so shall crave leave in some like passages following, (thoug in other things I shal labour to be more contrate,) that their children may see with what difficulties their fathers wrastled in going throug these things in their first beginnings, and how God brought them along notwithstanding all their weaknesses and infirmities. As allso that some use may be made hereof in after times by others in such like waightie imployments; and herewith I will end this chapter.

The 7. Chap.

Of their departure from Leyden, and other things ther aboute, with their arivall at South hamton, were they all mete togeather, and tooke in ther provissions.

AT length, after much travell and these debats, all things were got ready and provided. A smale ship[1] was bought, and fitted in Holand, which was intended as to serve to help to transport them, so to stay in the cuntrie and atend upon fishing and shuch other affairs as might be for the good and benefite of the colonie when they came ther. Another was hired at London, of burden about 9. score;[2] and all other

---

[1] "Of some 60 tune." (Br.) That its name was the *Speedwell* is not stated by Bradford, and first appears from the statement of his nephew Morton, in *New England's Memorial* (1669).

[2] The ship was the *Mayflower*, of 180 tons. Questions are often asked about her dimensions. At that time the method of computing the tonnage of a double-decked vessel (which we know she was, because Bradford says that when her main beam was sprung a post was placed under it resting on the lower deck), was as follows: Ascertain the length above the deck from the fore part of the stem to the after part of the stern-post, deduct three-fifths of the width, multiply the remainder by the width, multiply the product by one-half of the width and divide

things gott in readines. So being ready to departe, they had
a day of solleme humiliation, their pastor taking his texte
from Ezra 8. 21. *And ther at the river, by Ahava, I proclaimed
a fast, that we might humble ourselves before our God, and seeke
of him a right way for us, and for our children, and for all our
substance.* Upon which he spente a good parte of the day very
profitably, and suitable to their presente occasion. The rest
of the time was spente in powering out prairs to the Lord with
great fervencie, mixed with abundance of tears. And the
time being come that they must departe, they were accompanied with most of their brethren out of the citie, unto a
towne sundrie miles of called Delfes-Haven,[1] wher the ship lay
ready to receive them. So they lefte that goodly and pleasante
citie, which had been ther resting place near 12. years; but
they knew they were pilgrimes,[2] and looked not much on those
things, but lift up their eyes to the heavens, their dearest
cuntrie, and quieted their spirits. When they came to the
place they found the ship and all things ready; and shuch of
their freinds as could not come with them followed after them,
and sundrie also came from Amsterdame to see them shipte
and to take their leave of them. That night was spent with
litle sleepe by the most, but with freindly entertainmente and
christian discourse and other reall expressions of true christian
love. The next day, the wind being faire, they wente aborde,
and their freinds with them, where truly dolfull was the sight
of that sade and mournfull parting; to see what sighs and sobbs
and praires did sound amongst them, what tears did gush
from every eye, and pithy speeches peirst each harte; that
sundry of the Dutch strangers that stood on the key as specta-
tors, could not refraine from tears. Yet comfortable and sweete

the product by 95. If we assume the extreme length to have been 97½ feet, and
the width to have been twenty feet, we should under this rule have a vessel of 180
tons. The name *Mayflower* does not appear in Bradford, but is given in the
Plymouth Colony records of 1623. It was a common name for ships.
     [1] Delfshaven is on the Maas, just below Rotterdam. From Leyden one
would go to it by canal, 24 miles. The place of embarkation at Delfshaven has
recently been marked by a tablet.   [2] "Heb. 11."   (Br.)

it was to see shuch lively and true expressions of dear and
unfained love. But the tide (which stays for no man) caling
them away that were thus loath to departe, their Rev[er]end
pastor falling downe on his knees, (and they all with him,)
with watrie cheeks commended them with most fervente
praiers to the Lord and his blessing. And then with mutuall
imbrases and many tears, they tooke their leaves one of an
other; which proved to be the last leave to many of them.

Thus hoysing saile,[1] with a prosperus winde they came in
short time to Southhamton, wher they found the bigger ship
come from London, lying ready, with all the rest of their
company. After a joyfull wellcome, and mutuall congratulations, with othe[r] frendly entertainements, they fell to parley
aboute their bussines, how to dispatch with the best expedition;
as allso with their agents aboute the alteration of the conditions. Mr. Carver pleaded he was imployed hear at Hamton,[2]
and knew not well what the other had don at London. Mr.
Cushman answered, he had done nothing but what he was
urged too, partly by the grounds of equity, and more espetialy
by necessitie, other wise all had bene dasht and many undon.
And in the begining he aquainted his felow agents here with
who consented unto him, and left it to him to execute, and to
receive the money at London and send it downe to them at
Hamton, wher they made the provissions; the which he
accordingly did, though it was against his minde, and some of
the marchants, that they were their made. And for giveing
them notise at Leyden of this change, he could not well in
regarde of the shortnes of the time; againe, he knew it would
trouble them and hinder the bussines, which was already
delayed overlong in regard of the season of the year, which he
feared they would find to their cost. But these things gave
not contente at presente. Mr. Weston, likwise, came up from
London to see them dispatcht and to have the conditions confirmed; but they refused, and answered him, that he knew

---

[1] "This was about 22. of July." (Br.)   [2] Southampton.

right well that these were not according to the first agreemente
neither could they yeeld to them without the consente of the
rest that were behind. And indeed they had spetiall charge
when they came away, from the cheefe of those that were behind, not to doe it. At which he was much offended, and tould
them, they must then looke to stand on their owne leggs. So
he returned in displeasure, and this was the first ground of
discontent betweene them. And wheras ther wanted well near
100*li*. to clear things at their going away, he would not take
order to disburse a penie, but let them shift as they could.
So they were forst to selle of some of their provissions to stop
this gape, which was some 3. or 4. score firkins of butter, which
comoditie they might best spare, haveing provided too large
a quantitie of that kind. Then they write a leter to the
marchants and adventures aboute the diferances concerning
the conditions, as foloweth.

Aug. 3. An°: 1620.

Beloved freinds, sory we are that ther should be occasion of writing
at all unto you, partly because we ever expected to see the most of you
hear, but espetially because ther should any differance at all be conceived
betweene us. But seing it faleth out that we cannot conferr togeather,
we thinke it meete (though brefly) to show you the just cause and reason
of our differing from those articles last made by Robart Cushman, without our comission or knowledg. And though he might propound good
ends to himselfe, yet it no way justifies his doing it. Our maine diference
is in the 5. and 9. article, concerning the deviding or holding of house and
lands; the injoying wherof some of your selves well know, was one spetiall
motive, amongst many other, to provoke us to goe. This was thought so
reasonable, that when the greatest of you in adventure (whom we have
much cause to respecte), when he propounded conditions to us freely of
his owne accorde, he set this downe for one; a coppy wherof we have sent
unto you, with some additions then added by us; which being liked on
both sids, and a day set for the paimente of moneys, those of Holland paid
in theirs. After that, Robart Cushman, Mr. Peirce [1] and Mr. Martine,

---

[1] John Peirce was a citizen and clothworker of London. The first patent of
the Pilgrims, issued by the southern Virginia Company, was issued in his name and
finally surrendered. The patent issued by the Council for New England which
was brought over in the *Fortune* in 1621 was also issued in his name. The letter

brought them into a better forme, and write them in a booke now extante; and upon Robarts shewing them and delivering Mr. Mullins[1] a coppy therof under his hand (which we have), he payd in his money.   And we of Holland had never seen other before our coming to Hamton, but only as one got for him selfe a private coppy of them; upon sight wherof we manyfested uter dislike, but had put of our estats and were ready to come, and therfore was too late to rejecte the vioage.   Judge therfore we beseech you indiferently of things, and if a faulte have bene commited, lay it wher it is, and not upon us, who have more cause to stand for the one, then you have for the other.   We never gave Robart Cushman comission to make any one article for us, but only sent him to receive moneys upon articles before agreed on, and to further the provissions till John Carver came, and to assiste him in it.   Yet since you conceive your selves wronged as well as we, we thought meete to add a branch to the end of our 9. article, as will allmost heale that wound of it selfe, which you conceive to be in it. But that it may appeare to all men that we are not lovers of our selves only, but desire also the good and inriching of our freinds who have adventured your moneys with our persons, we have added our last article to the rest, promising you againe by leters in the behalfe of the whole company, that if large profits should not arise within the 7. years, that we will con- tinue togeather longer with you, if the Lord give a blessing.[2]   This we hope is sufficente to satisfie any in this case, espetialy freinds, since we are asured that if the whole charge was devided into 4. parts, 3. of them will not stand upon it, nether doe regarde it, etc.   We are in shuch a streate at presente, as we are forced to sell away 60*li.* worth of our provissions to cleare the Haven, and withall put our selves upon great extremities, scarce haveing any butter, no oyle, not a sole to mend a shoe, nor every man a sword to his side, wanting many muskets, much armoure, etc.   And yet we are willing to expose our selves to shuch eminente dangers as are like to insue, and trust to the good providence of God, rather then his name and truth should be evill spoken of for us.   Thus saluting all of you in love, and beseeching the Lord to give a blesing to our endeavore, and keepe all our harts in the bonds of peace and love, we take leave and rest,

Yours, etc.

Aug. 3. 1620.

in "Mourt's *Relation*," addressed to J. P. and signed R. G., was addressed to him.

[1] William Mullins, a member of the Leyden church, came in the *Mayflower* with wife and two children and died February 21, 1621.   His daughter was the Priscilla of Longfellow's *Courtship of Miles Standish*.

[2] "It was well for them that this was not accepted."   (Br.)

It was subscribed with many names of the cheefest of the company.

At their parting Mr. Robinson write a leter to the whole company, which though it hath already bene printed,[1] yet I thought good here likwise to inserte it; as also a breefe leter writ at the same time to Mr. Carver, in which the tender love and godly care of a true pastor appears.

My dear Brother,—I received inclosed in your last leter the note of information, which I shall carefully keepe and make use of as ther shall be occasion. I have a true feeling of your perplexitie of mind and toyle of body, but I hope that you who have allways been able so plentifully to administer comforte unto others in their trials, are so well furnished for your selfe as that farr greater difficulties then you have yet undergone (though I conceive them to have been great enough) cannot oppresse you, though they press you, as the Apostle speaks. The spirite of a man (sustained by the spirite of God) will sustaine his infirmitie, I dout not so will yours. And the beter much when you shall injoye the presence and help of so many godly and wise bretheren, for the bearing of part of your burthen, who also will not admitte into their harts the least thought of suspition of any the least negligence, at least presumption, to have been in you, what so ever they thinke in others. Now what shall I say or write unto you and your goodwife my loving sister?[2] even only this, I desire (and allways shall) unto you from the Lord, as unto my owne soule; and assure your selfe that my harte is with you, and that I will not forslowe my bodily coming at the first oppertunitie. I have writen a large leter to the whole, and am sorie I shall not rather speak then write to them; and the more, considering the wante of a preacher, which I shall also make sume spurr to my hastening after you. I doe ever commend my best affection unto you, which if I thought you made any doubte of, I would express in more, and the same more ample and full words. And the Lord in whom you trust and whom you serve ever in this bussines and journey, guid you with his hand, protecte you with his winge, and shew you and us his salvation in the end, and bring us in the mean while togeather in the place desired, if shuch be his good will, for his Christs sake. Amen.

Yours, etc.

July 27. 1620.   Jo: R.

---

[1] In the prefatory pages of "Mourt's *Relation*" (1622).

[2] This passage has led to the supposition that Katherine Carver, the governor's wife, was Robinson's sister.

This was the last letter that Mr. Carver lived to see from him.   The other follows.[1]

Lovinge Christian friends, I doe hartily and in the Lord salute you all, as being they with whom I am presente in my best affection, and most ernest longings after you, though I be constrained for a while to be bodily absente from you.   I say constrained, God knowing how willingly, and much rather then otherwise, I would have borne my part with you in this first brunt, were I not by strong necessitie held back for the present. Make accounte of me in the mean while, as of a man devided in my selfe with great paine, and as (naturall bonds set a side) having my beter parte with you.   And though I doubt not but in your godly wisdoms, you both foresee and resolve upon that which concerneth your presente state and condition, both severally and joyntly, yet have I thought it but my duty to add some furder spurr of provocation unto them, who rune allready, if not because you need it, yet because I owe it in love and dutie.   And first, as we are daly to renew our repentance with our God, espetially for our sines known, and generally for our unknowne trespasses, so doth the Lord call us in a singuler maner upon occasions of shuch difficultie and danger as lieth upon you, to a both more narrow search and carefull reformation of your ways in his sight; least he, calling to remembrance our sines forgotten by us or unrepented of, take advantage against us, and in judgmente leave us for the same to be swalowed up in one danger or other; wheras, on the contrary, sine being taken away by ernest repentance and the pardon therof from the Lord sealed up unto a mans conscience by his spirite, great shall be his securitie and peace in all dangers, sweete his comforts in all distresses, with hapie deliverance from all evill, whether in life or in death.

Now next after this heavenly peace with God and our owne consciences, we are carefully to provide for peace with all men what in us lieth, espetially with our associats, and for that watchfullnes must be had, that we neither at all in our selves doe give, no nor easily take offence being given by others.   Woe be unto the world for offences, for though it be necessarie (considering the malice of Satan and mans corruption) that offences come, yet woe unto the man or woman either by whom the offence cometh, saith Christ, Mat. 18. 7.   And if offences in the unseasonable use of things in them selves indifferent, be more to be feared then death itselfe, as the Apostle teacheth, 1. Cor. 9. 15. how much more in things simply evill, in which neither honour of God nor love of man is thought worthy to be regarded.   Neither yet is it sufficiente that we keepe

---

[1] "This Letter is omitted in Gov. Bradford's Collection of Letters." (Prince.)

our selves by the grace of God from giveing offence, exepte withall we be armed against the taking of them when they be given by others. For how unperfect and lame is the work of grace in that person, who wants charritie to cover a multitude of offences, as the scriptures speake. Neither are you to be exhorted to this grace only upon the commone grounds of Christianitie, which are, that persons ready to take offence, either wante charitie, to cover offences, of wisdome duly to waigh humane frailtie; or lastly, are grosse, though close hipocrites, as Christ our Lord teacheth, Mat. 7. 1, 2, 3, as indeed in my owne experience, few or none have bene found which sooner give offence, then shuch as easily take it; neither have they ever proved sound and profitable members in societies, which have nurished this touchey humor. But besids these, ther are diverse motives provoking you above others to great care and conscience this way: As first, you are many of you strangers, as to the persons, so to the infirmities one of another, and so stand in neede of more watchfullnes this way, least when shuch things fall out in men and women as you suspected not, you be inordinatly affected with them; which doth require at your hands much wisdome and charitie for the covering and preventing of incident offences that way. And lastly, your intended course of civill comunitie will minister continuall occasion of offence, and will be as fuell for that fire, excepte you dilligently quench it with brotherly forbearance. And if taking of offence causlesly or easilie at mens doings be so carefuly to be avoyded, how much more heed is to be taken that we take not offence at God him selfe, which yet we certainly doe so often as we doe murmure at his providence in our crosses, or beare impatiently shuch afflictions as wherwith he pleaseth to visite us. Store up therfore patience against the evill day, without which we take offence at the Lord him selfe in his holy and just works.

A 4. thing ther is carfully to be provided for, to witte, that with your commone imployments you joyne commone affections truly bente upon the generall good, avoyding as a deadly plague of your both commone and spetiall comfort all retirednes of minde for proper advantage, and all singularly affected any maner of way; let every man represe in him selfe and the whol body in each person, as so many rebels against the commone good, all private respects of mens selves, not sorting with the generall conveniencie. And as men are carfull not to have a new house shaken with any violence before it be well setled and the parts firmly knite, so be you, I beseech you, brethren, much more carfull, that the house of God which you are, and are to be, be not shaken with unnecessarie novelties or other oppositions at the first setling therof.

Lastly, wheras you are become a body politik, using amongst your selves civill govermente, and are not furnished with any persons of spetiall eminencie above the rest, to be chosen by you into office of goverment, let your wisdome and godlines appeare, not only in chusing shuch persons as doe entirely love and will promote the commone good, but also in yeelding unto them all due honour and obedience in their lawfull adminis-trations; not behoulding in them the ordinarinesse of their persons, but Gods ordinance for your good, not being like the foolish multitud who more honour the gay coate, then either the vertuous minde of the man, or glorious ordinance of the Lord.   But you know better things, and that the image of the Lords power and authoritie which the magistrate beareth, is honourable, in how meane persons soever.   And this dutie you both may the more willingly and ought the more conscionably to performe, because you are at least for the present to have only them for your or-dinarie governours, which your selves shall make choyse of for that worke.

Sundrie other things of importance I could put you in minde of, and of those before mentioned, in more words, but I will not so farr wrong your godly minds as to thinke you heedless of these things, ther being also diverce among you so well able to admonish both them selves and others of what concerneth them.   These few things therfore, and the same in few words, I doe ernestly commend unto your care and conscience, joyning therwith my daily incessante prayers unto the Lord, that he who hath made the heavens and the earth, the sea and all rivers of waters, and whose providence is over all his workes, espetially over all his dear children for good, would so guide and gard you in your wayes, as inwardly by his Spirite, so outwardly by the hand of his power, as that both you and we also, for and with you, may have after matter of praising his name all the days of your and our lives.   Fare you well in him in whom you trust, and in whom I rest.

An unfained wellwiller of your hapie
success in this hopefull voyage,

JOHN ROBINSON.

This letter, though large, yet being so frutfull in it selfe, and suitable to their occation, I thought meete to inserte in this place.

All things being now ready, and every bussines dispatched, the company was caled togeather, and this letter read amongst them, which had good acceptation with all and after fruit with many.   Then they ordered and distributed their company for either shipe, as they conceived for the best.   And chose a

Govr and 2. or 3. assistants for each shipe, to order the people by the way, and see to the dispossing of there provissions,
and shuch like affairs. All which was not only with the liking
of the maisters of the ships, but according to their desires.
Which being done, they sett sayle from thence aboute the 5.
of August; but what befell them further upon the coast of
England will appeare in the nexte chapter.

The 8. Chap.

*Off the troubls that befell them on the coaste, and at sea being
forced, after much trouble, to leave one of ther ships and
some of their companie behind them.*

BEING thus put to sea they had not gone farr, but Mr.
Reinolds the m^r of the leser ship complained that he found
his ship so leak as he durst not put further to sea till she was
mended. So the m^r of the biger ship (caled Mr. Jonas)[1] being consulted with, they both resolved to put into Dartmouth
and have her ther searched and mended, which accordingly
was done, to their great charg and losse of time and a faire
winde. She was hear thorowly searcht from steme to sterne,
some leaks were found and mended, and now it was conceived
by the workmen and all, that she was sufficiente, and they
might proceede without either fear or danger. So with good
hopes from hence, they put to sea againe, conceiving they should
goe comfortably on, not looking for any more lets of this kind;
but it fell out otherwise, for after they were gone to sea againe
above 100. leagues without the Lands End, houlding company

---

[1] Since the publication of Neill's *Virginia Company of London*, it has been
usual to identify this Captain Jones with Thomas Jones, who in the *Discovery*
sailed to Virginia in November, 1621, visited Plymouth the next summer (see p.
139, *post*), robbed he natives, and died in Virginia in 1624, under some suspicion of
piracy. This idenification has lent support to the view that he behaved with
treachery toward the Pilgrims off Cape Cod. But Mr. R. G. Marsden seems to
have proved, in the *English Historical Review*, XIX. 669–680, that the captain of
the *Mayflower* was Christopher Jones, a man against whose character nothing is
known. See also *New England Historic Genealogical Register*, XL. 62. Captain Christopher Jones died in 1622.

togeather all this while, the m^r of the small ship complained his ship was so leake as he must beare up or sinke at sea, for they could scarce free her with much pumping. So they came to consultation againe, and resolved both ships to bear up backe againe and put into Plimmoth, which accordingly was done. But no spetiall leake could be founde, but it was judged to be the generall weaknes of the shipe, and that shee would not prove sufficiente for the voiage. Upon which it was resolved to dismise her and parte of the companie, and proceede with the other shipe. The which (though it was greevous, and caused great discouragmente) was put in execution. So after they had tooke out such provission as the other ship could well stow, and concluded both what number and what persons to send bak, they made another sad parting, the one ship going backe for London, and the other was to proceede on her viage. Those that went bak were for the most parte such as were willing so to doe, either out of some discontente, or feare they conceived of the ill success of the vioage, seeing so many croses befale, and the year time so farr spente; but others, in regarde of their owne weaknes, and charge of many yonge children, were thought least usefull, and most unfite to bear the brunte of this hard adventure; unto which worke of God, and judgmente of their brethern, they were contented to submite. And thus, like Gedions armie, this small number was devided, as if the Lord by this worke of his providence thought these few to many for the great worke he had to doe. But here by the way let me show, how afterward it was found that the leaknes of this ship was partly by being over masted, and too much pressed with sayles; for after she was sould and put into her old trime, she made many viages and performed her service very sufficiently, to the great profite of her owners. But more espetially, by the cuning and deceite of the m^r and his company, who were hired to stay a whole year in the cuntrie, and now fancying dislike and fearing wante of victeles, they ploted this strategem to free them selves; as afterwards was knowne, and by some of them confessed. For they apprehended that the greater ship, being of force, and in whom most of the provissions were stowed, she would retayne enough for her selfe, what soever became of them or the passengers; and indeed shuch speeches had bene cast out by some of them; and yet, besids other incouragments, the cheefe of them that came from Leyden wente in this shipe to give the m^r contente. But so strong was self love and his fears, as he forgott all duty and former kindnesses, and delt thus falsly with them, though he pretended otherwise. Amongest those that returned was Mr. Cushman and his familie, whose hart and courage was gone from them before, as it seems, though his body was with them till now he departed; as may appear by a passionate letter he write to a freind in London from Dartmouth, whilst the ship lay ther a mending; the which, besids the expressions of his owne fears, it shows much of the providence of God working for their good beyonde man's expectation, and other things concerning their condition in these streats.[1] I will hear relate it. And though it discover some infirmities in him (as who under temtation is free), yet after this he continued to be a spetiall instrumente for their good, and to doe the offices of a loving freind and faithfull brother unto them, and pertaker of much comforte with them.

The letter is as followth.

To his loving friend Ed: S.[2] at Henige House in the Duks Place, these, etc

Dartmouth, Aug. 17.

Loving friend, my most kind remembrance to you and your wife, with loving E. M. etc. whom in this world I never looke to see againe. For besids the eminente dangers of this viage, which are no less then deadly, an infirmitie of body hath ceased me, which will not in all licelyhoode leave me till death. What to call it I know not, but it is a bundle

[1] Straits.

[2] "In Governor Bradford's Collection of Letters, this is Edward Southworth." (Prince.) Edward Southworth was a member of the Leyden congregation who did not go to New England. His widow, Alice, afterward became the second wife of Governor Bradford. Duke's Place is in London.

of lead, as it were, crushing my harte more and more these 14. days, as that allthough I doe the acctions of a liveing man, yet I am but as dead; but the will of God be done.   Our pinass will not cease leaking, els I thinke we had been halfe way at Virginia, our viage hither hath been as full of crosses, as our selves have been of crokednes.   We put in hear to trimme her, and I thinke, as others also, if we had stayed at sea but 3. or 4. howers more, shee would have sunke right downe.   And though she was twise trimmed at Hamton, yet now shee is open and leakie as a seive; and ther was a borde, a man might have puld of with his fingers, 2 foote longe, wher the water came in as at a mole hole.   We lay at Hamton 7. days, in fair weather, waiting for her, and now we lye hear waiting for her in as faire a wind as can blowe, and so have done these 4. days, and are like to lye 4. more, and by that time the wind will happily turne as it did at Hampton.   Our victualls will be halfe eaten up, I thinke, before we goe from the coaste of England, and if our viage last longe, we shall not have a months victialls when we come in the countrie.   Neare 700*li*. hath bene bestowed at Hampton, upon what I know not.   Mr. Martin saith he neither can nor will give any accounte of it, and if he be called upon for accounts he crieth out of unthankfullnes for his paines and care, that we are susspitious of him, and flings away, and will end nothing. Also he so insulteth over our poore people, with shuch scorne and con-tempte, as if they were not good enough to wipe his shoes.   It would break your hart to see his dealing,[1] and the mourning of our people.   They complaine to me, and alass! I can doe nothing for them; if I speake to him, he flies in my face, as mutinous, and saith no complaints shall be heard or received but by him selfe, and saith they are forwarde, and waspish, discontented people, and I doe ill to hear them.   Ther are others that would lose all they have put in, or make satisfaction for what they have had, that they might depart; but he will not hear them, nor suffer them to goe ashore, least they should rune away.   The sailors also are so offended at his ignorante bouldnes, in medling and controuling in things he knows not what belongs too, as that some threaten to misscheefe him, others say they will leave the shipe and goe their way.   But at the best this cometh of it, that he maks him selfe a scorne and laughing stock unto them.   As for Mr. Weston, excepte grace doe greatly swaye with him, he will hate us ten times more then ever he loved us, for not confirming the conditions.   But now, since some pinches have taken them, they begine to reveile the trueth, and say Mr. Robinson was in the falte who charged them never to consente to those conditions, nor chuse me into office, but

---

[1] "He was governour in the biger ship, and Mr. Cushman assistante."   (Br.)

indeede apointed them to chose them they did chose.[1]   But he and they
will rue too late, they may now see, and all be ashamed when it is too late,
that they were so ignorante, yea, and so inordinate in their courses.   I am
sure as they were resolved not to seale those conditions, I was not so resolute at Hampton to have left the whole bussines, excepte they would seale
them, and better the vioage to have bene broken of then, then to have
brought such miserie to our selves, dishonour to God, and detrimente to
our loving freinds, as now it is like to doe.   4. or 5. of the cheefe of them
which came from Leyden, came resolved never to goe on those conditions.
And Mr. Martine, he said he never received no money on those conditions,
he was not beholden to the marchants for a pine, they were bloudsuckers,
and I know not what.   Simple man, he indeed never made any conditions
with the marchants, nor ever spake with them.   But did all that money
flie to Hampton, or was it his owne?   Who will goe and lay out money
so rashly and lavishly as he did, and never know how he comes by it,
or on what conditions? 2^{ly}.   I tould him of the alteration longe agoe,
and he was contente; but now he dominires, and said I had betrayed them
into the hands of slaves; he is not beholden to them, he can set out 2.
ships him selfe to a viage.   When, good man?   He hath but $50li$. in,
and if he should give up his accounts he would not have a penie left him,
as I am persuaded,[2] etc.   Freind, if ever we make a plantation, God
works a mirakle; especially considering how scante we shall be of victualls,
and most of all ununited amongst our selves, and devoyd of good tutors
and regimente.   Violence will break all.   Wher is the meek and humble
spirite of Moyses? and of Nehemiah who reedified the wals of Jerusalem,
and the state of Israell?   Is not the sound of Rehoboams braggs daly
hear amongst us?   Have not the philosophers and all wise men observed
that, even in setled commone welths, violente governours bring either
them selves, or people, or boath, to ruine; how much more in the raising
of commone wealths, when the morter is yet scarce tempered that should
bind the wales.   If I should write to you of all things which promiscuously
forerune our ruine, I should over charge my weake head and greeve your
tender hart; only this, I pray you prepare for evill tidings of us every day.
But pray for us instantly, it may be the Lord will be yet entreated one way
or other to make for us.   I see not in reason how we shall escape even the
gasping of hunger starved persons; but God can doe much, and his will
be done.   It is better for me to dye, then now for me to bear it, which I
doe daly, and expecte it howerly; haveing received the sentance of death,
both within me and without me.   Poore William King and my selfe doe

---

[1] "I thinke he was deceived in these things."   (Br.)
[2] "This was found true afterward."   (Br.)

strive who shall be meate first for the fishes; but we looke for a glorious resurrection, knowing Christ Jesus after the flesh no more, but looking unto the joye that is before us, we will endure all these things and accounte them light in comparison of that joye we hope for.   Remember me in all love to our freinds as if I named them, whose praiers I desire ernestly, and wish againe to see, but not till I can with more comforte looke them in the face.   The Lord give us that true comforte which none can take from us.   I had a desire to make a breefe relation of our estate to some freind.   I doubte not but your wisdome will teach you seasonably to utter things as here after you shall be called to it.   That which I have writen is treue, and many things more which I have forborne.   I write it as upon my life, and last confession in England.   What is of use to be spoken of presently, you may speake of it, and what is fitt to conceile, conceall.   Pass by my weake maner, for my head is weake, and my body feeble, the Lord make me strong in him, and keepe both you and yours.

Your loving freind,

ROBART CUSHMAN.

Dartmouth, Aug. 17. 1620.

These being his conceptions and fears at Dartmouth, they must needs be much stronger now at Plimoth.

The 9. Chap.

Of their vioage, and how they passed the sea, and of their safe arrival at Cape Codd.

SEPT[R]: 6.   These troubles being blowne over, and now all being compacte togeather in one shipe,[1] they put to sea againe with a prosperus winde, which continued diverce days togeather, which was some incouragmente unto them; yet according to the usuall maner many were afflicted with seasicknes.   And I may not omite hear a spetiall worke of Gods providence.   Ther was a proud and very profane yonge man, one of the sea-men, of a lustie, able body, which made him the more hauty; he would allway be contemning the poore people in their sicknes, and cursing them dayly with greevous execrations, and did not let to tell them,[2] that he hoped to help

---

[1] For Governor Bradford's list of passengers in the *Mayflower*, see Appendix, No. I.   [2] Did not refrain from telling them.

to cast halfe of them over board before they came to their jurneys end, and to make mery with what they had; and if he were by any gently reproved, he would curse and swear most bitterly. But it plased God before· they came halfe seas over, to smite this yong man with a greeveous disease, of which he dyed in a desperate maner, and so was him selfe the first that was throwne overbord. Thus his curses light on his owne head; and it was an astonishmente to all his fellows, for they noted it to be the just hand of God upon him.

After they had injoyed faire winds and weather for a season, they were incountred many times with crosse winds, and mette with many feirce stormes, with which the shipe was shroudly[1] shaken, and her upper works made very leakie; and one of the maine beames in the midd ships was bowed and craked, which put them in some fear that the shipe could not be able to performe the vioage. So some of the cheefe of the company, perceiveing the mariners to feare the suffisiencie of the shipe, as appeared by their mutterings, they entred into serious consulltation with the m^r and other officers of the ship, to consider in time of the danger; and rather to returne then to cast them selves into a desperate· and inevitable perill. And truly ther was great distraction and differance of opinion amongst the mariners them selves; faine would they doe what could be done for their wages sake, (being now halfe the seas over,) and on the other hand they were loath to hazard their lives too desperately. But in examening of all opinions, the m^r and others affirmed they knew the ship to be stronge and firme under water; and for the buckling[2] of the maine beame, ther was a great iron scrue the passengers brought out of Holland, which would raise the beame into his place; the which being done, the carpenter and m^r affirmed that with a post put under it, set firme in the lower deck, and otherways bounde, he would make it sufficiente. And as for the decks and uper workes they would calke them as well as they could,

---

[1] Shrewdly, severely.   [2] Bending under strain.

and though with the workeing of the ship they would not longe keepe stanch, yet ther would otherwise be no great danger, if they did not overpress her with sails. So they commited them selves to the will of God, and resolved to proseede. In sundrie of these stormes the winds were so feirce, and the seas so high, as they could not beare a knote of saile, but were forced to hull,[1] for diverce days togither. And in one of them, as they thus lay at hull, in a mighty storme, a lustie yonge man (called John Howland) coming upon some occasion above the grattings, was, with a seele[2] of the shipe throwne into [the] sea; but it pleased God that he caught hould of the top-saile halliards, which hunge over board, and rane out at length; yet he held his hould (though he was sundrie fadomes under water) till he was hald up by the same rope to the brime of the water, and then with a boat hooke and other means got into the shipe againe, and his life saved; and though he was something ill with it, yet he lived many years after, and became a profitable member both in church and commone wealthe. In all this viage ther died but one of the passengers, which was William Butten,[3] a youth, servant to Samuell Fuller, when they drew near the coast. But to omite other things, (that I may be breefe,) after longe beating at sea they fell with that land which is called Cape Cod; the which being made and certainly knowne to be it, they were not a litle joyfull. After some deliberation had amongst them selves and with the m^r of the ship, they tacked aboute and resolved to stande for the southward (the wind and weather being faire) to finde some place aboute Hudsons river for their habitation. But after they had sailed that course aboute halfe the day,[4] they fell amongst deangerous

---

[1] To drift.   [2] The "seele" of a ship is the toss in a rough sea.

[3] William Butten, son of Robert, baptized in the Austerfield church February 12, 1598, O. S.

[4] As the *Mayflower* approached Cape Cod she probably had the wind north-west and when she changed her course she stood south-southwest until she reached Pollock Rip. From that point up the Sound the deep water course is west-northwest, leaving Shovel Full Shoal on the port hand. On that course the northwest wind would shrink upon her, as expressed by Bradford.

shoulds and roring breakers, and they were so farr intangled
ther with as they conceived them selves in great danger; and
the wind shrinking upon them withall, they resolved to bear
up againe for the Cape, and thought them selves hapy to gett
out of those dangers before night overtooke them, as by Gods
providence they did. And the next day they gott into the
Cape-harbor wher they ridd in saftie. A word or too by the
way of this cape; it was thus first named by Capten Gosnole
and his company, Anº: 1602,[1] and after by Capten Smith was
caled Cape James; but it retains the former name amongst
seamen. Also that pointe which first shewed those dangerous
shoulds unto them, they called Pointe Care, and Tuckers
Terrour; but the French and Dutch to this day call it Malabarr,[2] by reason of those perilous shoulds, and the losses
they have suffered their.

Being thus arived in a good harbor and brought safe to
land, they fell upon their knees and blessed the God of heaven,
who had brought them over the vast and furious ocean, and
delivered them from all the periles and miseries therof, againe
to set their feete on the firme and stable earth, their proper
elemente. And no marvell if they were thus joyfull, seeing
wise Seneca was so affected with sailing a few miles on the
coast of his owne Italy; as he affirmed,[3] that he had rather
remaine twentie years on his way by land, then pass by sea
to any place in a short time; so tedious and dreadfull was
the same unto him.

But hear I cannot but stay and make a pause, and stand
half amased at this poore peoples presente condition; and so
I thinke will the reader too, when he well considers the same.
Being thus passed the vast ocean, and a sea of troubles before
in their preparation (as may be remembred by that which

---

[1] "Because they tooke much of that fishe ther." (Br.) See *Early English
and French Voyages,* in this series, p. 331. The name Cape James appears on
Captain John Smith's map of New England; see page 112 of this volume.
[2] Cape Malabarr was the Mallebarre of Champlain. See his map, in *Voyages of Samuel de Champlain,* in this series. [3] "Epist: 53." (Br.)

wente before), they had now no freinds to wellcome them,
nor inns to entertaine or refresh their weatherbeaten bodys,
no houses or much less townes to repaire too, to seeke for succoure. It is recorded in scripture[1] as a mercie to the apostle
and his shipwraked company, that the barbarians shewed
them no smale kindnes in refreshing them, but these savage
barbarians, when they mette with them (as after will appeare)
were readier to fill their sids full of arrows then otherwise.
And for the season it was winter, and they that know the
winters of that cuntrie know them to be sharp and violent,
and subjecte to cruell and feirce stormes, deangerous to travill
to known places, much more to serch an unknown coast.
Besids, what could they see but a hidious and desolate wildernes, full of wild beasts and willd men? and what multituds ther
might be of them they knew not. Nether could they, as it
were, goe up to the tope of Pisgah, to vew from this willdernes
a more goodly cuntrie to feed their hops; for which way soever
they turnd their eys (save upward to the heavens) they could
have litle solace or content in respecte of any outward objects.
For summer being done, all things stand upon them with a
wetherbeaten face; and the whole countrie, full of woods and
thickets, represented a wild and savage heiw. If they looked
behind them, ther was the mighty ocean which they had passed,
and was now as a maine barr and goulfe to seperate them from
all the civill parts of the world. If it be said they had a ship
to sucour them, it is trew; but what heard they daly from the
m^r and company? but that with speede they should looke
out a place with their shallop, wher they would be at some
near distance; for the season was shuch as he would not stirr
from thence till a safe harbor was discovered by them wher
they would be, and he might goe without danger; and that
victells consumed apace, but he must and would keepe sufficient
for them selves and their returne. Yea, it was muttered by
some, that if they gott not a place in time, they would turne

[1] "Act. 28."   (Br.)

them and their goods ashore and leave them. Let it also be considred what weake hopes of supply and succoure they left behinde them, that might bear up their minds in this sade condition and trialls they were under; and they could not but be very smale. It is true, indeed, the affections and love of their brethren at Leyden was cordiall and entire towards them, but they had litle power to help them, or them selves; and how the case stode betweene them and the marchants at their coming away, hath allready been declared. What could now sustaine them but the spirite of God and his grace? May not and ought not the children of these fathers rightly say: *Our faithers were Englishmen which came over this great ocean, and were ready to perish in this willldernes;*[1] *but they cried unto the Lord, and he heard their voyce, and looked on their adversitie, etc. Let them therfore praise the Lord, because he is good, and his mercies endure for ever.*[2] *Yea, let them which have been redeemed of the Lord, shew how he hath delivered them from the hand of the oppressour. When they wandered in the deserte willldernes out of the way, and found no citie to dwell in, both hungrie, and thirstie, their sowle was overwhelmed in them. Let them confess before the Lord his loving kindnes, and his wonderfull works before the sons of men.*

The 10. Chap.

Showing how they sought out a place of habitation, and what befell them theraboute.

BEING thus arrived at Cap-Cod the 11. of November, and necessitie calling them to looke out a place for habitation, (as well as the maisters and mariners importunitie,) they having brought a large shalop with them out of England, stowed in quarters in the ship, they now gott her out and sett their carpenters to worke to trime her up; but being much brused and shatered in the shipe with foule weather, they saw she would

---

[1] "Deu: 26. 5, 7." (Br.)   [2] "107 Psa: v. 1, 2, 4, 5, 8." (Br.)

be longe in mending. Wherupon a few of them tendered them selves to goe by land and discovere those nearest places, whilst the shallop was in mending; and the rather because as they wente into that harbor ther seemed to be an opening some 2. or 3 leagues of, which the maister judged to be a river. It was conceived ther might be some danger in the attempte, yet seeing them resolute, they were permited to goe, being 16. of them well armed, under the conduct of Captain Standish,[1] having shuch instructions given them as was thought meete. They sett forth the 15. of Nove^{br}: and when they had marched aboute the space of a mile by the sea side, they espied 5. or 6. persons with a dogg coming towards them, who were salv-ages; but they fled from them, and ranne up into the woods, and the English followed them, partly to see if they could speake with them, and partly to discover if ther might not be more of them lying in ambush. But the Indeans seeing them selves thus followed, they againe forsooke the woods, and rane away on the sands as hard as they could, so as they could not come near them, but followed them by the tracte of their feet sundrie miles, and saw that they had come the same way. So, night coming on, they made their randevous and set out their sentinels, and rested in quiete that night, and the next morning followed their tracte till they had headed a great creake, and so left the sands, and turned an other way into the woods.

[1] Myles Standish is here mentioned for the first time in the history. He was born in Lancashire about 1586, and was in service in Holland during her war with Spain. During the twelve years' truce he found the Pilgrims in Leyden and came in the *Mayflower* with his wife Rose, who died January 29, 1620/1. He married a second wife, Barbara, who may have come in the *Anne* or *Little James* in 1623. In 1625 he went to England in behalf of the colony. He received a grant of land in Duxbury which he occupied as early as 1630. The state-ment often made that he was a Roman Catholic is probably not correct. The following entry in the Plymouth Colony records shows that he was a Protestant if not a full member of the Plymouth Church: "Anno 1632 Aprell 2—the names of those which promise to remove their families to live in the towne in the win-ter time that they may the better repaire to the worship of God—John Alden, Capt. Standish, Jonathan Brewster, Thomas Prence."

Of the explorations on Cape Cod, here described, there is a fuller account in "Mourt's *Relation.*"

But they still followed them by geuss, hopeing to find their dwellings; but they soone lost both them and them selves, falling into shuch thickets as were ready to tear their cloaths and armore in peeces, but were most distresed for wante of drinke. But at length they found water and refreshed them selves, being the first New-England water they drunke of, and was now in thir great thirste as pleasante unto them as wine or bear had been in for-times. Afterwards they directed their course to come to the other shore, for they knew it was a necke of land they were to crosse over, and so at length gott to the sea-side, and marched to this supposed river, and by the way found a pond of clear fresh water, and shortly after a good quantitie of clear ground wher the Indeans had formerly set corne, and some of their graves.[1] And proceeding furder they saw new-stuble wher corne had been set the same year, also they found wher latly a house had been, wher some planks and a great ketle was remaining, and heaps of sand newly padled with their hands, which they, digging up, found in them diverce faire Indean baskets filled with corne, and some in eares, faire and good, of diverce collours, which seemed to them a very goodly sight, (haveing never seen any shuch before). This was near the place of that supposed river they came to seeck;[2] unto which they wente and found it to open it selfe into 2. armes with a high cliffe of sand in the enterance, but more like to be crikes of salte water then any fresh, for ought they saw; and that ther was good harborige for their shalope; leaving it further to be discovered by their shalop when she was ready. So their time limeted them being expired, they returned to the ship, least they should be in fear of their saftie; and tooke with them parte of the corne, and buried up the rest, and so like the men from Eshcoll carried with them of the fruits of the land, and showed their breethren; of which, and

[1] Near Pond Village, in Truro.

[2] Pamet River, in the same township. The second "discovery" or exploration extended somewhat farther into the same region. The third extended quite around Cape Cod Bay.

their returne, they were marvelusly glad, and their harts incouraged.

After this, the shalop being got ready, they set out againe for the better discovery of this place, and the m^r of the ship desired to goe him selfe, so ther went some 30. men, but found it to be no harbor for ships but only for boats; ther was allso found 2. of their houses covered with matts, and sundrie of their implements in them, but the people were rune away and could not be seen; also ther was found more of their corne, and of their beans of various collours. The corne and beans they brought away, purposing to give them full satisfaction when they should meete with any of them (as about some 6. months afterward they did, to their good contente). And here is to be noted a spetiall providence of God, and a great mercie to this poore people, that hear they gott seed to plant them corne the next year, or els they might have starved, for they had none, nor any liklyhood to get any till the season had beene past (as the sequell did manyfest). Neither is it lickly they had had this, if the first viage had not been made, for the ground was now all covered with snow, and hard frozen. But the Lord is never wanting unto his in their greatest needs; let his holy name have all the praise.

The month of November being spente in these affairs, and much foule weather falling in, the 6. of Desem^r: they sente out their shallop againe with 10. of their principall men, and some sea men, upon further discovery, intending to circulate that deepe bay of Cap-codd. The weather was very could, and it frose so hard as the sprea of the sea lighting on their coats, they were as if they had been glased; yet that night betimes they gott downe into the botome of the bay, and as they drue nere the shore they saw some 10. or 12. Indeans very busie aboute some thing. They landed aboute a league or 2. from them, and had much a doe to put a shore any wher, it lay so full of flats. Being landed, it grew late, and they made them selves a barricade with loggs and bowes as well as they could in the time, and set out their sentenill and betooke them to rest, and saw the smoake of the fire the savages made that night. When morning was come they devided their company, some to coaste along the shore in the boate, and the rest marched throw the woods to see the land, if any fit place might be for their dwelling. They came allso to the place wher they saw the Indans the night before, and found they had been cuting up a great fish like a grampus, being some 2. inches thike of fate like a hogg, some peeces wher of they had left by the way; and the shallop found 2. more of these fishes dead on the sands, a thing usuall after storms in that place, by reason of the great flats of sand that lye of. So they ranged up and doune all that day, but found no people, nor any place they liked. When the sune grue low, they hasted out of the woods to meete with their shallop, to whom they made signes to come to them into a creeke hardby, the which they did at highwater; of which they were very glad, for they had not seen each other all that day, since the morning. So they made them a barri- cado (as usually they did every night) with loggs, staks, and thike pine bowes, the height of a man, leaving it open to lee- ward, partly to shelter them from the could and wind (mak- ing their fire in the midle, and lying round aboute it), and partly to defend them from any sudden assaults of the sav- ags, if they should surround them.[1] So being very weary, they betooke them to rest. But aboute midnight, they heard a hideous and great crie, and their sentinell caled, "Arme, arme"; so they bestired them and stood to their armes, and shote of a cupple of moskets, and then the noys seased. They concluded it was a companie of wolves, or such like willd beasts; for one of the sea men tould them he had often heard shuch a noyse in New-found land. So they rested till about 5. of the clock in the morning; for the tide, and ther purpose to goe from thence, made them be stiring betimes. So after praier they prepared for breakfast, and it being day dawning,

[1] Probably in or near Eastham.

it was thought best to be carring things downe to the boate. But some said it was not best to carrie the armes downe, others said they would be the readier, for they had laped them up in their coats from the dew.   But some 3. or 4. would not cary theirs till they wente them selves, yet as it fell out, the water being not high enough, they layed them downe on the banke side, and came up to breakfast.   But presently, all on the sudain, they heard a great and strange crie, which they knew to be the same voyces they heard in the night, though they varied their notes, and one of their company being abroad came runing in, and cried, "Men, Indeans, Indeans"; and withall, their arowes came flying amongst them.   Their men rane with all speed to recover their armes, as by the good providence of God they did.   In the mean time, of those that were ther ready, tow muskets were discharged at them, and 2. more stood ready in the enterance of ther randevoue, but were comanded not to shoote till they could take full aime at them; and the other 2. charged againe with all speed, for ther were only 4. had armes ther, and defended the baricado which was first assalted. The crie of the Indeans was dreadfull, espetially when they saw ther men rune out of the randevoue towourds the shallop, to recover their armes, the Indeans wheeling aboute upon them.   But some running out with coats of malle on, and cutlasses in their hands, they soone got their armes, and let flye amongs them, and quickly stopped their violence. Yet ther was a lustie man, and no less valiante, stood behind a tree within halfe a musket shot, and let his arrows flie at them.   He was seen shoot 3. arrowes, which were all avoyded.   He stood 3. shot of a musket, till one taking full aime at him, and made the barke or splinters of the tree fly about his ears, after which he gave an extraordinary shrike, and away they wente all of them.   They left some to keep the shalop, and followed them aboute a quarter of a mille, and shouted once or twise, and shot of 2. or 3. peces, and so returned.   This they did, that they might conceive that they were not affrade of them or any

way discouraged. Thus it pleased God to vanquish their enimies, and give them deliverance; and by his spetiall providence so to dispose that not any one of them were either
hurte, or hitt, though their arrows came close by them, and
on every side them, and sundry of their coats, which hunge
up in the barricado, were shot throw and throw. Aterwards
they gave God sollamne thanks and praise for their deliverance,
and gathered up a bundle of their arrows, and sente them
into England afterward by the m^r of the ship, and called
that place the first encounter. From hence they departed, and
costed all along, but discerned no place likly for harbor; and
therfore hasted to a place that their pillote, (one Mr. Coppin
who had bine in the cuntrie before)[1] did assure them was a good
harbor, which he had been in, and they might fetch it before
night; of which they were glad, for it begane to be foule
weather. After some houres sailing, it begane to snow and
raine, and about the midle of the afternoone, the wind increased, and the sea became very rough, and they broake their
rudder, and it was as much as 2. men could doe to steere her
with a cupple of oares. But their pillott bad them be of good
cheere, for he saw the harbor; but the storme increasing, and
night drawing on, they bore what saile they could to gett in,
while they could see. But herwith they broake their mast in
3. peeces, and their saill fell over bord, in a very grown sea, so
as they had like to have been cast away; yet by God's mercie
they recovered them selves, and having the floud with them,
struck into the harbore. But when it came too, the pillott
was deceived in the place, and said, the Lord be mercifull unto
them, for his eys never saw that place before; and he and
the m^r mate would have rune her ashore, in a cove full of
breakers, before the winde. But a lusty seaman which steered,
bad those which rowed, if they were men, about with her, or
ells they were all cast away; the which they did with speed.
So he bid them be of good cheere and row lustly, for ther was a

---

[1] Robert Coppin was second mate of the *Mayflower*.

faire sound before them, and he doubted not but they should
find one place or other wher they might ride in saftie. And
though it was very darke, and rained sore, yet in the end
they gott under the lee of a smalle iland, and remained ther
all that night in saftie.[1] But they knew not this to be an iland
till morning, but were devided in their minds; some would
keepe the boate for fear they might be amongst the Indians;
others were so weake and could, they could not endure, but got
a shore, and with much adoe got fire, (all things being so wett,)
and the rest were glad to come to them; for after midnight
the wind shifted to the north-west, and it frose hard. But
though this had been a day and night of much trouble and
danger unto them, yet God gave them a morning of comforte
and refreshing (as usually he doth to his children), for the
next day was a faire sunshining day, and they found them
sellvs to be on an iland secure from the Indeans, wher they
might drie their stufe, fixe their peeces, and rest them selves,
and gave God thanks for his mercies, in their manifould
deliverances. And this being the last day of the weeke,
they prepared ther to keepe the Sabbath. On Munday they
sounded the harbor, and founde it fitt for shipping; and
marched into the land,[2] and found diverse cornfeilds, and litle
runing brooks, a place (as they supposed) fitt for situation;
at least it was the best they could find, and the season,
and their presente necessitie, made them glad to accepte
of it. So they returned to their shipp againe with this news

[1] The rough sea and rain make it probable that the wind was east or east-
southeast. In my judgment the shallop passed over a part of what is called
Brown's Island, which, as Champlain's map made in 1605 shows, was a sand-
bar exposed at low tide, and approached Saquish Cove, thence steering up the
channel and anchoring for the night under the shelter of a little island. Saquish was at that time an island, as Champlain's map shows, and was probably
the little island which sheltered the shallop from the easterly wind. The record
states that during the night the wind changed to the northwest, and Clark's
Island with its southerly aspect undoubtedly became the resting place of the
shallop party until Monday the 11th.

[2] The landing on Plymouth Rock of the shallop party, December 11, O. S.,
December 21, N. S., was the historic landing.

to the rest of their people which did much comforte their
harts.

On the 15. of Desem[r]: they wayed anchor to goe to the
place they had discovered, and came within 2. leagues of it,
but were faine to bear up againe; but the 16. day the winde
came faire, and they arrived safe in this harbor. And after
wards tooke better view of the place, and resolved wher to
pitch their dwelling; and the 25. day begane to erecte the first
house for commone use to receive them and their goods.[1]

[1] The site of the house is marked by a bronze tablet erected in 1898 by the
Commonwealth of Massachusetts.

THE 2. BOOKE.

THE rest of this History (if God give me life, and opportunitie) I shall, for brevitis sake, handle by way of annalls, noteing only the heads of principall things, and passages as they fell in order of time, and may seeme to be profitable to know, or to make use of. And this may be as the 2. Booke.

The remainder of An°: 1620.

I SHALL a litle returne backe and begine with a combination[1] made by them before they came ashore, being the first foundation of their govermente in this place; occasioned partly by the discontented and mutinous speeches that some of the strangers amongst them had let fall from them in the ship—That when they came a shore they would use their owne libertie; for none had power to command them, the patente they had being for Virginia, and not for New-england, which belonged to an other Goverment, with which the Virginia Company had nothing to doe. And partly that shuch an acte by them done (this their condition considered) might be as firme as any patent, and in some respects more sure.

[1] Perhaps an undue significance has been attached to this combination or compact. The President and Council of New England, from whom the Pilgrims received their patent or grant, were authorized by their royal charter "to make, ordain and establish all manner of orders, laws, directions, instructions, forms and ceremonies of government and magistracy, fit and necessary for and concerning the government of the said colony and plantation." The patent issued to the Pilgrims by the Council, June 1, 1621, authorized them "to establish such Lawes and ordynaunces as are for their better government, and the same by such Officer or Officers as they shall by most voices elect and choose to put in execution." Thus the principle of the rule of the majority in the enactment of laws and the election of officers was recognized by both the patent and the royal charter. But landing outside the jurisdiction of the company which had granted the patent actually brought with them, they were obliged to assume, though on recognized principles, such authority as was needful. A similar course was afterward followed by the river towns of Connecticut, at New Haven, by the settlers at Dover and Exeter on the Piscataqua, at Providence and elsewhere.

The forme was as followeth.

In the name of God, Amen. We whose names are under-writen, the loyall subjects of our dread soveraigne Lord, King James, by the grace of God, of Great Britaine, Franc, and Ireland king, defender of the faith, etc., haveing undertaken, for the glorie of God, and advancemente of the Christian faith, and honour of our king and countrie, a voyage to plant the first colonie in the Northerne parts of Virginia, doe by these presents solemnly and mutualy in the presence of God, and one of another, covenant and combine our selves togeather into a civill body politick, for our better ordering and preservation and furtherance of the ends aforesaid; and by vertue hearof to enacte, constitute, and frame such just and equall lawes, ordinances, acts, constitutions, and offices, from time to time, as shall be thought most meete and convenient for the generall good of the Colonie, unto which we promise all due submission and obedience. In witnes wherof we have hereunder subscribed our names at Cap-Codd the 11. of November, in the year of the raigne of our soveraigne lord, King James, of England, France, and Ireland the eighteenth, and of Scotland the fiftie fourth. Anº: Dom. 1620.

After this they chose, or rather confirmed,[1] Mr. John Carver (a man godly and well approved amongst them) their Governour for that year. And after they had provided a place for their goods, or comone store, (which were long in unlading for want of boats, foulnes of winter weather, and sicknes of diverce,) and begune some small cottages for their habitation, as time would admitte, they mette and consulted of lawes and orders, both for their civill and military Govermente, as the necessitie of their condition did require, still adding therunto as urgent occasion in severall times, and as cases did require.

In these hard and difficulte beginings they found some discontents and murmurings arise amongst some, and mutinous speeches and carriags in other; but they were soone quelled and overcome by the wisdome, patience, and just and equall

[1] John Carver had been informally appointed governor of the *Mayflower* when she sailed from England, so that his formal election by the company after the compact was signed is called confirmation.

carrage of things by the Govr and better part, which clave
faithfully togeather in the maine. But that which was most
sadd and lamentable was, that in 2. or 3. moneths time halfe
of their company dyed, espetialy in Jan: and February, being
the depth of winter, and wanting houses and other comforts;
being infected with the scurvie and other diseases, which this
long vioage and their inacomodate condition had brought upon
them; so as ther dyed some times 2. or 3. of a day, in the foresaid time; that of 100. and odd persons, scarce 50. remained.[1]
And of these in the time of most distres, ther was but 6. or 7.
sound persons, who, to their great comendations be it spoken,
spared no pains, night nor day, but with abundance of toyle
and hazard of their owne health, fetched them woode, made
them fires, drest them meat, made their beads, washed their
lothsome cloaths, cloathed and uncloathed them; in a word,
did all the homly and necessarie offices for them which dainty
and quesie stomacks cannot endure to hear named; and all
this willingly and cherfully, without any grudging in the least,
shewing herein their true love unto their freinds and bretheren.
A rare example and worthy to be remembred.   Tow of these
7. were Mr. William Brewster, ther reverend Elder, and Myles
Standish, ther Captein and military comander, unto whom
my selfe, and many others, were much beholden in our low and
sicke condition.   And yet the Lord so upheld these persons,
as in this generall calamity they were not at all infected either
with sicknes, or lamnes.   And what I have said of these, I
may say of many others who dyed in this generall vissitation,
and others yet living, that whilst they had health, yea, or any
strength continuing, they were not wanting to any that had
need of them.   And I doute not but their recompence is with
the Lord.

But I may not hear pass by an other remarkable passage
not to be forgotten.   As this calamitie fell among the passengers that were to be left here to plant, and were hasted a

---

[1] The sickness was perhaps typhus or ship fever.

shore and made to drinke water, that the sea-men might have
the more bear,[1] and one in his sicknes desiring but a small
cann of beere, it was answered, that if he were their owne
father he should have none; the disease begane to fall amongst
them also, so as allmost halfe of their company dyed before
they went away, and many of their officers and lustyest men,
as the boatson, gunner, 3. quarter-maisters, the cooke, and
others. At which the m[r] was something strucken and sent
to the sick a shore and tould the Gov[r] he should send for
beer for them that had need of it, though he drunke water
homward bound. But now amongst his company ther was
farr another kind of carriage in this miserie then amongst the
passengers; for they that before had been boone companions
in drinking and joyllity in the time of their health and wellfare, begane now to deserte one another in this calamitie,
saing they would not hasard ther lives for them, they should
be infected by coming to help them in their cabins, and so, after
they came to dye by it, would doe litle or nothing for them,
but if they dyed let them dye. But shuch of the passengers
as were yet abord shewed them what mercy they could, which
made some of their harts relente, as the boatson (and some
others), who was a prowd yonge man, and would often curse
and scofe at the passengers; but when he grew weak, they had
compassion on him and helped him; then he confessed he did
not deserve it at their hands, he had abused them in word
and deed. O! saith he, you, I now see, shew your love like
Christians indeed one to another, but we let one another lye
and dye like doggs. Another lay cursing his wife, saing if it
had not ben for her he had never come this unlucky viage,
and anone cursing his felows, saing he had done this and that,
for some of them, he had spente so much, and so much, amongst
them, and they were now weary of him, and did not help him,
having need. Another gave his companion all he had, if he
died, to help him in his weaknes; he went and got a litle spise

[1] " Which was this author him selfe." (Br.)

and made him a mess of meat once or twise, and because he dyed not so soone as he expected, he went amongst his fellows, and swore the rogue would cousen him, he would see him choaked before he made him any more meate; and yet the pore fellow dyed before morning.

All this while the Indians came skulking about them, and would sometimes show them selves aloofe of, but when any aproached near them, they would rune away. And once they stoale away their tools wher they had been at worke, and were gone to diner. But about the 16. of March a certaine Indian came bouldly amongst them, and spoke to them in broken English, which they could well understand, but marvelled at it. At length they understood by discourse with him, that he was not of these parts, but belonged to the eastrene parts, wher some English-ships came to fhish, with whom he was aquainted, and could name sundrie of them by their names, amongst whom he had gott his language. He became proftable to them in aquainting them with many things concerning the state of the cuntry in the east-parts wher he lived, which was afterwards profitable unto them; as also of the people hear, of their names, number, and strength; of their situation and distance from this place, and who was cheefe amongst them. His name was Samaset;[1] he tould them also of another Indian whos name was Squanto,[2] a native of this place, who had been in England and could speake better English then him selfe. Being, after some time of entertainmente and gifts, dismist, a while after he came againe, and 5. more with him, and they brought againe all the tooles that were stolen away before, and made way for the coming of their great Sachem, called Massasoyt; who, about 4. or 5. days

[1] Samoset was a sagamore from Monhegan in Maine, and probably came to this region with Thomas Dermer and had not returned home. After his return to Maine he sold by deed in 1625 to John Brown of New Harbor twelve thousand acres of land for fifty beaver skins.

[2] Squanto, or Tisquantum, was of much use to the Pilgrims as guide and interpreter. He died in Chatham in November, 1622. His eventful story is fully told in C. F. Adams's *Three Episodes of Massachusetts History*, pp. 23–44.

after, came with the cheefe of his freinds and other attendance, with the aforesaid Squanto. With whom, after frendly
entertainment, and some gifts given him, they made a peace
with him (which hath now continued this 24. years)[1] in these
terms.

1. That neither he nor any of his, should injurie or doe
hurte to any of their peopl.

2. That if any of his did any hurte to any of theirs, he
should send the offender, that they might punish him.

3. That if any thing were taken away from any of theirs,
he should cause it to be restored; and they should doe the
like to his.

4. If any did unjustly warr against him, they would aide
him; if any did warr against them, he should aide them.

5. He should send to his neighbours confederats, to
certifie them of this, that they might not wrong them, but
might be likewise comprised in the conditions of peace.

6. That when ther men came to them, they should leave
their bows and arrows behind them.)

After these things he returned to his place caled Sowams,[2]
some 40. mile from this place, but Squanto continued with
them, and was their interpreter, and was a spetiall instrument
sent of God for their good beyond their expectation. He
directed them how to set their corne, wher to take fish, and to
procure other comodities, and was also their pilott to bring
them to unknowne places for their profitt, and never left them
till he dyed. He was a native of this place, and scarce any left
alive besids him selfe. He was caried away with diverce others
by one Hunt,[3] a m^r of a ship, who thought to sell them for

[1] It continued more than 50 years.

[2] On the present site of Warren, R. I.

[3] Thomas Hunt, captain of one of the ships in John Smith s expedition to
New England in 1614, captured twenty of the Patuxet Indians and seven Nausets
and carried them to Malaga, where he sold them. The friars caused them to
be released and Squanto found his way to England, where he was a servant of
Mr. John Slanie, a merchant of London. Before the return of Squanto to New
England the Patuxet tribe had been swept away by disease.

slaves in Spaine; but he got away for England, and was entertained by a marchante in London, and imployed to New-foundland and other parts, and lastly brought hither into these parts by one Mr. Dermer, a gentle-man imployed by Sr. Ferdinando Gorges and others, for discovery, and other designes in these parts. Of whom I shall say some thing, because it is mentioned in a booke set forth Anº: 1622. by the Presidente and Counsell for New-England,[1] that he made the peace betweene the salvages of these parts and the English; of which this plantation, as it is intimated, had the benefite. But what a peace it was, may apeare by what befell him and his men.

This Mr. Dermer was hear the same year that these people came, as apears by a relation written by him, and given me by a freind, bearing date June 30. Anº: 1620. And they came in Novembᵣ: following, so ther was but 4. months differance. In which relation to his honored freind, he hath these passages of this very place.

I will first begine (saith he) with that place from whence Squanto, or Tisquantem, was taken away; which in Cap: Smiths mape is called Plimoth:[2] and I would that Plimoth had the like comodities. I would that the first plantation might hear be seated, if ther come to the number of 50. persons, or upward. Otherwise at Charlton, because ther the savages are lese to be feared. The Pocanawkits,[3] which live to the west of Plimoth, bear an inveterate malice to the English, and are of more streingth then all the savags from thence to Penobscote. Their desire of revenge was occasioned by an English man, who having many of them

---

[1] "Page 19." (Br.) The reference is to *A briefe Relation of the Discovery and Plantation of New England* (London, 1622), reprinted in 1890 by the Prince Society in the first of its volumes on Gorges. See p. 221 of that volume.

[2] This map was first published in 1614. In later "states" of the map after the settlement, the name appears as New Plymouth. The adoption of the name by the Pilgrims was due to the nomenclature of Smith's map. Most of Smith's names for town-sites were not retained by the actual settlers. "Charlton," indeed, mentioned in the text above, lies not far from where Charlestown was actually established in 1630; but that name does not appear on the map till its later states.

[3] Pokanoket included what are now Bristol and Barrington in Rhode Island and parts of Swansea and Seekonk in Massachusetts.

on bord, made a great slaughter with their murderers and smale shot, when as (they say) they offered no injurie on their parts. Whether they were English or no, it may be douted; yet they beleeve they were, for the Frenche have so possest them; for which cause Squanto cannot deney but they would have kiled me when I was at Namasket,[1] had he not entreated hard for me. The soyle of the borders of this great bay, may be compared to most of the plantations which I have seene in Virginia. The land is of diverce sorts; for Patuxite is a hardy but strong soyle, Nawset and Saughtughtett are for the most part a blakish and deep mould, much like that wher groweth the best Tobacco in Virginia. In the botume of that great bay is store of Codd and basse, or mulett, etc.

But above all he comends Pacanawkite for the richest soyle, and much open ground fitt for English graine, etc.

Massachussets [2] is about 9. leagues from Plimoth, and situate in the mids betweene both, is full of ilands and peninsules very fertill for the most parte.

With sundrie shuch relations which I forbear to transcribe, being now better knowne then they were to him.

He was taken prisoner by the Indeans at Manamoiak[3] (a place not farr from hence, now well knowne). He gave them what they demanded for his liberty, but when they had gott what they desired, they kept him still and indevored to kill his men; but he was freed by seasing on some of them, and kept them bound till they gave him a cannows load of corne. Of which, see Purch: lib. 9. fol. 1778.[4] But this was Anº: 1619.

After the writing of the former relation he came to the Ile of Capawack [5] (which lyes south of this place in the way to Virginia), and the foresaid Squanto with him, wher he going a shore amongst the Indans to trad, as he used to doe, was betrayed and assaulted by them, and all his men slaine, but one

---

[1] Nemasket was in Middleborough, Patuxet in Plymouth, Nauset in Eastham, and Satucket in Brewster.

[2] Meaning Boston harbor.   [3] Chatham, on Cape Cod.

[4] The reference is to Samuel Purchas's *Pilgrimes* (London, 1625), vol. IV., fol. 1778, where a letter of Dermer's is printed, which he wrote to Purchas from Virginia, in December, 1619, recounting this and other adventures.

[5] Martha's Vineyard

that kept the boat; but him selfe gott abord very sore wounded, and they had cut of his head upon the cudy [1] of his boat, had not the man reskued him with a sword. And so they got away, and made shift to gett into Virginia, wher he dyed; whether of his wounds or the diseases of the cuntrie, or both togeather, is uncertaine. By all which it may appeare how farr these people were from peace, and with what danger this plantation was begune, save as the powerfull hand of the Lord did protect them. These thing[s] were partly the reason why they kept aloofe and were so long before they came to the English. An other reason (as after them selvs made known) was how aboute 3. years before, a French-ship was cast away at Cap-Codd, but the men gott ashore, and saved their lives, and much of their victails, and other goods; but after the Indeans heard of it, they geathered togeather from these parts, and never left watching and dogging them till they got advantage, and kild them all but 3. or 4. which they kept, and sent from one Sachem to another, to make sporte with, and used them worse then slaves; (of which the foresaid Mr. Dermer redeemed 2. of them;) and they conceived this ship was now come to revenge it.

Also, (as after was made knowne,) before they came to the English to make freindship, they gott all the Powachs [2] of the cuntrie, for 3. days togeather, in a horid and divellish maner to curse and execrate them with their cunjurations, which asembly and service they held in a darke and dismale swampe.

But to returne. The spring now approaching, it pleased God the mortalitie begane to cease amongst them, and the sick and lame recovered apace, which put as it were new life into them; though they had borne their sadd affliction with much patience and contentednes, as I thinke any people could doe. But it was the Lord which upheld them, and had beforehand prepared them; many having long borne the yoake,

[1] A small cabin.   [2] Powwows. or medicine men.

yea from their youth. Many other smaler maters I omite,
sundrie of them having been allready published in a Jurnall
made by one of the company;[1] and some other passages of
jurneys and relations allredy published, to which I referr
those that are willing to know them more perticulerly. And
being now come to the 25. of March I shall begine the year
1621.[2]

Anno. 1621.

THEY now begane to dispatch the ship away which broⁿght
them over, which lay tille aboute this time, or the begining of
Aprill.   The reason on their parts why she stayed so long, was
the necessitie and danger that lay upon them, for it was well
towards the ende of Desember before she could land any thing
hear, or they able to receive any thing ashore. Afterwards,
the 14. of Jan: the house which they had made for a generall
randevoze by casulty fell afire, and some were faine to retire
abord for shilter.   Then the sicknes begane to fall sore amongst
them, and the weather so bad as they could not make much
sooner any dispatch.   Againe, the Govʳ and cheefe of them,
seeing so many dye, and fall downe sick dayly, thought it
it no wisdom to send away the ship, their condition considered,
and the danger they stood in from the Indeans, till they
could procure some shelter; and therfore thought it better to
draw some more charge upon them selves and freinds, then
hazard all.   The mʳ and sea-men likewise, though before
they hasted the passengers a shore to be goone, now many of
their men being dead, and of the ablest of them, (as is before
noted,) and of the rest many lay sick and weake, the mʳ
durst not put to sea, till he saw his men begine to recover,
and the hart of winter over.

Afterwards they (as many as were able) began to plant
ther corne, in which servise Squanto stood them in great stead,
showing them both the maner how to set it, and after how to

---

[1] The journal referred to is that in "Mourt's *Relation*."   See the editor's Introduction.   [2] See p. 56, note 3.

dress and tend it.   Also he tould them excepte they gott fish and set with it (in these old grounds)[1] it would come to nothing, and he showed them that in the midle of Aprill they should have store enough come up the brooke, by which they begane to build, and taught them how to take it, and wher to get other provissions necessary for them; all which they found true by triall and experience.   Some English seed they sew, as wheat and pease, but it came not to good, eather by the badnes of the seed, or latenes of the season, or both, or some other defecte.

In this month of Aprill whilst they were bussie about their seed, their Gov[r] (Mr. John Carver) came out of the feild very sick, it being a hott day; he complained greatly of his head, and lay downe, and within a few howers his sences failed, so as he never spake more till he dyed, which was within a few days after.   Whoss death was much lamented, and caused great heavines amongst them, as ther was cause.   He was buried in the best maner they could, with some vollies of shott by all that bore armes; and his wife, being a weak woman, dyed within 5. or 6. weeks after him.

Shortly after William Bradford was chosen Gove[r] in his stead, and being not yet recoverd of his ilnes, in which he had been near the point of death, Isaak Allerton was chosen to be an Asistante unto him, who, by renewed election every year, continued sundry years togeather, which I hear note once for all.

May 12. was the first mariage in this place,[2] which, according to the laudable custome of the Low-Cuntries, in which they had lived, was thought most requisite to be performed by the magistrate, as being a civill thing, upon which many questions aboute inheritances doe depende, with other things most proper to their cognizans, and most consonante to the scripturs, Ruth

---

[1] *I. e.*, where the Indians had been accustomed to plant.

[2] This was the marriage of Edward Winslow, whose wife had died March 24, 1620/1, with Susanna White, whose husband, William White, had died February 21, 1620/1.

4. and no wher found in the gospell to be layed on the ministers as a part of their office. "This decree or law about mariage was published by the Stats of the Low-Cuntries An°: 1590. That those of any religion, after lawfull and open publication, coming before the magistrats, in the Town or Stat-house, were to be orderly (by them) maried one to another." Petets Hist. fol: 1029.[1] And this practiss hath continued amongst, not only them, but hath been followed by all the famous churches of Christ in these parts to this time,—An°: 1646.

Haveing in some sorte ordered their bussines at home, it was thought meete to send some abroad to see their new freind Massasoyet,[2] and to bestow upon him some gratuitie to bind him the faster unto them; as also that hearby they might veiw the countrie, and see in what maner he lived, what strength he had aboute him, and how the ways were to his place, if at any time they should have occasion. So the 2. of July they sente Mr. Edward Winslow[3] and Mr. Hopkins, with the foresaid

[1] J. F. le Petit, *La Grande Chronique Ancienne et Moderne de Hollande, Zeelande*, etc. (Dordrecht, 1601). The province of Holland had established civil marriage in 1580.

[2] For an account of the visit to Massasoit, see "Mourt's *Relation*" in Dexter's reprint, or Arber, *Story of the Pilgrim Fathers*, pp. 462–473.

[3] Edward Winslow was born in Droitwich, Worcestershire, October 19, 1595. He joined the Pilgrim company in Leyden in 1617. While there he engaged in the business of a printer, and married in 1618 Elizabeth Barker of Chester, England. He came with his wife in the *Mayflower* to Plymouth, where she died March 24, 1620/1. On May 12, 1621, he married Susanna, widow of William White. In 1623 he went to England as the agent of the colony, and returned in the *Charity* in 1624, bringing the first cattle introduced into the colony. While in England he published a book entitled *Good News from New England* (London, 1624). In 1633 he was chosen governor of the colony. He visited England again in 1634 and was imprisoned in the Fleet prison; see p. 316. He was again governor in 1636 and 1644. In 1646 he went to England for the fourth time and did not return. At that visit through his influence the Society for the Propagation of the Gospel among the Indians, which is still in existence, was established, in 1649. He published *Hypocrisie Unmasked* (London, 1646), and the next year published *New England's Salamander*. In the appendix of *Hypocrisie Unmasked* he gave an account of the farewell discourse of Robinson concerning new light, which has been much discussed. He was intimate with Cromwell, who consulted him about colonial affairs and issued to him various commissions, in the execution of one of which, for the settlement of Jamaica,

Squanto for ther guid, who gave him a suite of cloaths, and a horsemans coate, with some other small things, which were kindly accepted; but they found but short commons, and came both weary and hungrie home.   For the Indeans used then to have nothing so much corne as they have since the English have stored them with their hows,[1] and seene their industrie in breaking up new grounds therwith.   They found his place to be 40. miles from hence, the soyle good, and the people not many, being dead and abundantly wasted in the late great mortalitie which fell in all these parts aboute three years before the coming of the English,[2] wherin thousands of them dyed, they not being able to burie one another; ther sculs and bones were found in many places lying still above ground, where their houses and dwellings had been; a very sad spectackle to behould.   But they brought word that the Narighansets lived but on the other side of that great bay, and were a strong people, and many in number, living compacte togeather, and had not been at all touched with this wasting plague.

Aboute the later end of this month, one John Billington lost him selfe in the woods, and wandered up and downe some 5. days, living on beries and what he could find.   At length he light on an Indean plantation, 20. mils south of this place, called Manamet, they conveid him furder of, to Nawsett, among those peopl that had before set upon the English when they were costing, whilest the ship lay at the Cape, as is before noted.   But the Gove[r] caused him to be enquired for among the Indeans, and at length Massassoyt sent word wher he was, and the Gove[r] sent a shalop for him, and had

he died at sea May 8, 1655.   One of these commissions, a parchment containing a portrait of Cromwell, is preserved in Pilgrim Hall in Plymouth.   In 1651, while in London, a portrait of Winslow was painted, probably by Robert Walker, Cromwell's court painter; this is also in Pilgrim Hall, together with portraits of his son Josiah and wife, painted presumably by the same artist.

[1] Hoes.

[2] The nature of the great pestilence which fell on the Massachusetts is not certain.   It raged throughout the years 1616 and 1617.

him delivered. Those people also came and made their peace; and they gave full satisfaction to those whose corne they had found and taken when they were at Cap-Codd.

Thus ther peace and aquaintance was prety well establisht with the natives aboute them; and ther was an other Indean called Hobamack[1] come to live amongst them, a proper lustie man, and a man of accounte for his vallour and parts amongst the Indeans, and continued very faithfull and constant to the English till he dyed. He and Squanto being gone upon bussines amonge the Indeans, at their returne (whether it was out of envie to them or malice to the English) ther was a Sachem called Corbitant, alyed to Massassoyte, but never any good freind to the English to this day, mett with them at an Indean towne caled Namassakett[2] 14. miles to the west of this place, and began to quarell with them, and offered to stabe Hobamack; but being a lusty man, he cleared him selfe of him, and came running away all sweating and tould the Gov[r] what had befalne him, and he feared they had killed Squanto, for they threatened them both, and for no other cause but because they were freinds to the English, and servisable unto them. Upon this the Gove[r] taking counsell, it was conceivd not fitt to be borne; for if they should suffer their freinds and messengers thus to be wronged, they should have none would cleave unto them, or give them any inteligence, or doe them serviss afterwards; but nexte they would fall upon them selves. Whereupon it was resolved to send the Captaine and 14. men well armed, and to goe and fall upon them in the night; and if they found that Squanto was kild, to cut of Corbitants head, but not to hurt any but those that had a hand in it. Hobamack was asked if he would goe and be their guid, and bring them ther before day. He said he would, and

---

[1] Hobomok was one of the captains and counsellors of Massasoit. He early attached himself to the Pilgrims, whom he faithfully served until his death in old age. In the division of lands in 1624 a parcel was set to him which was known as "Hobomok's Ground."   [2] Middleborough.

bring them to the house wher the man lay, and show them which was he. So they set forth the 14. of August, and beset the house round; the Captin giving charg to let none pass out, entred the house to search for him. But he was goone away that day, so they mist him; but understood that Squanto was alive, and that he had only threatened to kill him, and made an offer to stabe him but did not. So they withheld and did no more hurte, and the people came trembling, and brought them the best provissions they had, after they were aquainted by Hobamack what was only intended. Ther was 3. sore wounded which broak out of the house, and asaid to pass through the garde. These they brought home with them, and they had their wounds drest and cured, and sente home. After this they had many gratulations from diverce sachims, and much firmer peace; yea, those of the Iles of Capawack sent to make frendship; and this Corbitant him selfe used the mediation of Massassoyte to make his peace, but was shie to come neare them a longe while after.

After this, the 18. of Sepemb^r: they sente out ther shalop to the Massachusets, with 10. men, and Squanto for their guid and interpreter, to discover and veiw that bay, and trade with the natives; the which they performed, and found kind entertainement. The people were much affraid of the Tarentins,[1] a people to the eastward which used to come in harvest time and take away their corne, and many times kill their persons. They returned in saftie, and brought home a good quanty of beaver, and made reporte of the place, wishing they had been ther seated; (but it seems the Lord, who assignes to all men the bounds of their habitations, had apoynted it for an other use). And thus they found the Lord to be with them in all their ways, and to blesse their outgoings and incommings, for which let his holy name have the praise for ever, to all posteritie.

---

[1] The Tarentins or Tarrantines were a fierce body of Indians living along the coast of Maine, who made bloody attacks on the weaker tribes.

They begane now to gather in the small harvest they had, and to fitte up their houses and dwellings against winter, being all well recovered in health and strenght, and had all things in good plenty; for as some were thus imployed in affairs abroad, others were excersised in fishing, aboute codd, and bass, and other fish, of which they tooke good store, of which every family had their portion. All the sommer ther was no wante. And now begane to come in store of foule, as winter aproached, of which this place did abound when they came first (but afterward decreased by degrees). And besids water foule, ther was great store of wild Turkies, of which they tooke many, besids venison, etc. Besids they had aboute a peck a meale a weeke to a person, or now since harvest, Indean corne to that proportion. Which made many afterwards write so largly of their plenty hear to their freinds in England, which were not fained, but true reports.

In Novemb^r, about that time twelfe month that them selves came, ther came in a small ship to them unexpected or loked for,[1] in which came Mr. Cushman (so much spoken of before) and with him 35. persons[2] to remaine and live in the plantation; which did not a litle rejoyce them. And they when they came a shore and found all well, and saw plenty of vitails in every house, were no less glade. For most of them were lusty yonge men, and many of them wild enough, who litle considered whither or aboute what they wente, till they came into the harbore at Cap-Codd, and ther saw nothing but a naked and barren place. They then begane to thinke what should become of them, if the people here were dead or cut of by the Indeans. They begane to consulte (upon some speeches that some of the sea-men had cast out) to take the sayls from the yeard least the ship should gett away and leave them ther. But the m^r hereing of it, gave them good words, and tould them

---

[1] "She came the 9. to the Cap." (Br.)

[2] For the list of passengers in the *Fortune*, see Davis's *Ancient Landmarks of Plymouth*, part I., page 51. The *Fortune* was of 55 tons.

if any thing but well should have befallne the people hear, he hoped he had vitails enough to cary them to Virginia, and whilst he had a bitt they should have their parte; which gave them good satisfaction.   So they were all landed; but ther was not so much as bisket-cake or any other victialls[1] for them, neither had they any beding, but some sory things they had in their cabins, nor pot, nor pan, to drese any meate in; nor overmany cloaths, for many of them had brusht away their coats and cloaks at Plimoth as they came.   But ther was sent over some burching-lane[2] suits in the ship, out of which they were supplied.   The plantation was glad of this addition of strenght, but could have wished that many of them had been of beter condition, and all of them beter furnished with pro-vissions; but that could not now be helpte.

In this ship Mr. Weston sent a large leter to Mr. Carver, the late Gove[r], now deseased, full of complaints and expostula-tions aboute former passagess at Hampton; and the keeping the shipe so long in the country, and returning her without lad-ing, etc., which for brevitie I omite.   The rest is as followeth:

Part of Mr. Westons letter.

I durst never aquainte the adventurers with the alteration of the conditions first agreed on betweene us, which I have since been very glad of, for I am well assured had they knowne as much as I doe, they would not have adventured a halfe-peny of what was necesary for this ship. That you sent no lading in the ship is wonderfull, and worthily distasted. I know you[r] weaknes was the cause of it, and I beleeve more weaknes of judgmente, then weaknes of hands.   A quarter of the time you spente in discoursing, arguing, and consulting, would have done much more; but that is past, etc.   If you mean, bona fide, to performe the conditions agreed upon, doe us the favore to coppy them out faire, and subscribe them with the principall of your names.   And likwise give us accounte as per-ticulerly as you can how our moneys were laid out.   And then I shall be able to give them some satisfaction, whom I am now forsed with good words to shift of.   And consider that the life of the bussines depends on

[1] "Nay, they were faine to spare the shipe some to carry her home."   (Br.)

[2] Birchen or Birchover Lane in London was a headquarters of the sellers of clothing.

the lading of this ship, which, if you doe to any good purpose, that I may be freed from the great sums I have disbursed for the former, and must doe for the later, *I promise you I will never quit the bussines, though all the other adventurers should.*

We have procured you a Charter,[1] the best we could, which is beter then your former, and with less limitation.   For any thing that is els worth writting, Mr. Cushman can informe you.   I pray write instantly for Mr. Robinson to come to you.   And so praying God to blesse you with all graces nessessary both for this life and that to come, I rest

Your very loving frend,
THO. WESTON.

London, July 6. 1621.

This ship (caled the *Fortune*) was speedily dispatcht away, being laden with good clapbord as full as she could stowe, and 2. hoggsheads of beaver and otter skins, which they gott with a few trifling comodities brought with them at first, being altogeather unprovided for trade; neither was ther any amongst them that ever saw a beaver skin till they came hear, and were informed by Squanto.   The fraight was estimated to be worth near 500*li.*   Mr. Cushman returned backe also with this ship, for so Mr. Weston and the rest had apoynted him, for their better information.   And he doubted not, nor them selves neither, but they should have a speedy supply; considering allso how by Mr. Cushmans perswation,[2] and letters received from Leyden, wherin they willed them so to doe, they yeel[d]ed to the afforesaid conditions, and subscribed them with their hands.   But it proved other wise, for Mr. Weston, who had made that large promise in his leter, (as is before noted,) that if all the rest should fall of, yet he would never quit the bussines,

---

[1] This patent from the President and Council of New England, dated June 1, 1621, was issued to John Pierce and his associates and was brought over in the *Fortune* in November, 1621.   The patent which the Pilgrims brought with them from the (southern) Virginia Company was surrendered.   That of 1621 is preserved in Pilgrim Hall, Plymouth.   For its text, see *Ancient Landmarks of Plymouth*, part I., page 40.

[2] Cushman came over probably as the agent of the London merchants to obtain the execution of the contract, which had never been signed.   The address which he delivered in the common house, and which has been called a sermon, was a speech to induce the colonists to sign the contract.

but stick to them, if they yeelded to the conditions, and sente some lading in the ship; and of this Mr. Cushman was confident, and confirmed the same from his mouth, and serious protestations to him selfe before he came.   But all proved but wind, for he was the first and only man that forsooke them, and that before he so much as heard of the returne of this ship, or knew what was done; (so vaine is the confidence in man.)   But of this more in its place.

A leter in answer to his write to Mr. Carver, was sente to him from the Govr, of which so much as is pertenente to the thing in hand I shall hear inserte.

Sr: Your large letter writen to Mr. Carver, and dated the 6. of July, 1621, I have received the 10. of Novemb^r, wherin (after the apologie made for your selfe) you lay many heavie imputations upon him and us all. Touching him, he is departed this life, and now is at rest in the Lord from all those troubls and incoumbrances with which we are yet to strive.   He needs not my appologie; for his care and pains was so great for the commone good, both ours and yours, as that therwith (it is thought) he oppressed him selfe and shortened his days; of whose loss we cannot sufficiently complaine.   At great charges in this adventure, I confess you have beene, and many losses may sustaine; but the loss of his and many other honest and industrious mens lives, cannot be vallewed at any prise. Of the one, ther may be hope of recovery, but the other no recompence can make good.   But I will not insiste in generalls, but come more perticulerly to the things them selves.   You greatly blame us for keping the ship so long in the countrie, and then to send her away emptie.   She lay 5. weks at Cap-Codd, whilst with many a weary step (after a long journey) and the indurance of many a hard brunte, we sought out in the foule winter a place of habitation.   Then we went in so tedious a time to make provission to sheelter us and our goods, aboute which labour, many of our armes and leggs can tell us to this day we were not necligent.   But it pleased God to vissite us then, with death dayly, and with so generall a disease, that the living were scarce able to burie the dead; and the well not in any measure sufficiente to tend the sick.   And now to be so greatly blamed, for not fraighting the ship, doth indeed goe near us, and much discourage us.   But you say you know we will pretend weaknes; and doe you think we had not cause?   Yes, you tell us you beleeve it, but it was more weaknes of judgmente, then of hands.   Our weaknes herin is great we confess, therfore we will bear this check patiently amongst the rest, till God send us wiser men.   But they which tould you we spent so much time in discoursing and consulting, etc., their harts can tell their toungs, they lye.   They cared not, so they might salve their owne sores, how they wounded others.   Indeed, it is our callamitie that we are (beyound expectation) yoked with some ill conditioned people, who will never doe good, but corrupte and abuse others, etc.

The rest of the letter declared how they had subscribed those conditions according to his desire, and sente him the former accounts very perticulerly; also how the ship was laden, and in what condition their affairs stood; that the coming of these people would bring famine upon them unavoydably, if they had not supply in time (as Mr. Cushman could more fully informe him and the rest of the adventurers).   Also that seeing he was now satisfied in all his demands, that offences would be forgoten, and he remember his promise, etc.

After the departure of this ship, (which stayed not above 14. days,) the Gove^r and his assistante haveing disposed these late commers into severall families, as they best could, tooke an exacte accounte of all their provissions in store, and proportioned the same to the number of persons, and found that it would not hould out above 6. months at halfe alowance, and hardly that.   And they could not well give less this winter time till fish came in againe.   So they were presently put to half alowance, one as well as an other, which begane to be hard, but they bore it patiently under hope of supply.

Soone after this ships departure, the great people of the Narigansets, in a braving maner, sente a messenger unto them with a bundl of arrows tyed aboute with a great sneak-skine; which their interpretours tould them was a threatening and a chaleng.   Upon which the Govr, with the advice of others sente them a round answere, that if they had rather have warre then peace, they might begine when they would; they had done them no wrong, neither did they fear them, or should they find them unprovided.   And by another messenger sente the sneake-skine back with bulits in it; but they would not receive it, but sent it back againe.   But these things I doe but mention, because they are more at large allready put forth in printe,[1] by Mr. Winslow, at the requeste of some freinds. And it is like the reason was their owne ambition, who, (since the death of so many of the Indeans,) thought to dominire and lord it over the rest, and conceived the English would be a barr in their way, and saw that Massasoyt took sheilter allready under their wings.

But this made them the more carefully to looke to them selves, so as they agreed to inclose their dwellings with a good strong pale, and make flankers in convenient places, with gates to shute, which were every night locked, and a watch kept and when neede required ther was also warding in the day time.   And the company was by the Captaine and the Gov[r] advise, devided into 4. squadrons, and every one had ther quarter apoynted them, unto which they were to repaire upon any suddane alarme.   And if ther should be any crie of fire, a company were appointed for a gard, with muskets, whilst others quenchet the same, to prevent Indean treachery. This was accomplished very cherfully, and the towne impayled round by the begining of March, in which evry family had a prety garden plote secured.   And herewith I shall end this year.   Only I shall remember one passage more, rather of mirth then of waight.   One the day called Chrismasday, the Gov[r] caled them out to worke, (as was used,) but the most of this new-company excused them selves and said it wente against their consciences to work on that day.   So the Gov[r] tould them that if they made it mater of conscience, he would spare them till they were better informed.   So he led-away the rest and left them; but when they came home at noone from their worke, he found them in the streete at play, openly; some pitching the barr and some at stoole-ball,[2] and shuch like sports.

---

[1] In *Good News from New England* (London, 1624).
[2] A play in which balls were driven from stool to stool.

So he went to them, and tooke away their implements, and tould them that was against his conscience, that they should play and others worke.   If they made the keeping of it mater of devotion, let them kepe their houses, but ther should be no gameing or revelling in the streets.   Since which time nothing hath been atempted that way, at least openly.

Anno 1622.

AT the spring of the year they had apointed the Massachusets to come againe and trade with them, and begane now to prepare for that vioag about the later end of March.   But upon some rumors heard, Hobamak, their Indean, tould them upon some jealocies he had, he feared they were joyned with the Narighansets and might betray them if they were not carefull.   He intimated also some jealocie of Squanto, by what he gathered from some private whisperings betweene him and other Indeans.   But they resolved to proseede, and sente out their shalop with 10. of their cheefe men aboute the begining of Aprill, and both Squanto and Hobamake with them, in regarde of the jelocie betweene them.   But they had not bene gone longe, but an Indean belonging to Squantos family came runing in seeming great fear, and tould them that many of the Narihgansets, with Corbytant, and he thought also Massasoyte, were coming against them; and he gott away to tell them, not without danger.   And being examined by the Govr, he made as if they were at hand, and would still be looking back, as if they were at his heels.   At which the Govr caused them to take armes and stand on their garde, and supposing the boat to be still within hearing (by reason it was calme) caused a warning peece or 2. to be shote of, the which they heard and came in.   But no Indeans apeared; watch was kepte all night, but nothing was seene.   Hobamak was confidente for Massasoyt, and thought all was false; yet the Govr caused him to send his wife privatly, to see what she could observe (pretening other occasions), but ther was nothing found, but all was quiet.

After this they proseeded on their vioge to the Massachusets, and had good trade, and returned in saftie, blessed be God.

But by the former passages, and other things of like nature, they begane to see that Squanto sought his owne ends, and plaid his owne game, by putting the Indeans in fear, and drawing gifts from them to enrich him selfe; making them beleeve he could stur up warr against whom he would, and make peece for whom he would. Yea, he made them beleeve they kept the plague buried in the ground, and could send it amongs whom they would, which did much terrifie the Indeans, and made them depend more on him, and seeke more to him then to Massasoyte, which proucured him envie, and had like to have cost him his life. For after the discovery of his practises, Massasoyt sought it both privatly and openly; which caused him to stick close to the English, and never durst goe from them till he dyed. They also made good use of the emulation that grue betweene Hobamack and him, which made them cary more squarely. And the Gov[r] seemed to countenance the one, and the Captaine the other, by which they had better intelligence, and made them both more diligente.

Now in a maner their provissions were wholy spent, and they looked hard for supply, but none came. But about the later end of May, they spied a boat at sea, which at first they thought had beene some Frenchman; but it proved a shalop which came from a ship which Mr. Weston and an other had set out a fishing, at a place called Damarins-cove,[1] 40. leagues to the eastward of them, wher were that year many more ships come a fishing. This boat brought 7. passengers and some letters, but no vitails, nor any hope of any. Some part of which I shall set downe.

Mr. Carver, in my last leters by the *Fortune*, in whom Mr. Cushman wente, and who I hope is with you, for we daly expecte the shipe back againe. She departed hence, the begining of July, with 35. persons, though not over well provided with necesaries, by reason of the parsemonie

---

[1] Now Damariscove Island, near the mouth of Damariscotta River, on the Maine coast.

of the adventure[r]s. I have solisited them to send you a supply of men and provissions before shee come. They all answer they will doe great maters, when they hear good news. Nothing before; so faithfull, constant, and carefull of your good, are your olde and honest freinds, that if they hear not from you, they are like to send you no supplie, etc. I am now to relate the occasion of sending this ship, hoping if you give credite to my words, you will have a more favourable opinion of it, then some hear, wherof Pickering is one, who taxed me to mind my owne ends, which is in part true, etc. Mr. Beachamp [1] and my selfe bought this litle ship, and have set her out, partly, if it may be, to uphold [2] the plantation, as well to doe others good as our selves; and partly to gett up what we are formerly out; though we are otherwise censured, etc. This is the occasion we have sent this ship and these passengers, on our owne accounte; whom we desire you will frendly entertaine and supply with shuch necesaries as you cane spare, and they wante, etc. And among other things we pray you lend or sell them some seed corne, and if you have the salt remaining of the last year, that you will let them have it for their presente use, and we will either pay you for it, or give you more when we have set our salt-pan to worke, which we desire may be set up in one of the litle ilands in your bay, etc. And because we intende, if God plase, (and the generallitie doe it not,) to send within a month another shipe, who, having discharged her passengers, shal goe to Virginia, etc. And it may be we shall send a small ship to abide with you on the coast, which I conceive may be a great help to the plantation. To the end our desire may be effected, which, I assure my selfe, will be also for your good, we pray you give them entertainmente in your houses the time they shall be with you, that they may lose no time, but may presently goe in hand to fell trees and cleave them, to the end lading may be ready and our ship stay not.

Some of the adventurers have sent you hearwith all some directions for your furtherance in the commone bussines, who are like those St. James speaks of, that bid their brother eat, and warme him, but give him nothing; so they bid you make salt, and uphold the plantation, but send you no means wherwithall to doe it, etc. By the next we purpose to send more people on our owne accounte, and to take a patente; that if your peopl should be as unhumane as some of the adventurers, not to admite

---

[1] John Beauchamp was one of the merchant adventurers. When eight of the leading members of the Pilgrim Colony made a settlement with the adventurers after the expiration of the seven years' contract, he, with James Shirley, Richard Andrews and Timothy Hatherley, endorsed the note which they gave to liquidate their indebtedness to the adventurers.

[2] "I know not which way." (Br.)

us to dwell with them, which were extreme barbarisme, and which will
never enter into my head to thinke you have any shuch Pickerings amongst
you.   Yet to satisfie our passengers I must of force doe it; and for some
other reasons not necessary to be writen, etc.   I find the generall so
backward, and your freinds at Leyden so could, that I fear you must stand
on your leggs, and trust (as they say) to God and your selves.

Subscribed,
your loving freind,

Jan: 12. 1621.[1]   Tho: Weston.

Sundry other things I pass over, being tedious and imperti-
nent.

All this was but could comfort to fill their hungrie bellies,
and a slender performance of his former late promiss; and as
litle did it either fill or warme them, as those the Apostle James
spake of, by him before mentioned.   And well might it make
them remember what the psalmist saith, Psa. 118.8.   *It is
better to trust in the Lord, then to have confidence in man.*   And
Psa. 146.   *Put not you trust in princes* (much less in the
marchants) *nor in the sone of man, for ther is no help in them.*
v. 5. *Blesed is he that hath the God of Jacob for his help, whose
hope is in the Lord his God.*   And as they were now fayled of
suply by him and others in this their greatest neede and wants,
which was caused by him and the rest, who put so great a company of men upon them, as the former company were, without
any food, and came at shuch a time as they must live almost
a whole year before any could be raised, excepte they had
sente some; so, upon the pointe they never had any supply of
vitales more afterwards (but what the Lord gave them otherwise); for all the company sent at any time was allways too
short for those people that came with it.

Ther came allso by the same ship other leters, but of later
date, one from Mr. Weston, an other from a parte of the adventurers, as foloweth.

Mr. Carver, since my last, to the end we might the more readily proceed to help the generall, at a meeting of some of the principall advent-

[1] I. e., 1622.

urers, a proposition was put forth, and alowed by all presente (save Pickering), to adventure each man the third parte of what he foi merly had done. And ther are some other that folow his example, and will adventure no furder. In regard wherof the greater part of the adventurers being willing to uphold the bussines, finding it no reason that those that are willing should uphold the bussines of those that are unwilling, whose backwardnes doth discourage those that are forward, and hinder other new-adventurers from coming in, we having well considered therof, have resolved, according to an article in the agreemente, (that it may be lawfull by a generall consente of the adventurers and planters, upon just occasion, to breake of their joynte stock,) to breake it of; and doe pray you to ratifie, and confirme the same on your parts. Which being done, we shall the more willingly goe forward for the upholding of you with all things necesarie. But in any case you must agree to the artickls, and send it by the first under your hands and seals. So I end.

Your loving freind,

Jan: 17. 1621.   THO: WESTON.

Another leter was write from part of the company of the adventurers to the same purpose, and subscribed with 9. of their names, wherof Mr. Westons and Mr. Beachamphs were tow. Thes things seemed strang unto them, seeing this unconstancie and shufling; it made them to thinke ther was some misterie in the matter. And therfore the Govr concealed these letters from the publick, only imparted them to some trustie freinds for advice, who concluded with him, that this tended to disband and scater them (in regard of their straits); and if Mr. Weston and others, who seemed to rune in a perticuler way, should come over with shiping so provided as his letters did intimate, they most would fall to him, to the prejudice of them selves and the rest of the adventure[r]s, their freinds, from whom as yet they heard nothing. And it was doubted whether he had not sente over shuch a company in the former ship, for shuch an end. Yet they tooke compassion of those 7. men which this ship, which fished to the eastward, had kept till planting time was over, and so could set no corne; and allso wanting vitals, (for they turned them off without any, and indeed wanted for them selves,) neither was their salt-pan come, so as they could not performe any of those things which Mr. Weston had apointed, and might have starved if the plantation had not succoured them; who, in their wants, gave them as good as any of their owne. The ship wente to Virginia, wher they sould both ship and fish, of which (it was conceived) Mr. Weston had a very slender accounte.

After this came another of his ships, and brought letters dated the 10. of Aprill, from Mr. Weston, as followeth.

Mr. Bradford, these, etc. The *Fortune* is arived, of whose good news touching your estate and proceedings, I am very glad to hear. And how soever he was robed on the way by the Frenchmen,[1] yet I hope your loss will not be great, for the conceite of so great a returne doth much animate the adventurers, so that I hope some matter of importance will be done by them, etc. As for my selfe, I have sould my adventure and debts unto them, so as I am quit [2] of you, and you of me, for that matter, etc. Now though I have nothing to pretend as an adventurer amongst you, yet I will advise you a litle for your good, if you can apprehend it. I perceive and know as well as another, the dispositions of your adventurers, whom the hope of gaine hath drawne on to this they have done; and yet I fear that hope will not draw them much furder. Besids, most of them are against the sending of them of Leyden, for whose cause this bussines was first begune, and some of the most religious (as Mr. Greene by name) [3] excepts against them. So that my advice is (you may follow it if you please) that you forthwith break of your joynte stock, which you have warente to doe, both in law and conscience, for the most parte of the adventurers have given way unto it by a former letter. And the means you have ther, which I hope will be to some purpose by the trade of this spring, may, with the help of some freinds hear, bear the charge of transporting those of Leyden; and when they are with you I make no question but by Gods help you will be able to subsist of your selves. But I shall leave you to your discretion.

I desired diverce of the adventurers, as Mr. Peirce, Mr. Greene, and others, if they had any thing to send you, either vitails or leters, to send them by these ships; and marvelling they sent not so much as a letter, I asked our passengers what leters they had, and with some dificultie one of them tould me he had one, which was delivered him with great charge of secrecie; and for more securitie, to buy a paire of new-shoes, and sow

---

[1] See the Introduction.   [2] "See how his promiss is fulfild." (Br.)
[3] William Greene was one of the merchant adventurers.

it betweene the soles for fear of intercepting.   I, taking the leter, wondering what mistrie might be in it, broke it open, and found this treacherous letter subscribed by the hands of Mr. Pickering and Mr. Greene.   Wich leter had it come to you[r] hands without answer, might have caused the hurt, if not the ruine, of us all.   For assuredly if you had followed their instructions, and shewed us that unkindness which they advise you unto, to hold us in distruste as enimise, etc., it might have been an occasion to have set us togeather by the eares, to the distruction of us all.   For I doe beleeve that in shuch a case, they knowing what bussines hath been betweene us, not only my brother, but others also, would have been violent, and heady against you, etc.   I mente to have setled the people I before and now send, with or near you, as well for their as your more securitie and defence, as help on all occasions.   But I find the adventurers so jealous and suspitious, that I have altered my resolution, and given order to my brother and those with him, to doe as they and him selfe shall find fitte. Thus, etc.

Your loving freind,

Aprill 10. 1621.   THO: WESTON.

Some part of Mr Pickerings letter before mentioned

To Mr. Bradford and Mr. Brewster, etc.

My dear love remembred unto you all, etc.   The company hath bought out Mr. Weston, and are very glad they are freed of him, he being judged a man that thought him selfe above the generall, and not expresing so much the fear of God as was meete in a man to whom shuch trust should have been reposed in a matter of so great importance.   I am sparing to be so plaine as indeed is clear against him; but a few words to the wise.

Mr. Weston will not permitte leters to be sent in his ships, nor any thing for your good or ours, of which ther is some reason in respecte of him selfe, etc.   His brother Andrew, whom he doth send as principall in one of these ships, is a heady yong man, and violente, and set against you ther, and the company hear; ploting with Mr. Weston their owne ends, which tend to your and our undooing in respecte of our estates ther, and prevention of our good ends.   For by credible testimoney we are informed his purpose is to come to your colonie, pretending he comes for and from the adventurers, and will seeke to gett what you have in readynes into his ships, as if they came from the company, and possessing all, will be so much profite to him selfe.   And further to informe them selves what spetiall places or things you have discovered, to the end that they may supres and deprive you, etc.

The Lord, who is the watchman of Israll and slepeth not, preserve you and deliver you from unreasonable men. I am sorie that ther is cause to admonish you of these things concerning this man; so I leave you to God, who bless and multiply you into thousands, to the advancemente of the glorious gospell of our Lord Jesus. Amen. Fare well.

Your loving freinds,
EDWARD PICKERING.
WILLIAM GREENE.

I pray conceale both the writing and deliverie of this leter, but make the best use of it. We hope to sete forth a ship our selves with in this month.

The heads of his answer.

Mr. Bradford, this is the leter that I wrote unto you of, which to answer in every perticuler is needles and tedious. My owne conscience and all our people can and I thinke will testifie, that my end in sending the ship *Sparrow* was your good, etc. Now I will not deney but ther are many of our people rude fellows, as these men terme them; yet I presume they will be governed by such as I set over them. And I hope not only to be able to reclaime them from that profanenes that may scandalise the vioage, but by degrees to draw them to God, etc. I am so farr from sending rude fellows to deprive you either by fraude or violence of what is yours, as I have charged the m^r· of the ship *Sparrow*, not only to leave with you 2000. of bread, but also a good quantitie of fish,[1] etc. But I will leave it to you to consider what evill this leter would or might have done, had it come to your hands and taken the effecte the other desired.

Now if you be of the mind that these men are, deale plainly with us, and we will seeke our residence els-wher. If you are as freindly as we have thought you to be, give us the entertainment of freinds, and we will take nothing from you, neither meat, drinke, nor lodging, but what we will, in one kind or other, pay you for, etc. I shall leave in the countrie a litle ship (if God send her safe thither) with mariners and fisher-men to stay ther, who shall coast, and trad with the savages, and the old plantation. It may be we shall be as helpfull to you, as you will be to us. I thinke I shall see you the next spring; and so I comend you to the protection of God, who ever keep you.

Your loving freind,
THO: WESTON.

---

[1] "But y^e [*he*] left not his own men a bite of bread." (Br.)

Thus all ther hops in regard of Mr. Weston were layed in the dust, and all his promised helpe turned into an empttie advice, which they apprehended was nether lawfull nor profitable for them to follow. And they were not only thus left destitute of help in their extreme wants, haveing neither vitails, nor any thing to trade with, but others prepared and ready to glean up what the cuntrie might have afforded for their releefe. As for those harsh censures and susspitions intimated in the former and following leters, they desired to judg as charitably and wisly of them as they could, waighing them in the ballance of love and reason; and though they (in parte) came from godly and loveing freinds, yet they conceived many things might arise from over deepe jealocie and fear, togeather with unmeete provocations, though they well saw Mr. Weston pursued his owne ends, and was imbittered in spirite. For after the receit of the former leters, the Govr received one from Mr. Cushman, who went home in the ship, and was allway intimate with Mr. Weston, (as former passages declare), and it was much marveled that nothing was heard from him, all this while. But it should seeme it was the difficulty of sending, for this leter was directed as the leter of a wife to her husband, who was here, and brought by him to the Govr. It was as followeth.

Beloved Sr: I hartily salute you, with trust of your health, and many thanks for your love. By Gods providence we got well home the 17. of Feb. Being robbed by the Frenchmen by the way, and carried by them into France, and were kepte ther 15. days, and lost all that we had that was worth taking; but thanks be to God, we escaped with our lives and ship. I see not that it worketh any discouragment hear. I purpose by Gods grace to see you shortly, I hope in June nexte, or before. In the mean space know these things, and I pray you be advertised a litle. Mr. Weston hath quite broken of from our company, through some discontents that arose betwext him and some of our adventurers, and hath sould all his adventurs, and hath now sent 3. smale ships for his perticuler plantation. The greatest wherof, being 100. tune, Mr. Reynolds goeth m^r and he with the rest purposeth to come him selfe; for what end I know not.

The people which they cary are no men for us, wherfore I pray you entertaine them not, neither exchainge man for man with them, excepte it be some of your worst. He hath taken a patente for him selfe. If they offerr to buy any thing of you, let it be shuch as you can spare, and let them give the worth of it. If they borrow any thing of you, let them leave a good pawne, etc. It is like he will plant to the southward of the Cape, for William Trevore [1] hath lavishly tould but what he knew or imagined of Capewack, Mohiggen, and the Narigansets. I fear these people will hardly deale so well with the savages as they should. I pray you therfore signifie to Squanto, that they are a distincte body from us, and we have nothing to doe with them, neither must be blamed for their falts, much less can warrente their fidelitie. We are aboute to recover our losses in France. Our freinds at Leyden are well, and will come to you as many as can this time. I hope all will turne to the best, wherfore I pray you be not discouraged, but gather up your selfe to goe thorow these dificulties cherfully and with courage in that place wherin God hath sett you, untill the day of refreshing come. And the Lord God of sea and land bring us comfortably togeather againe, if it may stand with his glorie.

Yours,   ROBART CUSHMAN.

On the other sid of the leafe, in the same leter, came these few lines from Mr. John Peirce, in whose name the patente was taken, and of whom more will follow, to be spoken in its place.

Worthy Sr: I desire you to take into consideration that which is writen on the other side, and not any way to damnifie your owne collony, whos strength is but weaknes, and may therby be more infeebled. And for the leters of association, by the next ship we send, I hope you shall receive satisfaction; in the mean time whom you admite I will approve. But as for Mr. Weston's company, I thinke them so base in condition (for the most parte) as in all apearance not fitt for an honest mans company. I wish they prove other wise. My purpose is not to enlarge my selfe, but cease in these few lins, and so rest

Your loving freind,
JOHN PEIRCE.

All these things they pondred and well considered, yet concluded to give his men frendly entertainmente; partly in regard of Mr. Weston him selfe, considering what he had been unto them, and done for them, and to some, more espetially;

---

[1] William Trevore came in the *Mayflower*, having been hired for a year, and returned to England.

and partly in compassion to the people, who were now come
into a willdernes, (as them selves were,) and were by the ship
to be presently put a shore, (for she was to cary other passengers to Virginia, who lay at great charge,) and they were
alltogeather unacquainted and knew not what to doe. So as
they had received his former company of 7. men, and vitailed
them as their owne hitherto, so they also received these (being
aboute 60. lusty men), and gave housing for them selves and
their goods; and many being sicke, they had the best means
the place could aford them. They stayed hear the most parte
of the sommer till the ship came back againe from Virginia.
Then, by his direction, or those whom he set over them, they
removed into the Massachusset Bay, he having got a patente
for some part ther, (by light of ther former discovery in leters
sent home).[1] Yet they left all ther sicke folke hear till they
were setled and housed. But of ther victails they had not
any, though they were in great wante, nor any thing els in
recompence of any courtecie done them; neither did they
desire it, for they saw they were an unruly company, and had
no good govermente over them, and by disorder would soone
fall into wants if Mr. Weston came not the sooner amongst
them; and therfore, to prevente all after occasion, would have
nothing of them.

Amids these streigths, and the desertion of those from
whom they had hoped for supply, and when famine begane
now to pinch them sore, they not knowing what to doe, the
Lord, (who never fails his,) presents them with an occasion,
beyond all expectation. This boat which came from the eastward brought them a letter from a stranger, of whose name they
had never heard before, being a captaine of a ship come ther a
fishing. This leter was as followeth. Being thus inscribed.

To all his good freinds at Plimoth, these, etc.

Freinds, cuntrimen, and neighbours: I salute you, and wish you all
health and hapines in the Lord. I make bould with these few lines to

---

[1] Weston's patent is not extant.

trouble you, because unless I were unhumane, I can doe no les. **Bad**
news doth spread it selfe too farr; yet I will so farr informe you that my
selfe, with many good freinds in the south-collonie of Virginia, have received shuch a blow, that 400. persons large will not make good our losses.
Therfore I doe intreat you (allthough not knowing you) that the old rule
which I learned when I went to schoole, may be sufficente.   That is,
Hapie is he whom other mens harmes doth make to beware.   And now
againe and againe, wishing all those that willingly would serve the Lord,
all health and happines in this world, and everlasting peace in the world
to come.   And so I rest,

Yours,

JOHN HUDLSTON.

By this boat the Govr returned a thankfull answer,
as was meete, and sent a boate of their owne with them, which
was piloted by them, in which Mr. Winslow was sente to procure what provissions he could of the ships, who was kindly
received by the foresaid gentill-man, who not only spared what
he could, but writ to others to doe the like.   By which means
he gott some good quantitie and returned in saftie, by which
the plantation had a duble benefite, first, a present refreshing
by the food brought, and secondly, they knew the way to
those parts for their benifite hearafter.   But what was gott,
and this small boat brought, being devided among so many,
came but to a litle, yet by Gods blesing it upheld them till
harvest.   It arose but to a quarter of a pound of bread a day
to each person; and the Govr caused it to be dayly given
them, otherwise, had it been in their owne custody, they
would have eate it up and then starved.   But thus, with what
els they could get, they made pretie shift till corne was ripe.

This sommer they builte a fort with good timber, both
strong and comly, which was of good defence, made with a
flate rofe and batelments, on which their ordnance were
mounted, and wher they kepte constante watch, espetially in
time of danger.   It served them allso for a meeting house, and
was fitted accordingly for that use.[1]   It was a great worke

An interesting description of the town and its fortifications, a few years
later, is given by Isaac de Rasières, secretary of New Netherland, who visited

for them in this weaknes and time of wants; but the deanger of the time required it, and both the continuall rumors of the fears from the Indeans hear, espetially the Narigansets, and also the hearing of that great massacre in Virginia, made all hands willing to despatch the same.

Now the wellcome time of harvest aproached, in which all had their hungrie bellies filled. But it arose but to a litle, in comparison of a full years supplie; partly by reason they were not yet well aquainted with the manner of Indean corne, (and they had no other,) allso their many other imployments, but cheefly their weaknes for wante of food, to tend it as they should have done. Also much was stolne both by night and day, before it became scarce eatable, and much more afterward. And though many were well whipt (when they were taken) for a few ears of corne, yet hunger made others (whom conscience did not restraine) to venture. So as it well appeared that famine must still insue the next year allso, if not some way prevented, or supplie should faile, to which they durst not trust. Markets there was none to goe too, but only the Indeans, and they had no trading comodities. Behold now another providence of God; a ship comes into the harbor, one Captain Jons being cheefe therin. They were set out by some marchants to discovere all the harbors betweene this and Virginia, and the shoulds of Cap-Cod, and to trade along the coast wher they could. This ship had store of English-beads (which were then good trade) and some knives, but would sell none but at dear rates, and also a good quantie togeather. Yet they weere glad of the occasion, and faine to buy at any rate; they were faine to give after the rate of cento per cento, if not more, and yet pay away coat-beaver at 3s. per *li.*, which in a few years after yeelded 20s. By this means they were fitted againe to trade for beaver and other things, and intended to buy what corne they could.

it in 1627. His letter is printed in the *Collections of the New York Historioai Society* second series, II. 351. See also pp. 225, 226, 234, *post.*

But I will hear take liberty to make a little digression. Ther was in this ship a gentle-man by name Mr. John Poory;[1] he had been secretarie in Virginia, and was now going home passenger in this ship.   After his departure he write a leter to the Gov[r] in the postscrite wherof he hath these lines.

To your selfe and Mr. Brewster, I must acknowledg my selfe many ways indebted, whose books I would have you thinke very well bestowed on him, who esteemeth them shuch juells.   My hast would not suffer me to remember (much less to begg) Mr. Ainsworths elaborate worke upon the 5. books of Moyses.   Both his and Mr. Robinsons doe highly comend the authors, as being most conversante in the scripturs of all others.   And what good (who knows) it may please God to worke by them, through my hands, (though most unworthy,) who finds shuch high contente in them.   God have you all in his keeping.

Your unfained and firme freind,

Aug. 28. 1622.   JOHN PORY.

These things I hear inserte for honour sake of the authors memorie, which this gentle-man doth thus ingeniusly ac-knowledg; and him selfe after his returne did this poore-plantation much credite amongst those of no mean ranck. But to returne.

Shortly after harvest Mr. Westons people who were now seated at the Massachusets, and by disorder (as it seems) had made havock of their provissions, begane now to perceive that want would come upon them.   And hearing that they hear had bought trading comodities and intended to trade for corne, they write to the Gov[r] and desired they might joyne with them, and they would imploy their small ship in the servise; and furder requested either to lend or sell them so much of their trading comodities as their part might come to, and they would undertake to make paymente when Mr. Weston

---

[1] A letter of Pory's describing conditions at Jamestown in 1619 is printed in *Narratives of Early Virginia*, in this series; its introduction gives an account of him.   He was a traveller and an experienced member of Parliament.   As speaker of the first elected legislative assembly in America, that which met in Jamestown in 1619, he drew up the journal of its proceedings, which is printed in the same volume.

or their supply, should come. The Gov[r] condesended upon equall terms of agreemente, thinkeing to goe aboute the Cap to the southward with the ship, wher some store of corne might be got. Althings being provided, Captaint Standish was apointed to goe with them, and Squanto for a guid and interpreter, about the latter end of September; but the winds put them in againe, and putting out the 2. time, he fell sick of a feavor, so the Gov[r] wente him selfe. But they could not get aboute the should of Cap-Cod, for flats and break-ers, neither could Squanto directe them better, nor the m[r] durst venture any further, so they put into Manamoyack Bay and got w[th] [what] they could ther. In this place Squanto fell sick of an Indean feavor, bleeding much at the nose (which the Indeans take for a simptome of death), and within a few days dyed ther; desiring the Gov[r] to pray for him, that he might goe to the Englishmens God in heaven, and be-queathed sundrie of his things to sundry of his English freinds, as remembrances of his love; of whom they had a great loss. They got in this vioage, in one place and other, about 26. or 28. hogsheads of corne and beans, which was more then the Indeans could well spare in these parts, for the set but a litle till they got English hows. And so were faine to returne, being sory they could not gett about the Cap, to have been better laden. After ward the Gov[r] tooke a few men and wente to the inland places, to get what he could, and to fetch it home at the spring, which did help them something.

After these things, in Feb: a messenger came from John Sanders, who was left cheefe over Mr. Weston's men in the bay of Massachusets, who brought a letter shewing the great wants they were falen into; and he would have borrowed a hh of corne of the Indeans, but they would lend him none. He desired advice whether he might not take it from them by force to succore his men till he came from the eastward, whither he was going. The Gov[r] and rest deswaded him by all means from it, for it might so exasperate the Indeans as

might endanger their saftie, and all of us might smart for it;
for they had already heard how they had so wronged the
Indeans by stealing their corne, etc. as they were much in-
censed against them. Yea, so base were some of their own
company, as they wente and tould the Indeans that their
Govr was purposed to come and take their corne by force.
The which with other things made them enter into a conspiracie against the English, of which more in the nexte.
Hear with I end this year.

Anno Dom: 1623.

It may be thought strang that these people should fall to
these extremities in so short a time, being left competently
provided when the ship left them, and had an addition by that
moyetie of corn that was got by trade, besids much they gott
of the Indans wher they lived, by one means and other. It
must needs be their great disorder, for they spent excesseivly
whilst they had, or could get it; and, it may be, wasted parte
away among the Indeans (for he that was their cheef was
taxed by some amongst them for keeping Indean women, how
truly I know not). And after they begane to come into
wants, many sould away their cloathes and bed coverings;
others (so base were they) became servants to the Indeans,
and would cutt them woode and fetch them water, for a cap
full of corne; others fell to plaine stealing, both night and day,
from the Indeans, of which they greevosly complained. In
the end, they came to that misery, that some starved and
dyed with could and hunger. One in geathering shell-fish was
so weake as he stuck fast in the mudd, and was found dead in
the place. At last most of them left their dwellings and
scatered up and downe in the woods, and by the water sids,
wher they could find ground nuts and clames, hear 6. and ther
ten. By which their cariages they became contemned and
scorned of the Indeans, and they begane greatly to insulte over
them in a most insolente maner; insomuch, many times as

they lay thus scatered abrod, and had set on a pot with ground nuts or shell-fish, when it was ready the Indeans would come and eate it up; and when night came, wheras some of them had a sorie blanket, or such like, to lappe them selves in, the Indeans would take it and let the other lye all nighte in the could; so as their condition was very lamentable. Yea, in the end they were faine to hange one of their men, whom they could not reclaime from stealing, to give the Indeans contente.

Whilst things wente in this maner with them, the Govr and people hear had notice that Massasoyte ther freind was sick and near unto death. They sent to vissete him, and withall sente him such comfortable things as gave him great contente, and was a means of his recovery; upon which occasion he discovers the conspiracie of these Indeans, how they were resolved to cutt of Mr. Westons people, for the continuall injuries they did them, and would now take opportunitie of their weaknes to doe it; and for that end had conspired with other Indeans their neighbours their aboute. And thinking the people hear would revenge their death, they therfore thought to doe the like by them, and had solisited him to joyne with them. He advised them therfore to prevent it, and that speedly by taking of some of the cheefe of them, before it was to late, for he asured them of the truth hereof.

This did much trouble them, and they tooke it into serious delibration, and found upon examenation other evidence to give light hear unto, to longe hear to relate. In the mean time, came one of them from the Massachucts, with a small pack at his back; and though he knew not a foote of the way, yet he got safe hither, but lost his way, which was well for him, for he was pursued, and so was mist. He tould them hear how all things stood amongst them, and that he durst stay no longer, he apprehended they (by what he observed) would be all knokt in the head shortly. This made them make the more hast, and dispatched a boate away with Capten Standish

and some men, who found them in a miserable condition, out
of which he rescued them, and helped them to some releef, cut
of some few of the cheefe conspirators, and, according to his
order, offered to bring them all hither if they thought good;
and they should fare no worse then them selves, till Mr.
Weston or some supplie came to them. Or, if any other
course liked them better, he was to doe them any helpfullnes
he could. They thanked him and the rest. But most of
them desired he would help them with some corne, and they
would goe with their smale ship to the eastward, wher hapily
they might here of Mr. Weston, or some supply from him,
seing the time of the year was for fishing ships to be in the
land. If not, they would worke among the fishermen for their
liveing, and get ther passage into England, if they heard nothing from Mr. Weston in time. So they shipped what. they
had of any worth, and he got them all the corne he could
(scarce leaving to bring him home), and saw them well out
of the bay, under saile at sea, and so came home, not takeing
the worth of a peny of any thing that was theirs. I have but
touched these things breefly, because they have allready been
published in printe more at large.[1]

This was the end of these that some time bosted of their
strength, (being all able lustie men,) and what they would
doe and bring to pass, in comparison of the people hear, who
had many women and children and weak ons amongst them;
and said at their first arivall; when they saw the wants hear,
that they would take an other course, and not to fall into
shuch a condition, as this simple people were come too. But
a mans way is not in his owne power; God can make the
weake to stand; let him also that standeth take heed least
he fall.

Shortly after, Mr. Weston came over with some of the
fishermen, under another name, and the disguise of a blacke-
smith, were [where] he heard of the ruine and disolution of

---

[1] "Mourt's *Relation*," published in London in 1622, is here referred to.

his colony. He got a boat and with a man or 2. came to see how things were. But by the way, for wante of skill, in a storme, he cast away his shalop in the botome of the bay between Meremek river and Pascataquack,[1] and hardly escaped with life, and afterwards fell into the hands of the Indeans, who pillaged him of all he saved from the sea, and striped him out of all his cloaths to his shirte. At last he got to Pascataquack, and borrowed a suite of cloaths, and got means to come to Plimoth. A strang alteration ther was in him to such as had seen and known him in his former florishing condition; so uncertaine are the mutable things of this unstable world. And yet men set their harts upon them, though they dayly see the vanity therof.

After many passages, and much discourse, (former things boyling in his mind, but bit in as was discernd,) he desired to borrow some beaver of them; and tould them he had hope of a ship and good supply to come to him, and then they should have any thing for it they stood in neede of. They gave litle credite to his supplie, but pitied his case, and remembered former curtesies. They tould him he saw their wants, and they knew not when they should have any supply; also how the case stood betweene them and their adventurers, he well knew; they had not much bever, and if they should let him have it, it were enoughe to make a mutinie among the people, seeing ther was no other means to procure them foode which they so much wanted, and cloaths allso. Yet they tould him they would help him, considering his necessitie, but must doe it secretly for the former reasons. So they let him have 100. beaver-skins, which waighed 170*li.* odd pounds. Thus they helpt him when all the world faild him, and with this means he went againe to the ships, and stayed his small ship and some of his men, and bought provissions and fited him selfe; and it was the only foundation of his after course. But he

---

[1] *I. e.*, near Hampton Beach, between the mouth of the Merrimac and the present site of Portsmouth.

requited them ill, for he proved after a bitter enimie unto
them upon all occasions, and never repayed them any thing
for it, to this day, but reproches and evill words. Yea, he
divolged it to some that were none of their best freinds, whilst
he yet had the beaver in his boat; that he could now set them
all togeather by the ears, because they had done more then
they could answer, in letting him have this beaver, and he did
not spare to doe what he could. But his malice could not
prevaile.

All this whille no supply was heard of, neither knew they
when they might expecte any. So they begane to thinke how
they might raise as much corne as they could, and obtaine a
beter crope then they had done, that they might not still thus
languish in miserie. At length, after much debate of things,
the Govr (with the advise of the cheefest amongest them)
gave way that they should set corne every man for his owne
perticuler, and in that regard trust to them selves; in all
other things to goe on in the generall way as before. And so
assigned to every family a parcell of land, according to the
proportion of their number for that end, only for present use
(but made no devission for inheritance), and ranged all boys
and youth under some familie. This had very good success;
for it made all hands very industrious, so as much more corne
was planted then other waise would have bene by any means
the Govr or any other could use, and saved him a great
deall of trouble, and gave farr better contente. The women
now wente willingly into the feild, and tooke their litle-ons
with them to set corne, which before would aledg weaknes,
and inabilitie; whom to have compelled would have bene
thought great tiranie and oppression.

The experience that was had in this commone course and
condition, tried sundrie years, and that amongst godly and
sober men, may well evince the vanitie of that conceite of
Platos and other .ancients, applauded by some of later times;
—that the taking away of propertie, and bringing in com-

munitie into a comone wealth, would make them happy and
florishing; as if they were wiser then God. For this comunitie
(so farr as it was) was found to breed much confusion and
discontent, and retard much imployment that would have
been to their benefite and comforte. For the yong-men that
were most able and fitte for labour and service did repine that
they should spend their time and streingth to worke for other
mens wives and children, with out any recompence. The
strong, or man of parts, had no more in devission of victails
and cloaths, then he that was weake and not able to doe a
quarter the other could; this was thought injuestice. The
aged and graver men to be ranked and equalised in labours,
and victails, cloaths, etc., with the meaner and yonger sorte,
thought it some indignite and disrespect unto them. And
for mens wives to be commanded to doe servise for other men,
as dresing their meate, washing their cloaths, etc., they deemd
it a kind of slaverie, neither could many husbands well brooke
it. Upon the poynte all being to have alike, and all to doe
alike, they thought them selves in the like condition, and one
as good as another; and so, if it did not cut of those relations
that God hath set amongest men, yet it did at least much
diminish and take of the mutuall respects that should be preserved amongst them. And would have bene worse if they
had been men of another condition. Let none objecte this is
men's corruption, and nothing to the course it selfe. I answer, seeing all men have this corruption in them, God in his
wisdome saw another course fiter for them.

But to returne. After this course setled, and by that[1]
their corne was planted, all ther victails were spente, and
they were only to rest on Gods providence; at night not many
times knowing wher to have a bitt of any thing the next day.
And so, as one well observed, had need to pray that God would
give them their dayly brade, above all people in the world.
Yet they bore these wants with great patience and allacritie

[1] By the time that.

of spirite, and that for so long a time as for the most parte of
2. years; which makes me remember what Peter Martire writs,
(in magnifying the Spaniards) in his 5. Decade, pag. 208.[1]
They (saith he) *led a miserable life for 5. days togeather, with the
parched graine of maize only, and that not to saturitie;* and then
concluds, *that shuch pains, shuch labours, and shuch hunger, he
thought none living which is not a Spaniard could have endured.*
But alass! these, when they had maize (that is, Indean corne)
they thought it as good as a feast, and wanted not only for
5. days togeather, but some time 2. or 3. months togeather,
and neither had bread nor any kind of corne.   Indeed, in an
other place, in his 2. Decade, page 94. he mentions how others
of them were worse put to it, wher they were faine to eate
doggs, toads, and dead men, and so dyed almost all.   From
these extremities they [the] Lord in his goodnes kept these his
people, and in their great wants preserved both their lives
and healthes; let his name have the praise.   Yet let me hear
make use of his conclusion, which in some sorte may be applied to this people: *That with their miseries they opened a
way to these new-lands; and after these stormes, with what ease
other men came to inhabite in them, in respecte of the calamities
these men suffered; so as they seeme to goe to a bride feaste wher
all things are provided for them.*

They haveing but one boat left and she not over well fitted,
they were devided into severall companies, 6. or 7. to a gangg
or company, and so wente out with a nett they had bought,
to take bass and such like fish, by course, every company
knowing their turne.   No sooner was the boate discharged of
what she brought, but the next company tooke her and wente
out with her.   Neither did they returne till they had cauight
something, though it were 5. or 6. days before, for they knew
there was nothing at home, and to goe home emptie would be
a great discouragemente to the rest.   Yea, they strive who

[1] Peter Martyr of Anghiera, *Decades de Rebus Oceanicis et Novo Orbe*, the
great Spanish history of America, translated into English by Richard Eden.

should doe best. If she stayed longe or got litle, then all went to seeking of shel-fish, which at low-water they digged out of the sands. And this was their living in the sommer time, till God sente them beter; and in winter they were helped with ground-nuts and foule. Also in the sommer they gott now and then a dear; for one or 2. of the fitest was apoynted to range the woods for that end, and what was gott that way was devided amongst them.

At length they received some leters from the adventurers, too long and tedious hear to record, by which they heard of their furder crosses and frustrations; begining in this maner.

Loving freinds, as your sorrows and afflictions have bin great, so our croses and interceptions in our proceedings hear, have not been small. For after we had with much trouble and charge sente the *Parragon* away to sea, and thought all the paine past, within 14. days after she came againe hither, being dangerously leaked, and brused with tempestious stormes, so as shee was faine to be had into the docke, and an 100*li.* bestowed upon her. All the passengers lying upon our charg for 6. or 7. weeks, and much discontent and distemper was occasioned hereby, so as some dangerous evente had like to insewed. But we trust all shall be well and worke for the best and your benefite, if yet with patience you can waite, and but have strength to hold in life. Whilst these things were doing, Mr. Westons ship came and brought diverce leters from you, etc. It rejoyseth us much to hear of those good reports that diverce have brought home from you, etc.

These letters were dated Des. 21: 1622.

So farr of this leter.

This ship was brought by Mr. John Peirce, and set out at his owne charge, upon hope of great maters. These passengers, and the goods the company sent in her, he tooke in for fraught, for which they agreed with him to be delivered hear. This was he in whose name their first patente was taken, by reason of aquaintance, and some aliance that some of their freinds had with him. But his name was only used in trust. But when he saw they were hear hopfully thus seated, and by the success God gave them had obtained the favour of the

Counsell of New-England, he goes and sues to them for another patent of much larger extente (in their names), which was easily obtained.[1] But he mente to keep it to him selfe and alow them what he pleased, to hold of him as tenants, and sue to his courts as cheefe Lord, as will appear by that which follows. But the Lord marvelously crost him; for after this first returne, and the charge above mentioned, when shee was againe fitted, he pesters him selfe and taks in more passengers, and those not very good to help to bear his losses, and sets out the 2. time. But what the event was will appear from another leter from one of the cheefe of the company, dated the 9. of Aprill, 1623. writ to the Govr hear, as followeth.

Loving freind, when I write my last leter, I hope to have received one from you well-nigh by this time. But when I write in Des: I litle thought to have seen Mr. John Peirce till he had brought some good tidings from you. But it pleased God, he brought us the wofull tidings of his returne when he was half-way over, by extraime tempest, werin the goodnes and mercie of God appeared in sparing their lives, being 109. souls. The loss is so great to Mr. Peirce, etc., and the companie put upon so great charge, as veryly, etc.

Now with great trouble and loss, we have got Mr. John Peirce to assigne over the grand patente to the companie, which he had taken in his owne name, and made quite voyd our former grante. I am sorie to writ how many hear thinke that the hand of God was justly against him, both the first and 2. time of his returne; in regard he, whom you and we so confidently trusted, but only to use his name for the company, should aspire to be lord over us all, and so make you and us tenants at his will and pleasure, our assurance or patente being quite voyd and disanuled by his means. I desire to judg charitably of him. But his unwillingnes to part with his royall Lordship, and the high-rate he set it at, which was 500li. which cost him but 50li., maks many speake and judg hardly of him. The company are out for goods in his ship, with charge aboute the passengers, 640li., etc.

[1] April 20, 1622, John Pierce surrendered to the Council for New England the patent of June 1, 1621, which he had obtained ostensibly for the benefit of the Pilgrims, and took a new patent of the same lands for himself alone. On the facts being presented to the Council, March 25, 1623, they assured to the colonists all the rights to which they had been entitled under the former patent.

We have agreed with 2. marchants for a ship of 140. tunes, caled the *Anne*, which is to be ready the last of this month, to bring 60. passengers and 60. tune of goods, etc.

This was dated Aprill 9. 1623.

These were ther owne words and judgmente of this mans dealing and proceedings; for I thought it more meete to render them in theirs then my owne words. And yet though ther was never got other recompence then the resignation of this patente, and the shares he had in adventure, for all the former great sumes, he was never quiet, but sued them in most of the cheefe courts in England, and when he was still cast, brought it to the Parlemente. But he is now dead, and I will leave him to the Lord.

This ship suffered the greatest extreemitie at sea at her 2. returne, that one shall lightly hear of, to be saved; as I have been informed by Mr. William Peirce who was then m^r of her, and many others that were passengers in her. It was aboute the midle of Feb: The storme was for the most parte of 14. days, but for 2. or 3. days and nights togeather in most violent extreemitie. After they had cut downe their mast, the storme beat of their round house and all their uper works; 3. men had worke enough at the helme, and he· that cund[1] the ship before the sea, was faine to be bound fast for washing away; the seas did so overrake them, as many times those upon the decke knew not whether they were within bord or withoute; and once she was so foundered in the sea as they all thought she would never rise againe. But yet the Lord preserved them, and brought them at last safe to Ports-mouth, to the wonder of all men that saw in what a case she was in, and heard what they had endured.

About the later end of June came in a ship, with Captaine Francis West,[2] who had a commission to be admirall of New-England, to restraine interlopers, and shuch fishing ships as came to fish and trade without a licence from the Counsell of

[1] "Conned," *i. e.*, directed.   [2] A brother of Lord Delaware.

New-England, for which they should pay a round sume of
money.   But he could doe no good of them, for they were to
stronge for him, and he found the fisher men to be stuberne
fellows.   And their owners, upon complainte made to the
Parlemente,[1] procured an order that fishing should be free.
He tould the Gov[r] they spooke with a ship at sea, and
were abord her, that was coming for this plantation, in which
were sundrie passengers, and they marvelled she was not
arrived, fearing some miscariage; for they lost her in a storme
that fell shortly after they had been abord.   Which relation
filled them full of fear, yet mixed with hope.   The m[r] of
this ship had some 2. ħħ of pease to sell, but seeing their
wants, held them at 9*li*. sterling a hoggshead, and under
8*li*. he would not take, and yet would have beaver at an
under rate.   But they tould him they had lived so long without, and would doe still, rather then give so unreasonably.
So they went from hence to Virginia.

[I may not here omite how, notwithstand all their great
paines and industrie, and the great hops of a large cropp, the
Lord seemed to blast, and take away the same, and to threaten
further and more sore famine unto them, by a great drought
which continued from the 3. weeke in May, till about the
midle of July, without any raine, and with great heat (for the
most parte), insomuch as the corne begane to wither away,
though it was set with fishe, the moysture wherof helped it
much.   Yet at length it begane to languish sore, and some of
the drier grounds were partched like withered hay, part
wherof was never recovered.   Upon which they sett a parte a
solemne day of humilliation, to seek the Lord by humble and
fervente prayer, in this great distrese.   And he was pleased to
give them a gracious and speedy answer, both to thier owne
and the Indeans admiration, that lived amongest them.   For
all the morning, and greatest part of the day, it was clear

---

[1] The attack was made a part of the general movement in Parliament against
monopolies.   See *Commons Journal*, I. 688-697.

weather and very hotte, and not a cloud or any signe of raine
to be seen, yet toward evening it begane to overcast, and
shortly after to raine, with shuch sweete and gentle showers,
as gave them cause of rejoyceing, and blesing God. It came,
without either wind, or thunder, or any violence, and by de-
greese in that abundance, as that the earth was thorowly wete
and soked therwith. Which did so apparently revive and
quicken the decayed corne and other fruits, as was wonderfull to see, and made the Indeans astonished to behold; and
afterwards the Lord sent them shuch seasonable showers, with
enterchange of faire warme weather, as, through his blessing,
caused a fruitfull and liberall harvest, to their no small comforte and rejoycing. For which mercie (in time conveniente)
they also sett aparte a day of thanksgiveing. This being overslipt in its place, I thought meet here to inserte the same.] [1]

About 14. days after came in this ship, caled the *Anne*,
wherof Mr. William Peirce was m[r], and aboute a weeke or
10. days after came in the pinass which in foule weather
they lost at sea, a fine new vessell of about 44. tune, which the
company had builte to stay in the cuntrie.[2] They brought
about 60. persons for the generall, some of them being very
usefull persons, and became good members to the body, and
some were the wives and children of shuch as were hear allready. And some were so bad, as they were faine to be at
charge to send them home againe the next year. Also, besids
these ther came a company, that did not belong to the generall body, but came one [on] their perticuler, and were to
have lands assigned them, and be for them selves, yet to be
subjecte to the generall Goverment; which caused some
diferance and disturbance amongst them, as will after ap-

[1] The above is written on the reverse of page 103 of the original, and should
properly be inserted here. This passage, "being overslipt in its place," the
author at first wrote it, or the most of it, under the preceding year; but, dis-
covering his error before completing it, drew his pen across it, and wrote beneath,
"This is to be here rased out, and is to be placed on page 103, wher it is inserted."

[2] These two vessels were the *Anne* and *Little James*. For their list of passengers, see *Ancient Landmarks of Plymouth*, part i., p. 52.

peare. I shall hear againe take libertie to inserte a few things
out of shuch leters as came in this shipe, desiring rather to
manefest things in ther words and apprehentions, then in my
owne, as much as may be, without tediousness.

Beloved freinds, I kindly salute you all, with trust of your healths
and wellfare, being right sorie that no supplie hath been made to you all
this while; for defence wher of, I must referr you to our generall leters.
Naitheir indeed have we now sent you many things, which we should and
would, for want of money. But persons, more then inough, (though not
all we should,) for people come flying in upon us, but monys come creep-
ing in to us. Some few of your old freinds are come, as, etc. So they
come droping to you, and by degrees, I hope ere long you shall enjoye
them all. And because people press so hard upon us to goe, and often
shuch as are none of the fitest, I pray you write ernestly to the Treasurer
and directe what persons should be sente. It greeveth me to see so
weake a company sent you, and yet had I not been hear they had been
weaker. You must still call upon the company hear to see that honest
men be sente you, and threaten to send them back if any other come, etc.
We are not any way so much in danger, as by corrupte an noughty persons. Shuch, and shuch, came without my consente; but the importunitie of their freinds got promise of our Treasurer in my absence. Neither
is ther need we should take any lewd men, for we may have honest men
enew, etc.

Your assured freind,

R. C.[1]

The following was from the genrall.

Loving freinds, we most hartily salute you in all love and harty
affection; being yet in hope that the same God which hath hithertoo
preserved you in a marvelous maner, doth yet continue your lives and
health, to his owne praise and all our comforts. Being right sory that you
have not been sent unto all this time, etc. We have in this ship sent shuch
women, as were willing and ready to goe to their husbands and freinds,
with their children, etc. We would not have you discontente, because
we have not sent you more of your old freinds, and in spetiall, him [2] on
whom you most depend. Farr be it from us to neclecte you, or contemne
him. But as the intente was at first, so the evente at last shall shew it,
that we will deal fairly, and squarly answer your expectations to the full.
Ther are also come unto you, some honest men to plant upon their par-

[1] Robert Cushman.
[2] "J. R." (Note by Bradford, meaning John Robinson.)

ticulers besids you. A thing which if we should not give way unto, we should wrong both them and you. Them, by puting them on things more inconveniente, and you, for that being honest men, they will be a strengthening to the place, and good neighbours unto you. Tow things we would advise you of, which we have likwise signified them hear. First, the trade for skins to be retained for the generall till the devidente; 2^{ly}. that their setling by you, be with shuch distance of place as is neither inconvenient for the lying of your lands, nor hurtfull to your speedy and easie assembling togeather.

We have sente you diverse fisher men, with salte, etc. Diverse other provissions we have sente you, as will appear in your bill of lading, and though we have not sent all we would (because our cash is small), yet it is that we could, etc.

And allthough it seemeth you have discovered many more rivers and fertill grounds then that wher you are, yet seeing by Gods providence that place fell to your lote, let it be accounted as your portion; and rather fixe your eyes upon that which may be done ther, then languish in hops after things els-wher. If your place be not the best, it is better, you shall be the less envied and encroached upon; and shuch as are earthly minded, will not setle too near your border.[1] If the land afford you bread, and the sea yeeld you fish, rest you a while contented, God will one day afford you better fare. And all men shall know you are neither fugetives nor discontents. But can, if God so order it, take the worst to your selves, with contend [content], and leave the best to your neighbours, with cherfullnes.

Let it not be greeveous unto you that you have been instruments to breake the ise for others who come after with less dificulty, the honour shall be yours to the worlds end, etc.

We bear you always in our brests, and our harty affection is towards you all, as are the harts of hundreds more which never saw your faces, who doubtles pray for your saftie as their owne, as we our selves both doe and ever shall, that the same God which hath so marvelously preserved you from seas, foes, and famine, will still preserve you from all future dangers, and make you honourable amongst men, and glorious in blise at the last day. And so the Lord be with you all and send us joyfull news from you, and inable us with one shoulder so to accomplish and perfecte this worke, as much glorie may come to Him that confoundeth the mighty by the weak, and maketh small thinges great. To whose greatnes, be all glorie for ever and ever.

---

[1] "This proved rather, a propheti, then advice." (Br.)

This leter was subscribed with 13. of their names.[1]

These passengers, when they saw their low and poore condition a shore, were much danted and dismayed, and according to their diverse humores were diversly affected; some wished them selves in England againe; others fell a weeping, fancying their own miserie in what they saw now in others; other some pitying the distress they saw their freinds had been long in, and still were under; in a word, all were full of sadnes.   Only some of their old freinds rejoysed to see them, and that it was no worse with them, for they could not expecte it should be better, and now hoped they should injoye better days togeather.   And truly it was no marvell they should be thus affected, for they were in a very low condition, many were ragged in aparell, and some litle beter then halfe naked; though some that were well stord before, were well enough in this regard.   But for food they were all alike, save some that had got a few pease of the ship that was last hear. The best dish they could presente their freinds with was a lobster, or a peece of fish, without bread or any thing els but a cupp of fair spring water.   And the long continuance of this diate, and their labours abroad, had something abated the freshnes of their former complexion.   But God gave them health and strength in a good measure; and showed them by experience the truth of that word, Deut. 8. 3.   *That man liveth not by bread only, but by every word that proceedeth out of the mouth of the Lord doth a man live.*

When I think how sadly the scripture speaks of the famine in Jaakobs time, when he said to his sonns, Goe buy us food, that we may live and not dye.   Gen. 42. 2. and 43. 1, that the famine was great, or heavie in the land; and yet they had such great herds, and store of catle of sundrie kinds, which, besids flesh, must needs produse other food, as milke,

---

[1] An answer to it, by Bradford and Allerton, found among the papers of the High Court of Admiralty in the British Public Record Office, is printed in the *American Historical Review*, VIII. 295–301.

butter and cheese, etc., and yet it was counted a sore affliction; theirs hear must needs be very great, therfore, who not
only wanted the staffe of bread, but all these things, and had
no Egipte to goe too. But God fedd them out of the sea for
the most parte, so wonderfull is his providence over his in
all ages; for his mercie endureth for ever.

On the other hand the old planters were affraid that their
corne, when it was ripe, should be imparted to the new-
commers, whose provissions which they brought with them
they feared would fall short before the year wente aboute (as
indeed it did). They came to the Govr and besought him
that as it was before agreed that they should set corne for
their perticuler, and accordingly they had taken extraordinary
pains ther aboute, that they might freely injoye the same, and
they would not have a bitte of the victails now come, but
waite till harvest for their owne, and let the new-commers
injoye what they had brought; they would have none of it,
excepte they could purchase any of it of them by bargaine or
exchainge. Their requeste was granted them, for it gave both
sides good contente; for the new-commers were as much afraid
that the hungrie planters would have eat up the provissions
brought, and they should have fallen into the like condition.

This ship was in a shorte time laden with clapbord, by the
help of many hands. Also they sente in her all the beaver
and other furrs they had, and Mr. Winslow was sent over with
her, to informe of all things, and procure such things as were
thought needfull for their presente condition. By this time
harvest was come, and in stead of famine, now God gave them
plentie, and the face of things was changed, to the rejoysing of
the harts of many, for which they blessed God. And the
effect of their perticuler planting was well seene, for all had,
one way and other, pretty well to bring the year aboute, and
some of the abler sorte and more industrious had to spare,
and sell to others, so as any generall wante or famine hath not
been amongst them since to this day.

Those that come on their perticuler looked for greater matters then they found or could attaine unto, aboute building great houses, and such pleasant situations for them, as them selves had fancied; as if they would be great men and rich, all of a sudaine; but they proved castls in the aire. These were the conditions agreed on betweene the colony and them.

First, that the Gov[r], in the name and with the consente of the company, doth in all love and frendship receive and imbrace them; and is to allote them competente places for habitations within the towne. And promiseth to shew them all such other curtesies as shall be reasonable for them to desire, or us to performe.

2. That they, on their parts, be subjecte to all such laws and orders as are already made, or hear after shall be, for the publick good.

3. That they be freed and exempte from the generall imployments of the said company, (which their presente condition of comunitie requireth,) excepte commune defence, and such other imployments as tend to the perpetuall good of the collony.

4[ly]. Towards the maintenance of Gov[rt], and publick officers of the said collony, every male above the age of 16. years shall pay a bushell of Indean wheat, or the worth of it, into the commone store.

5[ly]. That (according to the agreemente the marchants made with them before they came) they are to be wholy debared from all trade with the Indeans for all sorts of furrs, and such like commodities, till the time of the comunallitie be ended.

About the midle of September arrived Captaine Robart Gorges [1] in the Bay of the Massachusets, with sundrie pas-

---

[1] Robert Gorges, son of Sir Ferdinando Gorges, who had been a soldier in the Venetian wars, had a private patent for a district on the north side of Massachusetts Bay, but planted his colony at Weymouth, in the buildings deserted by Weymouth's men. His patent, dated December 30, 1622, is printed in the Prince Society's *Gorges*, II. 51–54

sengers and families, intending ther to begine a plantation; and pitched upon the place Mr. Weston's people had forsaken. He had a commission from the Counsell of New-England, to be generall Gove^r of the cuntrie, and they appoynted for his counsell and assistance, Captaine Francis West, the aforesaid admirall, Christopher Levite, Esquire,[1] and the Govr of Plimoth for the time beeing, etc. Allso, they gave him authoritie to chuse such other as he should find fit. Allso, they gave (by their commission) full power to him and his assistants, or any 3. of them, wherof him selfe was allway to be one, to doe and execute what to them should seeme good, in all cases, Capitall, Criminall, and Civill, etc., with diverce other instructions. Of which, and his comission, it pleased him to suffer the Govr hear to take a coppy.

He gave them notice of his arivall by letter, but before they could visite him he went to the eastward with the ship he came in; but a storme arising, (and they wanting a good pilot to harbor them in those parts,) they bore up for this harbor. He and his men were hear kindly entertained; he stayed hear 14. days. In the mean time came in Mr. Weston with his small ship, which he had now recovered. Captaine Gorges tooke hold of the opportunitie, and acquainted the Govr hear, that one occasion of his going to the eastward was to meete with Mr. Weston, and call him to accounte for some abuses he had to lay to his charge. Wherupon he called him before him, and some other of his assistants, with the Govr of this place; and charged him, first, with the ille carriage of his men at the Massachusets; by which means the peace of the cuntrie was disturbed, and him selfe and the people which he had brought over to plante in that bay were therby much prejudised. To this Mr. Weston easily answered, that what was that way done, was in his absence, and might have

---

[1] Christopher Levite (Levett) came to New England in 1623 and explored its eastern coast with a view to a settlement. On his return to England in 1624 he published an account of his voyage, which has been reprinted by the Gorges Society.

befalen any man; he left them sufficently provided, and conceived they would have been well governed; and for any
errour committed he had sufficiently smarted. This particuler was passed by. A 2^d. was, for an abuse done to his
father, Sr. Ferdenando Gorges, and to the State. The thing
was this; he used him and others of the Counsell of New-
England, to procure him a licence for the transporting of
many peeces of great ordnance for New-England, pretending
great fortification hear in the countrie, and I know not what
shipping. The which when he had obtained, he went and
sould them beyond seas for his private profite; for which (he
said) the State was much offended, and his father suffered a
shrowd check, and he had order to apprehend him for it. Mr.
Weston excused it as well as he could, but could not deney it;
it being one maine thing (as was said) for which he with-drew
himself. But after many passages, by the mediation of the
Govr and some other freinds hear, he was inclined to
gentlnes (though he aprehended the abuse of his father
deeply); which, when Mr. Weston saw, he grew more pre-
sumptuous, and gave such provocking and cutting speches, as
made him rise up in great indignation and distemper, and
vowed that he would either curb him, or send him home for
England. At which Mr. Weston was something danted, and
came privatly to the Govr hear, to know whether they
would suffer Captaine Gorges to apprehend him. He was
tould they could not hinder him, but much blamed him, that
after they had pacified things, he should thus breake out, by
his owne folly and rashnes, to bring trouble upon him selfe
and them too. He confest it was his passion, and prayd the
Govr to entreat for him, and pacifie him if he could. The
which at last he did, with much adoe; so he was called againe,
and the Govr was contente to take his owne bond to be
ready to make further answer, when either he or the lords
should send for him. And at last he tooke only his word, and
ther was a freindly parting on all hands.

But after he was gone, Mr. Weston in lue of thanks to the Gov[r] and his freinds hear, gave them this quib (behind their baks) for all their pains. That though they were but yonge justices, yet they wear good beggers. Thus they parted at this time, and shortly after the Gov[r] tooke his leave and went to the Massachusets by land, being very thankfull for his kind entertainemente. The ship stayed hear, and fitted her selfe to goe for Virginia, having some passengers ther to deliver; and with her returned sundrie of those from hence which came over on their perticuler, some out of dis-contente and dislike of the cuntrie; others by reason of a fire that broke out, and burnt the houses they lived in, and all their provisions so as they were necessitated therunto. This fire was occasioned by some of the sea-men that were roy-stering in a house wher it first begane, makeing a great fire in very could weather, which broke out of the chimney into the thatch, and burnte downe 3. or 4. houses, and consumed all the goods and provissions in them. The house in which it begane was right against their store-house, which they had much adoe to save, in which were their commone store and all their provissions; the which if it had been lost, the planta-tion had been overthrowne. But through Gods mercie it was saved by the great dilligence of the people, and care of the Gov[r] and some aboute him. Some would have had the goods throwne out; but if they had, ther would much have been stolne by the rude company that belonged to these 2. ships, which were allmost all ashore. But a trusty company was plased within, as well as those that with wet-cloaths and other means kept of the fire without, that if necessitie required they might have them out with all speed. For they suspected some malicious dealing, if not plaine treacherie, and whether it was only suspition or no, God knows; but this is certaine, that when the tumulte was greatest, ther was a voyce heard (but from whom it was not knowne) that bid them looke well aboute them, for all were not freinds that were near them.

And shortly after, when the vemencie of the fire was over, smoke was seen to arise within a shed that was joynd to the end of the store-house, which was watled up with bowes, in the withered leaves wherof the fire was kindled, which some, running to quench, found a longe firebrand of an ell longe, lying under the wale on the inside, which could not possibly come their by cassualtie, but must be laid ther by some hand, in the judgmente of all that saw it. But God kept them from this deanger, what ever was intended.

Shortly after Captaine Gorges, the generall Govr, was come home to the Massachusets, he sends a warrante to arrest Mr. Weston and his ship, and sends a m^r to bring her away thither, and one Captain Hanson (that belonged to him) to conducte him along. The Govr and others hear were very sory to see him take this course, and tooke exception at the warrante, as not legall nor sufficiente; and withall write to him to disswade him from this course, shewing him that he would but entangle and burthen him selfe in doing this; for he could not doe Mr. Weston a better turne, (as things stood with him); for he had a great many men that belonged to him in this barke, and was deeply ingaged to them for wages, and was in a manner out of victails (and now winter); all which would light upon him, if he did arrest his barke. In the mean time Mr. Weston had notice to shift for him selfe; but it was conceived he either knew not whither to goe, or how to mend him selfe, but was rather glad of the occasion, and so stirred not. But the Govr would not be perswaded, but sent a very formall warrente under his hand and seall, with strict charge as they would answere it to the state; he also write that he had better considered of things since he was hear, and he could not answer it to let him goe so; besids other things that were come to his knowledg since, which he must answer too. So he was suffered to proceede, but he found in the end that to be true that was tould him; for when an inventorie was taken of what was in the ship, ther was not vitailes

found for above 14. days, at a fare allowance, and not much
else of any great worth, and the men did so crie out of him
for wages and diate, in the mean time, as made him soone
weary. So as in conclusion it turned to his loss, and the expence of his owne provissions; and towards the spring they
came to agreement, (after they had bene to the eastward,)
and the Gov[r] restord him his vessell againe, and made
him satisfaction, in bisket, meal, and such like provissions,
for what he had made use of that was his, or what his men
had any way wasted or consumed. So Mr. Weston came
hither againe, and afterward shaped his course for Virginie,
and so for present I shall leave him.[1]

The Gov[r] and some that depended upon him returned
for England, haveing scarcly saluted the cuntrie in his Govermente, not finding the state of things hear to answer his
quallitie and condition. The peopl dispersed them selves,
some went for England, others for Virginia, some few remained, and were helped with supplies from hence. The
Gov[r] brought over a minister with him, one Mr. Morell,
who, about a year after the Gov[r] returned, tooke shipping
from hence.[2] He had I know not what power and authority
of superintendancie over other churches granted him, and
sundrie instructions for that end; but he never shewed it,
or made any use of it; (it should seeme he saw it was in
vaine;) he only speake of it to some hear at his going
away. This was in effect the end of a 2. plantation in that
place. Ther were allso this year some scatering beginings
made in other places, as at Paskataway, by Mr. David

[1] "He dyed afterwards at Bristoll, in the time of the warrs, of the sicknes in
that place." (Br.)

[2] Rev. William Morell came over with Robert Gorges with a commission to
regulate the religious affairs of the country and to compel the people to conform
to the Church of England. Finding little encouragement he abandoned his
mission and spent a year in Wessagusset without disclosing until his final departure the purpose of his coming. After his return to England he published a
Latin poem giving an account of his observations, which was published in the
first volume of the *Collections of the Massachusetts Historical Society.*

Thomson, at Monhigen, and some other places by sundrie others.[1]

It rests now that I speake a word aboute the pinnass spoken of before, which was sent by the adventurers to be imployed in the cuntrie. She was a fine vessell, and bravely set out,[2] and I fear the adventurers did over pride them selves in her, for she had ill success. How ever, they erred grosly in tow things aboute her; first, though she had a sufficiente maister, yet she was rudly manned,[3] and all her men were upon shars, and none was to have any wages but the m^r. 2^{ly}, wheras they mainly lookt at trade, they had sent nothing of any value to trade with. When the men came hear, and mette with ill counsell from Mr. Weston and his crue, with others of the same stampe, neither m^r nor Govr could scarce rule them, for they exclaimed that they were abused and deceived, for they were tould they should goe for a man of warr, and take I know not whom, French and Spaniards, etc. They would neither trade nor fish, excepte they had wages; in fine, they would obey no command of the maisters; so it was apprehended they would either rune away with the vessell, or get away with the ships, and leave her; so as Mr. Peirce and others of their freinds perswaded the Govr to chaing their condition, and give them wages; which was accordingly done. And she was sente about the Cape to the Narigansets to trade, but they made but a poore vioage of it. Some corne and beaver they got, but the Dutch used to furnish them with cloath and better commodities, they haveing only a few beads and knives, which were not ther much esteemed. Allso, in her returne home, at the very entrance into ther owne harbore, she had like to have been cast away in a

---

[1] David Thompson was a Scotsman, and agent of Mason and Gorges. In the spring of 1623 he began a settlement at Little Harbor, near the mouth of the Piscataqua, and near the present site of Portsmouth. About 1626 he took possession of the island in Boston harbor still called Thompson's Island; indeed he may have occupied it before his settlement at Paskataway.

[2] "With her flages, and streamers, pendents, and wastcloaths, etc." (Br.)

[3] See *American Historical Review*, VIII. 295.

storme, and was forced to cut her maine mast by the bord, to save herselfe from driving on the flats that lye without, caled Browns Ilands,[1] the force of the wind being so great as made her anchors give way and she drive right upon them; but her mast and takling being gone, they held her till the wind shifted.

Anno Dom: 1624.

THE time of new election of ther officers for this year being come, and the number of their people increased, and their troubls and occasions therwith, the Gov[r] desired them to chainge the persons, as well as renew the election;[2] and also to adde more Assistans to the Gov[r] for help and counsell, and the better carrying on of affairs. Showing that it was necessarie it should be so. If it was any honour or benefite, it was fitte others should be made pertakers of it; if it was a burthen, (as doubtles it was,) it was but equall others should help to bear it; and that this was the end[3] of Annuall Elections. The issue was, that as before ther was but one Assistante, they now chose 5. giving the Gov[r] a duble voyce; and aftwards they increased them to 7. which course hath continued to this day.

They having with some truble and charge new-masted and rigged their pinass, in the begining of March they sent her well vitaled to the eastward on fishing. She arrived safly at a place near Damarins cove,[4] and was there well harbored in a place wher ships used to ride, ther being also some ships allready arived out of England. But shortly after ther arose such a violent and extraordinarie storme, as the seas broak over such places in the harbor as was never seene before, and drive her against great roks, which beat such a hole in her bulke, as a horse and carte might have gone in, and after

---

[1] Brown's Island is a sand-bar in the outer harbor of Plymouth, which a false tradition says was once an island. See Champlain's map.

[2] Bradford was not permitted to retire.

[3] Purpose.   [4] See p. 128, note 1.

drive her into deep-water, wher she lay sunke. The m^r. was drowned, the rest of the men, all save one, saved their lives, with much a doe; all her provision, salt, and what els was in her, was lost. And here I must leave her to lye till afterward.

Some of those that still remained hear on their perticuler, begane privatly to nurish a faction, and being privie to a strong faction that was among the adventurers in England, on whom sundry of them did depend, by their private whispering they drew some of the weaker sorte of the company to their side, and so filld them with discontente, as nothing would satisfie them excepte they might be suffered to be in their perticuler allso; and made great offers, so they might be freed from the generall. The Govr consulting with the ablest of the generall body what was best to be done hear in, it was resolved to permitte them so to doe, upon equall conditions. The conditions were the same in effect with the former before related. Only some more added, as that they should be bound here to remaine till the generall partnership was ended. And also that they should pay into the store, the on halfe of all such goods and comodities as they should any waise raise above their food, in consideration of what charg had been layed out for them, with some such like things. This liberty granted, soone stopt this gape, for ther was but a few that undertooke this course when it came too; and they were as sone weary of it. For the other had perswaded them, and Mr. Weston togeather, that ther would never come more supply to the generall body; but the perticulers had such freinds as would carry all, and doe for them I know not what.

Shortly after, Mr. Winslow came over, and brought a prety good supply, and the ship came on fishing, a thing fatall to this plantation. He brought 3. heifers and a bull, the first begining of any catle of that kind in the land, with some cloathing and other necessaries, as will further appear; but withall the reporte of a strong faction amongst the ad-

venture[r]s against them, and espetially against the coming
of the rest from Leyden, and with what difficulty this supply
was procured, and how, by their strong and long opposision,
bussines was so retarded as not only they were now falne too
late for the fishing season, but the best men were taken up of
the fishermen in the west countrie, and he was forct to take
such a m^r. and company for that imployment as he could
procure upon the present.   Some letters from them shall beter
declare these things, being as followeth.

Most worthy and loving freinds, your kind and loving leters I have
received, and render you many thanks, etc.   It hath plased God to stirre
up the harts of our adventure[r]s to raise a new stock for the seting forth
of this shipe, caled the *Charitie*, with men and necessaries, both for the
plantation and the fishing, though accomplished with very great difficulty; in regard we have some amongst us which undoubtedly aime more
at their owne private ends, and the thwarting and opposing of some hear,
and other worthy instruments,[1] of Gods glory elswher, then at the generall
good and furtherance of this noble and laudable action.   Yet againe we
have many other, and I hope the greatest parte, very honest Christian
men, which I am perswaded their ends and intents are wholy for the
glory of our Lord Jesus Christ, in the propagation of his gospell, and hope
of gaining those poore salvages to the knowledg of God.   But, as we have
a proverbe, One scabed sheep may marr a whole flock, so these malecon-
tented persons, and turbulente spirits, doe what in them lyeth to withdraw
mens harts from you and your freinds, yea, even from the generall bussines;
and yet under show and pretence of godlynes and furtherance of the
plantation.   Wheras the quite contrary doth plainly appeare; as some
of the honester harted men (though of late of their faction) did make
manifest at our late meeting.   But what should I trouble you or my selfe
with these restles opposers of all goodnes, and I doubte will be continuall
disturbers of our frendly meetjngs and love.   On Thurs-day the 8. of
Jan: we had a meeting aboute the artickls betweene you and us; wher
they would rejecte that, which we in our late leters prest you to grante,
(an addition to the time of our joynt stock).   And their reason which they
would make known to us was, it trobled their conscience to exacte longer
time of you then was agreed upon at the first.   But that night they were
so followed and crost of their perverse courses, as they were even wearied,
and offered to sell their adventurs; and some were willing to buy.   But I,

[1] "He means Mr. Robinson."   (Br.)

doubting they would raise more scandale and false reports, and so diverse waise doe us more hurt, by going of in such a furie, then they could or can by continuing adventurers amongst us, would not suffer them.   But on the 12. of Jan: we had another meting, but in the interime diverse of us had talked with most of them privatly, and had great combats and reasoning, pro and con.   But at night when we mete to read the generall letter, we had the loveingest and frendlyest meeting that ever I knew[1] and our greatest enemise offered to lend us 50*li*.   So I sent for a potle of wine, (I would you could[2] doe the like,) which we dranke freindly together. Thus God can turne the harts of men when it pleaseth him, etc.   Thus loving freinds, I hartily salute you all in the Lord, hoping ever to rest,

Yours to my power,

Jan: 25. 1623.   JAMES SHERLEY.[3]

Another leter.

Beloved Sr., etc.   We have now sent you, we hope, men and means, to setle these 3. things, viz. fishing, salt making, and boat making; if you can bring them to pass to some perfection, your wants may be supplyed. I pray you bend you selfe what you can to setle these bussinesses.   Let the ship be fraught away as soone as you can, and sent to Bilbow.[4]   You must send some discreete man for factore, whom, once more, you must also authorise to confirme the conditions.   If Mr. Winslow could be spared, I could wish he came againe.   This ship carpenter is thought to be the fittest man for you in the land, and will no doubte doe you much good.   Let him have an absolute comand over his servants and such as you put to him.   Let him build you 2. catches, a lighter, and some 6. or 7. shalops, as soone as you can.   The salt-man is a skillfull and industrious man, put some to him, that may quickly apprehende the misterie of it.   The preacher we have sent is (we hope) an honest plaine man, though none of the most eminente and rare.   Aboute chusing him into

---

[1] "But this lasted not long, they had now provided Lyford and others to send over." (Br.)

[2] "It is worthy to be observed, how the Lord doth chaing times and things; for what is now more plentifull then wine? and that of the best, coming from Malago, the Cannaries, and other places, sundry ships lading in a year.   So as ther is now more cause to complaine of the excess and the abuse of wine (through mens corruption) even to drunkennes, then of any defecte or wante of the same. Witnes this year 1646.   The good Lord lay not the sins and unthankfullnes of men to their charge in this perticuler." (Br.)

[3] James Shirley, "citizen and goldsmith," of London, was the treasurer of the merchant adventurers.   The date is of course 1624 in new style.

[4] Bilbao, on the north coast of Spain.

office use your owne liberty and discretion; he knows he is no officer amongst you, though perhaps custome and universalitie may make him forget him selfe. Mr. Winslow and my selfe gave way to his going, to give contente to some hear, and we see no hurt in it, but only his great charge of children.

We have tooke a patente for Cap Anne, etc.[1] I am sory ther is no more discretion used by some in their leters hither.[2] Some say you are starved in body and soule; others, that you eate piggs and doggs, that dye alone; others, that the things hear spoaken of, the goodnes of the cuntry, are gross and palpable lyes; that ther is scarce a foule to be seene, or a fish to be taken, and many such like. I would such discontented men were hear againe, for it is a miserie when the whole state of a plantation shall be thus exposed to the passionate humors of some discontented men. And for my selfe I shall hinder for hearafter some that would goe, and have not better composed their affections; mean space it is all our crosses, and we must bear them.

I am sorie we have not sent you more and other things, but in truth we have rune into so much charge, to victaile the ship, provide salte and other fishing implements, etc. as we could not provid other comfortable things, as buter, suger, etc. I hope the returne of this ship and the *James*,[3] will put us in cash againe. The Lord make you full of courage in this troublesome bussines, which now must be stuck unto, till God give us rest from our labours. Fare well in all harty affection.

Your assured freind,

Jan: 24. 1623.   R. C.[4]

With the former lettter write by Mr. Sherley, there were sente sundrie objections concerning which he thus writeth. "These are the cheefe objections which they that are now returned make against you and the countrie. I pray you consider them, and answer them by the first conveniencie." These objections were made by some of those that came over

---

[1] The Council for New England had attempted to divide its coast among themselves individually. The patent alluded to was executed by Lord Sheffield in favor of Robert Cushman and Edward Winslow, for themselves and their associates, and bore date of January 1, 1623-4. Its text is given in J. W. Thornton, *The Landing at Cape Anne*, pp. 31-35. See also *American Historical Review*, VIII. 296.

[2] "This was John Oldome and his like." (Br.)

[3] The *Little James* was the pinnace which had accompanied the *Anne*.

[4] Robert Cushman.

on their perticuler[1] and were returned home, as is before mentioned, and were of the same suite with those that this other letter mentions.

I shall here set them downe, with the answers then made unto them, and sent over at the returne of this ship; which did so confound the objecters, as some confessed their falte, and others deneyed what they had said, and eate their words, and some others of them have since come over againe and heere lived to convince them selves sufficiently, both in their owne and other mens judgments.

1. obj. was diversitie aboute Religion. Ans: We know no such matter, for here was never any controversie or opposition, either publicke or private, (to our knowledg,) since we came.

2. ob: Neglecte of familie duties, one the Lords day.

Ans. We allow no such thing, but blame it in our selves and others; and they that thus reporte it, should have shewed their Christian love the more if they had in love tould the offenders of it, rather then thus to reproach them behind their baks. But (to say no more) we wish them selves had given better example.

3. ob: Wante of both the sacraments.

Ans. The more is our greefe, that our pastor is kept from us, by whom we might injoye them; for we used to have the Lords Supper every Saboth, and baptisme as often as ther was occasion of children to baptise.

4. ob: Children not catechised nor taught to read.

Ans: Neither is true; for diverse take pains with their owne as they can; indeede, we have no commone schoole for want of a fitt person, or hithertoo means to maintaine one; though we desire now to begine.

5. ob: Many of the perticuler members of the plantation will not work for the generall.

Ans: This allso is not wholy true; for though some doe it

---

[1] On their own account.

not willingly, and other not honestly, yet all doe it; and he that doth worst gets his owne foode and something besids. But we will not excuse them, but labour to reforme them the best we cane, or else to quitte the plantation of them.

6. ob: The water is not wholsome.

Ans: If they mean, not so wholsome as the good beere and wine in London, (which they so dearly love,) we will not dispute with them; but els, for water, it is as good as any in the world, (for ought we knowe,) and it is wholsome enough to us that can be contente therwith.

7. ob: The ground is barren and doth bear no grasse.

Ans: It is hear (as in all places) some better and some worse; and if they well consider their words, in England they shall not find such grasse in them, as in their feelds and meadows. The catle find grasse, for they are as fatt as need be; we wish we had but one for every hundred that hear is grase to keep. Indeed, this objection, as some other, are ridiculous to all here which see and know the contrary.

8. ob: The fish will not take salt to keepe sweete.

Ans: This is as true as that which was written, that ther is scarce a foule to be seene or a fish to be taken. Things likly to be true in a cuntrie wher so many sayle of ships come yearly a fishing; they might as well say, there can no aile or beere in London be kept from sowering.

9. ob: Many of them are theevish and steale on from an other.

Ans: Would London had been free from that crime, then we should not have been trobled with these here; it is well knowne sundrie have smarted well for it, and so are the rest like to doe, if they be taken.

10. ob: The countrie is anoyed with foxes and woules.[1]

Ans: So are many other good cuntries too; but poyson, traps, and other such means will help to destroy them.

[1] Wolves.

11. ob: The Dutch are planted nere Hudsons Bay,[1] and are likely to overthrow the trade.

Ans: They will come and plante in these parts, also, if we and others doe not, but goe home and leave it to them. We rather commend them, then condemne them for it.

12. ob: The people are much anoyed with muskeetoes.

Ans: They are too delicate and unfitte to begine new-plantations and collonies, that cannot enduer the biting of a muskeeto; we would wish such to keepe at home till at least they be muskeeto proofe. Yet this place is as free as any, and experience teacheth that the more the land is tild, and the woods cut downe, the fewer ther will be, and in the end scarse any at all.

Having thus dispatcht these things, that I may handle things togeather, I shall here inserte 2. other letters from Mr. Robinson their pastor; the one to the Gov[r], the other to Mr. Brewster their Elder, which will give much light to the former things; and express the tender love and care of a true pastor over them.

His leter to the Gov[r].

My loving and much beloved freind, whom God hath hithertoo preserved, preserve and keepe you still to his glorie, and the good of many; that his blessing may make your godly and wise endeavours answerable to the valuation which they ther have, and set upon the same. Of your love too and care for us here, we never doubted; so are we glad to take knowledg of it in that fullnes we doe. Our love and care to and for you, is mutuall, though our hopes of coming unto you be small, and weaker then ever. But of this at large in Mr. Brewsters letter, with whom you, and he with you, mutualy, I know, comunicate your letters, as I desire you may doe these, etc.

Concerning the killing of those poor Indeans, of which we heard at first by reporte, and since by more certaine relation, oh! how happy a thing had it been, if you had converted some, before you had killed any; besids, wher bloud is one begune to be shed, it is seldome stanched of a long time after. You will say they deserved it. I grant it; but upon what provocations and invitments by those heathenish Chris-

---

[1] Hudson's River is no doubt meant. Permanent settlement at its mouth has been supposed to have begun in 1623, but a trading post had been established there some years before that date.

tians?[1] Besids, you, being no magistrats over them, were to consider, not what they deserved, but what you were by necessitie constrained to inflicte. Necessitie of this, espetially of killing so many, (and many more, it seems, they would, if they could,) I see not. Methinks on or tow principals should have been full enough, according to that approved rule, The punishmente to a few, and the fear to many. Upon this occasion let me be bould to exhorte you seriouly to consider of the dispossition of your Captaine,[2] whom I love, and am perswaded the Lord in great mercie and for much good hath sent you him, if you use him aright. He is a man humble and meek amongst you, and towards all in ordinarie course. But now if this be meerly from an humane spirite, ther is cause to fear that by occasion, espetially of provocation, ther may be wanting that tendernes of the life of man (made after Gods image) which is meete. It is also a thing more glorious in mens eyes, then pleasing in Gods, or conveniente for Christians, to be a terrour to poore barbarous people; and indeed I am afraid least, by these occasions, others should be drawne to affecte a kind of rufling course in the world. I doubt not but you will take in good part these things which I write, and as ther is cause make use of them. It were to us more comfortable and convenient, that we comunicated our mutuall helps in presence, but seeing that canot be done, we shall always long after you, and love you, and waite Gods apoynted time. The adventurers it seems have neither money nor any great mind of us, for the most parte. They deney it to be any part of the covenants betwixte us, that they should transporte us, neither doe I looke for any further help from them, till means come from you. We hear are strangers in effecte to the whole course, and so both we and you (save as your owne wisdoms and worths have intressed you further) of principals intended in this bussines, are scarce accessaries, etc. My wife, with me, resalute you and yours. Unto him who is the same to his in all places, and nere to them which are farr from one an other, I comend you and all with you, resting,

Yours truly loving,

Leyden, Des: 19. 1623.   JOHN ROBINSON.

His to Mr. Brewster.

Loving and dear freind and brother: That which I most desired of God in regard of you, namly, the continuance of your life and health, and the safe coming of these sent unto you, that I most gladly hear of, and praise God for the same. And I hope Mrs. Brewsters weake and decayed state of body will have some reparing by the coming of her daughters, and the provissions in this and former ships, I hear is made for you; which maks

---

[1] "Mr. Westons men." (Br.)   [2] Standish.

us with more patience bear our languishing state, and the deferring of our desired transportation; which I call desired, rather than hoped for, whatsoever you are borne in hand by any others. For first, ther is no hope at all, that I know, or can conceive of, of any new stock to be raised for that end; so that all must depend upon returns from you, in which are so many uncertainties, as that nothing with any certaintie can thence be concluded. Besids, howsoever for the presente the adventurers aledg nothing but want of money, which is an invincible difculty, yet if that be taken away by you, others without doubte will be found. For the beter clearing of this, we must dispose the adventurers into 3. parts; and of them some 5. or 6. (as I conceive) are absolutly bent for us, above any others. Other 5. or 6. are our bitter professed adversaries. The rest, being the body, I conceive to be honestly minded, and loveingly also towards us; yet such as have others (namly the forward preachers) nerer unto them, then us, and whose course so farr as ther is any differance, they would rather advance then ours. Now what a hanck [1] these men have over the professors, you know. And I perswade my selfe, that for me, they of all others are unwilling I should be transported, espetially such of them as have an eye that way them selves; as thinking if I come ther, ther market will be mard in many regards. And for these adversaries, if they have but halfe the witte to their malice, they will stope my course when they see it intended, for which this delaying serveth them very opportunly. And as one restie jade can hinder, by hanging back, more then two or 3. can (or will at least, if they be not very free) draw forward, so will it be in this case. A notable experimente of this, they gave in your messengers presence, constraining the company to promise that none of the money now gathered should be expended or imployed to the help of any of us towards you. Now touching the question propounded by you, I judg it not lawfull for you, being a ruling Elder, as Rom. 12. 7. 8. and 1. Tim. 5. 17. opposed to the Elders that teach and exhorte and labore in the word and doctrine, to which the sacraments are annexed, to administer them, nor convenient if it were lawfull. Whether any larned man will come unto you or not, I know not; if any doe, you must *Consilium capere in arena.* [2] Be you most hartily saluted, and your wife with you, both from me and _nine. Your God and ours, and the God of all his, bring us together if it be his will, and keep us in the mean while, and allways to his glory, and make us servisable to his majestie, and faithfull to the end. Amen.

Your very loving brother,

Leyden, Des: 20. 1623.   JOHN ROBINSON.

[1] Hold.   [2] Take counsel at the moment, or on the spot.

These things premised, I shall now prosecute the proced-
ings and afairs here. And before I come to other things I
must speak a word of their planting this year; they having
found the benifite of their last years harvest, and setting
corne for their particuler, having therby with a great deale of
patience overcome hunger and famine. Which maks me remember a saing of Senecas, *Epis:* 123. *That a great parte of
libertie is a well governed belly, and to be patiente in all wants.*
They begane now highly to prise corne as more pretious then
silver, and those that had some to spare begane to trade one
with another for smale things, by the quarte, potle, and peck,
etc.; for money they had none, and if any had, corne was
prefered before it. That they might therfore encrease their
tillage to better advantage, they made suite to the Govr
to have some portion of land given them for continuance, and
not by yearly lotte, for by that means, that which the more
industrious had brought into good culture (by much pains)
one year, came to leave it the nexte, and often another might
injoye it; so as the dressing of their lands were the more
sleighted over, and to lese profite. Which being well considered, their request was granted. And to every person was
given only one acrre of land, to them and theirs, as nere the
towne as might be, and they had no more till the 7. years were
expired. The reason was, that they might be kept close together both for more saftie and defence, and the better im-
provement of the generall imployments. Which condition of
theirs did make me often thinke, of what I had read in Plinie[1]
of the Romans first beginings in Romulus time. How every
man contented him selfe with 2. Acres of land, and had no
more assigned them. And chap. 3. It was thought a great
reward, to receive at the hands of the people of Rome a pinte
of corne. And long after, the greatest presente given to a
Captaine that had gotte a victory over their enemise, was as

[1] "Plin: lib: 18. chap. 2." (Br.) The reference is to Pliny's *Natural
History.*

much ground as they could till in one day. And he was not counted a good, but a dangerous man, that would not contente him selfe with 7. Acres of land. As also how they did pound their corne in morters, as these people were forcte to doe many years before they could get a mille.

The ship which brought this supply,[1] was speedily discharged, and with her m^r. and company sente to Cap-Anne (of which place they had gott a patente, as before is shewed) on fishing, and because the season was so farr spente some of the planters were sent to help to build their stage,[2] to their owne hinderance. But partly by the latenes of the year, and more espetialy by the basnes of the m^r., one Baker, they made a poore viage of it. He proved a very drunken beast, and did nothing (in a maner) but drink, and gusle, and consume away the time and his victails; and most of his company followed his example; and though Mr. William Peirce was to over see the busines, and to be m^r. of the ship home, yet he could doe no good amongst them, so as the loss was great, and would have bene more to them, but that they kept one a trading ther, which in those times got some store of skins, which was some help unto them.

The ship-carpenter that was sent them, was an honest and very industrious man, and followed his labour very dilligently, and made all that were imployed with him doe the like; he quickly builte them 2 very good and strong shalops (which after did them greate service), and a great and strong lighter, and had hewne timber for 2. catches; but that was lost, for he fell into a feaver in the hote season of the year, and though he had the best means the place could aforde, yet he dyed; of whom they had a very great loss, and were very sorie for his death. But he whom they sent to make salte was an ignorante, foolish, self-willd fellow; he bore them in hand he could doe great matters in making salt-works, so he was sente to seeke out fitte ground for his purpose; and after some serch he tould

---

[1] The *Charity*. [2] Frames or scaffolds for drying fish.

the Govr that he had found a sufficente place, with a good botome to hold water, and otherwise very conveniente, which he doubted not but in a short time to bring to good perfection, and to yeeld them great profite; but he must have 8. or ten men to be constantly imployed. He was wisht to be sure that the ground was good, and other things answerable, and that he could bring it to perfection; otherwise he would bring upon them a great charge by imploying him selfe and so many men. But he was, after some triall, so confidente, as he caused them to send carpenters to rear a great frame for a large house, to receive the salte and such other uses. But in the end all proved vaine. Then he layed fault of the ground, in which he was deceived; but if he might have the lighter to cary clay, he was sure then he could doe it. Now though the Govr and some other foresaw that this would come to litle, yet they had so many malignant spirits amongst them, that would have laid it upon them, in their letters of complainte to the adventurers, as to be their falte that would not suffer him to goe on to bring his work to perfection; for as he by his bould confidence and large promises deceived them in England that sente him, so he had wound him selfe in to these mens high esteeme hear, so as they were faine to let him goe on till all men saw his vanity. For he could not doe any thing but boyle salt in pans, and yet would make them that were joynd with him beleeve ther was so grat a misterie in it as was not easie to be attained, and made them doe many unnecessary things to blind their eys, till they discerned his sutltie. The next yere he was sente to Cap-Anne, and the pans were set up ther wher the fishing was; but before sommer was out, he burnte the house, and the fire was so vehemente as it spoyld the pans, at least some of them, and this was the end of that chargable bussines.

The 3$^{d.}$ eminente person (which the letters before mention) was the minister which they sent over, by name Mr. John Lyford, of whom and whose doing I must be more large, though I shall abridg things as much as I can. When this man first came a shore, he saluted them with that reverence and humilitie as is seldome to be seen, and indeed made them ashamed, he so bowed and cringed unto them, and would have kissed their hands if they would have suffered him;[1] yea, he wept and shed many tears, blessing God that had brought him to see their faces; and admiring the things they had done in their wants, etc. as if he had been made all of love, and the humblest person in the world. And all the while (if we may judg by his after cariags) he was but like him mentioned in Psa: 10. 10. That croucheth and boweth, that heaps of poore may fall by his might. Or like to that dissembling Ishmaell,[2] who, when he had slaine Gedelia, went out weeping and mette them that were coming to offer incence in the house of the Lord; saing, Come to Gedelia, when he ment to slay them. They gave him the best entertainment they could, (in all simplisitie,) and a larger alowans of food out of the store then any other had, and as the Gov[r] had used in all waightie affairs to consulte with their Elder, Mr. Brewster, (togeither with his assistants,) so now he caled Mr. Liford also to counsell with them in their waightiest bussineses. After some short time he desired to joyne himselfe a member to the church hear, and was accordingly received. He made a large confession of his faith, and an acknowledgemente of his former disorderly walking, and his being intangled with many corruptions, which had been a burthen to his conscience, and blessed God for this opportunitie of freedom and libertie to injoye the ordinances of God in puritie among his people, with many more such like expressions. I must hear speake a word also of Mr. John Oldom, who was a copartner with him in his after courses. He had bene a cheefe sticler in the former faction among the perticulers, and an intelligencer to those in England. But now, since the coming of this ship and he saw the supply that came, he tooke occasion to open his minde to some of the

---

[1] "Of which were many witnesses." (Br.)   [2] "Jer. 41. 6." (Br.)

cheefe amongst them heere, and confessed he had done them wrong both by word and deed, and writing into England; but he now saw the eminente hand of God to be with them, and his blesing upon them, which made his hart smite him, neither should those in England ever use him as an instrumente any longer against them in any thing; he also desired former things might be forgotten, and that they would looke upon him as one that desired to close with them in all things, with such like expressions. Now whether this was in hipocrisie, or out of some sudden pange of conviction (which I rather thinke), God only knows. Upon it they shew all readynes to imbrace his love, and carry towards him in all frendlynes, and called him to counsell with them in all cheefe affairs, as the other, without any distrust at all.

Thus all things seemed to goe very comfortably and smothly on amongst them, at which they did much rejoyce; but this lasted not long, for both Oldom and he grew very perverse, and shewed a spirite of great malignancie, drawing as many into faction as they could; were they never so vile or profane, they did nourish and back them in all their doings; so they would but cleave to them and speak against the church hear; so as ther was nothing but private meetings and whisperings amongst them; they feeding themselves and others with what they should bring to pass in England by the faction of their freinds their, which brought others as well as them selves into a fools paradise. Yet they could not cary so closly but much of both their doings and sayings were discovered, yet outwardly they still set a faire face of things.

At lenght when the ship was ready to goe, it was observea Liford was long in writing, and sente many letters, and could not forbear to comunicate to his intimats such things as made them laugh in their sleeves, and thought he had done ther errand sufficiently. The Govr and some other of his freinds knowing how things stood in England, and what hurt

these things might doe, tooke a shalop and wente out with the
ship a league or 2. to sea, and caled for all Lifords and Old-
ums letters.   Mr. William Peirce being m^r of the ship, (and
knew well their evill dealing both in England and here,) afforded him all the assistance he could.   He found above 20.
of Lyfords letters, many of them larg, and full of slanders, and
false accusations, tending not only to their prejudice, but to
their ruine and utter subversion.   Most of the letters they let
pas, only tooke copys of them, but some of the most materiall
they sent true copyes of them, and kept the originalls, least he
should deney them, and that they might produce his owne
hand against him.   Amongst his letters they found the coppyes of tow letters which he sent inclosed in a leter of his to
Mr. John Pemberton, a minister, and a great opposite of theirs.
These 2. letters of which he tooke the coppyes were one of them
write by a gentle-man in England to Mr. Brewster here, the
other by Mr. Winslow to Mr. Robinson, in Holand, at his coming away, as the ship lay at Gravsend.   They lying sealed in
the great cabin, (whilst Mr. Winslow was bussie aboute the
affairs of the ship,) this slye marchante taks and opens them,
taks these coppys, and seals them up againe; and not only
sends the coppyes of them thus to his friend and their adversarie, but adds thertoo in the margente many scurrilous
and flouting anotations.   This ship went out towards evning,
and in the night the Govr returned.   They were somwaht
blanke at it, but after some weeks, when they heard nothing,
they then were as briske as ever, thinking nothing had been
knowne, but all was gone currente, and that the Govr
went but to dispatch his owne letters.   The reason why the
Govr and rest concealed these things the longer, was to
let things ripen, that they might the better• discover their
intents and see who were their adherents.   And the rather
because amongst the rest they found a letter of one of their
confederats, in which was writen that Mr. Oldame and Mr.
Lyford intended a reformation in church and commone wealth;

and, as soone as the ship was gone, they intended to joyne togeather, and have the sacrements, etc.

For Oldame, few of his leters were found, (for he was so
bad a scribe as his hand was scarce legible,) yet he was as deepe
in the mischeefe as the other. And thinking they were now
strong enough, they begane to pick quarells at every thing.
Oldame being called to watch (according to order) refused to
come, fell out with the Capten, caled him raskell, and beggerly raskell, and resisted him, drew his knife at him; though
he offered him no wrong, nor gave him no ille termes, but with
all fairnes required him to doe his duty. The Govr, hearing the tumulte, sent to quiet it, but he ramped more like a
furious beast then a man, and cald them all treatours, and
rebells, and other such foule language as I am ashamed to
remember; but after he was clapt up a while, he came to him
selfe, and with some slight punishmente was let goe upon his
behaviour for further censure.

But to cutt things shorte, at length it grew to this esseue,
that Lyford with his complicies,[1] without ever speaking one
word either to the Govr, Church, or Elder, withdrewe them
selves and set up a publick meeting aparte, on the Lord's
day; with sundry such insolente cariages, too long here to
relate, begining now publikly to acte what privatly they had
been long plotting.

It was now thought high time (to prevent further mischeefe) to calle them to accounte; so the Govr called a
courte and summoned the whol company to appeare. And
then charged Lyford and Oldom with such things as they were
guilty of. But they were stiffe, and stood resolutly upon
the deneyall of most things, and required proofe. They first
alledged what was write to them out of England, compared
with their doings and practises hear; that it was evident they
joyned in plotting against them, and disturbing their peace,
both in respecte of their civill and church state, which was

[1] Accomplices.

most injurious; for both they and all the world knew they came hither to injoye the libertie of their conscience and the free use of Gods ordinances; and for that end had ventured their lives and passed throwgh so much hardshipe hithertoo, and they and their freinds had borne the charg of these beginings, which was not small. And that Lyford for his parte was sent over on this charge, and that both he and his great family was maintained on the same, and also was joyned to the church, and a member of them; and for him to plote against them and seek their ruine, was most unjust and perfidious. And for Oldam or any other that came over at their owne charge, and were on ther perticuler, seeing they were received in curtesie by the plantation, when they came only to seeke shelter and protection under their wings, not being able to stand alone, that they, (according to the fable,) like the Hedghogg whom the conny in a stormy day in pittie received into her borrow, would not be content to take part with her, but in the end with her sharp pricks forst the poore conny to forsake her owne borrow; so these men with the like injustice indevored to doe the same to thos that entertained them.

Lyford denyed that he had any thing to doe with them in England, or knew of their courses, and made other things as strange that he was charged with. Then his letters were prodused and some of them read, at which he was struck mute. But Oldam begane to rage furiously, because they had intercepted and opened his letters, threatening them in very high language, and in a most audacious and mutinous maner stood up and caled upon the people, saying, My maisters, wher is your harts? now shew your courage, you have oft complained to me so and so; now is the time, if you will doe any thing, I will stand by you, etc. Thinking that every one (knowing his humor) that had soothed and flattered him, or other wise in their discontente uttered any thing unto him, would now side with him in open rebellion. But he was deceived, for not a man opened his mouth, but all were silent, being strucken with the injustice of the thing. Then the Govr turned his speech to Mr. Lyford, and asked him if he thought they had done evill to open his letters; but he was silente, and would not say a word, well knowing what they might reply. Then the Govr shewed the people he did it as a magistrate, and was bound to it by his place, to prevent the mischeefe and ruine that this conspiracie and plots of theirs would bring on this poor colony. But he, besids his evill dealing hear, had delte trecherusly with his freinds that trusted him, and stole their letters and opened them, and sent coppies of them, with disgracefull annotations, to his freinds in England. And then the Govr produced them and his other letters under his owne hand, (which he could not deney,) and caused them to be read before all the people; at which all his freinds were blanke, and had not a word to say.

It would be too long and tedious here to inserte his letters (which would almost fill a volume), though I have them by me. I shall only note a few of the cheefe things collected out of them, with the answers to them as they were then given; and but a few of those many, only for instance, by which the rest may be judged of.

1. First, he saith, the church would have none to live hear but them selves. 2^{ly}. Neither are any willing so to doe if they had company to live elswher.

Ans: Their answer was, that this was false, in both the parts of it; for they were willing and desirous that any honest men may live with them, that will cary them selves peacably, and seek the commone good, or at least doe them no hurte. And againe, ther are many that will not live els wher so long as they may live with them.

2. That if ther come over any honest men that are not of the seperation, they will quickly distast them, etc.

A. Ther answer was as before, that it was a false callumniation, for they had many amongst them that they liked well of, and were glad of their company; and should be of any such like that should come amongst them.

3.   That they excepted against him for these 2. doctrins raised from 2. Sam: 12. 7.   First, that ministers must sume times perticulerly apply their doctrine to spetiall persons; 2^{ly}, that great men may be reproved as well as meaner.

A.   Their answer was, that both these were without either truth or colour of the same (as was proved to his face), and that they had taught and beleeved these things long before they knew Mr. Liford.

4.   That they utterly sought the ruine of the perticulers; as appeareth by this, that they would not suffer any of the generall either to buy or sell with them, or to exchaing one commoditie for another.

Ans: This was a most malicious slander and voyd of all truth, as was evidently proved to him before all men; for any of them did both buy, sell, or exchaing with them as often as they had any occation.   Yea, and allso both lend and give to them when they wanted; and this the perticuler persons them selves could not deney, but freely confest in open court. But the ground from whence this arose made it much worse, for he was in counsell with them.   When one was called before them, and questioned for receiving powder and bisket from the gunner of the small ship, which was the companys, and had it put in at his window in the night, and allso for buying salt of one, that had no right to it, he not only stood to back him (being one of these perticulers) by excusing and extenuating his falte, as long as he could, but upon this builds this mischeevous and most false slander: That because they would not suffer them to buy stolne goods, ergo, they sought their utter ruine.   Bad logick for a devine.

5.   Next he writs, that he chocked them with this; that they turned men into their perticuler, and then sought to starve them, and deprive them of all means of subsistance.

A.   To this was answered, he did them manifest wrong,

for they turned none into their perticuler; it was their owne importunitie and ernest desire that moved them, yea, constrained them to doe it. And they apealed to the persons them selves for the truth hereof. And they testified the same against him before all present, as allso that they had no cause to complaine of any either hard or unkind usage.

6. He accuseth them with unjust distribution, and writeth, that it was a strang difference, that some have bene alowed 16*li*. of meale by the weeke, and others but 4*li*. And then (floutingly) saith, it seems some mens mouths and bellies are very litle and slender over others.

Ans: This might seeme strange indeed to those to whom he write his leters in England, which knew not the reason of it; but to him and others hear, it could not be strange, who knew how things stood. For the first commers had none at all, but lived on their corne. Those which came in the *Anne*, the August before, and were to live 13. months of the provissions they brought, had as good alowance in meal and pease as it would extend too, the most part of the year; but a litle before harvest, when they had not only fish, but other fruits began to come in, they had but 4*li*. having their libertie to make their owne provisions. But some of these which came last, as the ship carpenter, and sawiers, the salte-men and others that were to follow constante imployments, and had not an howers time, from their hard labours, to looke for any thing above their alowance; they had at first, 16*li*. alowed them, and afterwards as fish, and other food coued be gott, they had as balemente,[1] to 14. and 12. yea some of them to 8. as the times and occasions did vary. And yet those which followed planting and their owne occasions, and had but 4*li*. of meall a week, lived better then the other, as was well knowne to all. And yet it must be remembered that Lyford and his had allwais the highest alowance.

Many other things (in his letters) he accused them of, with

[1] Bailment, delivery of goods on trust, in advance of payment.

many aggravations; as that he saw exseeding great wast of tools and vesseles; and this, when it came to be examened, all the instance he could give was, that he had seen an old hogshed or too fallen to peeces, and a broken how or tow lefte carlesly in the feilds by some. Though he also knew that a godly, honest man was appointed to looke to these things. But these things and such like was write of by him, to cast disgrace and prejudice upon them; as thinking what came from a minister would pass for currente. Then he tells them that Winslow should say, that ther was not above 7. of the adventurers that souight the good of the collony. That Mr. Oldam and him selfe had had much to doe with them, and that the faction here might match the Jesuits for politie. With many the like greevious complaints and accusations.

1. Then, in the next place, he comes to give his freinds counsell and directtion. And first, that the Leyden company (Mr. Robinson and the rest) must still be kepte back, or els all will be spoyled. And least any of them should be taken in privatly somewher on the coast of England, (as it was feared might be done,) they must chaing the m^r. of the ship (Mr. William Peirce), and put another allso in Winslows stead, for marchante,[1] or els it would not be prevented.

2. Then he would have such a number provided as might oversway them hear. And that the perticulers should have voyces in all courts and elections, and be free to bear any office. And that every perticuler should come over as an adventurer, if he be but a servante; some other venturing 10*li*., the bill may be taken out in the servants name, and then assigned to the party whose money it was, and good covenants drawn betweene them for the clearing of the matter; and this (saith he) would be a means to strengthen this side the more.

3. Then he tells them that if that Capten they spoake of should come over hither as a generall,[2] he was perswaded

---

[1] Merchant in the sense of cape merchant or supercargo.
[2] *I. e.*, as one of the colony.

he would be chosen Capten; for this Captaine Standish looks like a silly boy, and is in utter contempte.

4. Then he shows that if by the forementioned means they cannot be strengthened to cary and overbear things, it will be best for them to plant els wher by them selves; and would have it artickled by them that they might make choyse of any place that they liked best within 3. or 4. myls distance, shewing ther were farr better places for plantation then this.

5. And lastly he concluds, that if some number came not over to bear them up here, then ther would be no abiding for them, but by joyning with these hear. Then he adds: Since I begane to write, ther are letters come from your company, wherin they would give sole authoritie in diverce things unto the Govr here; which, if it take place, then, *Ve Nobis.*[1] But I hope you will be more vigilante hereafter, that nothing may pass in such a manner. I suppose (saith he) Mr. Oldame will write to you further of these things. I pray you conceall me in the discovery of these things, etc.

Thus I have breefly touched some cheefe things in his leters, and shall now returne to their procceeding with him. After the reading of his leters before the whole company, he was demanded what he could say to these things. But all the answer he made was, that Billington and some others had informed him of many things, and made sundrie complaints, which they now deneyed. He was againe asked if that was a sufficiente ground for him thus to accuse and traduse them by his letters, and never say word to them, considering the many bonds betweene them. And so they went on from poynte to poynte; and wisht him, or any of his freinds and confederats, not to spare them in any thing; if he or they had any proofe or witnes of any corrupte or evill dealing of theirs, his or their evidence must needs be ther presente, for ther was the whole company and sundery strangers. He said he had been abused by others in their informations, (as he now well saw,) and so had abused them. And this was all the answer they could have, for none would take his parte in any thing; but Billington, and any whom he named, deneyed the things, and protested he wronged them, and would have drawne them to such and such things which they could not consente too, though they were sometimes drawne to his meetings. Then they delte with him aboute his dissembling with them aboute the church, and that he professed to concur with them in all things, and what a large confession he made at his admittance, and that he held not him selfe a minister till he had a new calling, etc. And yet now he contested against them, and drew a company aparte, and sequestred him selfe; and would goe minister the sacraments (by his Episcopall caling) without ever speaking a word unto them, either as magistrats or bretheren. In conclusion, he was fully convicted, and burst out into tears, and "confest he feared he was a reprobate, his sinns were so great that he doubted God would not pardon them, he was unsavorie salte, etc.; and that he had so wronged them as he could never make them amends, confessing all he had write against them was false and nought, both for matter and manner." And all this he did with as much fullnes as words and tears could express.

After their triall and conviction, the court censured them to be expeld the place; Oldame presently, though his wife and family had liberty to stay all winter, or longer, till he could make provission to remove them comfortably. Lyford had liberty to stay 6. months. It was, indeede, with some eye to his release, if he caried him selfe well in the meane time, and that his repentance proved sound. Lyford acknowledged his censure was farr less than he deserved.

Afterwards, he confest his sin publikly in the church, with tears more largly then before. I shall here put it downe as I find it recorded by some who tooke it from his owne words, as him selfe utered them. Acknowledging "That he had don very evill, and slanderously abused them; and thinking most of the people would take parte with him, he thought to cary all by violence and strong hand against them. And that God might justly lay innocente blood to his charge, for he knew not what hurt might have come of these his writings, and blest God they were stayed. And that he spared not to take knowledg from any, of any evill that was spoaken, but shut his eyes and ears against all the good; and if God should make him a vacabund in the earth, as was Caine, it was but just, for he had sined in envie and malice against his brethren as he did. And he confessed 3. things to be the ground and causes of these his doings: pride, vaine-glorie, and selfe love." Amplifying these heads with many other sade expressions, in the perticulers of them.

So as they begane againe to conceive good thoughts of him upon this his repentance, and admited him to teach amongst them as before; and Samuell Fuller (a deacon amongst them), and some other tender harted men amongst them, were so taken with his signes of sorrow and repentance, as they professed they would fall upon their knees to have his censure released.

But that which made them all stand amased in the end, and may doe all others that shall come to hear the same, (for a rarer president can scarse be showne,) was, that after a month or 2. notwithstand all his former conffessions, convictions, and publick acknowledgments, both in the face of the church and whole company, with so many tears and sadde censures of him selfe before God and men, he should goe againe to justifie what he had done.

For secretly he write a 2^d. leter to the adventurers in England, in which he justified all his former writings, (save in some things which tended to their damage,) the which, because it is brefer then the former, I shall here inserte.

Worthy Srs: Though the filth of mine owne doings may justly be cast in my face, and with blushing cause my perpetuall silence, yet that the truth may not herby be injuried, your selves any longer deluded, nor in[j]urious dealing caried out still, with bould out facings, I have ad·

ventured once more to write unto you. Firest, I doe freely confess I delte very indiscreetly in some of my perticuler leters which I wrote to private freinds, for the courses in coming hither and the like; which I doe in no sorte seeke to justifie, though stired up ther unto in the beholding the indirecte courses held by others, both hear, and ther with you, for effecting their designes. But am hartily sory for it, and doe to the glory of God and mine owne shame acknowledg it. Which leters being intercepted by the Gov[r], I have for the same undergone the censure of banishmente. And had it not been for the respecte I have unto you, and some other matters of private regard, I had returned againe at this time by the pinass for England; for hear I purpose not to abide, unless I receive better incouragmente from you, then from the church (as they call them selves) here I doe receive. I purposed before I came, to undergoe hardnes, therfore I shall I hope cherfully bear the conditions of the place, though very mean; and they have chainged my wages ten times allready. I suppose my letters, or at least the coppies of them, are come to your hands, for so they hear reporte; which, if it be so, I pray you take notice of this, that I have writen nothing but what is certainly true, and I could make so apeare planly to any indifferente men, whatsoever colours be cast to darken the truth, and some ther are very audatious this way; besids many other matters which are farre out of order hear. My mind was not to enlarge my selfe any further, but in respecte of diverse poore souls here, the care of whom in parte belongs to you, being here destitute of the means of salvation. For how so ever the church are provided for, to their contente, who are the smalest number in the collony, and doe so appropriate the ministrie to them selves, houlding this principle, that the Lord hath not appointed any ordinary ministrie for the conversion of those that are without, so that some of the poor souls have with tears complained of this to me, and I was taxed for preaching to all in generall. Though in truth they have had no ministrie here since they came, but such as may be performed by any of you, by their owne possition, what soever great pretences they make; but herin they equivocate, as in many other things they doe. But I exceede the bounds I set my selfe, therfore resting thus, untill I hear further from you, so it be within the time limited me. I rest, etc.,

Remaining yours ever,

Dated Aug: 22. An°: 1624.   JOHN LYFORD, Exille.

They made a breefe answer to some things in this leter, but referred cheefly to their former. The effecte was to this purpose: That if God in his providence had not brought these things to their hands (both the former and later), they might have been thus abused, tradused, and calumniated, over-throwne, and undone; and never have knowne by whom, nor for what. They desired but this equall favoure, that they would be pleased to hear their just defence, as well as his accusations, and waigh them in the balance of justice and reason, and then censure as they pleased. They had write breefly to the heads of things before, and should be ready to give further answer as any occasion should require; craving leave to adde a word or tow to this last.

1. And first, they desire to examene what filth that was that he acknowledgeth might justly be throwne in his face, and might cause blushing and perpetuall silence; some great mater sure! But if it be looked into, it amounts to no more then a poynte of indiscretion, and thats all; and yet he licks of that too with this excuse, that he was stired up therunto by beholding the indirecte course here. But this point never troubled him here, it was counted a light matter both by him and his freinds, and put of with this,—that any man might doe so, to advise his private freinds to come over for their best advantage. All his sorrow and tears here was for the wrong and hurt he had done us, and not at all for this he pretends to be done to you: it was not counted so much as indiscretion.

2. Having thus payed you full satisfaction, he thinks he may lay load of us here. And first complains that we have changed his wages ten times. We never agreed with him for any wages, nor made any bargen at all with him, neither know of any that you have made. You sent him over to teach amongst us, and desired he might be kindly used; and more then this we know not. That he hath beene kindly used, (and farr beter then he deserves from us,) he shall be judged first of his owne mouth. If you please to looke upon that writing of his, that was sent you amongst his leters, which he cals a generall relation, in which, though he doth otherwise

traduse us, yet in this he him selfe clears us. In the latter
end therof he hath these words. *I speak not this* (saith he)
out of any ill affection to the men, for I have found them very
kind and loving to me. You may ther see these to be his owne
words under his owne hand. 2^{ly}. It will appere by this that
he hath ever had a larger alowance of food out of the store
for him and his then any, and clothing as his neede hath
required; a dwelling in one of our best houses, and a man
wholy at his owne command to tend his private affairs. What
cause he hath therfore to complaine, judge ye; and what he
means in his speech we know not, except he aluds to that of
Jaacob and Laban. If you have promised him more or other
wise, you may doe it when you please.

3. Then with an impudente face he would have you
take notice, that (in his leters) he hath write nothing but
what is certainly true, yea, and he could make it so appeare
plainly to any indifferente men. This indeed doth astonish
us and causeth us to tremble at the deceitfullnes and desperate wickednes of mans harte. This is to devoure holy things,
and after voues to enquire. It is admirable that after such
publick confession, and acknowledgmente in court, in church,
before God, and men, with such sadd expressions as he used,
and with such melting into teares, that after all this he shoud
now justifie all againe. If things had bene done in a corner,
it had been some thinge to deney them; but being done in
the open view of the cuntrie and before all men, it is more
then strange now to avow to make them plainly appeare to
any indifferente men; and here wher things were done, and
all the evidence that could be were presente, and yet could
make nothing appeare, but even his freinds condemnd him and
gave their voyce to his censure, so grose were they; we leave
your selves to judge herein. Yet least this man should triumph in his wikednes, we shall be ready to answer him, when,
or wher you will, to any thing he shall lay to our charg, though
we have done it sufficiently allready.

4. Then he saith he would not inlarge, but for some poore souls here who are destiute of the means of salvation, etc. But all his soothing is but that you would use means, that his censure might be released that he might here continue; and under you (at least) be sheltered, till he sees what his freinds (on whom he depends) can bring about and effecte. For such men pretend much for poor souls, but they will looke to their wages and conditions; if that be not to their content, let poor souls doe what they will, they will shift for them selves, and seek poore souls some wher els among richer bodys.

Next he fals upon the church, that indeed is the burthensome stone that troubls him. First, he saith they hold this principle, that the Lord hath not apointed any ordinarie ministrie for the converssion of those without. The church needs not be ashamed of what she houlds in this, haveing Gods word for her warrente; that ordinarie officers are bound cheefly to their flocks, Acts 20. 28. and are not to be extravagants, to goe, come, and leave them at their pleasurs to shift for them selves, or to be devoured of wolves. But he perverts the truth in this as in other things, for the Lord hath as well appoynted them to converte, as to feede in their severall charges; and he wrongs the church to say other wise. Againe, he saith he was taxed for preaching to all in generall. This is a meere untruth, for this dissembler knows that every Lords day some are appointed to visite suspected places, and if any be found idling and neglecte the hearing of the word, (through idlnes or profanes,) they are punished for the same. Now to procure all to come to hear, and then to blame him for preaching to all, were to play the mad men.

6. Next (he saith) they have had no ministrie since they came, what soever pretences they make, etc. We answer, the more is our wrong, that our pastor is kept from us by these mens means, and then reproach us for it when they have done. Yet have we not been wholy distitute of the means of

salvation, as this man would make the world beleeve; for our reve[d] Elder hath laboured diligently in dispencing the word of God unto us, before he came; and since hath taken equalle pains with him selfe in preaching the same; and, be it spoaken without ostentation, he is not inferriour to Mr. Lyford (and some of his betters) either in gifts or larning, though he would never be perswaded to take higher office upon him. Nor ever was more pretended in this matter. For equivocating, he may take it to him selfe; what the church houlds, they have manifested to the world, in all plaines,[1] both in open confession, doctrine, and writing.

This was the sume of ther answer, and hear I will let them rest for the presente. I have bene longer in these things then I desired, and yet not so long as the things might require, for I pass many things in silence, and many more deserve to have been more largly handled. But I will returne to other things, and leave the rest to its place.

The pinass[2] that was left sunck and cast away near Damarins-cove, as is before showed, some of the fishing maisters said it was a pity so fine a vessell should be lost, and sent them word that, if they would be at the cost, they would both directe them how to waygh her, and let them have their carpenters to mend her. They thanked them, and sente men aboute it, and beaver to defray the charge, (without which all had been in vaine). So they gott coopers to trime, I know not how many tune of cask, and being made tight and fastened to her at low-water, they boyed her up; and then with many hands hald her on shore in a conveniente place wher she might be wrought upon; and then hired sundrie carpenters to work upon her, and other to saw planks, and at last fitted her and got her home. But she cost a great deale of money, in thus recovering her, and buying riging and seails for her, both now and when before she lost her mast; so as she proved a chargable vessell to the poor plantation. So they

---

[1] Plainness.   [2] The *James*.

sent her home, and with her Lyford sent his last letter, in great secrecie; but the party intrusted with it gave it the Govr.

The winter was passed over in ther ordinarie affairs, without any spetiall mater worth noteing; saveing that many who before stood something of from the church, now seeing Lyfords unrighteous dealing, and malignitie against the church, now tendered them selves to the church, and were joyned to the same; proffessing that it was not out of the dislike of any thing that they had stood of so long, but a desire to fitte them selves beter for such a state, and they saw now the Lord cald for their help. And so these troubls prodused a quite contrary effecte in sundrie hear, then these adversaries hoped for. Which was looked at as a great worke of God, to draw on men by unlickly means; and that in reason which might rather have set them further of. And thus I shall end this year.

Anno Dom: 1625.

AT the spring of the year, about the time of their Election Court,[1] Oldam came againe amongst them; and though it was a part of his censure for his former mutinye and miscariage, not to returne without leave first obtained, yet in his dareing spirite, he presumed without any leave at all, being also set on and hardened by the ill counsell of others. And not only so, but suffered his unruly passion to rune beyond the limits of all reason and modestie; in so much that some strangers which came with him were ashamed of his outrage, and rebuked him; but all reprofes were but as oyle to the fire, and made the flame of his coller greater. He caled them all to nought, in this his mad furie, and a hundred rebells and traytors, and I know not what. But in conclusion they commited him till he was tamer, and then apointed a gard of musketers which he was to pass throw, and ever one was ordered to give him a thump on the brich, with the but end of

---

[1] Annual meeting for election of officers of the colony.

his musket, and then was conveied to the water side, wher a
boat was ready to cary him away.   Then they bid him goe and
mende his maners.

Whilst this was a doing, Mr. William Peirce and Mr. Winslow came up from the water side, being come from England;
but they were so busie with Oldam, as they never saw them
till they came thus upon them.   They bid them not spare
either him or Liford, for they had played the vilans with
them.   But that I may hear make an end with him, I shall
hear once for all relate what befell concerning him in the
future, and that breefly.   After the removall of his familie
from hence, he fell into some straits, (as some others did,)
and aboute a year or more afterwards, towards winter, he
intended a vioage for Virginia; but it so pleased God that the
barke that caried him, and many other passengers, was in
that danger, as they dispaired of life; so as many of them,
as they fell to prayer, so also did they begine to examine their
consciences and confess such sins as did most burthen them.
And Mr. Ouldame did make a free and large confession of the
wrongs and hurt he had done to the people and church here,
in many perticulers, that as he had sought their ruine, so God
had now mette with him and might destroy him; yea, he
feared they all fared the worce for his sake; he prayed God to
forgive him, and made vowes that, if the Lord spard his life,
he would become otherwise, and the like.   This I had from
some of good credite, yet living in the Bay, and were them
selves partners in the same dangers on the shoulds of Cap-
Codd, and heard it from his owne mouth.   It pleased God to
spare their lives, though they lost their viage; and in time
after wards, Ouldam caried him selfe fairly towards them,
and acknowledged the hand of God to be with them, and
seemed to have an honourable respecte of them; and so farr
made his peace with them, as he in after time had libertie
to goe and come, and converse with them, at his pleasure.   He
went after this to Virginia, and had ther a great sicknes, but

recovered and came back againe to his familie in the Bay, and ther lived till some store of people came over. At lenght going a trading in a smale vessell among the Indians, and being weakly mand, upon some quarell they knockt him on the head with a hatched, so as he fell downe dead, and never spake word more. 2. litle boys that were his kinsmen were saved, but had some hurte, and the vessell was strangly recovered from the Indeans by another that belonged to the Bay of Massachusets; and this his death was one ground of the Pequente[1] warr which followed.

I am now come to Mr. Lyford. His time being now expired, his censure was to take place. He was so farre from answering their hopes by amendmente in the time, as he had dubled his evill, as is before noted. But first behold the hand of God conceirning him, wherin that of the Psalmist is verified. Psa: 7. 15. He hath made a pitte, and digged it, and is fallen into the pitte he made. He thought to bring shame and disgrace upon them, but in stead therof opens his owne to all the world. For when he was delte with all aboute his second letter, his wife was so affected with his doings, as she could no longer conceaill her greefe and sorrow of minde, but opens the same to one of their deacons and some other of her freinds, and after uttered the same to Mr. Peirce upon his arrivall. Which was to this purpose, that she feared some great judgment of God would fall upon them, and upon her, for her husbands cause; now that they were to remove, she feared to fall into the Indeans hands, and to be defiled by them, as he had defiled other women; or some shuch like judgmente, as God had threatened David, 2. Sam. 12. 11. I will raise up evill against thee, and will take thy wives and give them, etc. And upon it showed how he had wronged her, as first he had a bastard by another before they were maried, and she having some inkling of some ill cariage that way, when he was a suitor to her, she tould him what she heard, and

[1] Pequot.

deneyd him; but she not certainly knowing the thing, other wise then by some darke and secrete muterings, he not only stifly denied it, but to satisfie her tooke a solemne oath ther was no shuch matter. Upon which she gave consente, and maried with him; but afterwards it was found true, and the bastard brought home to them. She then charged him with his oath, but he prayed pardon, and said he should els not have had her. And yet afterwards she could keep no maids but he would be medling with them, and some time she hath taken him in the maner, as they lay at their beds feete, with shuch other circumstances as I am ashamed to relate. The woman being a grave matron and of good cariage all the while she was hear, and spoake these things out of the sorrow of her harte, sparingly, and yet with some further intimations. And that which did most seeme to affecte her (as they conceived) was, to see his former cariage in his repentance, not only hear with the church, but formerly about these things; sheding tears, and using great and sade expressions, and yet eftsone fall into the like things.

Another thing of the same nature did strangly concurr herewith. When Mr. Winslow and Mr. Peirce were come over, Mr. Winslow informed them that they had had the like bickering with Lyfords freinds in England, as they had with him selfe and his freinds hear, aboute his letters and accusations in them. And many meetings and much clamour was made by his freinds theraboute, crying out, a minister, a man so godly, to be so esteemed and taxed they held a great skandale, and threated to prosecute law against them for it. But things being referred to a further meeting of most of the adventurers, to heare the case and decide the matters, they agreed to chose 2. eminente men for moderators in the bussines. Lyfords faction chose Mr. White, a counselor at law, the other parte chose Rev͂e^d. Mr. Hooker,[1] the minister, and

---

[1] Rev. Thomas Hooker, afterward the famous minister of Hartford; at this time he was rector of Esher in Surrey.

many freinds on both sids were brought in, so as ther was a great assemblie. In the mean time, God in his providence had detected Lyford's evill cariage in Ireland to some freinds amongst the company, who made it knowne to Mr. Winslow, and directed him to 2. godly and grave witnesses, who would testifie the same (if caled therunto) upon their oath. The thing was this; he being gott into Ireland, had wound him selfe into the esteeme of sundry godly and zelous professours in those parts, who, having been burthened with the ceremonies in England, found their some more liberty to their consciences; amongst whom were these 2. men, which gave this evidence. Amongst the rest of his hearers, ther was a godly yonge man that intended to marie, and cast his affection on a maide which lived their aboute; but desiring to chose in the Lord, and preferred the fear of God before all other things, before he suffered his affection to rune too farr, he resolved to take Mr. Lyfords advise and judgmente of this maide, (being the minister of the place,) and so broak the matter unto him; and he promised faithfully to informe him, but would first take better knowledg of her, and have private conferance with her; and so had sundry times; and in conclusion commended her highly to the young man as a very fitte wife for him. So they were maried togeather; but some time after mariage the woman was much troubled in mind, and afflicted in conscience, and did nothing but weepe and mourne, and long it was before her husband could get of her what was the cause. But at length she discovered the thing, and prayed him to forgive her, for Lyford had overcome her, and defiled her body before marriage, after he had comended him unto her for a husband, and she resolved to have him, when he came to her in that private way. The circumstances I forbear, for they would offend chast ears to hear them related, (for though he satisfied his lust on her, yet he indeaoured to hinder conception.) These things being thus discovered, the womans husband tooke some godly freinds with

him, to deale with Liford for this evill.   At length he confest
it, with a great deale of seeming sorrow and repentance, but
was forct to leave Irland upon it, partly for shame, and partly
for fear of further punishmente, for the godly withdrew them
selves from him upon it; and so comming into England un-
hapily he was light upon and sente hither.

But in this great assembly, and before the moderators, in
handling the former matters aboute the letters, upon provocation, in some heate of replie to some of Lyfords defenders, Mr.
Winslow let fall these words, That he had delte knavishly;
upon which on of his freinds tooke hold, and caled for witneses, that he cald a minister of the gospell knave, and would
prosecute law upon it, which made a great tumulte, upon
which (to be shorte) this matter broke out, and the witnes
were prodused, whose persons were so grave, and evidence so
plaine, and the facte so foule, yet delivered in such modest
and chast terms, and with such circumstances, as strucke all
his freinds mute, and made them all ashamed; insomuch as
the moderators with great gravitie declared that the former
matters gave them cause enough to refuse him and to deal
with him as they had done, but these made him unmeete for
ever to bear ministrie any more, what repentance soever he
should pretend; with much more to like effecte, and so wisht
his freinds to rest quiete.   Thus was this matter ended.

From hence Lyford wente to Natasco,[1] in the Bay of the
Massachusets, with some other of his freinds with him, wher
Oldom allso lived.   From thence he removed to Namkeke,
since called Salem; but after ther came some people over,
wheather for hope of greater profite, or what ends els I know
not, he left his freinds that followed him, and went from thence
to Virginia, wher he shortly after dyed, and so I leave him to
the Lord.   His wife afterwards returned againe to this cuntry,
and thus much of this matter.

This storme being thus blowne over, yet sundrie sad effects

[1] Nantasket.

followed the same; for the Company of Adventurers broake in peeces here upon, and the greatest parte wholy deserted the colony in regarde of any further supply, or care of their subsistance. And not only so, but some of Lyfords and Oldoms freinds, and their adherents, set out a shipe on fishing, on their owne accounte, and getting the starte of the ships that came to the plantation, they tooke away their stage, and other necessary provisions that they had made for fishing at Cap-Anne the year before, at their great charge, and would not restore the same, excepte they would fight for it. But the Govr sent some of the planters to help the fisher men to build a new one, and so let them keepe it. This shipe also brought them some small supply, of little value; but they made so pore a bussines of their fishing, (neither could these men make them any returne for the supply sente,) so as, after this year, they never looked more after them.

Also by this ship, they, some of them, sent (in the name of the rest) certaine reasons of their breaking of from the plantation, and some tenders, upon certaine conditions, of reuniting againe. The which because they are longe and tedious, and most of them aboute the former things already touched, I shall omite them; only giveing an instance in one, or tow. 1. reason, they charged them for dissembling with his majestie in their petition, and with the adventurers about the French discipline, etc.[1] 2^ly, for receiv[ing] a man[2] into their church, that in his conffession renownced all, universall, nationall, and diocessan churches, etc., by which (say they) it appears, that though they deney the name of Brownists,[3] yet

---

[1] See p. 51, p. 56 and note 4, and p. 57.

[2] "This was Lyford himselfe." (Br.)

[3] Robert Browne, whose followers were called Brownists, was the son of a sheriff of Rutlandshire and was educated at Cambridge. First a schoolmaster, he became a preacher at Cambridge, and in 1580 separated from the Church. He was twice imprisoned for non-conformity, and escaping to Holland organized a church at Middelburg, and wrote works setting forth the congregational church polity. He returned to England before long, and, becoming reconciled to the Church, obtained in 1591 a living in Northamptonshire. Finally, being imprisoned for

they practiss the same, etc. And therfore they should sinne against God in building up such a people.

Then they adde: Our dislikes thus laid downe, that we may goe on in trade with better contente and credite, our desires are as followeth. First, that as we are partners in trade, so we may be in Gov͠rt ther, as the patente doth give us power, etc.

2. That the French discipline may be practised in the plantation, as well in the circumstances theirof, as in the substance; wherby the scandallous name of the Brownists, and other church differences, may be taken away.

3. Lastly, that Mr. Robinson and his company may not goe over to our plantation, unless he and they will recon- cile themselves to our church by a recantation under their hands, etc.

Their answer in part to these things was then as foloweth.

Wheras you taxe us for dissembling with his majestie and the ad- venturers aboute the French discipline, you doe us wrong, for we both hold and practice the discipline of the French and other reformed churches, (as they have published the same in the Harmony of Confessions,) [1] according to our means, in effecte and substance. But wheras you would tye us to the French discipline in every circumstance, you derogate from the libertie we have in Christ Jesus. The Apostle Paule would have none to follow him in any thing but wherin he follows Christ, much less ought any Christian or church in the world to doe it. The French may erre, we may erre, and other churches may erre, and doubtless doe in many circumstances. That honour therfore belongs only to the infallible word of God, and pure Testamente of Christ, to be propounded and followed as the only rule and pattern for direction herin to all churches and Christians. And it is too great arrogancie for any man, or church to thinke that he or they have so sounded the word of God to the bottome, as precislie to sett downe the churches discipline, without error in sub- stance or circumstance, as that no other without blame may digress or

striking a constable, he died in Northampton gaol in 1633 at the age of about 83. After his recantation the Separatists repudiated the name of Brownists.

[1] A book entitled *An Harmony of the Confessions of the Faith of the Christian and Reformed Churches with verie shorte Notes, translated out of Latine into English* (1586).

differ in any thing from the same. And it is not difficulte to shew, that the reformed churches differ in many circumstances amongest them selves.

The rest I omitte, for brevities sake, and so leave to prosecute these men or their doings any further, but shall returne to the rest of their freinds of the company, which stuck to them. And I shall first inserte some part of their letters as followeth; for I thinke it best to render their minds in ther owne words.

To our loving freinds, etc.

Though the thing we feared be come upon us, and the evill we strove against have overtaken us, yet we cannot forgett you, nor our freindship and fellowship which togeather we have had some years; wherin though our expressions have been small, yet our harty affections towards you (unknown by face) have been no less then to our nearest freinds, yea, to our owne selves. And though this your freind Mr. Winslow can tell you the state of things hear, yet least we should seeme to neglecte you, to whom, by a wonderfull providence of God, we are so nearly united, we have thought good once more to write unto you, to let you know what is here befallen, and the resons of it; as also our purposes and desirs toward you for hereafter.

The former course for the generalitie here is wholy dissolved from what it was; and wheras you and we were formerly sharers and partners, in all viages and deallings, this way is now no more, but you and we are left to bethinke our sellves what course to take in the future, that your lives and our monies be not lost.

The reasons and causes of this allteration have been these. First and mainly, the many losses and crosses at sea, and abuses of sea-men, which have caused us to rune into so much charge, debts, and ingagements, as our estats and means were not able to goe on without impoverishing our selves, except our estats had been greater, and our associats cloven beter unto us. 2^{ly}, as here hath been a faction and siding amongst us now more then 2. years, so now there is an uter breach and sequestration amongst us, and in too parts of us a full dissertion and forsaking of you, without any intente or purpose of medling more with you. And though we are perswaded the maine cause of this their doing is wante of money, (for neede wherof men use to make many excuses,) yet other things are pretended, as that you are Brownists, etc. Now what use you or we ought to make of these things, it remaineth to be considered, for we know the hand of God to be in all these things, and no doubt he would admonish some thing therby, and to looke what is amise.   And allthough it be now too late for us or you to prevent and stay these things, yet is it not to late to exercise patience, wisdom, and conscience in bearing them, and in caring our selves in and under them for the time to come.

And as we our selves stand ready to imbrace all occasions that may tend to the furthrance of so hopefull a work, rather admiring of what is, then grudging for what is not; so it must rest in you to make all good againe.   And if in nothing else you can be approved, yet let your honestie and conscience be still approved, and lose not one jote of your innocencie, amids your crosses and afflictions.   And surly if you upon this allteration behave your selves wisly, and goe on fairly, as men whose hope is not in this life, you shall need no other weapon to wound your adversaries; for when your righteousnes is revealled as the light, they shall cover their faces with shame, that causlesly have sought your overthrow.

Now we thinke it but reason, that all such things as ther apertaine to the generall, be kept and preserved togeather, and rather increased dayly, then any way be dispersed or imbeseled away for any private ends or intents whatsoever.   And after your necessities are served, you gather togeather such commodities as the cuntrie yeelds, and send them over to pay debts and clear ingagements hear, which are not less then 1400*li*. And we hope you will doe your best to free our ingagements, etc.   Let us all indeavor to keep a faire and honest course, and see what time will bring forth, and how God in his providence will worke for us.   We still are perswaded you are the people that must make a plantation in those remoate places when all others faile and returne.   And your experience of Gods providence and preservation of you is such as we hope your harts will not faile you, though your freinds should forsake you (which we our selves shall not doe whilst we live, so long as your honestie so well appereeth).   Yet surly help would arise from some other place whilst you waite on God, with uprightnes, though we should leave you allso.

And lastly be you all intreated to walke circumspectly, and carry your selves so uprightly in all your ways, as that no man may make just exceptions against you.   And more espetially that the favour and countenance of God may be so toward you, as that you may find abundante joye and peace even amids tribulations, that you may say with David, Though my father and mother should forsake me, yet the Lord would take me up.

We have sent you hear some catle, cloath, hose, shoes, leather, etc., but in another nature then formerly, as it stood us in hand to doe; we have committed them to the charge and custody of Mr. Allerton and Mr. Winslow, as our factours, at whose discretion they are to be sould, and commodities to be taken for them, as is fitting. And by how much the more they will be chargable unto you, the bet[ter] they had need to be husbanded, etc. Goe on, good freinds, comfortably, pluck up your spirits, and quitte your selves like men in all your difficulties, that not-withstanding all displeasure and threats of men, yet the work may goe on you are aboute, and not be neglected. Which is so much for the glorie of God, and the furthrance of our countrie-men, as that a man may with more comforte spend his life in it, then live the life of Mathusala, in wasting the plentie of a tilled land, or eating the fruite of a growne tree. Thus with harty salutations to you all, and harty prayers for you all, we lovingly take our leaves, this 18. of Des: 1624.

Your assured freinds to our powers,

J. S.   W. C.   T. F.   R. H.   etc.[1]

By this leter it appears in what state the affairs of the plantation stood at this time. These goods they bought, but they were at deare rates, for they put 40. in the hundred upon them, for profite and adventure, outward bound; and be-cause of the venture of the paiment homeward, they would have 30.[2] in the 100. more, which was in all 70. p^r. cent; a thing thought unreasonable by some, and too great an op-pression upon the poore people, as their case stood. The catle were the best goods, for the other being ventured ware, were neither at the best (some of them) nor at the best prises. Sundrie of their freinds disliked these high rates, but comming from many hands, they could not help it.

They sent over also 2. ships on fishing on their owne acounte; the one was the pinass that was cast away the last year hear in the cuntrie, and recovered by the planters, (as was before related,) who, after she came home, was attached by one of the company for his perticuler debte, and now sent againe on this accounte. The other was a great ship, who was well fitted with an experienced m^r and company of fisher-men, to make a viage, and to goe to Bilbo or Sabastians[3]

---

[1] James Shirley, William Collier (who later emigrated to Plymouth), Thomas Fletcher and Robert Holland.

[2] "If I mistake not, it was not much less."   (Br.)

[3] Bilbao or San Sebastian, both on the north coast of Spain.

with her fish; the lesser, her order was to load with cor-fish,[1] and to bring the beaver home for England that should be received for the goods sould to the plantation. This bigger ship made a great viage of good drie fish, the which, if they had gone to a market with, would have yeelded them (as such fish was sould that season) 1800*li.* which would have enriched them.   But because ther was a bruite of warr with France, the m[r] neglected (through timerousnes) his order, and put first into Plimoth, and after into Portsmouth, and so lost their opportunitie, and came by the loss. The lesser ship had as ill success, though she was as hopfull as the other for the marchants profite; for they had fild her with goodly cor-fish taken upon the banke, as full as she could swime; and besids she had some 800*li.* weaight of beaver, besids other furrs to a good value from the plantation. The m[r] seeing so much goods come, put it abord the biger ship, for more saftie; but Mr. Winslow (their factor in this busines) was bound in a bond of 500*li.* to send it to London in the smale ship; ther was some contending between the m[r] and him aboute it. But he tould the m[r] he would follow his order aboute it; if he would take it out afterward, it should be at his perill. So it went in the smale ship, and he sent bills of lading in both. The m[r] was so carfull being both so well laden, as they went joyfully home togeather, for he towed the leser ship at his sterne all the way over bound, and they had such fayr weather as he never cast her of till they were shott deep in to the English Chanell, almost within the sight of Plimoth; and yet ther she was unhaply taken by a Turks man of warr, and carried into Saly,[2] wher the m[r] and men were made slaves, and many of the beaver skins were sould for 4*d.* a peece. Thus was all their hops dasht, and the joyfull news they ment to cary home turned to heavie tidings. Some thought this a hand of God for their too great exaction of the poore plantation, but Gods judgments are unseerchable, neither dare I be bould therwith;

---

[1] Salt codfisk   [2] Sallee, on the coast of Morocco.

but however it shows us the uncertainty of all humane things, and what litle cause ther is of joying in them or trusting to them.

In the bigger of these ships was sent over Captine Standish from the plantation, with leters and instructions, both to their freinds of the company which still clave to them, and also to the Honourable Counsell of New-England. To the company to desire that seeing that they ment only to let them have goods upon sale, that they might have them upon easier termes, for they should never be able to bear such high intrest, or to allow so much per cent; also that what they would doe in that way that it might be disburst in money, or such goods as were fitte and needfull for them, and bought at best hand; and to aquainte them with the contents of his leters to the Counsell above said, which was to this purpose, to desire their favour and help; that such of the adventurers as had thus forsaken and deserted them, might be brought to some order, and not to keepe them bound, and them selves be free. But that they might either stand to ther former covenants, or ells come to some faire end, by dividente, or composition. But he came in a very bad time, for the Stat was full of trouble, and the plague very hote in London, so as no bussines could be done; yet he spake with some of the Honourd Counsell, who promised all helpfullnes to the plantation which lay in them. And sundrie of their freinds the adventurers were so weakened with their losses the last year, by the losse of the ship taken by the Turks, and the loss of their fish, which by reason of the warrs they were forcte to land at Portsmouth, and so came to litle; so as, though their wills were good, yet theyr power was litle. And ther dyed such multituds weekly of the plague, as all trade was dead, and litle money stirring. Yet with much adooe he tooke up 150*li*. (and spent a good deal of it in expences) at 50. per cent. which he bestowed in trading goods and such other most needfull comodities as he knew requiset for their use; and so returned passengers in a fhishing ship, haveing prepared a good way for the compossition that was afterward made.

In the mean time it pleased the Lord to give the plantation peace and health and contented minds, and so to blese ther labours, as they had corne sufficient, (and some to spare to others,) with other foode; neither ever had they any supply of foode but what they first brought with them. After harvest this year, they sende out a boats load of corne 40. or 50. leagues to the eastward, up a river called Kenibeck; it being one of those 2. shalops which their carpenter had built them the year before; for bigger vessell had they none. They had laid a litle deck over her midships to keepe the corne drie, but the men were faine to stand it out all weathers without shelter; and that time of the year begins to growe tempestious. But God preserved them, and gave them good success, for they brought home 700*li.* of beaver, besids some other furrs, having litle or nothing els but this corne, which them selves had raised out of the earth. This viage was made by Mr. Winslow and some of the old standers, for seamen they had none.

Anno Dom: 1626.

About the begining of Aprill they heard of Captain Standish his arrivall, and sent a boat to fetch him home, and the things he had brought. Welcome he was, but the news he broughte was sadd in many regards; not only in regarde of the former losses, before related, which their freinds had suffered, by which some in a maner were undon, others much disabled from doing any further help, and some dead of the plague, but also that Mr. Robinson, their pastor, was dead, which struck them with much sorrow and sadnes, as they had cause. His and their adversaries had been long and continually plotting how they might hinder his coming hither, but the Lord had appointed him a better place; concerning whose death and the maner therof, it will appere by these few lines write to the Gov[r] and Mr. Brewster.

Loving and kind frinds, etc. I know not whether this will ever come to your hands, or miscarie, as other my letters have done; yet in regard of the Lords dealing with us hear, I have had a great desire to write unto you, knowing your desire to bear a parte with us, both in our joyes, and sorrows, as we doe with you. These are therfore to give you to understand, that it hath pleased the Lord to take out of this vaell of tears, your and our loving and faithfull pastor, and my dear and Rev[d] brother, Mr. John Robinson, who was sick some 8. days. He begane to be sick on Saturday in the morning, yet the next day (being the Lords day) he taught us twise. And so the weeke after grew weaker, every day more then other; yet he felt no paine but weaknes all the time of his sicknes. The phisick he tooke wrought kindly in mans judgmente, but he grew weaker every day, feeling litle or no paine, and sensible to the very last. He fell sicke the 22. of Feb: and departed this life the 1. of March.[1] He had a continuall inwarde ague, but free from infection, so that all his freinds came freely to him. And if either prayers, tears, or means, would have saved his life, he had not gone hence. But he having faithfully finished his course, and performed his worke which the Lord had appointed him here to doe, he now resteth with the Lord in eternall hapines. We wanting him and all Church Gov[rs], yet we still (by the mercie of God) continue and hould close togeather, in peace and quietnes; and so hope we shall doe, though we be very weake. Wishing (if such were the will of God) that you and we were againe united togeather in one, either ther or here; but seeing it is the will of the Lord thus to dispose of things, we must labour with patience to rest contented, till it please the Lord otherwise to dispose. For news, is here not much; only as in England we have lost our old king James, who departed this life aboute a month agoe, so here they have lost the old prince, Grave Mourise;[2] who both departed this life since my brother Robinson. And as in England

---

[1] Robinson was buried three days after his death under the pavement of St. Peter's church in Leyden, nearly opposite his house. A tablet in memory of him has been set up on the outer wall of the church, and another on the front of the house now occupying the site of his dwelling in the Kloksteeg, near which many of his congregation also dwelt.

[2] King James I. of England died March 27, 1625. Count Maurice of Nassau, Prince of Orange, stadholder of the Netherlands, second son of William the Silent, died April 23, 1625 (new style, which was at this time followed in Holland). He was succeeded as prince and as stadholder by his brother, Count Frederick Henry.

we have a new-king Charls, of whom ther is great hope, so hear they have made prince Hendrick Generall in his brothers place, etc.   Thus with my love remembred, I take leave and rest,

Your assured loving freind,

ROGER WHITE.[1]

Leyden, Aprill 28.
An°: 1625.

Thus these too great princes, and their pastor, left this world near aboute one time.   Death maks no difference.

He further brought them notice of the death of their anciente freind, Mr. Cush-man, whom the Lord tooke away allso this year, and aboute this time, who was as their right hand with their freinds the adventurers, and for diverce years had done and agitated all their bussines with them to ther great advantage.   He had write to the Gove[r] but some few months before, of the sore sicknes of Mr. James Sherley, who was a cheefe freind to the plantation, and lay at the pointe of death, declaring his love and helpfullnes, in all things; and much bemoned the loss they should have of him, if God should now take him away, as being the stay and life of the whole bussines.   As allso his owne purposs this year to come over, and spend his days with them.   But he that thus write of anothers sicknes, knew not that his owne death was so near. It shows allso that a mans ways are not in his owne power, but in his hands who hath the issues of life and death.   Man may purpose, but God doth dispose.

Their other freinds from Leyden writ many leters to them full of sad laments for ther heavie loss; and though their wills were good to come to them, yet they saw no probabilitie of means, how it might be effected, but concluded (as it were) that all their hopes were cutt of; and many, being aged, begane to drop away by death.

All which things (before related) being well weighed and laied togither, it could not but strick them with great perplexi-

<hr>

[1] The writer was Robinson's brother-in-law, Robinson having married Bridget White, his sister.

tie; and to looke humanly on the state of things as they presented them selves at this time, it is a marvell it did not wholy
discourage them, and sinck them. But they gathered up
their spirits, and the Lord so helped them, whose worke they
had in hand, as now when they were at lowest[1] they begane
to rise againe, and being striped (in a maner) of all humane
helps and hops, he brought things aboute other wise, in his
devine providence, as they were not only upheld and sustained, but their proccedings both honoured and imitated by
others; as by the sequell will more appeare, if the Lord spare
me life and time to declare the same.

Haveing now no fishing busines, or other things to intend,
but only their trading and planting, they sett them selves to
follow the same with the best industrie they could. The
planters finding their corne, what they could spare from ther
necessities, to be a commoditie, (for they sould it at 6s. a
bushell,) used great dilligence in planting the same. And
the Gove[r] and such as were designed to manage the trade,
(for it was retained for the generall good, and none were to
trade in perticuler,) they followed it to the best advantage
they could; and wanting trading goods, they understoode
that a plantation which was at Monhigen, and belonged to
some marchants of Plimoth was to breake up, and diverse
usefull goods was ther to be sould; the Gove[r] and Mr. Winslow
tooke a boat and some hands and went thither. But Mr.
David Thomson, who lived at Pascataway,[2] understanding
their purpose, tooke oppertunitie to goe with them, which was
some hinderance to them both; for they, perceiving their
joynte desires to buy, held their goods at higher rates; and
not only so, but would not sell a parcell of their trading goods,
excepte they sould all. So, lest they should further prejudice
one an other, they agreed to buy all, and devid them equally
between them. They bought allso a parcell of goats, which
they distributed at home as they saw neede and occasion, and

<hr>

[1] "Note." (Br.)   [2] See p. 164, and note 1.

tooke corne for them of the people, which gave them good
content. Their moyety of the goods came to above 400*li*.
starling. Ther was allso that spring a French ship cast away
at Sacadahock, in which were many Biscaie ruggs and other
commodities, which were falen into these mens hands, and
some other fisher men at Damerins-cove, which were allso
bought in partnership, and made their parte arise to above
500*li*. This they made shift to pay for, for the most part,
with the beaver and comodities they had gott the winter before, and what they had gathered up that somer. Mr. Thomson having some things overcharged him selfe, desired they
would take some of his, but they refused except he would let
them have his French goods only; and the marchant (who
was one of Bristol) would take their bill for to be paid the
next year. They were both willing, so they became ingaged
for them and tooke them. By which means they became very
well furnished for trade; and tooke of therby some other ingagments which lay upon them, as the money taken up by
Captaine Standish, and the remains of former debts. With
these goods, and their corne after harvest, they gott good
store of trade, so as they were enabled to pay their ingagements
against the time, and to get some cloathing for the people, and
had some comodities before hand. But now they begane to
be envied, and others wente and fild the Indeans with corne,
and beat downe the prise, giveing them twise as much as they
had done, and under traded them in other comodities allso.

This year they sent Mr. Allerton into England, and gave
him order to make a composition with the adventurers, upon
as good termes as he could (unto which some way had ben
made the year before by Captaine Standish); but yet injoyned
him not to conclud absolutly till they knew the termes, and
had well considered of them; but to drive it to as good an
issew as he could, and referr the conclusion to them. Also
they gave him a commission under their hands and seals to
take up some money, provided it exeeded not such a summe

specified, for which they engaged them selves, and gave him order how to lay out the same for the use of the plantation.

And finding they ranne a great hazard to goe so long viages in a smale open boat, espetialy the winter season, they begane to thinke how they might gett a small pinass; as for the reason afforesaid, so also because others had raised the prise with the Indeans above the halfe of what they had formerly given, so as in such a boat they could not carry a quantity sufficient to answer their ends. They had no ship-carpenter amongst them, neither knew how to get one at presente; but they having an ingenious man that was a house carpenter, who also had wrought with the ship carpenter (that was dead) when he built their boats, at their request he put forth him selfe to make a triall that way of his skill; and tooke one of the bigest of ther shalops and sawed her in the midle, and so lenthened her some 5. or 6. foote, and strengthened her with timbers, and so builte her up, and laid a deck on her; and so made her a conveniente and wholsome vessell, very fitt and comfortable for their use, which did them servise 7. years after; and they gott her finished, and fitted with sayles and anchors, the insuing year. And thus passed the affairs of this year.

Anno Dom: 1627.

AT the usuall season of the coming of ships Mr. Allerton returned, and brought some usfull goods with him, according to the order given him. For upon his commission he tooke up 200*li.* which he now got at 30. per cent. The which goods they gott safly home, and well conditioned, which was much to the comfort and contente of the plantation. He declared unto them, allso, how, with much adoe and no small trouble, he had made a composition with the adventurers, by the help of sundrie of their faithfull freinds ther, who had allso tooke much pains ther about. The agreement or bargen he had brought a draught of, with a list of ther names ther too annexed, drawne by the best counsell of law they could get, to make it firme. The heads wherof I shall here inserte.

To all Christian people, greeting, etc. Whereas at a meeting the 26. of October last past, diverse and sundrie persons, whose names to the one part of these presents are subscribed in a schedule hereunto annexed, Adventurers to New-Plimoth in New-England in America, were contented and agreed, in consideration of the sume of one thousand and eight hundred pounds sterling to be paid, (in maner and forme folling,) to sell, and make sale of all and every the stocks, shares, lands, marchandise, and chatles, what soever, to the said adventurers, and other ther fellow adventurers to New Plimoth aforesaid, any way accruing, or belonging to the generalitie of the said adventurers aforesaid; as well by reason of any sume or sumes of money, or marchandise, at any time heretofore adventured or disbursed by them, or other wise howsoever; for the better expression and setting forth of which said agreemente, the parties to these presents subscribing, doe for them selves severally, and as much as in them is, grant, bargan, alien, sell, and transfere all and every the said shares, goods, lands, marchandice, and chatles to them belonging as aforesaid, unto Isaack Alerton, one of the planters resident at Plimoth afforesaid, assigned, and sent over as agente for the rest of the planters ther, and to such other planters at Plimoth afforesaid as the said Isack, his heirs, or assignes, at his or ther arrivall, shall by writing or otherwise thinke fitte to joyne or partake in the premisses, their heirs, and assignes, in as large, ample, and beneficiall maner and forme, to all intents and purposes, as the said subscribing adventurers here could or may doe, or performe. All which stocks, shares, lands, etc. to the said adven: in severallitie alloted, apportioned, or any way belonging, the said adven: doe warrant and defend unto the said Isaack Allerton, his heirs and assignes, against them, their heirs and assignes, by these presents. And therfore the said Isaack Allerton doth, for him, his heirs and assigns, covenant, promise, and grant too and with the adven: whose names are here unto subscribed, ther heirs, etc. well and truly to pay, or cause to be payed, unto the said adven: or 5. of them which were, at that meeting afforsaid, nominated and deputed, viz. John Pocock, John Beachamp, Robart Keane, Edward Base, and James Sherley, marchants, their heirs, etc. too and for the use of the generallitie of them, the sume of 1800*li*. of lawfull money of England, at the place appoynted for the receipts of money, on the west side of the Royall Exchaing in London, by 200*li*. yearly, and every year, on the feast of St.

Migchell,[1] the first paiment to be made An°: 1628, etc. Allso the said Isaack is to indeavor to procure and obtaine from the planters of N. P. aforesaid, securitie, by severall obligations, or writings obligatory, to make paiment of the said sume of 1800*li*. in forme afforsaid, according to the true meaning of these presents. In testimonie wherof to this part of these presents remaining with the said Isaack Allerton, the said sub-scribing adven: have sett to their names, etc.[2] And to the other part remaining with the said adven: the said Isaack Allerton hath subscribed his name, the 15. Nov^br. An°: 1626. in the 2. year of his Majesties raigne.

This agreemente was very well liked of, and approved by all the plantation, and consented unto; though they knew not well how to raise the payment and discharge their other in-gagements, and supply the yearly wants of the plantation, seeing they were forced for their necessities to take up money or goods at so high intrests. Yet they undertooke it, and 7. or 8. of the cheefe of the place became joyntly bound for the paimente of this 1800*li*. (in the behalfe of the rest) at the severall days. In which they rane a great adventure, as their present state stood, having many other heavie burthens all-

---

[1] Michaelmas, September 29.

[2] Below are the names of the adventurers subscribed to this paper, taken from Bradford's letter-book, in the *Collections of the Massachusetts Historical Society*, first series, III. 48.

John White,	Samuel Sharpe,	Thomas Hudson,
John Pocock,	Robert Holland,	Thomas Andrews,
Robert Kean,	James Sherley,	Thomas Ward,
Edward Bass,	Thomas Mott,	Fria. Newbald,
William Hobson,	Thomas Fletcher,	Thomas Heath,
William Penington,	Timothy Hatherly,	Joseph Tilden,
William Quarles,	Thomas Brewer,	William Perrin,
Daniel Poynton,	John Thorned,	Eliza Knight,
Richard Andrews,	Myles Knowles,	Thomas Coventry,
Newman Rookes,	William Collier,	Robert Allden,
Henry Browning,	John Revell,	Lawrence Anthony,
Richard Wright,	Peter Gudburn,	John Knight,
John Ling,	Emnu. Alltham,	Matthew Thornhill
Thomas Goffe,	John Beauchamp,	Thomas Millsop.

To this list Dr. Azel Ames, *The Mayflower and Her Log*, p. 58, suggests that we may perhaps add, as belonging to the original number, the names of William Greene, Christopher Martin, William Mullens, Edward Pickering, John Pierce, William Thomas, John White, John Wincob and Richard Wright.

ready upon them, and all things in an uncertaine condition amongst them. So the next returne it was absolutely confirmed on both sids, and the bargen fairly ingrossed in partchmente and in many things put into better forme, by the advice of the learnedest counsell they could gett; and least any forfeiture should fall on the whole for none paimente at any of the days, it rane thus: to forfite 30s. a weeke if they missed the time; and was concluded under their hands and seals, as may be seen at large by the deed it selfe.

Now though they had some untowarde persons mixed amongst them from the first, which came out of England, and more afterwards by some of the adventurers, as freindship or other affections led them,—though sundrie were gone, some for Virginia, and some to other places,—yet diverse were still mingled amongst them, about whom the Gove^r and counsell with other of ther cheefe freinds had serious consideration, how to setle things in regard of this new bargen or purchas made, in respecte of the distribution of things both for the presente and future. For the present, excepte peace and union were preserved, they should be able to doe nothing, but indanger to over throw all, now that other tyes and bonds were taken away. Therfore they resolved, for sundrie reasons, to take in all amongst them, that were either heads of families, or single yonge men, that were of abillity, and free, (and able to governe them selvs with meete descretion, and their affairs, so as to be helpfull in the comone-welth,) into this partnership or purchass. First, they considered that they had need of men and strength both for defence and carrying on of bussinesses. 2^{ly}, most of them had borne ther parts in former miseries and wants with them, and therfore (in some sort) but equall to partake in a better condition, if the Lord be pleased to give it. But cheefly they saw not how peace would be preserved without so doing, but danger and great disturbance might grow to their great hurte and prejudice other wise. Yet they resolved to keep such a mean in distribution of lands, and other courses, as should not hinder their growth in others coming to them.

So they caled the company togeather, and conferred with them, and came to this conclusion, that the trade should be managed as before, to help to pay the debts; and all such persons as were above named should be reputed and inrouled for purchasers; single free men to have a single share, and every father of a familie to be alowed to purchass so many shares as he had persons in his family; that is to say, one for him selfe, and one for his wife, and for every child that he had living with him, one. As for servants, they had none, but what either their maisters should give them out of theirs, or their deservings should obtaine from the company afterwards. Thus all were to be cast into single shares according to the order abovesaid; and so every one was to pay his part according to his proportion towards the purchass, and all other debts. what the profite of the trade would not reach too; viz. a single man for a single share, a maister of a famalie for so many as he had. This gave all good contente. And first accordingly the few catle which they had were devided,[1] which arose to this proportion; a cowe to 6. persons or shars, and 2. goats to the same, which were first equalised for age and goodnes, and then lotted for; single persons consorting with others, as they thought good, and smaler familys likwise; and swine though more in number, yet by the same rule. Then they agreed that every person or share should have 20. acres of land devided unto them, besids the single acres they had allready; and they appoynted were to begin first on the one side of the towne, and how farr to goe; and then on the other side in like maner; and so to devid it by lotte; and appointed sundrie by name to doe it, and tyed them to certaine ruls to proceed by; as that they should only lay out settable or tillable land, at least such of it as should butt on the water side, (as the most they were to lay out did,) and pass by the rest as refuse and

[1] For the division of cattle, see *Plymouth Colony Records*, XII. 9.

commune; and what they judged fitte should be so taken. And they were first to agree of the goodnes and fitnes of it before the lott was drawne, and so it might as well prove some of ther owne, as an other mans; and this course they were to hould throwout. But yet seekeing to keepe the people to-gither, as much as might be, they allso agreed upon this order, by mutuall consente, before any lots were cast: that whose lotts soever should fall next the towne, or most conveninte for nearnes, they should take to them a neigboure or tow, whom they best liked; and should suffer them to plant corne with them for 4. years; and afterwards they might use as much of theirs for as long time, if they would. Allso every share or 20. acers was to be laid out 5. acres in breadth by the water side, and 4. acres in lenght, excepting nooks and corners, which were to be measured as they would bear to best advantage. But no meadows were to be laid out at all, nor were not of many years after, because they were but streight of meadow grounds; and if they had bene now given out, it would have hindred all addition to them afterwards; but every season all were appoynted wher they should mowe, according to the pro-portion of catle they had. This distribution gave generally good contente, and setled mens minds. Also they gave the Gove^r and 4. or 5. of the spetiall men amongst them, the houses they lived in; the rest were valued and equalised at an in-diferent rate, and so every man kept his owne, and he that had a better alowed some thing to him that had a worse, as the vaulation wente.

Ther is one thing that fell out in the begining of the winter before, which I have refferred to this place, that I may handle the whole matter togeither. Ther was a ship, with many pas-sengers in her and sundrie goods, bound for Virginia.[1]   They

[1] A vessel bound to Virginia was wrecked on Cape Cod in the winter of 1626-1627, called according to tradition the *Sparrow-Hawk*. She was aban-doned and finally buried by the sand at a place which has been known since as "Old Ship Harbor." She was occasionally exposed by storms at sufficiently short intervals of time to become a familiar object to generation after generation.

had lost them selves at sea, either by the insufficiencie of the maister, or his ilnes; for he was sick and lame of the scurvie, so that he could but lye in the cabin dore, and give direction; and it should seeme was badly assisted either with mate or mariners; or else the fear and unrulines of the passengers were such, as they made them stear a course betweene the south-west and the norwest, that they might fall with some land, what soever it was they cared not. For they had been 6. weeks at sea, and had no water, nor beere, nor any woode left, but had burnt up all their emptie caske; only one of the company had a hogshead of wine or 2. which was allso allmost spente, so as they feared they should be starved at sea, or con-sumed with diseases, which made them rune this desperate course. But it plased God that though they came so neare the shoulds of Cap-Codd or else ran stumbling over them in the night, they knew not how, they came right before a small blind harbore, that lyes about the midle of Manamoyake Bay, to the southward of Cap-Codd,[1] with a small gale of wind; and about high water toucht upon a barr of sand that lyes before it, but had no hurte, the sea being smoth; so they laid out an anchore. But towards the evening the wind sprunge up at sea, and was so rough, as broake their cable, and beat them over the barr into the harbor, wher they saved their lives and goods, though much were hurte with salt water; for with beating they had sprung the but end of a planke or too, and beat out ther occome;[2] but they were soone over, and ran on a drie flate within the harbor, close by a beach; so at low water they gatt out their goods on drie shore, and dried those that were wette, and saved most of their things without any great loss; neither was the ship much hurt, but shee might be mended, and made servisable againe. But though they were not a litle glad that they had thus saved their lives, yet when

In 1863 she became sufficiently exposed to admit of the removal of her timbers, and she may now be seen in Pilgrim Hall, Plymouth, where she has been set up.

[1] Somewhere in Chatham; but the outline of this sandy coast has greatly changed in 280 years.	Oakum

they had a litle refreshed them selves, and begane to thinke
on their condition, not knowing wher they were, nor what
they should doe, they begane to be strucken with sadnes.
But shortly after they saw some Indians come to them in
canows, which made them stand upon their gard. But when
they heard some of the Indeans speake English unto them,
they were not a litle revived, especially when they heard them
demand if they were the Gove^r of Plimoths men, or freinds;
and that they would bring them to the English houses, or
carry their letters.

They feasted these Indeans, and gave them many giftes;
and sente 2. men and a letter with them to the Gove^r, and did
intreat him to send a boat unto them, with some pitch, and
occume, and spiks, with divers other necessaries for the mending of ther ship (which was recoverable). Allso they besought
him to help them with some corne and sundrie other things
they wanted, to enable them to make their viage to Virginia;
and they should be much bound to him, and would make satisfaction for any thing they had, in any comodities they had
abord. After the Gove^r was well informed by the messengers
of their condition, he caused a boate to be made ready, and
such things to be provided as they write for; and because
others were abroad upon trading, and such other affairs, as
had been fitte to send unto them, he went him selfe, and allso
carried some trading comodities, to buy them corne of the
Indeans. It was no season of the year to goe withoute the
Cape, but understanding wher the ship lay, he went into the
bottom of the bay, on the inside, and put into a crick called
Naumskachett,[1] wher it is not much above 2. mile over land
to the bay wher they were, wher he had the Indeans ready to
cary over any thing to them. Of his arrivall they were very
glad, and received the things to mend ther ship, and other
necessaries. Allso he bought them as much corne as they

[1] Naumskachett Creek is on the inside of Cape Cod between Brewster and
Orleans.

would have; and wheras some of their sea-men were rune
away amonge the Indeans, he procured their returne to the
ship, and so left them well furnished and contented, being very
thankfull for the curtesies they receaved. But after the
Gove^r thus left them, he went into some other harbors ther
aboute and loaded his boat with corne, which he traded, and
so went home. But he had not been at home many days, but
he had notice from them, that by the violence of a great storme,
and the bad morring of their ship (after she was mended) she
was put a shore, and so beatten and shaken as she was now
wholy unfitte to goe to sea. And so their request was that
they might have leave to repaire to them, and soujourne with
them, till they could have means to convey them selves to
Virginia; and that they might have means to transport their
goods, and they would pay for the same, or any thing els wher
with the plantation should releeve them. Considering their
distres, their requests were granted, and all helpfullnes done
unto them; their goods transported, and them selves and
goods sheltered in their houses as well as they could.

The cheefe amongst these people was one Mr. Fells and
Mr. Sibsie, which had many servants belonging unto them,
many of them being Irish. Some others ther were that had
a servante or 2. a peece; but the most were servants, and
such as were ingaged to the former persons, who allso had the
most goods. Affter they were hither come, and some thing
setled, the maisters desired some ground to imploye ther servants upon; seing it was like to be the latter end of the year
before they could have passage for Virginia, and they had now
the winter before them; they might clear some ground, and
plant a crope (seeing they had tools, and necessaries for the
same) to help to bear their charge, and keep their servants in
imployment; and if they had oppertunitie to departe before
the same was ripe, they would sell it on the ground. So they
had ground appointed them in convenient places, and Fells
and some other of them raised a great deall of corne, which they

sould at their departure. This Fells, amongst his other servants had a maid servante which kept his house and did his
household affairs, and by the intimation of some that belonged
unto him, he was suspected to keep her, as his concubine; and
both of them were examined ther upon, but nothing could be
proved, and they stood upon their justification; so with ad-
monition they were dismiste. But afterward it appeard she
was with child, so he gott a small boat, and ran away with her,
for fear of punishmente. First he went to Cap-Anne, and
after into the bay of the Massachussets, but could get no passage, and had like to have been cast away; and was forst to
come againe and submite him selfe; but they pact him away
and those that belonged unto him by the first oppertunitie,
and dismiste all the rest as soone as could, being many untoward people amongst them; though ther were allso some that
caried them selves very orderly all the time they stayed. And
the plantation had some benefite by them, in selling them
corne and other provisions of food for cloathing; for they had
of diverse kinds, as cloath, perpetuanes, and other stuffs,
besids hose, and shoes, and such like commodities as the
planters stood in need of. So they both did good, and
received good one from another; and a cuple of barks caried
them away at the later end of sommer. And sundrie of them
have acknowledged their thankfullness since from Virginia.

That they might the better take all convenient opportunitie
to follow their trade, both to maintaine them selves, and to
disingage them of those great sumes which they stood charged
with, and bound for, they resoloved to build a smale pinass at
Manamet,[1] a place 20. mile from the plantation, standing on
the sea to the southward of them, unto which, by an other
creeke on this side, they could cary their goods, within 4. or 5.
miles, and then transport them over land to their vessell; and
so avoyd the compasing of Cap-Codd, and those deangerous
shoulds, and so make any vioage to the southward in much

_____
[1] The place referred to lies near Buzzard's Bay, south of Plymouth.

shorter time, and with farr less danger. Also for the saftie of their vessell and goods, they builte a house their, and kept some servants, who also planted corne, and reared some swine, and were allwayes ready to goe out with the barke when ther was occasion. All which tooke good effecte, and turned to their profite.

They now sent (with the returne of the ships) Mr. Allerton againe into England, giveing him full power, under their hands and seals, to conclude the former bargaine with the adventurers; and sent ther bonds for the paimente of the money. Allso they sent what beaver they could spare to pay some of their ingagementes, and to defray his chargs; for those deepe interests still kepte them low. Also he had order to procure a patente for a fitt trading place in the river of Kenebec; for being emulated both by the planters at Pascataway and other places to the eastward of them, and allso by the fishing ships, which used to draw much profite from the Indeans of those parts, they threatened to procure a grante, and shutte them out from thence; espetially after they saw them so well furnished with commodities, as to carie the trade from them. They thought it but needfull to prevente such a thing, at least that they might not be excluded from free trade ther, wher them selves had first begune and discovered the same, and brought it to so good effecte. This year allso they had letters, and messengers from the Dutch-plantation, sent unto them from the Govr ther, writen both in Dutch and French. The Dutch had traded in these southerne parts, diverse years before they came; but they begane no plantation hear till 4. or 5. years after their coming, and here begining.[1] Ther letters were as followeth. It being their maner to be full of complementall titles.

Eedele, Eerenfeste Wyse Voorsinnige Heeren, den Goveerneur, ende Raeden in Nieu-Pliemuen residerende; onse seer Goede vrinden.

Den directeur ende Raed van Nieu-Nederlande, wensen uwe Edn:

---

[1] See p. 172, note 1.

eerenfesten, ende wijse voorsinnige geluck salichitt [gelukzaligheid?], In
Christi Jesu onsen Heere; met goede voorspoet, ende gesonthijt, naer
Siele, ende Lichaem.   Amen.[1]

The rest I shall render in English, leaving out the repeti-
tion of superfluous titles.

We have often before this wished for an opportunitie or an occasion
to congratulate you, and your prosperous and praise-worthy undertake-
ings, and Goverment of your colony ther.   And the more, in that we also
have made a good begining to pitch the foundation of a collonie hear;
and seeing our native countrie lyes not farr from yours, and our fore-
fathers (diverse hundred years agoe) have made and held frendship and
alliance with your ancestours, as sufficiently appears by the old contractes,
and entrecourses,[2] confirmed under the hands of kings and princes, in the
pointe of warr and trafick; as may be seene and read by all the world in
the old chronakles.   The which are not only by the king now reigning
confirmed, but it hath pleased his majesty, upon mature deliberation, to
make a new covenante,[3] (and to take up armes,) with the States Generall
of our dear native country, against our commone enemie the Spaniards,
who seeke nothing else but to usurpe and overcome other Christian kings
and princes lands, that so he might obtaine and possess his pretended
monarchie over all Christendom; and so to rule and command, after his
owne pleasure, over the consciences of so many hundred thousand sowles,
which God forbid.

And also seeing it hath some time since been reported unto us, by
some of our people, that by occasion came so farr northward with their
shalop, and met with sundry of the Indeans, who tould them that they
were within halfe a days journey of your plantation, and offered ther
service to cary letters unto you; therfore we could not forbear to salute
you with these few lines, with presentation of our good will and servise
unto you, in all frendly-kindnes and neighbourhood.   And if it so fall
out that any goods that comes to our hands from our native countrie, may
be serviceable unto you, we shall take our selves bound to help and ac-

---

[1] "Noble, worshipful, wise, and prudent Lords, the Governor and Council-
lors residing in New Plymouth, our very good friends:—The Director and Council
of New Netherland wish to your Lordships, worshipful, wise, and prudent,
happiness in Christ Jesus our Lord, with prosperity and health, in soul and
body.   Amen."

[2] *Intercursus* was a usual Latin word for the Anglo-Dutch commercial
treaties; *e. g.*, the Intercursus Magnus of 1496 between Henry VII. of England
and the Duke of Burgundy as Count of Flanders.

[3] The Treaty of Southampton, September 8, 1625.

commadate you ther with; either for beaver or any other wares or marchandise that you should be pleased to deale for.   And if in case we have
no commodity at present that may give you contente, if you please to sell
us any beaver, or otter, or such like comodities as may be usefull for us,
for ready money, and let us understand therof by this bearer in writing,
(whom we have apoynted to stay 3. or 4. days for your answer,) when we
understand your minds therin, we shall depute one to deale with you, at
such place as you shall appointe.   In the mean time we pray the Lord to take
you, our honoured good freinds and neighbours, into his holy protection.

By the appointment of the Govr and Counsell, etc.

Isaak de Rasier, Secretaris.[1]

From the Manhatas, in the fort Amsterdam,
March 9. An°: 1627.

To this they returned answer as followeth, on the other
side.

To the Honoured, etc.

The Gove^r and Counsell of New-Plim: wisheth, etc.   We have
received your leters, etc. wherin appeareth your good wills and frendship
towards us; but is expresed with over high titls, more then belongs to us,
or is meete for us to receive.   But for your good will, and congratulations
of our prosperitie in these smale beginings of our poore colonie, we are
much bound unto you, and with many thanks doe acknowledg the same;
taking it both for a great honour done unto us, and for a certaine testimoney
of your love and good neighbourhood.

Now these are further to give your Wor^{pps} to understand, that it is
to us no smale joye to hear, that his majestie hath not only bene pleased
to confirme that ancient amitie, aliance, and frendship, and other contracts, formerly made and ratified by his predecessors of famous memorie,
but hath him selfe (as you say) strengthened the same with a new-union
the better to resist the prid of that commone enemy the Spaniard, from
whose cruelty the Lord keep us both, and our native countries.   Now
forasmuch as this is sufficiente to unite us togeather in love and good
neighbourhood, in all our dealings, yet are many of us further obliged,
by the good and curteous entreaty which we have found in your countrie;
haveing lived ther many years, with freedome, and good contente, as also
many of our freinds doe to this day; for which we, and our children after us,

---

[1] Isaac de Rasières had come out to New Netherland in 1626, and remained
there two years as chief commissary and secretary of the colony under Director
Minuit.   The date of his letter is shown by Bradford's letter-book to be a new-
style date, after the practice of the Dutch.

are bound to be thankfull to your Nation, and shall never forgett the same, but shall hartily desire your good and prosperity, as our owne, for ever.

Likwise for your freindly tender, and offer to acommodate and help us with any comodities or marchandise you have, or shall come to you, either for beaver, otters, or other wares, it is to us very acceptable, and we doubte not but in short time we may have profitable commerce and trade togeather.[1]   But for this year we are fully supplyed with all necessaries, both for cloathing and other things; but hereafter it is like we shall deale with you, if your rates be reasonable.   And therfore when you please to send to us againe by any of yours, we desire to know how you will take beaver, by the pounde, and otters, by the skine; and how you will deale per cent. for other comodities, and what you can furnishe us with.   As likwise what other commodities from us may be acceptable unto you, as tobaco, fish, corne, or other things, and what prises you will give, etc.

Thus hoping that you will pardon and excuse us for our rude and imperfecte writing in your language, and take it in good parte, because for wante of use we cannot so well express that we understand, nor hapily understand every thing so fully as we should.   And so we humbly pray the Lord for his mercie sake, that he will take both us and you into his keeping and gratious protection.

By the Gove[r] and Counsell of New-Plimoth,

Your Wor[pps] very good freinds and neigbours, etc.

New-Plim: March 19.

After this ther was many passages betweene them both by letters and other entercourse;[2] and they had some profitable com-

[1] Bradford here, as is shown by his letter-book, *Collections of the Massachusetts Historical Society*, III. 52, omits the following important passage which was in his original letter: "But you may please to understand that we are but one particular colony or plantation in this land, there being divers others besides, unto whom it hath pleased those Honorable Lords of his Majesty's Council for New England to grant the like commission, and ample privileges to them (as to us) for their better profit and subsistence; namely to expulse, or make prize of any, either strangers or other English, which shall attempt either to trade or plant within their limits (without their special license and commission) which extend to forty degrees.   Yet for our parts, we shall not go about to molest or trouble you in anything, but continue all good neighborhood and correspondence as far as we may; only we desire that you would forbear to trade with the natives in this bay, and river of Naragansett and Sowames, which is (as it were) at our doors: The which if you do, we think no other English will go about any way to trouble or hinder you; which otherwise are resolved to solicit his Majesty for redress, if otherwise they cannot help themselves."

[2] Portions of this correspondence appear in Bradford's letter-book, *Coll. Mass. Hist. Soc.*, III. 53–55.

merce togither for diverce years, till other occasions interrupted
the same, as may happily appear afterwards, more at large.

Before they sent Mr. Allerton away for England this year,
the Gove^r and some of their cheefe freinds had serious consideration, not only how they might discharge those great ingagments, which lay so heavily upon them, and is affore
mentioned but also how they might (if possiblie they could)
devise means to help some of their freinds and breethren of
Leyden over unto them, who desired so much to come to them,
and they desired as much their company.   To effecte which,
they resolved to rune a high course, and of great adventure,
not knowing otherwise how to bring it aboute.   Which was
to hire the trade of the company for certaine years, and in
that time to undertake to pay that 1800li. and all the rest of
the debts that then lay upon the plantation, which was aboute
some 600li. more; and so to set them free, and returne the
trade to the generalitie againe at the end of the terme.   Upon
which resolution they called the company togeither, and made
it clearly appear unto all what their debts were, and upon what
terms they would undertake to pay them all in such a time,
and sett them clear.   But their other ends they were faine to
keepe secrete, haveing only privatly acquaynted some of their
trusty freinds therwith; which were glad of the same, but
doubted how they would be able to performe it.   So after some
agitation of the thing with the company, it was yeelded unto,
and the agreemente made upon the conditions following.

Articles of agreemente betweene the collony of New-Plimmoth of the
    one partie, and William Bradford, Captein Myles Standish, Isaack
    Allerton, etc. one the other partie; and shuch others as they shall
    thinke good to take as partners and undertakers with them,[1] con-
    cerning the trade for beaver and other furrs and comodities, etc.;
    made July, 1627.

[1] The names of the undertakers were William Bradford, Myles Standish,
Isaac Allerton, Edward Winslow, William Brewster, John Howland, John Alden,
and Thomas Prence of the colony and James Sherley, John Beauchamp, Richard
Andrews, and Timothy Hatherley of London.

First, it is agreed and covenanted betweexte the said parties, that the afforsaid William Bradford, Captain Myles Standish, and Isaack Allerton, etc. have undertaken, and doe by these presents, covenante and agree to pay, discharge, and acquite the said collony of all the debtes both due for the purchass, or any other belonging to them, at the day of the date of these presents.

Secondly, the above-said parties are to have and freely injoye the pinass latly builte, the boat at Manamett, and the shalop, called the Bass-boat, with all other implements to them belonging, that is in the store of the said company; with all the whole stock of furrs, fells, beads, corne, wampampeak,[1] hatchets, knives, etc. that is now in the storre, or any way due unto the same uppon accounte.

3ly. That the above said parties have the whole trade to them selves, their heires and assignes, with all the privileges therof, as the said collonie doth now, or may use the same, for 6. full years, to begine the last of September next insuing.

4ly.   In furder consideration of the discharge of the said debtes, every severall purchaser doth promise and covenante yearly to pay, or cause to be payed, to the above said parties, during the full terme of the said 6. years, 3. bushells of corne, or 6li. of tobaco, at the undertakers choyse.

5ly.   The said undertakers shall dureing the afforesaid terme bestow 50li. per annum, in hose and shoese, to be brought over for the collonies use, to be sould unto them for corne at 6s. per bushell.

6ly.   That at the end of the said terme of 6. years, the whole trade shall returne to the use and benefite of the said collonie, as before.

Lastly, if the afforesaid undertakers, after they have aquainted their freinds in England with these covenants, doe (upon the first returne) resolve to performe them, and undertake to discharge the debtes of the said collony, according to the true meaning and intente of these presents, then they are (upon such notice given) to stand in full force; otherwise all things to remaine as formerly they were, and a true accounte to be given to the said collonie, of the disposing of all things according to the former order.

Mr. Allerton carried a coppy of this agreemente with him into England, and amongst other his instructions had order given him to deale with some of their speciall freinds, to joyne with them in this trade upon the above recited conditions; as allso to imparte their further ends that moved them to take this course, namly, the helping over of some of their freinds

[1] See page 235, note 1, *post.*

from Leyden, as they should be able; in which if any of them would joyne with them they should thankfully acceptt of their love and partnership herein. And with all (by their letters) gave them some grounds of their hops of the accomplishmente of these things with some advantage.

Anno Dom: 1628.

AFTER Mr. Allertons arivall in England, he aquainted them with his comission and full power to conclude the forementioned bargan and purchas; upon the veiw wherof, and the delivery of the bonds for the paymente of the money yearly, (as is before mentioned,) it was fully concluded, and a deede[1] fairly ingrossed in partchmente was delivered him, under their hands and seals confirming the same. Morover he delte with them aboute other things according to his instructions. As to admitt some of these their good freinds into this purchass if they pleased, and to deale with them for moneys at better rates, etc. Touching which I shall hear inserte a letter of Mr. Sherleys, giving light to what followed therof, writ to the Gov[r] as followeth.

Sr: I have received yours of the 26. of May by Mr. Gibs, and Mr. Goffe, with the barrell of otter skins, according to the contents; for which I got a bill of store, and so tooke them up, and sould them togeather at 78*li*. 12*s*. sterling; and since, Mr. Allerton hath received the money, as will apear by the accounte. It is true (as you write) that your ingagments are great, not only the purchass, but you are yet necessitated to take up the stock you work upon; and that not at 6. or 8. p[r] cent. as it is here let out, but at 30. 40. yea, and some at 50. p[r] cent. which, were not your gaines great, and Gods blessing on your honest indeaours more then ordinarie, it could not be that you should longe subsiste in the maintaining of, and upholding of your worldly affaires. And this your honest and discreete agente, Mr. Allerton, hath seriously considered, and deeply laid to mind, how to ease you of it. He tould me you were contented to accepte of me and some few others, to joyne with you in the purchass, as partners; for which I kindly thanke you and all the rest, and doe willingly accepte of it. And though absente, shall willingly be at shuch charge as

---

[1] "Nov. 6, 1627. Page 238." (Note by Bradford, referring to the page of his manuscript. See under 1641, *post*.)

you and the rest shall thinke meete; and this year am contented to forbear my former 50*li*. and 2. years increase for the venture, both which now makes it 80*li*. without any bargaine or condition for the profite, you (I mean the generalitie) stand to the adventure, outward, and homeward. I have perswaded Mr. Andrews and Mr. Beachamp to doe the like, so as you are eased of the high rate, you were at the other 2. yeares; I say we leave it freely to your selves to alow us what you please, and as God shall blesse. What course I rune, Mr. Beachamp desireth to doe the same; and though he have been or seemed somwhat harsh heretofore, yet now you shall find he is new moulded. I allso see by your letter, you desire I should be your agente or factore hear. I have ever found you so faithfull, honest, and upright men, as I have even resolved with my selfe (God assisting me) to doe you all the good lyeth in my power; and therfore if you please to make choyse of so weak a man, both for abillities and body, to performe your bussines, I promise (the Lord enabling me) to doe the best I can according to those abillities he hath given me; and wherin I faile, blame your selves, that you made no better choyce. Now, because I am sickly, and we are all mortall, I have advised Mr. Allerton to joyne Mr. Beachamp with me in your deputation, which I conceive to be very necessary and good for you; your charge shall be no more, for it is not your salarie maks me undertake your bussines. Thus comending you and yours, and all Gods people, unto the guidance and protection of the Allmightie, I ever rest,

Your faithfull loving freind,

London, Nov. 17. 1628.   JAMES SHERLEY.

Another leter of his, that should have bene placed before:—

We cannot but take notice how the Lord hath been pleased to crosse our proseedings, and caused many disasters to befale us therin. I conceive the only reason to be, we, or many of us, aimed at other ends then Gods glorie; but now I hope that cause is taken away; the bargen being fully concluded, as farr as our powers will reach, and confirmed under our hands and seals, to Mr. Allerton and the rest of his and your copartners. But for my owne parte, I confess as I was loath to hinder the full confirming of it, being the first propounder ther of at our meeting; so on the other side, I was as unwilling to set my hand to the sale, being the receiver of most part of the adventurs, and a second causer of much of the ingagments; and one more threatened, being most envied and aimed at (if they could find any stepe to ground their malice on) then any other whosoever. I profess I know no just cause they ever had, or have, so to doe; neither shall it ever be proved that I have wronged them or any of the adventurers,

wittingly or willingly, one peny in the disbursing of so many pounds in
those 2. years trouble.   No, the sole cause why they maligne me (as I
and others conceived) was that I would not side with them against you,
and the going over of the Leyden people.   But as I then card not, so now
I litle fear what they can doe; yet charge and trouble I know they may
cause me to be at.   And for these reasons, I would gladly have perswaded
the other 4. to have sealed to this bargaine, and left me out, but they
would not; so rather then it should faile, Mr. Alerton having taken so
much pains, I have sealed with the rest; with this proviso and promise
of his, that if any trouble arise hear, you are to bear halfe the charge.
Wherfore now I doubt not but you will give your generallitie good contente,
and setle peace amongst your selves, and peace with the natives; and then
no doubt but the God of Peace will blese your going out and your returning,
and cause all that you sett your hands unto to prosper; the which I shall
ever pray the Lord to grante if it be his blessed will.   Asuredly unless the
Lord be mercifull unto us and the whole land in generall, our estate and
condition is farr worse then yours.   Wherfore if the Lord should send
persecution or trouble hear, (which is much to be feared,) and so should
put into our minds to flye for refuge, I know no place safer then to come
to you, (for all Europ is at varience one with another, but cheefly with us,)
not doubting but to find such frendly entertainmente as shall be honest
and conscionable, notwithstanding what hath latly passed.   For I profess
in the word of an honest man, had it not been to procure your peace and
quiet from some turbulent spirites hear, I would not have sealed to this
last deed; though you would have given me all my adventure and debte
ready downe.   Thus desiring the Lord to blesse and prosper you, I cease
ever resting,

Your faithfull and loving freind,
to my power,

Des: 27.   JAMES SHERLEY.[1]

With this leter they sent a draught of a formall deputation
to be hear sealed and sent back unto them, to authorise them
as their agents, according to what is mentioned in the above
said letter; and because some inconvenience grue therby
afterward I shall here inserte it.

To all to whom these prẽts shall come greeting; know yee that we,
William Bradford, Govr of Plimoth, in N. E. in America, Isaak

[1] The above letter was written on the reverse of a page (154) of the original
manuscript.

Allerton, Myles Standish, William Brewster, and Ed: Winslow, of Plimoth aforesaid, marchants, doe by these presents for us, and in our names, make, substitute, and appointe James Sherley, Goldsmith, and John Beachamp, Salter, citizens of London, our true and lawfull agents, factors, substitutes, and assignes; as well to take and receive all such goods, wares, and marchandise what soever as to our said substitutes or either of them, or to the citie of London, or other place of the Relme of Engl: shall be sente, transported, or come from us or any of us, as allso to vend, sell, barter, or exchaing the said goods, wares, and marchandise so from time to time to be sent to such person or persons upon credite, or other wise in such maner as to our said agents and factors joyently, or to either of them severally shall seeme meete.   And further we doe make and or-daine our said substituts and assignes joyntly and severally for us, and to our uses, and accounts, to buy and consigne for and to us into New-Engl: aforesaid, such goods and marchandise to be provided here, and to be returned hence, as by our said assignes, or either of them, shall be thought fitt.   And to recover, receive, and demand for us and in our names all such debtes and sumes of money, as now are or hereafter shall be due incidente accruing or belonging to us, or any of us, by any wayes or means; and to acquite, discharge, or compound for any debte or sume of money, which now or hereafter shall be due or oweing by any person or persons to us, or any of us.   And generally for us and in our names to doe, performe, and execute every acte and thing which to our said assignes, or either of them, shall seeme meete to be done in or aboute the premissies, as fully and effectually, to all intents and purposes, as if we or any of us were in person presente.   And whatsoever our said agents and factors joyntly or severally shall doe, or cause to be done, in or aboute the premis-ses, we will and doe, and every of us doth ratifie, alow, and confirme, by these presents.   In wittnes wherof we have here unto put our hands and seals.   Dated 18. Nov^{br} 1628.

This was accordingly confirmed by the above named, and 4. more of the cheefe of them under their hands and seals, and delivered unto them. Also Mr. Allerton formerly had au-thoritie under their hands and seals for the transacting of the former bussines, and taking up of moneys, etc. which still he retained whilst he was imployed in these affaires; they mis-trusting neither him nor any of their freinds faithfullnes, which made them more remisse in looking to shuch acts as had passed under their hands, as necessarie for the time; but letting them rune on to long unminded or recaled, it turned to their harme afterwards, as will appere in its place.

Mr. Allerton having setled all things thus in a good and hopfull way, he made hast to returne in the first of the spring to be hear with their supply for trade, (for the fishermen with whom he came used to sett forth in winter and be here betimes.) He brought a resonable supply of goods for the plantation, and without those great interests as before is noted; and brought an accounte of the beaver sould, and how the money was disposed for goods, and the paymente of other debtes, having paid all debts abroad to others, save to Mr. Sherley, Mr. Beachamp, and Mr. Andrews; from whom likwise he brought an accounte which to them all amounted not to above 400*li*. for which he had passed bonds. Allso he had payed the first paymente for the purchass, being due for this year, viz. 200*li*. and brought them the bonde for the same canselled; so as they now had no more foreine debtes but the abovesaid 400*li*. and odde pownds, and the rest of the yearly purchass monie. Some other debtes they had in the cuntrie, but they were without any intrest, and they had wherwith to discharge them when they were due. To this pass the Lord had brought things for them. Also he brought them further notice that their freinds, the abovenamed, and some others that would joyne with them in the trad and purchass, did intend for to send over to Leyden, for a competente number of them, to be hear the next year without fayle, if the Lord pleased to blesse their journey. He allso brought them a patente for Kenebeck,[1] but it was so straite and ill bounded, as they were faine to renew and inlarge it the next year, as allso that which they had at home, to their great charge, as will after appeare. Hithertoo Mr. Allerton did them good and faithfull service; and well had it been if he had so continued,

---

[1] The Kennebec Purchase of 1628 was better defined in the patent of January 13, 1629/30, which was granted by the Council for New England and covered both the region of New Plymouth and the Kennebec grant.

or els they had now ceased for imploying him any longer thus into England. But of this more afterwards.

Having procured a patente (as is above said) for Kenebeck, they now erected a house up above in the river in the most convenientest place for trade,[1] as they conceived, and furnished the same with commodities for that end, both winter and sommer, not only with corne, but also with such other commodities as the fishermen had traded with them, as coats, shirts, ruggs, and blankets, biskett, pease, prunes, etc.; and what they could not have out of England, they bought of the fishing ships, and so carried on their bussines as well as they could.

This year[2] the Dutch sent againe unto them from their plantation, both kind leterss, and also diverse comodities, as suger, linen cloth, Holand finer and courser stufes, etc. They came up with their barke to Manamete, to their house ther, in which came their Secretarie Rasier;[3] who was accompanied with a noyse of trumpeters, and some other attendants; and desired that they would send a boat for him, for he could not travill so farr over land. So they sent a boat to Manonscussett, and brought him to the plantation, with the cheefe of his company. And after some few days entertainmente, he returned to his barke, and some of them wente with him, and bought sundry of his goods; after which begining thus made, they sente often times to the same place, and had entercourse togeather for diverce years; and amongst other comodities, they vended much tobaco for linen cloath, stuffs, etc., which was a good benefite to the people, till the Virginians found out their plantation. But that which turned most to their profite,

---

[1] Now Augusta, Maine.

[2] The dates in Bradford's letter-book, however, show that the episode occurred in October, 1627.

[3] His account of the visit, a very interesting document, may be found in a letter he wrote to a friend in Holland, printed in the *Collections of the New York Historical Society*, second series, II. 351. Manomet (now Monument) was at the head of Buzzard's Bay; Manonscussett was on the opposite side of the isthmus, on Cape Cod Bay, in the present town of Bourne.

in time, was an entrance into the trade of Wampampeake;[1] for they now bought aboute 50*li*. worth of it of them; and they tould them how vendable it was at their forte Orania;[2] and did perswade them they would find it so at Kenebeck; and so it came to pass in time, though at first it stuck, and it was 2. years before they could put of this small quantity, till the inland people knew of it; and afterwards they could scarce ever gett enough for them, for many years togeather. And so this, with their other provissions, cutt of they trade quite from the fisher-men, and in great part from other of the stragling planters. And strange it was to see the great all-teration it made in a few years among the Indeans them selves; for all the Indeans of these parts, and the Massachus-sets, had none or very litle of it,[3] but the sachems and some spetiall persons that wore a litle of it for ornamente. Only it was made and kepte amonge the Nariganssets, and Pequents, which grew rich and potent by it, and these people were poore and begerly, and had no use of it. Neither did the English of this plantation, or any other in the land, till now that they had knowledg of it from the Dutch, so much as know what it was, much less that it was a comoditie of that worth and valew. But after it grue thus to be a comoditie in these parts, these Indeans fell into it allso, and to learne how to make it; for the

---

[1] The wampumpeake, of which De Rasières brought specimens to Plymouth, was made by the Long Island Indians from the thick quahaug shells and cut in the shape of oblong beads with holes by which they were strung. The wampum made by the Plymouth colonists was evidently made from the common clam-shell, cut in the shape of small button-moulds; a specimen is to be seen in Pil-grim Hall in Plymouth. There are several spots in Plymouth where the soil is filled with small pieces of clam-shells, which may have been the places where the wampum was cut. Wampum became at a later period a legal tender among the colonists, the value of which was from time to time fixed by law. I have seen a specimen of another kind of wampum made apparently of burned white clay, as hard and smooth as porcelain, about three-eighths of an inch in diameter and a quarter of an inch thick, with intervening thin discs of shell. The Indian grave in East Bridgewater in which this specimen was found contained a few bones almost destroyed by decay, and thus suggesting great antiquity.

[2] Fort Aurania, or Orange, was on the site of the present city of Albany.

[3] "Peag." (Br.)

Narigansets doe geather the shells of which they make it from their shors. And it hath now continued a current comoditie aboute this 20. years, and it may prove a drugg in time. In the mean time it maks the Indeans of these parts rich and power full and also prowd therby; and fills them with peeces, powder, and shote, which no laws can restraine, by reasone of the bassnes of sundry unworthy persons, both English, Dutch, and French, which may turne to the ruine of many. Hither-too the Indeans of these parts had no peeces nor other armes but their bowes and arrowes, nor of many years after; nether durst they scarce handle a gune, so much were they affraid of them; and the very sight of one (though out of kilter) was a terrour unto them. But those Indeans to the east parts, which had commerce with the French, got peces of them, and they in the end made a commone trade of it; and in time our English fisher-men, led with the like covetoussnes, followed their example, for their owne gaine; but upon complainte against them, it pleased the kings majestie to prohibite the same by a stricte proclaimation,[1] commanding that no sorte of armes, or munition, should by any of his subjects be traded with them.

Aboute some 3. or 4. years before this time, ther came over one Captaine Wolastone,[2] (a man of pretie parts,) and with him 3. or 4. more of some eminencie, who brought with them a great many servants, with provissions and other implments for to begine a plantation; and pitched them selves in a place within the Massachusets, which they called, after their Captains name, Mount-Wollaston. Amongst whom was one Mr. Morton,[3] who, it should seeme, had some small ad-

[1] Probably the reference is to the proclamation of November 24, 1630, "forbidding disorderly trade with the savages of New England."

[2] Captain Wolastone came over about 1625 with some partners and about thirty servants and began a plantation at what is now Quincy.

[3] Thomas Morton, the celebrated author of the *New English Canaan* (London, 1637), had first visited New England, according to his own statement, in June, 1622 (coming no doubt in the *Charity*), and had been charmed with the region.

venture (of his owne or other mens) amongst them; but had
litle respecte amongst them, and was sleghted by the meanest
servants.   Haveing continued ther some time, and not finding
things to answer their expectations, nor profite to arise as they
looked for, Captaine Wollaston takes a great part of the
sarvants, and transports them to Virginia, wher he puts them
of at good rates, selling their time to other men; and writs
back to one Mr. Rassdall, one of his cheefe partners, and
accounted their marchant, to bring another parte of them to
Verginia likewise, intending to put them of ther as he had
done the rest.   And he, with the consente of the said Rasdall,
appoynted one Fitcher to be his Livetenante, and governe the
remaines of the plantation, till he or Rasdall returned to take
further order theraboute.   But this Morton abovesaid, haveing
more craft then honestie, (who had been a kind of petie-
fogger, of Furnefells Inne,)[1] in the others absence, watches
an oppertunitie, (commons being but hard amongst them,) and
gott some strong drinck and other junkats, and made them a
feast; and after they were merie, he begane to tell them, he
would give them good counsell.   You see (saith he) that many
of your fellows are carried to Virginia; and if you stay till
this Rasdall returne, you will also be carried away and sould
for slaves with the rest.   Therfore I would advise you to thruste
out this Levetenant Fitcher; and I, having a parte in the
plantation, will receive you as my partners and consociats;
so may you be free from service, and we will converse, trad,
plante, and live togeather as equalls, and supporte and protecte one another, or to like effecte.   This counsell was easily
received; so they tooke oppertunitie, and thrust Levetenante
Fitcher out a dores, and would suffer him to come no more
amongst them, but forct him to seeke bread to eate, and other
releefe from his neigbours, till he could gett passage for
England.   After this they fell to great licenciousnes, and led a

---

[1] On the title-page of his book he describes himself as "Thomas Morton, of
Clifford's Inn, Gent."

dissolute life, powering out them selves into all profanenes. And Morton became lord of misrule, and maintained (as it were) a schoole of Athisme. And after they had gott some good into their hands, and gott much by trading with the Indeans, they spent it as vainly, in quaffing and drinking both wine and strong waters in great exsess, and, as some reported, 10*li*. worth in a morning.   They allso set up a May-pole, drinking and dancing aboute it many days togeather, inviting the Indean women, for their consorts, dancing and frisking togither, (like so many fairies, or furies rather,) and worse practises.   As if they had anew revived and celebrated the feasts of the Roman Goddes Flora, or the beasly practieses of the madd Bacchinalians.   Morton likwise (to shew his poetrie) composed sundry rimes and verses, some tending to lasciviousnes, and others to the detraction and scandall of some persons, which he affixed to this idle or idoll May-polle.   They chainged allso the name of their place, and in stead of calling it Mounte Wollaston, they call it Meriemounte, as if this joylity would have lasted ever.   But this continued not long, for after Morton was sent for England, (as follows to be declared,) shortly after came over that worthy gentlman, Mr. John Indecott, who brought over a patent under the broad seall,[1] for the govermente of the Massachusets, who visiting those parts caused that May-polle to be cutt downe, and rebuked them for their profannes, and admonished them to looke ther should be better walking; so they now, or others, changed the name of their place againe, and called it Mounte-Dagon.

Now to maintaine this riotous prodigallitie and profuse excess, Morton, thinking him selfe lawless, and hearing what gaine the French and fisher-men made by trading of peeces, powder, and shotte to the Indeans, he, as the head of this consortship, begane the practise of the same in these parts; and

---

[1] Endicott did not bring over a patent under the broad seal. He was sent over before the royal charter of March 4, 1628/9, was granted.

first he taught them how to use them, to charge, and discharg, and what proportion of powder to give the peece, according to the sise or bignes of the same; and what shotte to
use for foule, and what for deare. And having thus instructed
them, he imployed some of them to hunte and fowle for him,
so as they became farr more active in that imploymente then
any of the English, by reason of ther swiftnes of foote, and
nimblnes of body, being also quick-sighted, and by continuall
exercise well knowing the hants of all sorts of game. So as
when they saw the execution that a peece would doe, and the
benefite that might come by the same, they became madd, as
it were, after them, and would not stick to give any prise they
could attaine too for them; accounting their bowes and arrowes but bables in comparison of them.

And here I may take occasion to bewaile the mischefe that
this wicked man began in these parts, and which since base
covetousnes prevailing in men that should know better, has
now at length gott the upper hand, and made this thing commone, notwithstanding any laws to the contrary; so as the
Indeans are full of peeces all over, both fouling peeces, muskets,
pistols, etc. They have also their moulds to make shotte, of
all sorts, as muskett bulletts, pistoll bullets, swane and gose
shote, and of smaler sorts; yea, some have seen them have
their scruplats to make scrupins[1] them selves, when they
wante them, with sundery other implements, wherwith they
are ordinarily better fited and furnished then the English them
selves. Yea, it is well knowne that they will have powder
and shot, when the English want it, nor cannot gett it; and
that in a time of warr or danger, as experience hath manifested,
that when lead hath been scarce, and men for their owne defence would gladly have given a groat a *li.*, which is dear
enoughe, yet hath it bene bought up and sent to other places,
and sould to shuch as trade it with the Indeans, at 12. pence
the *li.*; and it is like they give 3. or 4.*s.* the pound, for they will

---

[1] Screw-plates, screw-pins.

have it at any rate. And these things have been done in the same times, when some of their neigbours and freinds are daly killed by the Indeans, or are in deanger therof, and live but at the Indeans mercie. Yea, some (as they have aquainted them with all other things) have tould them how gunpowder is made, and all the materialls in it, and that they are to be had in their owne land; and I am confidente, could they attaine to make saltpeter, they would teach them to make powder. O the horiblnes of this vilanie! how many both Dutch and English have been latly slaine by those Indeans, thus furnished; and no remedie provided, nay, the evill more increased, and the blood of their brethren sould for gaine, as is to be feared; and in what danger all these colonies are in is too well known. Oh! that princes and parlements would take some timly order to prevente this mischeefe, and at length to suppress it, by some exemplerie punishmente upon some of these gaine thirstie murderers, (for they deserve no better title,) before their collonies in these parts be over throwne by these barbarous savages, thus armed with their owne weapons, by these evill instruments, and traytors to their neigbors and cuntrie.[1] But I have forgott my selfe, and have been to longe in this digression; but now to returne. This Morton having thus taught them the use of peeces, he sould them all he could spare; and he and his consorts detirmined to send for many out of England, and had by some of the ships sente for above a score. The which being knowne, and his neigbours meeting the Indeans in the woods armed with guns in this sorte, it was a terrour unto them, who lived straglingly, and were of no strenght in any place. And other places (though more remote) saw this mischeefe would quictly spread over all, if not prevented. Besides, they saw they should keep no servants, for Morton would entertaine any, how vile soever, and all the

---

[1] See the similar remarks of Captain John Smith on this subject, in *Narratives of Early Virginia*, of this series, pp. 346, 400, and the Virginian act of 1619, *ibid.*, 270.

scume of the countrie, or any discontents, would flock to him
from all places, if this nest was not broken; and they should
stand in more fear of their lives and goods (in short time)
from this wicked and deboste[1] crue, then from the salvages
them selves.

So sundrie of the cheefe of the stragling plantations, meeting togither, agreed by mutuall consente to sollissite those of
Plimoth (who were then of more strength then them all) to
joyne with them, to prevente the further grouth of this mischeefe, and suppress Morton and his consortes before they
grewe to further head and strength.   Those that joyned in
this acction (and after contributed to the charge of sending
him for England) were from Pascataway, Namkeake, Winisi-
mett, Weesagascusett, Natasco,[2] and other places wher any
English were seated.   Those of Plimoth being thus sought too
by their messengers and letters, and waying both their reasons,
and the commone danger, were willing to afford them their
help; though them selves had least cause of fear or hurte.
So, to be short, they first resolved joyntly to write to him, and
in a freindly and neigborly way to admonish him to forbear
these courses, and sent a messenger with their letters to bring
his answer.   But he was so highe as he scorned all advise, and
asked who had to doe with him; he had and would trade peeces
with the Indeans in dispite of all, with many other scurillous
termes full of disdaine.   They sente to him a second time, and
bad him be better advised, and more temperate in his termes,
for the countrie could not beare the injure he did; it was
against their comone saftie, and against the king's proclamation.   He answerd in high terms as before, and that the kings
proclaimation was no law;[3] demanding what penaltie was upon
it.   It was answered, more then he could bear, his majesties
displeasure.   But insolently he persisted, and said the king

[1] Debauched.

[2] *I. e.*, the settlements at or near the present Portsmouth or Dover, Salem,
Chelsea, Weymouth, and Nantasket, respectively.

[3] See p. 236, note 1, above.

was dead and his displeasure with him, and many the like things; and threatened withall that if any came to molest him, let them looke to them selves, for he would prepare for them. Upon which they saw ther was no way but to take him by force; and having so farr proceeded, now to give over would make him farr more hautie and insolente. So they mutually resolved to proceed, and obtained of the Govr of Plimoth to send Captaine Standish, and some other aide with him, to take Morton by force. The which accordingly was done; but they found him to stand stifly in his defence, having made fast his dors, armed his consorts, set diverse dishes of powder and bullets ready on the table; and if they had not been over armed with drinke, more hurt might have been done. They sommaned him to yeeld, but he kept his house, and they could gett nothing but scofes and scorns from him; but at length, fearing they would doe some violence to the house, he and some of his crue came out, but not to yeeld, but to shoote; but they were so steeld with drinke as their peeces were to heavie for them; him selfe with a carbine (over charged and allmost halfe fild with powder and shote, as was after found) had thought to have shot Captaine Standish; but he stept to him, and put by his peece, and tooke him. Neither was ther any hurte done to any of either side, save that one was so drunke that he rane his owne nose upon the pointe of a sword that one held before him as he entred the house; but he lost but a litle of his hott blood. Morton they brought away to Plimoth, wher he was kepte, till a ship went from the Ile of Shols for England, with which he was sente to the Counsell of New-England; and letters writen to give them information of his course and cariage; and also one was sent at their commone charge to informe their Ho^{rs} more perticulerly, and to prosecute against him. But he foold of the messenger, after he was gone from hence, and though he wente for England, yet nothing was done to him, not so much as rebukte, for ought was heard; but returned the nexte year. Some of the worst

of the company were disperst, and some of the more modest
kepte the house till he should be heard from.   But I have
been too long aboute so unworthy a person, and bad a cause.

This year Mr. Allerton brought over a yonge man for a
minister to the people hear, wheather upon his owne head, or
at the motion of some freinds ther, I well know not, but it was
without the churches sending; for they had bene so bitten by
Mr. Lyford, as they desired to know the person well whom
they should invite amongst them.   His name was Mr. Rogers;
but they perceived, upon some triall, that he was crased in his
braine; so they were faine to be at further charge to send him
back againe the nexte year, and loose all the charge that was
expended in his hither bringing, which was not smalle by Mr.
Allerton's accounte, in provissions, aparell, bedding, etc.
After his returne he grue quite distracted, and Mr. Allerton was
much blamed that he would bring such a man over, they
having charge enough otherwise.

Mr. Allerton, in the years before, had brought over some
small quantie of goods, upon his owne perticuler, and sould
them for his owne private benefite; which was more then any
man had yet hithertoo attempted.   But because he had other
wise done them good service, and also he sould them among
the people at the plantation, by which their wants were supplied, and he aledged it was the love of Mr. Sherley and some
other freinds that would needs trust him with some goods,
conceiveing it might doe him some good, and none hurte, it
was not much lookt at, but past over.   But this year he brought
over a greater quantitie, and they were so intermixte with the
goods of the generall, as they knew not which were theirs, and
which was his, being pact up together; so as they well saw
that, if any casualty had beefalne at sea, he might have laid
the whole on them, if he would; for ther was no distinction.
Allso what was most vendible, and would yeeld presente pay,
usualy that was his; and he now begane allso to sell abroad to
others of forine places, which, considering their commone

course, they began to dislike. Yet because love thinkes no
evill, nor is susspitious, they tooke his faire words for excuse,
and resolved to send him againe this year for England; considering how well he had done the former bussines, and what
good acceptation he had with their freinds ther; as also seeing
sundry of their freinds from Leyden were sente for, which
would or might be much furthered by his means. Againe,
seeing the patente for Kenebeck must be inlarged, by reason
of the former mistaks in the bounding of it, and it was conceived
in a maner, the same charge would serve to inlarge this at home
with it, and he that had begane the former the last year would
be the fittest to effecte this; so they gave him instructions and
sente him for England this year againe. And in his instructions bound him to bring over no goods on their accounte, but
50*li.* in hose and shoes, and some linen cloth, (as they were
bound by covenante when they tooke the trad;) also some
trading goods to such a value; and in no case to exseed his
instructions, nor runne them into any further charge; he well
knowing how their state stood. Also that he should so provide
that their trading goods came over betimes, and what so ever
was sent on their accounte should be pact up by it selfe, marked
with their marke, and no other goods to be mixed with theirs.
For so he prayed them to give him such instructions as they
saw good, and he would folow them, to prevente any jellocie or
farther offence, upon the former forementioned dislikes. And
thus they conceived they had well provided for all things.

Anno Dom: 1629.

Mr. Allerton safly arriving in England, and delivering
his leters to their freinds their, and aquainting them with his
instructions, found good acceptation with them, and they were
very forward and willing to joyne with them in the partnership of trade, and in the charge to send over the Leyden people;
a company wherof were allready come out of Holand, and
prepared to come over, and so were sent away before Mr.

Allerton could be ready to come. They had passage with the ships that came to Salem, that brought over many godly persons to begine the plantations and churches of Christ ther, and in the Bay of Massachussets; so their long stay and keeping back was recompensed by the Lord to ther freinds here with a duble blessing, in that they not only injoyed them now beyond ther late expectation, (when all their hops seemed to be cutt of,) but, with them, many more godly freinds and Christian breethren, as the begining of a larger harvest unto the Lord, in the increase of his churches and people in these parts, to the admiration of many, and allmost wonder of the world; that of so small beginings so great things should insue, as time after manifested; and that here should be a resting place for so many of the Lords people, when so sharp a scourge came upon their owne nation. But it was the Lords doing, and it ought to be marvellous in our eyes.

But I shall hear inserte some of their freinds letters, which doe best expresse their owne minds in these thir proceedings.

A leter of Mr. Sherleys to the Gov.

May 25, 1629.[1]

Sr: etc. Here are now many of your and our freinds from Leyden coming over, who, though for the most parte be but a weak company, yet herein is a good parte of that end obtained which was aimed at, and which hath been so strongly opposed by some of our former adventurers. But God hath his working in these things, which man cannot frustrate. With them we have allso sent some servants in the ship called the *Talbut*, that wente hence latly; but these come in the *May-flower*. Mr. Beachamp and my selfe, with Mr. Andrews and Mr. Hatherly,[2] are, with your love and liking, joyned partners with you, etc.

Your deputation we have received, and the goods have been taken up and sould by your freind and agente, Mr. Allerton, my selfe having

[1] "1629, May 25, the first letter concerning the former company of Leyden people." (Note by Rev. Thomas Prince.)

Timothy Hatherley was one of the London adventurers, and arrived at Boston in the ship *Friendship* July 14, 1631. He came first in the *Anne* in 1623 and returned to England. He came again to Plymouth in 1632 in the ship *Barnstaple*, sailing from Barnstaple, England, and settled in Scituate.

bine nere 3. months in Holland, at Amsterdam and other parts in the Low-Countries. I see further the agreemente you have made with the generallitie, in which I cannot understand but you have done very well, both for them and you, and also for your freinds at Leyden. Mr. Beachamp, Mr. Andrews, Mr. Hatherley, and my selfe, doe so like and approve of it, as we are willing to joyne with you, and, God directing and inabling us, will be assisting and helpfull to you, the best that possiblie we can. Nay, had you not taken this course, I doe not see how you should accomplish the end you first aimed at, and some others indevored these years past. We know it must keep us from the profite, which otherwise by the blessing of God and your indeaours, might be gained; for most of those that came in May, and these now sente, though I hope honest and good people, yet not like to be helpfull to raise profite, but rather, ney, certaine must, some while, be chargable to you and us; at which it is lickly, had not this wise and discreete course been taken, many of your generalitie would have grudged. Againe, you say well in your letter, and I make no doubte but you will performe it, that now being but a few, on whom the burthen must be, you will both menage it the beter, and sett too it more cherfully, haveing no discontente nor contradiction, but so lovingly to joyne togeither, in affection and counsell, as God no doubte will blesse and prosper your honest labours and indeavors. And therfore in all respects I doe not see but you have done marvelously discreetly, and advisedly, and no doubt but it gives all parties good contente; I mean that are reasonable and honest men, such as make conscience of giving the best satisfaction they be able for their debts, and that regard not their owne perticuler so much as the accomplishing of that good end for which this bussines was first intended, etc. Thus desiring the Lord to blese and prosper you, and all yours, and all our honest endeavors, I rest

Your unfained and ever loving freind,

JAMES SHERLEY.

Lon: March 8. 1629.[1]

That I may handle things together, I have put these 2. companies that came from Leyden in this place; though they came at 2. severall times, yet they both came out of England this year. The former company, being 35. persons, were shiped in May, and arived here aboute August. The later were shiped in the begining of March, and arived hear the later

---

[1] "1629-30, March 8th, the second letter concerning the latter company of Leyden people." (Note by Prince.)

end of May, 1630. Mr. Sherleys 2. letters, the effect wherof I have before related, (as much of them as is pertinente,) mentions both. Their charge, as Mr. Allerton brought it in afterwards on accounte, came to above 550*li*. besids ther fetching hither from Salem and the Bay, wher they and their goods were landed; viz. their transportation from Holland to England, and their charges lying ther, and passages hither, with clothing provided for them. For I find by accounte for the one company, 125. yeards of karsey,[1] 127. ellons of linen cloath, shoes, 66. p^r, with many other perticulers. The charge of the other company is reckoned on the severall families, some 50*li*., some 40*li*., some 30*li*., and so more or less, as their number and expencess were. And besids all this charg, their freinds and bretheren here were to provid corne and other provissions for them, till they could reap a crope which was long before. Those that came in May were thus maintained upward of 16. or 18. months, before they had any harvest of their owne, and the other by proportion. And all they could doe in the mean time was to gett them some housing, and prepare them grounds to plant on, against the season. And this charg of maintaining them all this while was litle less then the former sume. These things I note more perticulerly, for sundry regards. First, to shew a rare example herein of brotherly love, and Christian care in performing their promises and covenants to their bretheren, too, and in a sorte beyonde their power; that they should venture so desperatly to ingage them selves to accomplish this thing, and bear it so cheerfully; for they never demanded, much less had, any repaymente of all these great sumes thus disbursed. 2^ly. It must needs be that ther was more then of man in these acheevements, that should thus readily stire up the harts of shuch able frinds to joyne in partnership with them in shuch a case, and cleave so faithfullie to them as these did, in so great adventures; and the more because the most of

---

[1] Kersey is coarse woollen cloth, usually ribbed. An ellon, or ell, was 45 inches.

them never saw their faces to this day; ther being neither kindred, aliance, or other acquaintance or relations betweene any of them, then hath been before mentioned; it must needs be therfore the spetiall worke and hand of God. 3^{ly}. That these poore people here in a wilderness should, notwithstanding, be inabled in time to repay all these ingagments, and many more unjustly brought upon them through the unfaithfullnes of some, and many other great losses which they sustained, which will be made manifest, if the Lord be pleased to give life and time. In the mean time, I cannot but admire his ways and workes towards his servants, and humbly desire to blesse his holy name for his great mercies hithertoo.

The Leyden people being thus come over, and sundry of the generalitie seeing and hearing how great the charg was like to be that was that way to be expended, they begane to murmure and repin eat it, notwithstanding the burden lay on other mens shoulders; espetially at the paying of the 3. bushells of corne a year, according to the former agreemente, when the trad was lett for the 6. years aforesaid. But to give them contente herein allso, it was promised them, that if they could doe it in the time without it, they would never demand it of them; which gave them good contente. And indeed it never was paid, as will appeare by the sequell.

Concerning Mr. Allertons proceedings about the inlarging and confirming of their patent, both that at home and Kenebeck, will best appere by another leter of Mr. Sherleys; for though much time and money was expended aboute it, yet he left it unaccomplisht this year, and came without it. See Mr. Sherleys letter.

Most worthy and loving freinds, etc.

Some of your leters I received in July, and some since by Mr. Peirce, but till our maine bussines, the patent, was granted,[1] I could not setle my

---

[1] This patent or grant was made January 13, 1629/30, to William Bradford, his heirs, associates and assigns, by the Council for New England, and was in 1640 assigned by Bradford to the colony, as may be seen under that year, *post*. It defined the territorial limits of the Plymouth Colony, and confirmed the Ken-

mind nor pen to writing. Mr. Allerton was so turrmoyled about it, as
verily I would not nor could not have undergone it, if I might have had a
thousand pounds; but the Lord so blessed his labours (even beyond expectation in these evill days) as he obtained the love and favore of great
men in repute and place. He got granted from the Earle of Warwick[1]
and Sr. Ferdinando Gorge all that Mr. Winslow desired in his letters to
me, and more also, which I leave to him to relate.   Then he sued to the
king to confirme their grante, and to make you a corporation, and so to
inable you to make and execute lawes, in such large and ample maner as
the Massachusett plantation hath it; which the king graciously granted,
referring it to the Lord Keeper to give order to the solisiter to draw it up,
if ther were a presidente for it.[2] So the Lord Keeper furthered it all he
could, and allso the solissiter; but as Festus said to Paule, With no small
sume of money obtained I this freedom; for by the way many ridells
must be resolved, and many locks must be opened with the silver, ney,
the golden key.   Then it was to come to the Lord Treasurer, to have his
warrente for freeing the custume for a certaine time; but he would not
doe it, but refferd it to the Counsell table.   And ther Mr. Allerton attended day by day, when they sate, but could not gett his petition read.
And by reason of Mr. Peirce his staying with all the passengers at Bristoll,
he was forct to leave the further prosecuting of it to a solissiter.   But ther
is no fear nor doubte but it will be granted, for he hath the cheefe of them
to freind; yet it will be marvelously needfull for him to returne by the
first ship that comes from thence; for if you had this confirmed, then were
you compleate, and might bear such sway and goverment as were fitt

nebec grant. No royal charter was ever granted to the colony. In 1685 the
colony was divided into three counties, Plymouth, Barnstable, and Bristol, and
the town of Bristol, now in Rhode Island, was made the shire town of Bristol
County. The patent included a strip of territory afterwards claimed by Rhode
Island under a charter granted in 1644 to Providence Plantations by the parlia-
mentary government, and also under a new charter granted in 1663 by Charles
II. During the controversy between Massachusetts and Rhode Island concerning the boundary line it became necessary to exhibit the Old Colony patent in
support of the Massachusetts claim, and after some search it was found in an
old Bradford house in Plympton. By order of Council under date of January
20, 1748, it was placed in the Plymouth registry of deeds where it now is. For
its text, see Ebenezer Hazard's *Historical Collections*, I. 298–303, or Davis,
History of Plymouth, pp. 146–155.
[1] A Puritan earl, at this time a leading member of the Council for New
England.
[2] For the forms and processes used in the preparation and issue of letters
patent by the Crown, see Dr. Charles Deane's paper in the *Proceedings of the
Massachusetts Historical Society*, XI. 168.

for your ranke and place that God hath called you unto; and stope the mouethes of base and scurrulous fellowes, that are ready to question and threaten you in every action you doe. And besids, if you have the custome free for 7. years inward, and 21. outward, the charge of the patent will be soone recovered, and ther is no fear of obtaining [1] it. But such things must work by degrees; men cannot hasten it as they would; werefore we (I write in behalfe of all our partners here) desire you to be ernest with Mr. Allerton to come, and his wife to spare him this one year more, to finish this great and waighty bussines, which we conceive will be much for your good, and I hope for your posteritie, and for many generations to come.

Thus much of this letter. It was dated the 19. March, 1629.[2]

By which it appears what progress was made herein, and in part what charge it was, and how left unfinished, and some reason of the same; but in truth (as was afterwards appehended the meaine reason was Mr. Allerton's policie, to have an opportunitie to be sent over againe, for other regards; and for that end procured them thus to write. For it might then well enough have been finshed, if not with that clause aboute the custumes, which was Mr. Allertons and Mr. Sherleys device, and not at all thought on by the colony here, nor much regarded, yet it might have been done without it, without all queston, having passed the kings hand; nay it was conceived it might then have beene done with it, if he had pleased; but covetousnes never brings ought home, as the proverb is, for this oppertunytie being lost, it was never accomplished, but a great deale of money veainly and lavishly cast away aboute it, as doth appear upon their accounts. But of this more in its place.

Mr. Alerton gave them great and just ofence in this (which I had omited [3] and almost forgotten),—in bringing over this year, for base gaine, that unworthy man, and instrumente of

---

[1] This word is here substituted for *recovering* in the manuscript, on the authority of Bradford's letter-book.   [2] 1629/30.

[3] This paragraph is written on the reverse of the page immediately preceding, in the original manuscript.

mischeefe, Morton, who was sent home but the year before for his misdemenors. He not only brought him over, but to the towne (as it were to nose them), and lodged him at his owne house, and for a while used him as a scribe to doe his bussines, till he was caused to pack him away. So he wente to his old nest in the Massachusets, wher it was not long but by his miscariage he gave them just occation to lay hands on him; and he was by them againe sent prisoner into England, wher he lay a good while in Exeter Jeole. For besids his miscariage here, he was vemently suspected for the murder of a man that had adventured moneys with him, when he came first into New-England. And a warrente was sente from the Lord-Cheefe Justice to apprehend him, by vertue wherof he was by the Govr of the Massachusets sent into England; and for other his misdemenors amongst them, they demolisht his house, that it might be no longer a roost for shuch unclaine birds to nestle in. Yet he got free againe, and write an infamouse and scurrillous booke[1] against many godly and cheefe men of the cuntrie; full of lyes and slanders, and fraight with profane callumnies against their names and persons, and the ways of God. After sundry years, when the warrs were hott in England, he came againe into the cuntrie, and was imprisoned at Boston for this booke and other things, being grown old in wickednes.

Concerning the rest of Mr. Allertons instructions, in which they strictly injoyned him not to exceed above that 50li. in the goods before mentioned, not to bring any but trading commodities, he followed them not at all, but did the quite contrarie; bringing over many other sorts of retaile goods, selling what he could by the way on his owne accounte, and delivering the rest, which he said to be theirs, into the store; and for trading goods brought but litle in comparison; excusing

---

[1] Thomas Morton's *New English Canaan* (Amsterdam, 1637). Returning to New England in 1643, Morton was allowed to spend the winter in Plymouth, but, venturing incautiously within the jurisdiction of Massachusetts, he was arrested, in September, 1644, imprisoned for a year, and fined heavily. Two years after, he died in Maine.

the matter, they had laid out much about the Laiden people, and patent, etc.   And for other goods, they had much of them of ther owne dealings, without present disbursemente, and to like effect.   And as for passing his bounds and instructions, he laid it on Mr. Sherley, etc., who, he said, they might see his mind in his leters; also that they had sett out Ashley at great charg; but next year they should have what trading goods they would send for, if things were now well setled, etc.   And thus were they put off; indeed Mr. Sherley write things tending this way, but it is like he was overruled by Mr. Allerton, and harkened more to him then to their letters from hence.

Thus he further writs in the former leter.

I see what you write in your leters concerning the overcomming and paying of our debts, which I confess are great, and had need be carfully looked unto; yet no doubt but we, joyning in love, may soone over-come them; but we must follow it roundly and to purpose, for if we pedle out the time of our trad, others will step in and nose us.   But we know that you have that aquaintance and experience in the countrie, as none have the like; wherfore, freinds and partners, be no way discouraged with the greatnes of the debt, etc., but let us not fulfill the proverbe, to bestow 12*d.* on a purse, and put 6*d.* in it; but as you and we have been at great charg, and undergone much for setling you ther, and to gaine experience, so as God shall enable us, let us make use of it.   And think not with 50*li.* pound a yeare sent you over, to rayse shuch means as to pay our debts.   We see a possibillitie of good if you be well supplied, and fully furnished; and cheefly if you lovingly agree.   I know I write to godly and wise men, such as have lerned to bear one an others infirmities, and rejoyce at any ones prosperities; and if I were able I would press this more, because it is hoped by some of your enimies, that you will fall out one with another, and so over throw your hopfull bussines.   Nay, I have heard it crediblie reported, that some have said, that till you be disjoynted by discontents and fractions[1] amongst your sellves, it bootes not any to goe over, in hope of getting or doing good in those parts.   But we hope beter things of you, and that you will not only bear one with another, but banish such thoughts, and not suffer them to lodg in your brests.   God grant you may disap-pointe the hopes of your foes, and procure the hartie desire of your selves and freinds in this perticuler.

[1] Factions.

By this it appears that ther was a kind of concurrance betweene Mr. Allerton and them in these things, and that they gave more regard to his way and course in these things, then to the advise from hence; which made him bould to presume above his instructions, and to rune on in the course he did, to their greater hurt afterwards, as will appear. These things did much trouble them hear, but they well knew not how to help it, being loath to make any breach or contention hear aboute; being so premonished as before in the leter above recited. An other more secrete cause was herewith concurrente; Mr. Allerton had maried the daughter of their Reverend Elder, Mr. Brewster[1] (a man beloved and honoured amongst them, and who tooke great paines in teaching and dispenceing the word of God unto them), whom they were loath to greeve or any way offend, so as they bore with much in that respecte. And with all Mr. Allerton carried so faire with him, and procured such leters from Mr. Sherley to him, with shuch applause of Mr. Allertons wisdom, care, and faithfullnes, in the bussines; and as things stood none were so fitte to send aboute them as he; and if any should suggest other wise, it was rather out of envie, or some other sinister respecte then other wise. Besids, though private gaine, I doe perswade my selfe, was some cause to lead Mr. Allerton aside in these beginings, yet I thinke, or at least charitie caries me to hope, that he intended to deale faithfully with them in the maine, and had such an opinion of his owne abillitie, and some experience of the benefite that he had made in this singuler way, as he conceived he might both raise him selfe an estate, and allso be a means to bring in such profite to Mr. Sherley, (and it may be the rest,) as might be as lickly to bring in their moneys againe with advantage, and it may be sooner then from the generall way; or at least

---

[1] Isaac Allerton of London married in Leyden in 1611 Mary Norris of Newbury, England, and came in the *Mayflower* with wife and three children, Bartholomew, Remember, and Mary. His wife died February 25, 1620/1, and in 1626 he married Fear, daughter of William Brewster. She died in 1634. He married a third wife, Joanna.

it was looked upon by some of them to be a good help ther unto; and that neither he nor any other did intend to charge the generall accounte with any thing that rane in perticuler; or that Mr. Sherley or any other did purposs but that the generall should be first and fully supplyed. I say charitie makes me thus conceive; though things fell out other wise, and they missed of their aimes, and the generall suffered abundantly hereby, as will afterwards apear.

Togeither herewith sorted an other bussines contrived by Mr. Allerton and them ther, without any knowledg of the partners, and so farr proceeded in as they were constrained to allow therof, and joyne in the same, though they had no great liking of it, but feared what might be the evente of the same. I shall relate it in a further part of Mr. Sherley's leter as foloweth.

I am to aquainte you that we have thought good to joyne with one Edward Ashley (a man I thinke that some of you know); but it is only of that place wherof he hath a patente in Mr. Beachamps name;[1] and to that end have furnished him with larg provissions, etc. Now if you please to be partners with us in this, we are willing you shall; for after we heard how forward Bristoll men (and as I hear some able men of his owne kindrid) have been to stock and supply him, hoping of profite, we thought it fitter for us to lay hould of such an opportunitie, and to keep a kind of running plantation, then others who have not borne the burthen of setling a plantation, as we have done. And he, on the other side, like an understanding yonge man, thought it better to joyne with those that had means by a plantation to supply and back him ther, rather then strangers, that looke but only after profite. Now it is not knowne that you are partners with him; but only we 4., Mr. Andrews, Mr. Beachamp, my selfe, and Mr. Hatherley, who desired to have the patente, in consideration of our great loss we have allready sustained in setling the first plantation ther; so we agreed togeather to take it in our names. And now, as I said before, if you please to joyne with us, we are willing you should. Mr. Allerton had no power from you to make this new contracte, neither was he willing

---

[1] Apparently this is that patent which the Council for New England gave to John Beauchamp and Thomas Leverett on March 13, 1629/30, for a tract of some 900 square miles lying between the Penobscot and Muscongus Bay. At a later time it was known as the Waldo Patent.

to doe any thing therin without your consente and approbation. Mr. William Peirce is joyned with us in this, for we thought it very conveniente, because of landing Ashley and his goods ther, if God please; and he will bend his course accordingly. He hath a new boate with him, and boards to make another, with 4. or 5. lustie fellowes, wherof one is a carpenter. Now in case you are not willing in this perticuler to joyne with us, fearing the charge and doubting the success, yet thus much we intreate of you, to afford him all the help you can, either by men, commodities, or boats; yet not but that we will pay you for any thing he hath. And we desire you to keep the accounts apart, though you joyne with us; becase ther is, as you see, other partners in this then the other; so, for all mens wages, boats-hire, or comodities, which we shall have of you, make him debtore for it; and what you shall have of him, make the plantation or your selves debtore for it to' him, and so ther will need no mingling of the accounts.

And now, loving freinds and partners, if you joyne in Ashles patent and bussines, though we have laid out the money and taken up much to stock this bussines and the other, yet I thinke it conscionable and reasonable that you should beare your shares and proportion of the stock, if not by present money, yet by securing us for so much as it shall come too; for it is not barly the interest that is to be alowed and considered of, but allso the adventure; though I hope in God, by his blessing and your honest indeavors, it may soon be payed; yet the years that this partnership holds is not long, nor many; let all therfore lay it to harte, and make the best use of the time that possiblie we cann, and let every man put too his shoulder, and the burthen will be the lighter. I know you are so honest and conscionable men, as you will consider hereof, and returne shuch an answer as may give good satisfaction. Ther is none of us that would venture as we have done, were it not to strengthen and setle you more then our owne perticuler profite.

Ther is no liclyhood of doing any good in buying the debte for the purchas. I know some will not abate the interest, and therfore let it rune its course; they are to be paied yearly, and so I hope they shall, according to agreemente. The Lord grant that our loves and affections may still be united, and knit togeither; and so we rest your ever loving friends,

JAMES SHERLEY.
TIMOTHY HATHERLEY.

Bristoll, March 19. 1629.[1]

This mater of the buying the debts of the purchass was parte of Mr. Allertons instructions, and in many of them it

[1] 1629/30.

might have been done to good profite for ready pay (as some
were); but Mr. Sherley had no mind to it. But this bussines
aboute Ashley did not a litle trouble them; for though he had
wite and abillitie enough to menage the bussines, yet some of
them knew him to be a very profane yonge man; and he had
for some time lived amonge the Indeans as a savage, and wente
naked amongst them, and used their maners (in which time
he got their language), so they feared he might still rune into
evill courses (though he promised better), and God would not
prosper his ways. As soone as he was landed at the place intended, caled Penobscote, some 4. score leagues from this place,
he write (and afterwards came) for to desire to be supplyed
with Wampampeake, corne against winter, and other things.
They considered these were of their cheefe commodities, and
would be continually needed by him, and it would much
prejudice their owne trade at Kenebeck if they did not joyne
with him in the ordering of things, if thus they should supply
him; and on the other hand, if they refused to joyne with
him, and allso to afford any supply unto him, they should
greatly offend their above named friends, and might hapily
lose them hereby; and he and Mr. Allerton, laying their
craftie wits togither, might gett supplies of these things els
wher; besids, they considered that if they joyned not in the
bussines, they knew Mr. Allerton would be with them in it, and
so would swime, as it were, betweene both, to the prejudice
of boath, but of them selves espetially. For they had reason
to thinke this bussines was cheefly of his contriving, and
Ashley was a man fitte for his turne and dealings. So they,
to prevente a worse mischeefe, resolved to joyne in the bussines,
and gave him supplies in what they could, and overlooked his
proceedings as well as they could; the which they did the better, by joyning an honest yonge man[1] that came from Leyden,

---

[1] "Thomas Willett." (Br.) Thomas Willett came to Plymouth about 1630
and was selected by the united colonies for mayor of New York after its capture
from the Dutch in 1664.

with him as his fellow (in some sorte), and not merely as a servante. Which yonge man being discreete, and one whom they could trust, they so instructed as keept Ashley in some good mesure within bounds. And so they returned their answer to their freinds in England, that they accepted of their motion, and joyned with them in Ashleys bussines; and yet withall tould them what their fears were concerning him.

But when they came to have full notice of all the goods brought them that year, they saw they fell very short of trading goods, and Ashley farr better suppleyed then themselves; so as they were forced to buy of the fisher men to furnish them selves, yea, and cottens and carseys and other such like cloath (for want of trading cloath) of Mr. Allerton himselfe, and so to put away a great parte of their beaver, at under rate, in the countrie, which they should have sente home, to help to discharge their great ingagementes; which was to their great vexation; but Mr. Allerton prayed them to be contente, and the nexte yere they might have what they would write for. And their ingagmentes of this year were great indeed when they came to know them, (which was not wholy till 2. years after); and that which made them the more, Mr. Allerton had taken up some large summes at Bristoll at 50. p^r cent. againe, which he excused, that he was forcte to it, because other wise he could at the spring of year get no goods transported, such were their envie against their trade. But wheither this was any more then an excuse, some of them doubted; but however, the burden did lye on their backs, and they must bear it, as they did many heavie loads more in the end.

This paying of 50. p^r cent. and dificulty of having their goods transported by the fishing ships at the first of the year, (as was beleeved,) which was the cheefe season for trade, put them upon another projecte. Mr. Allerton, after the fishing season was over, light of a bargan of salte, at a good fishing place, and bought it; which came to aboute 113li.; and shortly after he might have had 30li. cleare profite for it,

without any more trouble aboute it.   But Mr. Winslow coming
that way from Kenebeck, and some other of ther partners
with him in the barke, they mett with Mr. Allerton, and falling
into discourse with him, they stayed him from selling the
salte; and resolved, if it might please the rest, to keep it for
them selves, and to hire a ship in the west cuntrie to come on
fishing for them, on shares, according to the coustome; and
seeing she might have her salte here ready, and a stage ready
builte and fitted wher the salt lay safely landed and housed.
In stead of bringing salte, they might stowe her full of trading
goods, as bread, pease, cloth, etc., and so they might have a
full supply of goods without paing fraight, and in due season,
which might turne greatly to their advantage.   Coming home,
this was propounded, and considered on, and aproved by all
but the Govr, who had no mind to it, seeing they had allway
lost by fishing; but the rest were so ernest, as thinkeing that
they might gaine well by the fishing in this way; and if they
should but save, yea, or lose some thing by it, the other benefite
would be advantage inough; so, seeing their ernestnes, he gave
way, and it was referd to their freinds in England to alow, or
disalow it.   Of which more in its place.

Upon the consideration of the bussines about the paten,
and in what state it was left, as is before remembred, and Mr.
Sherleys ernest pressing to have Mr. Allerton to come over
againe to finish it, and perfect the accounts, etc., it was concluded to send him over this year againe; though it was with
some fear and jeolocie; yet he gave them fair words and
promises of well performing all their bussineses according to
their directions, and to mend his former errors.   So he was
accordingly sent with full instructions for all things, with large
letters to Mr. Sherley and the rest, both aboute Ashleys bussines
and their owne suply with trading comodities, and how much
it did concerne them to be furnished therwith, and what they
had suffered for wante therof; and of what litle use other goods
were in comparison therof; and so likewise aboute this fishing

ship, to be thus hired, and fraught with trading goods, which might both supply them and Ashley, and the benefite therof: which was left to their consideration to hire and set her out, or not; but in no case not to send any, exepte she was thus fraighte with trading goods. But what these things came too will appere in the next years passages.

I had like to have omited an other passage that fell out the begining of this year. Ther was one Mr. Ralfe Smith,[1] and his wife and familie, that came over into the Bay of the Massachusets, and sojourned at presente with some stragling people that lived at Natascoe; here being a boat of this place putting in ther on some occasion, he ernestly desired that they would give him and his, passage for Plimoth, and some such things as they could well carrie; having before heard that ther was liklyhood he might procure house-roome for some time, till he should resolve to setle ther, if he might, or els-wher as God should disposs; for he was werie of being in that uncoth place, and in a poore house that would neither keep him nor his goods drie. So, seeing him to be a grave man, and understood he had been a minister, though they had no order for any such thing, yet they presumed and brought him. He was here accordingly kindly entertained and housed, and had the rest of his goods and servants sente for, and exercised his gifts amongst them, and afterwards was chosen into the ministrie, and so remained for sundrie years.

It was before noted that sundry of those that came from Leyden, came over in the ships that came to Salem, wher Mr.

[1] Rev. Ralf Smith came over with Higginson in 1629 in the ship *Talbot*. Matthew Cradock, the governor in England of the Massachusetts Company, suspected him of Separatism and sent an order to Endicott to forbid his continuance in Massachusetts unless he conformed to the Church. Smith, fearing trouble, went to Nantasket and thence to Plymouth, where he became the first settled pastor of the Plymouth Church after the ministrations of Elder Brewster. Mr. Smith was graduated at Cambridge in 1613. In 1633, while in Plymouth, he married Mary (Goodall), widow of Richard Masterson. He dissolved his connection with the church in 1636 after a pastorate of seven years, remaining, however, in Plymouth several years longer, after which he preached in Manchester and died in Boston in 1662.

Endecott had cheefe command; and by infection that grue
amonge the passengers at sea, it spread also among them a
shore, of which many dyed, some of the scurvie, other of an
infectious feaoure, which continued some time amongst them
(though our people, through Gods goodnes, escaped it).
Upon which occasion he write hither for some help, understanding here was one that had some skill that way, and had
cured diverse of the scurvie, and others of other diseases, by
letting blood, and other means. Upon which his request the
Gov[r] hear sent him unto them, and also write to him, from
whom he received an answere; the which, because it is breefe,
and shows the begining of their aquaintance, and closing in
the truth and ways of God, I thought it not unmeete, nor
without use, hear to inserte it; and an other showing the begining of their fellowship and church estate ther.
    Being as followeth.

Right worthy Sr:
    It is a thing not usuall, that servants to one m[r] and of the same
houshold should be strangers; I assure you I desire it not, nay, to speake
more plainly, I cannot be so to you. Gods people are all marked with one
and the same marke, and sealed with one and the same seale, and have
for the maine, one and the same harte, guided by one and same spirite of
truth; and wher this is, ther can be no discorde, nay, here must needs
be sweete harmonie. And the same request (with you) I make unto the
Lord, that we may, as Christian breethren, be united by a heavenly and
unfained love; bending all our harts and forces in furthering a worke beyond our strength, with reverence and fear, fastening our eyse allways on
him that only is able to directe and prosper all our ways. I acknowledge
my selfe much bound to you for your kind love and care in sending Mr.
Fuller[1] among us, and rejoyce much that I am by him satisfied touching
your judgments of the outward forme of Gods worshipe. It is, as farr
as I can yet gather, no other then is warrented by the evidence of truth,
and the same which I have proffessed and maintained ever since the Lord
in mercie revealed him selfe unto me; being farr from the commone reporte that hath been spread of you touching that perticuler. But Gods

[1] Samuel Fuller, physician of the colony and deacon of the Plymouth church
(as he had been in that of Leyden), came in the *Mayflower*. His wife came in the
Anne in 1623. He died in 1633.

children must not looke for less here below, and it is the great mercie of God, that he strengthens them to goe through with it. I shall not neede at this time to be tedious unto you, for, God willing, I purpose to see your face shortly. In the mean time, I humbly take my leave of you, commiting you to the Lords blessed protection, and rest,

Your assured loving friend,

Jo: ENDECOTT.

Naumkeak, May 11. An°. 1629.

This second leter sheweth ther proceedings in their church affaires at Salem, which was the 2. church erected in these parts; and afterwards the Lord established many more in sundrie places.

Sr: I make bould to trouble you with a few lines, for to certifie you how it hath pleased God to deale with us, since you heard from us. How, notwithstanding all opposition that hath been hear, and els wher, it hath pleased God to lay a foundation, the which I hope is agreeable to his word in every thing. The 20. of July, it pleased the Lord to move the hart of our Govr to set it aparte for a solemne day of humilliation for the choyce of a pastor and teacher. The former parte of the day being spente in praier and teaching, the later parte aboute the election, which was after this maner.[1] The persons thought on (who had been ministers in England) were demanded concerning their callings; they acknowledged ther was a towfould calling, the one an inward calling, when the Lord moved the harte of a man to take that calling upon him, and fitted him with guiftes for the same; the second was an outward calling, which was from the people, when a company of beleevers are joyned togither in covenante, to walke togither in all the ways of God, and every member (being men) are to have a free voyce in the choyce of their officers, etc. Now, we being perswaded that these 2. men were so quallified, as the apostle speaks to Timothy, wher he saith, A bishop must be blamles, sober, apte to teach, etc., I thinke I may say, as the eunuch said unto Philip, What should let from being baptised, seeing ther was water? and he beleeved. So these 2. servants of God, clearing all things by their answers, (and being thus fitted,) we saw noe reason but we might freely give our voyces for their election, after this triall. So Mr. Skelton was chosen pastor, and Mr. Higgison to be teacher; and they accepting

---

[1] At this election by the Salem church the written ballot was used for the first time in America, as appears from the fuller copy of the letter in Bradford's letter-book. The transition to the congregational system of church polity is marked, and was important. The influence of the Plymouth example is obvious.

the choyce, Mr. Higgison, with 3. or 4. of the gravest members of the church, laid their hands on Mr. Skelton, using prayer therwith. This being done, ther was imposission of hands on Mr. Higgison also. And since that time, Thursday (being, as I take it, the 6. of August) is appoynted for another day of humilliation, for the choyce of elders and deacons, and ordaining of them.

And now, good Sr, I hope that you and the rest of Gods people (who are aquainted with the ways of God) with you, will say that hear was a right foundation layed, and that these 2. blessed servants of the Lord came in at the dore, and not at the window. Thus I have made bould to trouble you with these few lines, desiring you to remember us, etc. And so rest,

At your service in what I may,

CHARLES GOTT.

Salem, July 30. 1629.

Anno Dom: 1630.

ASHLEY, being well supplyed, had quickly gathered a good parcell of beaver, and like a crafty pate he sent it all home, and would not pay for the goods he had had of the plantation hear, but lett them stand still on the score, and tooke up still more. Now though they well enough knew his aime, yet they let him goe on, and write of it into England. But partly the beaver they received, and sould, (of which they weer sencible,) and partly by Mr. Allertons extolling of him, they cast more how to supplie him then the plantation, and something to upbraid them with it. They were forct to buy him a barke allso, and to furnish her with a m^r and men, to transporte his corne and provissions (of which he put of much); for the Indeans of those parts have no corne growing, and at harvest, after corne is ready, the weather grows foule, and the seas dangerous, so as he could doe litle good with his shallope for that purposs.

They looked ernestly for a timely supply this spring, by the fishing ship which they expected, and had been at charg to keepe a stage for her; but none came, nor any supply heard of for them. At length they heard sume supply was sent to Ashley by a fishing ship, at which they something marvelled, and the more that they had no letters either from Mr. Allerton

or Mr. Sherley; so they went on in their bussines as well as
they could. At last they heard of Mr. Peirce his arivall in the
Bay of the Massachusetts, who brought passengers and goods
thither. They presently sent a shallop, conceiving they should
have some thing by him. But he tould them he had none;
and a ship was sett out on fishing, but after 11. weeks beating
at sea, she mett with shuch foull weather as she was forcte
back againe for England, and, the season being over, gave off
the vioage. Neither did he hear of much goods in her for the
plantation, or that she did belong to them, for he had heard
some thing from Mr. Allerton tending that way. But Mr.
Allerton had bought another ship, and was to come in her, and
was to fish for bass to the eastward, and to bring goods, etc.
These things did much trouble them, and half astonish them.
Mr. Winslow haveing been to the eastward, brought nuese of
the like things, with some more perticulers, and that it was like
Mr. Allerton would be late before he came. At length they,
having an oppertunitie, resolved to send Mr. Winslow, with
what beaver they had ready, into England, to see how the
squars wente, being very jeolouse of these things, and Mr.
Allertons courses; and writ shuch leters, and gave him shuch
instructions, as they thought meet; and if he found things not
well, to discharge Mr. Allerton for being any longer agent for
them, or to deal any more in the bussines, and to see how the
accounts stood, etc.

Aboute the midle of sommer arrives Mr. Hatherley in
the Bay of the Massachusetts, (being one of the partners,) and
came over in the same ship that was set out on fhishing
(called the *Frendship*). They presently sent to him, making
no question but now they had goods come, and should know
how all things stood. But they found the former news true,
how this ship had been so long at sea, and spente and spoyled
her provissions, and overthrowne the viage. And he being
sent over by the rest of the partners, to see how things wente
hear, being at Bristoll with Mr. Allerton, in the shipe bought

(called the *White-Angell*), ready to set sayle, over night came
a messenger from Bastable[1] to Mr. Allerton, and tould him
of the returne of the ship, and what had befallen.   And he not
knowing what to doe, having a great charge under hand, the
ship lying at his rates, and now ready to set sayle, got him to
goe and discharg the ship, and take order for the goods.   To
be short, they found Mr. Hatherley some thing reserved, and
troubled in him selfe, (Mr. Allerton not being ther,) not knowing how to dispose of the goods till he came; but he heard he
was arived with the other ship to the eastward, and expected
his coming.   But he tould them ther was not much for them
in this ship, only 2. packs of Bastable ruggs, and 2. hoggsheads
of meatheglin,[2] drawne out in wooden flackets (but when these
flackets came to be received, ther was left but 6. gallons of the
2. hogsheads, it being drunke up under the name leackage, and
so lost).   But the ship was filled with goods for sundrie gentle-
men, and others, that were come to plant in the Massachusets,
for which they payed fraight by the tun.   And this was all the
satisfaction they could have at presente, so they brought this
small parcell of goods and returned with this nues, and a letter
as obscure; which made them much to marvell therat.   The
letter was as followeth.

Gentle-men, partners, and loving friends, etc.
   Breefly thus: wee have this year set forth a fishing ship, and a trading
ship, which later we have bought; and so have disbursed a great deale
of money, as may and will appeare by the accounts.   And because this
ship (called the *White Angell*) is to acte 2. parts, (as I may say,) fishing
for bass, and trading; and that while Mr. Allerton was imployed aboute
the trading, the fishing might suffer by carlesnes or neglecte of the sailors,
we have entreated your and our loving friend, Mr. Hatherley, to goe over
with him, knowing he will be a comforte to Mr. Allerton, a joye to you,
to all a carfull and loving friend, and a great stay to the bussines; and so
great contente to us, that if it should please God the one should faile, (as
God forbid,) yet the other would keepe both recconings, and things up-

   [1] Barnstaple is in Devonshire, about 70 miles from Bristol.
   [2] Metheglin, or mead, was a liquor made of honey and water boiled and
fermented, often enriched with spices.

righte. For we are now out great sumes of money, as they will acquainte you withall, etc. When we were out but 4. or 5. hundred pounds a peece, we looked not much after it, but left it to you, and your agente, (who, without flaterie, deserveth infinite thanks and comendations, both of you and us, for his pains, etc.); but now we are out double, nay, trible a peece, some of us, etc.; which maks us both write, and send over our friend, Mr. Hatherley, whom we pray you to entertaine kindly, of which we doubte not of. The main end of sending him is to see the state and accounte of all the bussines, of all which we pray you informe him fully, though the ship and bussines wayte for it and him. For we should take it very unkindly that we should intreat him to take such a journey, and that, when it pleaseth God he returnes, he could not give us contente and satisfaction in this perticuler, through defaulte of any of you. But we hope you will so order bussines, as neither he nor we shall have cause to complaine, but to doe as we ever have done, thinke well of you all, etc. I will not promise, but shall indeaour and hope to effecte the full desire and grant of your patente, and that ere it be longe. I would not have you take any thing unkindly. I have not write out of jeolocie of any unjuste dealing. Be you all kindly saluted in the Lord, so I rest,

Yours in what I may,
JAMES SHERLEY.

March 25. 1630.[1]

It needs not be thought strange, that these things should amase and trouble them; first, that this fishing ship should be set out, and fraight with other mens goods, and scarce any of theirs; seeing their maine end was (as is before remembred) to bring them a full supply, and their speatiall order not to sett out any excepte this was done. And now a ship to come on their accounte, clean contrary to their both end and order, was a misterie they could not understand; and so much the worse, seeing she had shuch ill success as to lose both her vioage and provissions. The 2. thing, that another ship should be bought and sente out on new designes, a thing not so much as once thought on by any here, much less, not a word intimated or spoaken of by any here, either by word or letter, neither could they imagine why this should be. Bass fishing was never lookt at by them, but as soone as ever they heard on it, they looked

---

[1] By error for March 25, 1631.

at it as a vaine thing, that would certainly turne to loss.   And
for Mr. Allerton to follow any trade for them, it was never in
their thoughts.   And 3^ly, that their friends should complaine
of disbursements, and yet rune into such great things, and
charge of shiping and new projects of their owne heads, not
only without, but against, all order and advice, was to them
very strang.   And 4^ly, that all these matters of so great charg
and imployments should be thus wrapped up in a breefe and
obscure letter, they knew not what to make of it.   But amids
all their doubts they must have patience till Mr. Allerton and
Mr. Hatherley should come.   In the mean time Mr. Winslow
was gone for England; and others of them were forst to folow
their imployments with the best means they had, till they could
hear of better.

At length Mr. Hatherley and Mr. Allerton came unto them,
(after they had delivered their goods,) and finding them
strucken with some sadnes aboute these things, Mr. Allerton
tould them that the ship *Whit-Angele* did not belong to them,
nor their accounte, neither neede they have any thing to doe
with her, excepte they would.   And Mr. Hatherley confirmed
the same, and said that they would have had him to have
had a parte, but he refused; but he made question whether
they would not turne her upon the generall accounte, if ther
came loss (as he now saw was like), seeing Mr. Allerton laid
downe this course, and put them on this projecte.   But for the
fishing ship, he tould them they need not be so much troubled,
for he had her accounts here, and showed them that her first
seting out came not much to exceed 600*li.* as they might
see by the accounte, which he showed them; and for this later
viage, it would arrise to profite by the fraight of the goods, and
the salle of some katle which he shiped and had allready sould,
and was to be paid for partly here and partly by bills into England, so as they should not have this put on their acounte at
all, except they would.   And for the former, he had sould so
much goods out of her in England, and imployed the money

in this 2. viage, as it, togeither with such goods and implements as Mr. Allerton must need aboute his fishing, would rise to a good parte of the money; for he must have the sallt and nets, allso spiks, nails, etc.; all which would rise to nere 400*li.*; so, with the bearing of their parts of the rest of the loses (which would not be much above 200*li.*), they would clear them of this whole accounte. Of which motion they were glad, not being willing to have any accounts lye upon them; but aboute their trade, which made them willing to harken therunto, and de-mand of Mr. Hatherly how he could make this good, if they should agree their unto, he tould them he was sent over as their agente, and had this order from them, that whatsoever he and Mr. Allerton did togeather, they would stand to it; but they would not alow of what Mr. Allerton did alone, except they liked it; but if he did it alone, they would not gaine say it. Upon which they sould to him and Mr. Allerton all the rest of the goods, and gave them present possession of them; and a writing was made, and confirmed under both Mr. Hatherleys and Mr. Allertons hands, to the effecte afforesaide. And Mr. Allertone, being best aquainted with the people sould away presenly all shuch goods as he had no need of for the fishing, as 9. shallop sails, made of good new canvas, and the roaps for them being all new, with sundry such usefull goods, for ready beaver, by Mr. Hatherleys allowance. And thus they thought they had well provided for them selvs. Yet they rebuked Mr. Allerton very much for runing into these courses, fearing the success of them. Mr. Allerton and Mr. Hatherley brought to the towne with them (after he had sould what he could abroad) a great quantity of other goods besids trading comodities; as linen cloath, bedticks, stockings, tape, pins, ruggs, etc., and tould them they were to have them, if they would; but they tould Mr. Allerton that they had forbid him before for bringing any such on their accounte; it would hinder their trade and returnes. But he and Mr. Hatherley said, if they would not have them, they would sell them, them selves, and take corne

for what they could not otherwise sell.   They tould them they
might, if they had order for it.   The goods of one sorte and
other came to upward of 500*li*.

After these things, Mr. Allerton wente to the ship aboute
his bass fishing; and Mr. Hatherley, (according to his order,)
after he tooke knowledg how things stood at the plantation,
(of all which they informed him fully,) he then desired a boate
of them to goe and visite the trading houeses, both Kenebeck,
and Ashley at Penobscote; for so they in England had injoyned
him.   They accordingly furnished him with a boate and men
for the viage, and aquainted him plainly and thorowly with all
things; by which he had good contente and satisfaction, and
saw plainly that Mr. Allerton plaid his owne game, and rane a
course not only to the great wrong and detrimente of the plantation, who imployed and trusted him, but abused them in
England also, in possessing them with prejudice against the
plantation; as that they would never be able to repaye their
moneys (in regard of their great charge), but if they would
follow his advice and projects, he and Ashley (being well supplyed) would quickly bring in their moneys with good advantage.   Mr. Hatherley disclosed also a further projecte
aboute the setting out of this ship, the *White-angell;* how, she
being wel fitted with good ordnance, and known to have made
a great fight at sea (when she belonged to Bristoll) and caried
away the victory, they had agreed (by Mr. Allerton's means)
that, after she had brought a fraight of goods here into the
countrie, and fraight her selfe with fish, she should goe from
hence to Port of porte,[1] and ther be sould, both ship, goods,
and ordenance; and had, for this end, had speech with a
factore of those parts, beforehand, to whom she should have
been consigned.   But this was prevented at this time, (after
it was known,) partly by the contrary advice given by their
freinds hear to Mr. Allerton and Mr. Hatherley, showing how
it might insnare their friends in England, (being men of estate,)

[1] Oporto in Portugal.

if it should come to be knowne; and for the plantation, they did and would disalow it, and protest against it; and partly by their bad viage, for they both came too late to doe any good for fishing, and allso had such a wicked and drunken company as neither Mr. Allerton nor any els could rule; as Mr. Hatherley, to his great greefe and shame, saw, and beheld, and all others that came nere them.

Ashley likwise was taken in a trape, (before Mr. Hatherley returned,) for trading powder and shote with the Indeans; and was ceased upon by some in authoritie, who allso would have confiscated above a thousand weight of beaver; but the goods were freed, for the Govr here made it appere, by a bond under Ashleys hand, wherin he was bound to them in 500li. not to trade any munition with the Indeans, or other wise to abuse him selfe; it was also manifest against him that he had commited uncleannes with Indean women, (things that they feared at his first imployment, which made them take this strict course with him in the begining); so, to be shorte, they gott their goods freed, but he was sent home prisoner. And that I may make an end concerning him, after some time of imprisonmente in the Fleet,[1] by the means of friends he was set at liberty, and intended to come over againe, but the Lord prevented it; for he had a motion made to him, by some marchants, to goe into Russia, because he had such good skill in the beaver trade, the which he accepted of, and in his returne home was cast away at sea; this was his end.

Mr. Hatherley, fully understanding the state of all things, had good satisfaction, and could well informe them how all things stood betweene Mr. Allerton and the plantation. Yea, he found that Mr. Allerton had gott within him, and got all the goods into his owne hands, for which Mr. Hatherley stood joyntly ingaged to them hear, aboute the ship-*Freindship*, as also most of the fraigte money, besids some of his owne per-ticuler estate; about which more will appear here after. So

---

[1] The celebrated prison on the Fleet market, in the city of London.

he returned into England, and they sente a good quantity of beaver with him to the rest of the partners; so both he and it was very wellcome unto them.

Mr. Allerton followed his affaires, and returned with his *White Angell*, being no more imployed by the plantation; but these bussinesses were not ended till many years after, nor well understood of a longe time, but foulded up in obscuritie, and kepte in the clouds, to the great loss and vexation of the plantation, who in the end were (for peace sake) forced to bear the unjust burthen of them, to their allmost undoing, as will appear, if God give life to finish this history.

They sent their letters also by Mr. Hatherley to the partners ther, to show them how Mr. Hatherley and Mr. Allerton had discharged them of the *Friendship* accounte, and that they boath affirmed that the *White-Angell* did not at all belong to them; and therfore desired that their accounte might not be charged therwith. Also they write to Mr. Winslow, their agente, that he in like maner should (in their names) protest against it, if any such thing should be intended, for they would never yeeld to the same. As allso to signifie to them that they renounsed Mr. Allerton wholy, for being their agente, or to have any thing to doe in any of their bussines.

This year John Billinton the elder (one that came over with the first) was arrained, and both by grand and petie jurie found guilty of willfull murder, by plaine and notorious evidence. And was for the same accordingly executed. This, as it was the first execution amongst them, so was it a mater of great sadnes unto them. They used all due means about his triall, and tooke the advice of Mr. Winthrop and other the ablest gentle-men in the Bay of the Massachusets, that were then new-ly come over, who concured with them that he ought to dye, and the land to be purged from blood. He and some of his had been often punished for miscariags before, being one of the profanest families amongst them. They came from London, and I know not by what freinds shufled into their company. His facte was, that he way-laid a yong-man, one John New-comin, (about a former quarell,) and shote him with a gune, wherof he dyed.[1]

Having by a providence a letter or to that came to my hands concerning the proceedings of their Re[d]: freinds in the Bay of the Massachusets, who were latly come over, I thought it not amise here to inserte them, (so farr as is pertenente, and may be usefull for after times,) before I conclude this year.

Sr: Being at Salem the 25. of July, being the saboath, after the evening exercise, Mr. Johnson received a letter from the Gov[r], Mr. John Winthrop, manifesting the hand of God to be upon them, and against them at Charles-towne, in visiting them with sicknes, and taking diverse from amongst them, not sparing the righteous, but partaking with the wicked in these bodily judgments. It was therfore by his desire taken into the Godly consideration of the best hear, what was to be done to pacifie the Lords wrath, etc. Wher it was concluded, that the Lord was to be sought in righteousnes; and to that end, the 6. day (being Friday) of this present weeke, is set aparte, that they may humble them selves before God, and seeke him in his ordenances; and that then also such godly persons that are amongst them, and known each to other, may publickly, at the end of their exercise, make known their Godly desire, and practise the same, viz. solemnly to enter into covenante with the Lord to walke in his ways. And since they are so disposed of in their outward estats, as to live in three distinct places, each having men of abilitie amongst them, ther to observe the day, and become 3. distincte bodys; not then intending rashly to proceed to the choyce of officers, or the admitting of any other to their societie then a few, to witte, such as are well knowne unto them; promising after to receive in such by confession of faith, as shall appeare to be fitly qualified for the estate. They doe ernestly entreate that the church of Plimoth would set apparte the same day, for the same ends, beseeching the Lord, as to withdraw his hand of correction from them, so also to establish and direct them in his wayes. And though the time be shorte, we pray you be provocked to this godly worke, seing the causes are so urgente; wherin God will be honoured, and they and we undoubtedly have sweete comforte. Be you all kindly saluted, etc.

Salem, July 26. 1630.   Your brethren in Christ, etc.

[1] This paragraph was written on the reverse of a page (180) of the original manuscript, near this place.

Sr: etc. The sadd news here is, that many are sicke, and many are dead; the Lord in mercie looke upon them. Some are here entered into church covenante; the first were 4. namly, the Govr, Mr. John Winthrop, Mr. Johnson, Mr. Dudley, and Mr. Willson;[1] since that 5. more are joyned unto them, and others, it is like, will adde them selves to them dayly; the Lord increase them, both in number and in holines for his mercie sake. Here is a gentleman, one Mr. Cottington, (a Boston man,) who tould me, that Mr. Cottons charge at Hamton was, that they should take advise of them at Plimoth, and should doe nothing to offend them. Here are diverce honest Christians that are desirous to see us, some out of love which they bear to us, and the good perswasion they have of us; others to see whether we be so ill as they have heard of us. We have a name of holines, and love to God and his saincts; the Lord make us more and more answerable, and that it may be more then a name, or els it will doe us no good. Be you lovingly saluted, and all the rest of our friends. The Lord Jesus blese us, and the whole Israll of God. Amen.

Your loving brother, etc.

Charles-towne, Aug. 2. 1630.

Thus out of smalle beginings greater things have been produced by his hand that made all things of nothing, and gives being to all things that are; and as one small candle may light a thousand, so the light here kindled hath shone to many, yea in some sorte to our whole nation; let the glorious name of Jehova have all the praise.

Anno Dom: 1631.

ASHLEY being thus by the hand of God taken away, and Mr. Allerton discharged of his imploymente for them, their bussines began againe to rune in one chanell, and them selves better able to guide the same, Penobscote being wholy now at

---

[1] Governor Winthrop, Isaac Johnson and Thomas Dudley of the court of assistants, and Rev. John Wilson, subsequently elected teacher of the church, united in a covenant to form the church, then admitted others. Rev. John Cotton, mentioned just below, was a famous Puritan divine of Boston, England, who three years later became teacher of this church formed at Charlestown but soon transferred to Boston. Wilson became its pastor. The person mentioned below as "Mr. Cottington" was William Coddington, a native of Boston in England, now a member of the court of assistants, afterwards banished for sympathy with Mrs. Hutchinson, and a founder and governor of Rhode Island.

their disposing.   And though Mr. William Peirce had a parte
ther as is before noted, yet now, as things stood, he was glad to
have his money repayed him, and stand out.   Mr. Winslow,
whom they had sent over, sent them over some supply as
soone as he could; and afterwards when he came, which was
something longe by reason of bussines, he brought a large
supply of suitable goods with him, by which ther trading
was well carried on.   But by no means either he, or the
letters they write, could take off Mr. Sherley and the rest
from putting both the *Friendship* and *Whit-Angell* on the
generall accounte; which caused continuall contention betweene them, as will more appeare.

I shall inserte a leter of Mr. Winslow's about these things,
being as foloweth.

Sr: It fell out by Gods providence, that I received and brought your
leters p^r Mr. Allerton from Bristoll, to London; and doe much feare
what will be the event of things.   Mr. Allerton intended to prepare the
ship againe, to set forth upon fishing.   Mr. Sherley, Mr. Beachamp, and
Mr. Andrews, they renounce all perticulers, protesting but for us they
would never have adventured one penie into those parts; Mr. Hatherley
stands inclinable to either.   And wheras you write that he and Mr.
Allerton have taken the *Whit-Angell* upon them, for their partners here,
they professe they neiver gave any such order, nor will make it good; if
them selves will cleare the accounte and doe it, all shall be well.   What
the evente of these things will be, I know not.   The Lord so directe and
assiste us, as he may not be dishonoured by our divissions.   I hear (p^r
a freind) that I was much blamed for speaking wth [what] I heard in the
spring of the year, concerning the buying and setting forth of that ship;[1]
sure, if I should not have tould you what I heard so peremtorly reported
(which report I offered now to prove at Bristoll), I should have been
unworthy my imploymente.   And concerning the commission so long
since given to Mr. Allerton, the truth is, the thing we feared is come
upon us; for Mr. Sherley and the rest have it, and will not deliver it,
that being the ground of our agents credite to procure shuch great sumes.
But I looke for bitter words, hard thoughts, and sower looks, from
sundrie, as well for writing this, as reporting the former.   I would I had

---

[1] "This was about the selling the ship in Spaine." (Br.)   Oporto, like the
rest of Portugal, was a part of the Spanish monarchy from 1580 to 1640.

a more thankfull imploymente; but I hope a good conscience shall make it comefortable, etc.

Thus farr he. Dated Nov: 16. 1631.

The comission above said was given by them under their hand and seale, when Mr. Allerton was first imployed by them, and redemanded of him in the year 29. when they begane to suspecte his course. He tould them it was amongst his papers, but he would seeke it out and give it them before he wente. But he being ready to goe, it was demanded againe. He said he could not find it, but it was amongst his papers, which he must take with him, and he would send it by the boat from the eastward; but ther it could not be had neither, but he would seeke it up at sea. But whether Mr. Sherley had it before or after, it is not certaine; but having it, he would not let it goe, but keeps it to this day. Wherfore, even amongst freinds, men had need be carfull whom they trust, and not lett things of this nature lye long unrecaled.

Some parts of Mr. Sherley's letters aboute these things, in which the truth is best manifested.

Sr: Yours I have received by our loving friends, Mr. Allerton and Mr. Hatherley, who, blesed be God, after a long and dangerous passage with the ship *Angell*, are safely come to Bristoll. Mr. Hatherley is come up, but Mr. Allerton I have not yet seen. We thanke you, and are very glad you have disswaded him from his Spanish viage, and that he did not goe on in these designes he intended; for we did all uterly dislick of that course, as allso of the fishing that the *Freindship* should have performed; for we wished him to sell the salte, and were unwilling to have him undertake so much bussines, partly for the ill success we formerly had in those affaires, and partly being loath to disburse so much money. But he perswaded us this must be one way that must repay us, for the plantation would be long in doing of it; ney, to my rememberance, he doubted you could not be able, with the trade ther, to maintaine your charge and pay us. And for this very cause he brought us on that bussines with Ed: Ashley, for he was a stranger to us, etc.

For the fishing ship, we are sorie it proves so heavie, and will be willing to bear our parts. What Mr. Hatherley and Mr. Allerton have done, no doubt but them selves will make good;[1] we gave them no order to make any composition, to seperate you and us in this or any other. And I thinke you have no cause to forsake us, for we put you upon no new thing, but what your agent perswaded us to, and you by your letters desired. If he exceede your order, I hope you will not blame us, much less cast us of, when our moneys be layed out, etc. But I fear neither you nor we have been well delte withall, for sure, as you write, halfe 4000*li*., nay, a quarter, in fitting comodities, and in seasonable time, would have furnished you beter then you were. And yet for all this, and much more I might write, I dare not but thinke him honest, and that his desire and intente was good; but the wisest may faile. Well, now that it hath pleased God to give us hope of meeting, doubte not but we will all indeavore to perfecte these accounts just and right, as soone as possibly we can. And I suppos you sente over Mr. Winslow, and we Mr. Hatherley, to certifie each other how the state of things stood. We have received some contente upon Mr. Hatherley's returne, and I hope you will receive good contente upon Mr. Winslow's returne. Now I should come to answer more perticulerly your letter, but herin I shall be very breefe. The coming of the *White Angele* on your accounte could not be more strang to you, then the buying of her was to us; for you gave him commission [2] that what he did you would stand too; we gave him none, and yet for his credite, and your saks, payed what bills he charged on us, etc. For that I write she was to acte tow parts, fishing and trade; beleeve me, I never so much as thought of any perticuler trade, nor will side with any that doth, if I conceive it may wrong you; for I ever was against it, useing these words: They will eate up and destroy the generall.

[1] "They were too short in resting on Mr. Hatherleys honest word, for his order to discharg them from the *Friendship's* accounte, when he and Mr. Allerton made the bargane with them, and they delivered them the rest of the goods; and therby gave them oppertunitie also to receive all the fraight of boath viages, without seeing an order (to have such power) under their hands in writing, which they never doubted of, seeing he affirmed he had power; and they both knew his honestie, and that he was spetially imployed for their agente at this time. And he was as shorte in resting on a verball order from them; which was now denyed, when it came to a perticuler of loss; but he still affirmed the same. But they were both now taught how to deale in the world, espetially with marchants, in such cases. But in the end this light upon these here also, for Mr. Allerton had gott all into his owne hand, and Mr. Hatherley was not able to pay it, except they would have uterlie undon him, as the sequell will manifest." (Note by Bradford.)

[2] "This commission is abused; he never had any for shuch end, as they well knew, nether had they any to pay this money, nor would have paid a peny, if they had not pleased for some other respecte." (Br.)

Other things I omite as tedious, and not very pertenente. This was dated Novr. 19. 1631.

In an other leter bearing date the 24. of this month, being an answer to the generall order, he hath these words:—

For the *White Angell*, against which you write so ernestly, and say we thrust her upon you, contrary to the intente of the buyer, herin we say you forgett your selves, and doe us wrong. We will not take uppon us to devine what the thougts or intents of the buyer was, but what he spack we heard, and that we will affirme, and make good against any that oppose it; which is, that unles shee were bought, and shuch a course taken, Ashley could not be supplyed; and againe, if he weer not supplyed, we could not be satisfied what we were out for you. And further, you were not able to doe it; and he gave some reasons which we spare to relate, unless by your unreasonable refusall you will force us, and so hasten that fire which is a kindling too fast allready, etc.

Out of another of his, bearing date Jan. 2. 1631.

We purpose to keep the *Freindship* and the *Whit Angell*, for the last year viages, on the generall accounte, hoping togeither they will rather produse profite then loss, and breed less confution in our accounts, and less disturbance in our affections. As for the *White Angell*, though we layed out the money, and tooke bills of salle in our owne names, yet none of us had so much as a thought (I dare say) of deviding from you in any thing this year, because we would not have the world (I may say Bristoll) take notice of any breach betwixte Mr. Allerton and you, and he and us; and so disgrace him in his proceedings o[n] in his intended viage. We have now let him the ship at 30*li*. p^r month, by charter-partie, and bound him in a bond of a 1000*li*. to performe covenants, and bring her to London (if God please). And what he brings in her for you, shall be marked with your marke, and bils of laden taken, and sent in Mr. Winslows letter, who is this day riding to Bristoll about it. So in this viage, we deale and are with him as strangers. He hath brought in 3. books of accounts, one for the company, an other for Ashley's bussines, and the third for the *Whit-Angell* and *Freindship*. The books, or coppies, we purpose to send you, for you may discover the errours in them better then we. We can make it appear how much money he hath had of us, and you can charg him with all the beaver he hath had of you. The totall sume, as he hath put it, is 7103. 17. 1. Of this he hath expended, and given to Mr. Vines and others, aboute 543*li*. ode money, and then by your books you will find whether you had such, and so much goods, as he chargeth you with all; and this is all that I can say at presente concerning these accounts. He thought to dispatch them in a few howers, but he and Straton and Fogge were above a month aboute them; but he could not stay till we had examined them, for losing his fishing viage, which I fear he hath allready done, etc.

We blese God, who put both you and us in mind to send each to other, for verily had he rune on in that desperate and chargable course one year more, we had not been able to suport him; nay, both he and we must have lyen in the ditch, and sunck under the burthen, etc. Had ther been an orderly course taken, and your bussines better managed, assuredly (by the blessing of God) you had been the ablest plantation that, as we think, or know, hath been undertaken by Englishmen, etc.

Thus farr of these letters of [Mr. Sherley's.][1]

A few observations from the former letters, and then I shall set downe the simple truth of the things (thus in controversie betweene them), at least as farr as by any good evidence it could be made to appeare; and so laboure to be breefe in so tedious and intricate a bussines, which hunge in expostulation betweene them many years before the same was ended. That though ther will be often occasion to touch these things about other passages, yet I shall not neede to be large therin; doing it hear once for all.

First, it seemes to appere clearly that Ashley's bussines, and the buying of this ship, and the courses framed ther upon, were first contrived and proposed by Mr. Allerton, as also that the pleaes and pretences which he made, of the inablitie of the plantation to repaye their moneys, etc., and the hops he gave them of doing it with profite, was more beleeved and rested on by them (at least some of them) then any thing the plantation did or said.

2. It is like, though Mr. Allerton might thinke not to wrong the plantation in the maine, yet his owne gaine and private ends led him a side in these things; for it came to be knowne, and I have it in a letter under Mr. Sherley's hand, that in the first 2. or 3. years of his imploymente, he had cleared up

[1] The last two words not found in the manuscript, but obviously intended.

400*li.* and put it into a brew-house of Mr. Colliers in London, at first under Mr. Sherley's name, etc.; besids what he might have other wise. Againe, Mr. Sherley and he had perticuler dealings in some things; for he bought up the beaver that seamen and other passengers brought over to Bristoll, and at other places, and charged the bills to London, which Mr. Sherley payed; and they got some time 50*li.* a peece in a bargen, as was made knowne by Mr. Hatherley and others, besids what might be other wise; which might make Mr. Sherley harken unto him in many things; and yet I beleeve, as he in his forementioned leter write, he never would side in any perticuler trade which he conceived would wrong the plantation, and eate up and destroy the generall.

3^{ly}. It may be perceived that, seeing they had done so much for the plantation, both in former adventures and late disbursements, and allso that Mr. Allerton was the first occasioner of bringing them upon these new designes, which at first seemed faire and profitable unto them, and unto which they agreed; but now, seeing them to turne to loss, and decline to greater intanglments, they thought it more meete for the plantation to bear them, then them selves, who had borne much in other things allready, and so tooke advantage of such comission and power as Mr. Allerton had formerly had as their agente, to devolve these things upon them.

4^{ly}. With pitie and compassion (touching Mr. Allerton) I may say with the apostle to Timothy, 1. Tim. 6. 9. *They that will be rich fall into many temtations and snares, etc., and pearce them selves throw with many sorrows, etc.; for the love of money is the roote of all evill,* v. 10. God give him to see the evill in his failings, that he may find mercie by repentance for the wrongs he hath done to any, and this pore plantation in spetiall. They that doe such things doe not only bring them selves into snares, and sorrows, but many with them, (though in an other kind,) as lamentable experience shows; and is too manifest in this bussines.

Now about these ships and their setting forth, the truth, as
farr as could be learned, is this. The motion aboute setting
forth the fishing ship (caled the *Frindship*) came first from the
plantation, and the reasons of it, as is before remembered;
but wholy left to them selves to doe or not to doe, as they saw
cause. But when it fell into consideration, and the designe
was held to be profitable and hopefull, it was propounded by
some of them, why might not they doe it of them selves, seeing
they must disburse all the money, and what need they have
any refferance to the plantation in that; they might take the
profite them selves, towards other losses, and need not let the
plantation share therin; and if their ends were other wise
answered for their supplyes to come too them in time, it would
be well enough. So they hired her, and set her out, and
fraighted her as full as she could carry with passengers goods
that belonged to the Massachussets, which rise to a good sume
of money; intending to send the plantations supply in the
other ship. The effecte of this Mr. Hatherley not only declared afterward upon occasion, but affirmed upon othe, taken
before the Govr and Dep: Govr of the Massachusets, Mr.
Winthrop and Mr. Dudley: That this ship-*Frindship* was
not sett out nor intended for the joynt partnership of the plantation, but for the perticuler accounte of Mr. James Sherley,
Mr. Beachampe, Mr. Andrews, Mr. Allerton, and him selfe.
This deposition was taken at Boston the 29. of Aug: 1639.
as is to be seen under their hands; besids some other concurente
testimonies declared at severall times to sundrie of them.

Aboute the *Whit-Angell*, though she was first bought, or
at least the price beaten, by Mr. Allerton (at Bristoll), yet that
had been nothing if Mr. Sherley had not liked it, and disbursed
the money. And that she was not intended for the plantation
appears by sundrie evidences;[1] as, first, the bills of sale, or

---

[1] "About the *Whit-Angell* they all mette at a certaine taverne in London,
wher they had a diner prepared, and had a conference with a factore aboute
selling of her in Spaine, or at Port a porte, as hath been before mentioned; as
Mr. Hatherley manifested, and Mr. Allerton could not deney." (Br.)

charter-parties, were taken in their owne names, without any mention or refferance to the plantation at all; viz. Mr. Sherley, Mr. Beachampe, Mr. Andrews, Mr. Denison, and Mr. Allerton; for Mr. Hatherley fell off, and would not joyne with them in this. That she was not bought for their accounte, Mr. Hatherley tooke his oath before the parties afforesaid, the day and year above writen.

Mr. Allerton tooke his oath to like effecte concerning this ship, the *Whit-Angell*, before the Govr and Deputie, the 7. of Sep: 1639. and likewise deposed, the same time, that Mr. Hatherley and him selfe did, in the behalfe of them selves and the said Mr. Sherley, Mr. Andrews, and Mr. Beachamp, agree and undertake to discharge, and save harmless, all the rest of the partners and purchasers, of and from the said losses of *Freindship* for 200*li.*, which was to be discounted therupon; as by ther depossitions (which are in writing) may appeare more at large, and some other depositions and other testemonies by Mr. Winslow,[1] etc. But I suppose these may be sufficente to evince the truth in these things, against all pretences to the contrary. And yet the burthen lay still upon the plantation; or, to speake more truly and rightly, upon those few that were ingaged for all, for they were faine to wade through these things without any help from any.

Concerning Mr. Allerton's accounts, they were so larg and intrecate, as they could not well understand them, much less examine and correcte them, without a great deale of time and help, and his owne presence, which was now hard to gett

---

[1] "Mr. Winslow deposed, the same time, before the Govr afore said, etc. that when he came into England, and the partners inquired of the success of the *Whit Angell*, which should have been laden with bass and so sent for Port, of Porting-gall, and their ship and goods to be sould; having informed them that they were like to faile in their lading of bass, that then Mr. James Sherley used these termes: Feck, we must make one accounte of all; and ther upon presed him, as agente for the partners in Neu-England, to accepte the said ship *Whit-Angell*, and her accounte, into the joynte partner-ship; which he refused, for many reasons; and after received instructions from New-Engl: to refuse her if she should be offered, which instructions he shewed them; and wheras he was often pressed to accept her, he ever refused her, etc." (Note by Bradford.)

amongst them; and it was 2. or 3. years before they could bring them to any good pass, but never make them perfecte.   I know not how it came to pass, or what misterie was in it, for he tooke upon him to make up all accounts till this time, though Mr. Sherley was their agente to buy and sell their goods, and did more then he therin; yet he past in accounts in a maner for all disbursments, both concerning goods bought, which he never saw, but were done when he was hear in the cuntrie or at sea; and all the expences of the Leyden people, done by others in his absence; the charges aboute the patente, etc. In all which he made them debtore to him above 300*li.* and demanded paimente of it.   But when things came to scaning, he was found above 2000*li.* debtore to them, (this wherin Mr. Hatherley and he being joyntly ingaged, which he only had, being included,) besids I know not how much that could never be cleared; and interest moneys which ate them up, which he never accounted.   Also they were faine to alow such large bills of charges as were intolerable; the charges of the patent came to above 500*li.* and yet nothing done in it but what was done at first without any confirmation; 30*li.* given at a clape, and 50*li.* spent in a journey.   No marvell therfore if Mr. Sherley said in his leter, if their bussines had been better managed, they might have been the richest plantation of any English at that time.   Yea, he scrued[1] up his poore old father in law's accounte to above 200*li.* and brought it on the generall accounte, and to befreind him made most of it to arise out of those goods taken up by him at Bristoll, at 50. per cent., because he knew they would never let it lye on the old man, when, alass! he, poore man, never dreamte of any such thing, nor that what he had could arise nere that valew; but thought that many of them had been freely bestowed on him and his children by Mr. Allerton.   Nither in truth did they come nere that valew in worth, but that sume was blowne up by interest and high prises, which the company did for the most parte bear,

[1] Screwed.

(he deserving farr more,) being most sory that he should have a name to have much, when he had in effecte litle.

This year also Mr. Sherley sent over an accounte, which was in a maner but a cash accounte what Mr. Allerton had had of them, and disbursed, for which he referd to his accounts; besids an account of beaver sould, which Mr. Winslow and some others had carried over, and a large supply of goods which Mr. Winslow had sent and brought over, all which was comprised in that accounte, and all the disbursements aboute the *Freind-ship*, and *Whit-Angell*, and what concerned their accounts from first to last; or any thing else he could charg the partners with.   So they were made debtor in the foote of that accounte 4770*li*. 19. 2.[1] besids 1000*li*. still due for the purchase yet unpayed; notwithstanding all the beaver, and returnes that both Ashley and they had made, which were not small.

In these accounts of Mr. Sherley's some things were obscure, and some things twise charged, as a 100. of Bastable ruggs which came in the *Freindship*, and cost 75*li*., charged before by Mr. Allerton, and now by him againe, with other perticulers of like nature doubtfull, to be twise or thrise charged;   as also a sume of 600*li*. which Mr. Allerton deneyed, and they could never understand for what it was.   They sent a note of these and such like things afterward to Mr. Sherley by Mr. Winslow; but (I know not how it came to pass) could never have them explained.

Into these deepe sumes had Mr. Allerton rune them in tow years, for in the later end of the year 1628. all their debts did not amounte to much above 400*li*., as was then noted;   and now come to so many thousands.   And wheras in the year

[1] "So as a while before, wheras their great care was how to pay the purchase, and those other few debts which were upon them, now it was with them as it was some times with Saule's father, who left careing for the Asses, and sorrowed for his sonn. 1. Sam. 10. 2.   So that which before they looked at as a heavie burthen, they now esteeme but a small thing and a light mater, in comparison of what was now upon them.   And thus the Lord oftentimes deals with his people to teach them, and humble them, that he may doe them good in the later end."   (Br.)

1629. Mr. Sherley and Mr. Hatherley being at Bristoll, and write a large letter from thence, in which they had given an account of the debts, and what sumes were then disbursed, Mr. Allerton never left begging and intreating of them till they had put it out. So they bloted out 2. lines in that leter in which the sumes were contained, and write upon it so as not a word could be perceived; as since by them was confessed, and by the leters may be seene. And thus were they kept hoodwinckte, till now they were so deeply ingaged. And wheras Mr. Sherley did so ernestly press that Mr. Allerton might be sent over to finish the great bussines aboute the patente, as may be seen in his leter write 1629. as is before recorded, and that they should be ernest with his wife to suffer him to goe, etc., he hath since confessed by a letter under my hands, that it was Mr. Allerton's owne doings, and not his, and he made him write his words, and not his owne. The patent was but a pretence, and not the thing. Thus were they abused in their simplicitie, and no beter then bought and sould, as it may seeme.

And to mend the matter, Mr. Allerton doth in a sorte wholy now deserte them; having brought them into the briers, he leaves them to gett out as they can. But God crost him mightily, for he having hired the ship of Mr. Sherly at 30*li.* a month, he set forth againe with a most wicked and drunken crue, and for covetousnes sake did so over lade her, not only filling her hould, but so stufed her betweene decks, as she was walte,[1] and could not bear sayle, and they had like to have been cast away at sea, and were forced to put for Millford Havene,[2] and new-stow her, and put some of ther ordnance and more heavie goods in the botome; which lost them time, and made them come late into the countrie, lose ther season, and made a worse viage then the year before. But being come into the countrie, he sells trading comodities to any that will

---

[1] Walty, crank, liable to roll over.
[2] Milford Haven is a harbor in Pembrokeshire, in the southwest part of Wales.

buy, to the great prejudice of the plantation here; but that which is worse, what he could not sell, he trustes; and sets up a company of base felows and maks them traders, to rune into every hole, and into the river of Kenebeck, to gleane away the trade from the house ther, aboute the patente and priviledge wherof he had dasht away so much money of theirs here; and now what in him lay went aboute to take away the benefite therof, and to overthrow them. Yea, not only this, but he furnishes a company, and joyns with some consorts, (being now deprived of Ashley at Penobscote,) and sets up a trading house beyoned Penobscote, to cute of the trade from thence also. But the French perceiving that that would be greatly to their damage allso, they came in their begining before they were well setled, and displanted them, slue 2. of their men, and tooke all their goods to a good valew, the loss being most, if not all, Mr. Allerton's; for though some of them should have been his partners, yet he trusted them for their partes; the rest of the men were sent into France, and this was the end of that projecte. The rest of those he trusted, being lose and drunken fellows, did for the most parte but coussen and cheate him of all they got into their hands; that howsoever he did his friends some hurte hereby for the presente, yet he gate litle good, but wente by the loss by Gods just hand. After in time, when he came to Plimmoth, the church caled him to accounte for these, and other his grosse miscarrages; he confessed his faulte, and promised better walking, and that he would wind him selfe out of these courses as soone as he could, etc.

This year also Mr. Sherley would needs send them over a new-acountante; he had made mention of such a thing the year before, but they write him word, that their charge was great allready, and they neede not increase it, as this would; but if they were well delte with, and had their goods well sent over, they could keep their accounts hear them selves. Yet he now sente one, which they did not refuse, being a yonger brother of Mr. Winslows, whom they had been at charge to instructe at London before he came. He came over in the *White Angell* with Mr. Allerton, and ther begane his first imploymente; for though Mr. Sherley had so farr befreinded Mr. Allerton, as to cause[1] Mr. Winslow to ship the supply sente to the partners here in this ship, and give him 4*li*. p^r tune wheras others carried for 3. and he made them pay their fraight ready downe, before the ship wente out of the harbore, wheras others payed upon certificate of the goods being delivered, and their fraight came to upward of 6. score pounds, yet they had much adoe to have their goods delivered, for some of them were chainged, as bread and pease; they were forced to take worse for better, neither could they ever gett all. And if Josias Winslow had not been ther, it had been worse; for he had the invoyce, and order to send them to the trading houses.

This year their house at Penobscott was robed by the French, and all their goods of any worth they carried away, to the value of 400. or 500*li*. as the cost first peny worth; in beaver 300*li*. waight; and the rest in trading goods, as coats, ruggs, blankett, biskett, etc. It was in this maner. The m^r of the house, and parte of the company with him, were come with their vessell to the westward to fecth a supply of goods which was brought over for them. In the mean time comes a smale French ship into the harbore (and amongst the company was a false Scott); they pretended they were nuly come from the sea, and knew not wher they were, and that their vesell was very leake, and desired they might hale her a shore and stop their leaks. And many French complements they used, and congees they made; and in the ende, seeing but 3. or 4. simple men, that were servants, and by this Scoth-man understanding that the maister and the rest of the company were gone from home, they fell of comending their gunes and muskets, that lay upon racks by the wall side, and tooke them

---

[1] This word is obscure in the manuscript.

downe to looke on them, asking if they were charged. And when they were possesst of them, one presents a peece ready charged against the servants, and another a pistoll; and bid them not sturr, but quietly deliver them their goods, and carries some of the men aborde, and made the other help to carry away the goods. And when they had tooke what they pleased, they sett them at liberty, and wente their way, with this mocke, biding them tell their m^r when he came, that some of the Ile of Rey gentlemen had been ther.[1]

This year,[2] on[e] Sr Christopher Gardener, being, as him selfe said, descended of that house that the Bishop of Winchester[3] came of (who was so great a persecutor of Gods saincts in Queene Maries days), and being a great traveler, received his first honour of knighthood at Jerusalem, being made Knight of the Sepulcher ther. He came into these parts under pretence of forsaking the world, and to live a private life, in a godly course, not unwilling to put him selfe upon any meane imployments, and take any paines for his living; and some time offered him selfe to joyne to the churchs in sundry places. He brought over with him a servante or 2. and a comly yonge woman, whom he caled his cousin, but it was suspected, she (after the Italian maner) was his concubine. Living at the Massachusets, for some miscariages which he

[1] The above paragraph was written on the reverse of a page (188) of the original manuscript. The Isle of Ré or Rhé is an island off Rochelle. During the recent war between England and France, in 1627, the Duke of Buckingham's expedition to Rochelle was made a failure by his repulse at the Isle of Ré.

[2] The following account of Sir Christopher Gardiner, with the documents accompanying it, extending to page 290, does not appear in the text of the original manuscript,—having been perhaps inadvertently omitted,—but was written on the reverse of certain neighboring pages (189–191). The mysterious Sir Christopher Gardiner came over as an agent of Gorges. Letters arriving from two wives, one of whom he had left in Paris, the other in London, and who had come together in the search for him and compared notes, the Massachusetts government, in February, 1631, ordered that he should be apprehended and sent back to England. After his capture and his delivery to the authorities of the Bay Colony, he was not tried nor punished, but went up into Maine for a year, and then returned to England. An article upon him will be found in the *Proceedings of the Massachusetts Historical Society*, XX. 60–88.   [3] Stephen Gardiner.

should have answered, he fled away from authority, and gott amonge the Indeans of these parts; they sent after him, but could not gett him, and promissed some reward to those that should find him. The Indeans came to the Gov[r] here, and tould wher he was, and asked if they might kill him; he tould them no, by no means, but if they could take him and bring him hither, they should be payed for their paines. They said he had a gune and a rapier, and he would kill them if they went aboute it; and the Massachuset Indeans said they might kille him. But the Gov[r] tould them no, they should not kill him, but watch their opportunitie, and take him. And so they did, for when they light of him by a river side, he got into a canowe to get from them, and when they came nere him, whilst he presented his peece at them to keep them of, the streame carried the canow against a rock, and tumbled both him and his peece and rapier into the water; yet he got out, and having a litle dagger by his side, they durst not close with him, but getting longe pols they soone beat his dagger out of his hand, so he was glad to yeeld; and they brought him to the Gov[r]. But his hands and armes were swolen and very sore with the blowes they had given him. So he used him kindly, and sent him to a lodging wher his armes were bathed and anoynted, and he was quickly well againe, and blamed the Indeans for beating him so much. They said that they did but a litle whip him with sticks. In his lodging, those that made his bed found a litle note booke that by accidente had slipt out of his pockett, or some private place, in which was a memoriall what day he was reconciled to the pope and church of Rome, and in what universitie he tooke his scapula,[1] and such and such degrees. It being brought to the Gov[r], he kept it, and sent the Gov[r] of the Massachusets word of his taking, who sent for him. So the Gov[r] sent him and these notes to the Gov[r] ther, who tooke it very thankfuly; but after he gott for England he shewed his malice, but God prevented him.

[1] academic hood.

See the Gov[r] leter on the other side.[1]

Sr: It hath pleased God to bring Sr Christopher Gardener safe to us, with thos that came with him.   And howsoever I never intended any hard measure to him, but to respecte and use him according to his qualitie, yet I let him know your care of him, and that he shall speed the better for your mediation.   It was a spetiall providence of God to bring those notes of his to our hands; I desire that you will please to speake to all that are privie to them, not to discovere them to any one, for that may frustrate the means of any further use to be made of them.   The good Lord our God who hath allways ordered things for the good of his poore churches here, directe us in this arighte, and dispose it to a good issue.   I am sorie we put you to so much trouble about this gentleman, espetialy at this time of great imploymente, but I know not how to avoyed it.   I must againe intreate you, to let me know what charge and troble any of your people have been at aboute him, that it may be recompenced.   So with the true affection of a frind, desiring all happines to your selfe and yours, and to all my worthy friends with you (whom I love in the Lord), I comende you to his grace and good providence, and rest

Your most assured friend,

John Winthrop.

Boston, May 5. 1631.

By occation wherof I will take a litle libertie to declare what fell out by this mans means and malice, complying with others.   And though I doubt not but it will be more fully done by my honourd friends, whom it did more directly concerne, and have more perticuler knowledg of the matter, yet I will here give a hinte of the same, and Gods providence in preventing the hurte that might have come by the same.   The intelligence I had by a letter from my much hon[d] and beloved freind, Mr. John Winthrop, Gov[r] of the Massachusets.

Sr: Upon a petition exhibited by Sr. Christo: Gardner, Sr. Ferd: Gorges, Captaine Masson, etc., against you and us, the cause was heard before the lords of the Privie Counsell, and after reported to the king, the sucsess wherof maks it evident to all, that the Lord hath care of his people hear. The passages are admirable, and too long to write. I hartily wish an opportunitie to imparte them unto you, being many sheets of paper. But the conclusion was (against all mens expectation) an order for our

<hr>

[1] That is, in the original manuscript.

incouragmente, and much blame and disgrace upon the adversaries, which calls for much thankfullnes from us all, which we purpose (the Lord willing) to express in a day of thanks-giving to our mercifull God, (I doubt not but you will consider, if it be not fitt for you to joyne in it,) who, as he hath humbled us by his late correction, so he hath lifted us up, by an abundante rejoysing, in our deliverance out of so desperate a danger; so as that which our enemies builte their hopes upon to ruine us by, He hath mercifully disposed to our great advantage, as I shall further aquainte you, when occasion shall serve.

The coppy of the order follows.

At the courte at Whit-hall the 19. Jan: 1632.[1]

Present

Sigillum Lord Privie Seale	Lord Cottinton
Ea: of Dorsett	Mr. Tre^r
Lo: Vi: Falkland	Mr. Vic Chamb^r
Lo: Bp: of London	Mr. Sec: Cooke

Maister Sec: Windebanck

Wheras his Matie hath latly been informed of great distraction and much disorder in that plantation in the parts of America called New-England, which, if they be true, and suffered to rune on, would tende to the great dishonour of this kingdome, and utter ruine of that plantation. For prevention wherof, and for the orderly settling of goverment, according to the intention of those patents which have been granted by his Matie and from his late royall father king James, it hath pleased his Matie that the lords and others of his most honourable Privie Counsell, should take the same into consideration. Their lordships in the first place thought fitt to make a comitie of this bord, to take examination of the matters informed; which comitties having called diverse of the principall adventurers in that plantation, and heard those that are complanants against them, most of the things informed being deneyed, and resting to be proved by parties that must be called from that place, which required a long expence of time; and at presente their lordships finding the adventurers were upon dispatch of men, victles, and marchandice for that place, all which would be at a stand, if the adventurers should have discouragmente, or take suspition that the state hear had no good opinion of that plantation; their lordships, not laying the faulte or fancies (if any be) of some perticuler men upon the generall govermente, or principall adventurers, (which in due time is further to be inquired into,) have thought fitt in the meane time to declare, that the appearences were so

[1] *I. e.*, 1633 of new style.

faire, and hopes so greate, that the countrie would prove both beneficiall
to this kingdom, and profitable to the perticuler adventurers, as that the
adventurers had cause to goe on cherfully with their undertakings, and rest
assured, if things were carried as was pretended when the patents were
granted, and accordingly as by the patentes it is appointed, his Majestie
would not only maintaine the liberties and privileges heretofore granted,
but supply any thing further that might tend to the good govermente,
prosperitie, and comforte of his people ther of that place, etc.

WILLIAM TRUMBALL.

Anno Dom: 1632.

MR. ALLERTON, returning for England, litle regarded his
bound of a 1000*li*. to performe covenants; for wheras he was
bound by the same to bring the ship to London, and to pay 30*li*.
per month for her hire, he did neither of boath, for he carried
her to Bristoll againe, from whence he intended to sett her out
againe, and so did the 3. time, into these parts (as after will
appear); and though she had been 10. months upon the former
viage, at 30*li*. p^r month, yet he never payed peney for hire.
It should seeme he knew well enough how to deale with Mr.
Sherley.   And Mr. Sherley, though he would needs tye her
and her accounte upon the generall, yet he would dispose of
her as him selfe pleased; for though Mr. Winslow had in their
names protested against the receiving her on that accounte,
or if ever they should hope to preveile in shuch a thing, yet
never to suffer Mr. Allerton to have any more to doe in her,
yet he the last year let her wholy unto him, and injoyned them
to send all their supplye in her to their prejudice, as is before
noted.   And now, though he broke his bonds, kepte no covenante, paid no hire, nor was ever like to keep covenants, yet
now he goes and sells him all, both ship, and all her accounts,
from first to last (and in effecte he might as well have given
him the same); and not only this, but he doth as good as provide a sanctuary for him, for he gives him one years time to
prepare his accounte, and then to give up the same to them
here; and then another year for him to make paymente of

what should be due upon that accounte. And in the mean time writs ernestly to them not to interupte or hinder him from his bussines, or stay him aboute clearing accounts, etc.; so as he in the mean time gathers up all monies due for fraighte, and any other debtes belonging either to her, or the *Frindship's* accounts, as his owne perticuler; and after, sells ship, and ordnans, fish, and what he had raised, in Spaine, according to the first designe, in effecte; and who had, or what became of the money, he best knows. In the mean time their hands were bound, and could doe nothing but looke on, till he had made all away into other mens hands (save a few catle and a litle land and some small maters he had here at Plimoth), and so in the end removed, as he had allready his person, so all his from hence. This will better appere by Mr. Sherley's leter.

Sr: These few lines are further to give you to understand, that seeing you and we, that never differed yet but aboute the *White-Angell*, which somewhat troubleth us, as I perceive it doth you. And now Mr. Allerton beeing here, we have had some confferance with him about her, and find him very willing to give you and us all contente that possiblie he can, though he burthen him selfe. He is contente to take the *White-Angell* wholy on him selfe, notwithstanding he mett with pirates nere the coast of Ierland, which tooke away his best sayles and other provissions from her; so as verily if we should now sell her, she would yeeld but a small price, besids her ordnance. And to set her forth againe with fresh money we would not, she being now at Bristoll. Wherfore we thought it best, both for you and us, Mr. Allerton being willing to take her, to accepte of his bond of tow thousand pounds, to give you a true and perfecte accounte, and take the whole charge of the *Whit-Angell* wholy to him selfe, from the first to the last. The accounte he is to make and perfecte within 12. months from the date of this letter, and then to pay you at 6. and 6. months after, what soever shall be due unto you and us upon the foote of that accounte. And verily, notwithstanding all the disasters he hath had, I am perswaded he hath enough to pay all men here and ther. Only they must have patience till he can gather in what is due to him ther. I doe not write this slightly, but upon some ground of what I have seen (and perhaps you know not of) under the hands and seals of some, etc. I rest

Your assured friend,

Des: 6. 1632. JAMES SHERLEY.

But heres not a word of the breach of former bonds and covenants, or paimente of the ships hire; this is passt by as if no such thing had been; besids what bonds or obligments so ever they had of him, ther never came any into the hands or sight of the partners here. And for this that Mr. Sherley seems to intimate (as a secrete) of his abilitie, under the hands and seals of some, it was but a trick, having gathered up an accounte of what was owing from such base fellows as he had made traders for him, and other debts; and then got Mr. Mahue, and some others, to affirme under their hand and seale, that they had seen shuch accounts that were due to him.

Mr. Hatherley came over againe this year, but upon his owne occasions, and begane to make preparation to plant and dwell in the countrie. He with his former dealings had wound in what money he had in the patnership into his owne hands, and so gave off all partnership (excepte in name), as was found in the issue of things; neither did he medle, or take any care aboute the same; only he was troubled about his ingagmente aboute the *Friendship*, as will after appeare. And now partly aboute that accounte, in some reconings betweene Mr. Allerton and him, and some debts that Mr. Allerton other-wise owed him upon dealing between them in perticuler, he drue up an accounte of above 2000*li.*, and would faine have ingaged the partners here with it, because Mr. Allerton had been their agent. But they tould him they had been fool'd longe enough with such things, and shewed him that it no way belonged to them; but tould him he must looke to make good his ingagment for the *Freindship*, which caused some trouble betweene Mr. Allerton and him.

Mr. William Peirce did the like, Mr. Allerton being wound into his debte also upon particuler dealings; as if they had been bound to make good all mens debts. But they easily shooke off these things. But Mr. Allerton herby rane into much trouble and vexation, as well as he had troubled others, for Mr. Denison sued him for the money he had disbursed for the 6. part of the *Whit-Angell*, and recovered the same with damages.

Though the partners were thus plunged into great ingagments, and oppresed with unjust debts, yet the Lord prospered their trading, that they made yearly large returnes, and had soone wound them selves out of all, if yet they had otherwise been well delt with all; as will more appear here after. Also the people of the plantation begane to grow in their owtward estats, by rea[son] of the flowing of many people into the cuntrie, espetially into the Bay of the Massachusets; by which means corne and catle rose to a great prise, by which many were much inriched, and commodities grue plentifull; and yet in other regards this benefite turned to their hurte, and this accession of strength to their weaknes. For now as their stocks increased, and the increse vendible, ther was no longer any holding them togeather, but now they must of necessitie goe to their great lots;[1] they could not other wise keep their katle; and having oxen growne, they must have land for plowing and tillage. And no man now thought he could live, except he had catle and a great deale of ground to keep them; all striving to increase their stocks. By which means they were scatered all over the bay, quickly, and the towne, in which they lived compactly till now, was left very thine, and in a short time allmost desolate. And if this had been all, it had been less, thoug to much; but the church must also be devided, and those that had lived so long togeather in Christian and comfortable fellowship must now part and suffer many divissions. First, those that lived on their lots on the other side of the bay (called Duxberie) they could not long bring their wives and children to the publick worship and church meetings here, but with such burthen, as, growing to some competente number, they sued to be dismissed and become a

---

[1] The landed property assigned to each family in Plymouth consisted of a small home lot in the village, sufficient for house and garden, and of larger lots at a greater distance.

body of them selves; and so they were dismiste (about this time), though very unwillingly. But to touch this sadd matter, and handle things together that fell out after ward. To prevent any further scatering from this place, and weakning of the same, it was thought best to give out some good farms to spetiall persons, that would promise to live at Plimoth, and lickly to be helpfull to the church or comonewelth, and so tye the lands to Plimoth as farmes for the same; and ther they might keepe their catle and tillage by some servants, and re-taine their dwellings here. And so some spetiall lands were granted at a place generall, called Greens Harbor,[1] wher no allotments had been in the former divission, a plase very weell meadowed, and fitt to keep and rear catle, good store. But alass! this remedy proved worse then the disease; for within a few years those that had thus gott footing ther rente them selves away, partly by force, and partly wearing the rest with importunitie and pleas of necessitie, so as they must either suf-fer them to goe, or live in continuall opposition and contention. And others still, as they conceived them selves straitened, or to want accommodation, break away under one pretence or other, thinking their owne conceived necessitie, and the example of others, a warrente sufficente for them. And this, I fear, will be the ruine of New-England, at least of the churches of God ther, and will provock the Lords displeasure against them.

This year, Mr. William Perce came into the cuntry, and brought goods and passengers, in a ship caled the *Lyon*, which belonged cheefly to Mr. Sherley, and the rest of the London partners, but these hear had nothing to doe with her. In this ship (besides beaver which they had sent home before) they sent upwards of 800*li.* in her, and some otter skines; and also the coppies of Mr. Allertons accounts, desiring that they would also peruse and examene them, and rectifie shuch things as they should find amise in them; and rather because they were

[1] Green's Harbor was incorporated March 2, 1640, under the name of Rex-ham, but the name was later changed to Marshfield.

better acquaynted with the goods bought ther, and the disbursments made, then they could bee here; yea, a great part were done by them selves, though Mr. Allerton brougt in the accounte, and sundry things seemed to them obscure and had need of clearing. Also they sente a booke of exceptions against his accounts, in such things as they could manifest, and doubted not but they might adde more therunto. And also shewed them how much Mr. Allerton was debtor to the accounte; and desired, seeing they had now put the ship *White-Angell,* and all, wholy into his power, and tyed their hands here, that they could not call him to accounte for any thinge, till the time was expired which they had given him, and by that time other men would get their debts of him, (as sume had done already by suing him,) and he would make all away here quickly out of their reach; and therfore prayed them to looke to things, and gett paymente of him ther, as it was all the reason they should, seeing they kept all the bonds and covenants they made with him in their owne hands; and here they could doe nothing by the course they had taken, nor had any thing to show if they should goe aboute it. But it pleased God, this ship, being first to goe to Verginia before she wente home was cast away on that coast, not farr from Virginia, and their beaver was all lost (which was the first loss they sustained in that kind); but Mr. Peirce and the men saved their lives, and also their leters, and gott into Virginia, and so safly home. The accounts were now sent from hence againe to them. And thus much of the passages of this year.

A part of Mr. Peirce his leter from Virginia.[1]

It was dated in Des: 25. 1632. and came to their hand the 7. of Aprill, before they heard any thing from England.

Dear freinds, etc. The bruit of this fatall stroke that the Lord hath brought both on me and you all will come to your ears before this commeth to your hands, (it is like,) and therfore I shall not need to inlarg in per-

[1]This letter was written on the reverse of a neighboring folio (192) of the original manuscript, and may properly be inserted here.

ticulers, etc. My whole estate (for the most parte) is taken away; and so yours, in a great measure, by this and your former losses [he means by the French and Mr. Allerton]. It is time to looke aboute us, before the wrath of the Lord breake forth to utter destruction. The good Lord give us all grace to search our harts and trie our ways, and turne unto the Lord, and humble our selves under his mightie hand, and seeke atonemente, etc. Dear freinds, you may know that all your beaver, and the books of your accounts, are swallowed up in the sea; your letters remaine with me, and shall be delivered, if God bring me home. But what should I more say? Have we lost our outward estates? yet a hapy loss if our soules may gaine; ther is yet more in the Lord Jehova than ever we had yet in the world. Oh that our foolish harts could yet be wained from the things here below, which are vanity and vexation of spirite; and yet we fooles catch after shadows, that flye away, and are gone in a momente, etc. Thus with my continuall remembrance of you in my poore desires to the throne of grace, beseeching God to renew his love and favoure towards you all, in and through the Lord Jesus Christ, both in spirituall and temporall good things, as may be most to the glory and praise of his name, and your everlasting good. So I rest,

Your afflicted brother in Christ,

Virginia, Des: 25. 1632.   WILLIAM PEIRCE.

Anno Dom: 1633.

THIS year Mr. Ed: Winslow was chosen Governor.

By the first returne this year, they had leters from Mr. Sherley of Mr. Allertons further ill success, and the loss by Mr. Peirce, with many sadd complaints; but litle hope of any thinge to be gott of Mr. Allerton, or how their accounts might be either eased, or any way rectified by them ther; but now saw plainly that the burthen of all would be cast on their backs. The spetiall passages of his letters I shall here inserte, as shall be pertinente to these things; for though I am weary of this tedious and uncomfortable subjecte, yet for the clearing of the truth I am compelled to be more larg in the opening of these matters, upon which so much trouble hath insued, and so many hard censures have passed on both sids. I would not be partiall to either, but deliver the truth in all, and, as nere as I can, in their owne words and passages, and so leave it to the impartiall judgment of any that shall come to read, or veiw these things. His leters are as folow, dated June 24. 1633.

Loving friends, my last[1] was sente in the *Mary and John*, by Mr. William Collier,[2] etc. I then certified you of the great, and uncomfortable, and unseasonable loss you and we had, in the loss of Mr. Peirce his ship, the *Lyon*; but the Lords holy name be blessed, who gives and taks as it pleaseth him; his will be done, Amen. I then related unto you that fearfull accidente, or rather judgmente, the Lord pleased to lay on London Bridge, by fire,[3] and therin gave you a touch of my great loss; the Lord, I hope, will give me patience to bear it, and faith to trust in him, and not in these slipery and uncertaine things of this world.

I hope Mr. Allerton is nere upon sayle with you by this; but he had many disasters here before he could gett away; yet the last was a heavie one; his ship, going out of the harbor at Bristoll, by stormie weather was so farr driven on the shore, as it cost him above 100*li*. before shee could be gott off againe. Verily his case was so lamentable as I could not but afford him some help therin (and so did some were strangers to him); besids, your goods were in her, and if he had not been supported, he must have broke off his viage, and so loss could not have been avoyded on all sides. When he first bought her, I thinke he had made a saving match, if he had then sunck her, and never set her forth. I hope he sees the Lords hand against him, and will leave of these viages. I thinke we did well in parting with her; she would have been but a clogge to the accounte from time to time, and now though we shall not gett much by way of satisfaction, yet we shall lose no more. And now, as before I have writte, I pray you finish all the accounts and reconings with him there; for here he hath nothing, but many debtes that he stands ingaged to many men for. Besids, here is not a man that will spend a day, or scarce an hower, aboute the accounts but my selfe, and that bussines will require more time and help then I can afford. I shall not need to say any more; I hope you will doe that which shall be best and just, to which adde mercie, and consider his intente, though he failed in many perticulers, which now cannot be helped, etc.

To morrow, or next day at furthest, we are to pay 300*li*. and Mr. Beachamp is out of the towne, yet the bussines I must doe. Oh the greefe and trouble that man, Mr. Allerton, hath brought upon you and us! I

---

[1] "March 22." (Br.)

[2] William Collier was one of the London adventurers.

[3] In 1632 London Bridge, on which at that time many houses and shops were situated, was swept from end to end by fire.

cannot forgett it, and to thinke on it draws many   sigh from my harte, and teares from my eyes.   And now the Lord hath visited me with an other great loss, yet I can undergoe it with more patience.   But this I have follishly pulled upon my selfe, etc.   [And in another, he hath this passage:] By Mr. Allertons faire propositions and large promises, I have over rune my selfe; verily, at this time greefe hinders me to write, and tears will not suffer me to see; wherfore, as you love those that ever loved you, and that plantation, thinke upon us.   Oh what shall I say of that man, who hath abused your trust and wronged our loves! but now to complaine is too late, nither can I complaine of your backwardnes, for I am perswaded it lys as heavie on your harts, as it doth on our purses or credites.   And had the Lord sent Mr. Peirce safe home, we had eased both you and us of some of those debts; the Lord I hope will give us patience to bear these crosses; and that great God, whose care and providence is every where, and spetially over all those that desire truly to fear and serve him, direct, guid, prosper, and blesse you so, as that you may be able (as I perswade my selfe you are willing) to discharge and take off this great and heavie burthen which now lyes upon me for your saks; and I hope in the ende for the good of you, and many thousands more; for had not you and we joyned and continued togeather, New-England might yet have been scarce knowne, I am perswaded, not so replenished and inhabited with honest English people, as it now is.   The Lord increase and blesse them, etc. So, with my continuall praiers for you all, I rest

Your assured loving friend,

June 24. 1633.   JAMES SHERLEY.

By this it apperes when Mr. Sherly sould him the ship and all her accounts, it was more for Mr. Allertons advantage then theirs; and if they could get any there, well and good, for they were like to have nothing here.   And what course was held to hinder them there, hath allready beene manifested. And though Mr. Sherley became more sinsible of his owne condition, by these losses, and therby more sadly and plainly to complaine of Mr. Allerton, yet no course was taken to help them here, but all left unto them selves; not so much as to examene and rectifie the accounts, by which (it is like) some hundereds of pounds might have been taken off.   But very probable it is, the more they saw was taken off, the less might come unto them selves.   But I leave these maters, and come to other things.

Mr. Roger Williams [1] (a man godly and zealous, having many precious parts, but very unsettled in judgmente) came over first to the Massachusets, but upon some discontente left that place, and came hither, (wher he was friendly entertained, according to their poore abilitie,) and exercised his gifts amongst them, and after some time was admitted a member of the church; and his teaching well approoved, for the benefite wherof I still blese God, and am thankfull to him, even for his sharpest admonitions and reproufs, so farr as they agreed with truth. He this year begane to fall into some strang oppinions, and from opinion to practise; which caused some controversie betweene the church and him, and in the end some discontente on his parte, by occasion wherof he left them some thing abruptly. Yet after wards sued for his dismission to the church of Salem, which was granted, with some caution to them concerning him, and what care they ought to have of him. But he soone fell into more things ther, both to their and the goverments troble and disturbance. I shall not need to name perticulers, they are too well knowen now to all, though for a time the church here wente under some hard censure by his occasion, from some that afterwards smarted them selves. But he is to be pitied, and prayed for, and so I shall leave the matter, and desire the Lord to shew him his errors, and reduse him into the way of truth, and give him a setled judgment and constancie in the same; for I hope he belongs to the Lord, and that he will shew him mercie.

Having had formerly converse and famliarity with the Dutch, (as is before remembred,) they, seeing them seated, here in a barren quarter, tould them of a river called by them the Fresh River, but now is known by the name of Conighte-cute-River, which they often commended unto them for a fine

---

[1] Roger Williams is so familiar to readers that it is needless to write a sketch of him here. See the work of Rev. Dr. Henry Martyn Dexter, entitled *As to Roger Williams and his Banishment* (Boston, 1876). He was an assistant of Rev. Ralf Smith in Plymouth from 1631 to 1633, when, owing to the liberality of the Pilgrim in their treatment of members of the established Church, he retired to Salem

place both for plantation and trade, and wished them to make use of it. But their hands being full otherwise, they let it pass. But afterwards ther coming a company of banishte Indeans into these parts, that were drivene out from thence by the potencie of the Pequents, which usurped upon them, and drive them from thence, they often sollisited them to goe thither, and they should have much trad, espetially if they would keep a house ther. And having now good store of comodities, and allso need to looke out wher they could advantage them selves to help them out of their great ingagments, they now begane to send that way to discover the same, and trade with the natives. They found it to be a fine place, but had no great store of trade; but the Indeans excused the same in regard of the season, and the fear the Indans were in of their enemise. So they tried diverce times, not with out profite, but saw the most certainty would be by keeping a house ther, to receive the trad when it came down out of the inland. These Indeans, not seeing them very forward to build ther, solisited them of the Massachusets in like sorte (for their end was to be restored to their countrie againe); but they in the Bay being but latly come, were not fitte for the same; but some of their cheefe made a motion to joyne with the partners here, to trad joyntly with them in that river, the which they were willing to imbrace, and so they should have builte, and put in equall stock togeather. A time of meeting was appointed at the Massachusets, and some of the cheefe here was appointed to treat with them, and went accordingly; but they cast many fears of deanger and loss and the like, which was perceived to be the maine obstacles, though they alledged they were not provided of trading goods. But those hear offered at presente to put in sufficiente for both, provided they would become ingaged for the halfe, and prepare against the nexte year. They conffessed more could not be offered, but thanked them, and tould them they had no mind to it. They then answered, they hoped it would be no offerce unto them, if them sellves wente on without them, if they saw it meete. They said ther was no reason they should; and thus this treaty broake of, and those here tooke conveniente time to make a begining ther; and were the first English that both discovered that place, and built in the same, though they were litle better then thrust out of it afterward as may appeare.

But the Dutch begane now to repente, and hearing of their purpose and preparation, indevoured to prevente them, and gott in a litle before them, and made a slight forte, and planted 2. peeces of ordnance, thretening to stopp their passage.[1] But they having made a smale frame of a house ready, and haveing a great new-barke, they stowed their frame in her hold, and bords to cover and finishe it, having nayles and all other provisions fitting for their use. This they did the rather that they might have a presente defence against the Indeans, who weare much offended that they brought home and restored the right Sachem of the place (called Natawanute); so as they were to incounter with a duble danger in this attempte, both the Dutch and the Indeans. When they came up the river, the Dutch demanded what they intended, and whither they would goe; they answered, up the river to trade (now their order was to goe and seat above them). They bid them strike, and stay, or els they would shoote them; and stood by ther ordnance ready fitted. They answered they had commission from the Gov[r] of Plimoth to goe up the river to such a place, and if they did shoote, they must obey their order and proceede; they would not molest them, but would goe one.[2] So they passed along, and though the Dutch threatened them hard, yet they shoot not. Comming to their place, they clapt up their

---

[1] In June, 1633, the Dutch bought from the Pequots a tract of land on the "Fresh River" (Connecticut), where Hartford now stands. Here they built Fort Good Hope. The name Dutch Point still survives, matched by Plymouth Meadow in Windsor.

[2] "On." The commander of the expedition was Lieut. William Holmes of Plymouth, who next to Standish was the military man of the colony. The place was the site of the present town of Windsor, Connecticut, the time September, 1633.

house quickly, and landed their provissions, and left the companie appoynted, and sent the barke home; and afterwards
palisadoed their house aboute, and fortified them selves better.
The Dutch sent word home to the Monhatas[1] what was done;
and in proces of time, they sent a band of aboute 70. men, in
warrlike maner, with collours displayed, to assaulte them;
but seeing them strengtened, and that it would cost blood, they
came to parley, and returned in peace. And this was their
enterance ther, who deserved to have held it, and not by
freinds to have been thrust out, as in a sorte they were, as will
after appere. They did the Dutch no wrong, for they took not
a foote of any land they bought, but went to the place above
them, and bought that tracte of land which belonged to these
Indeans which they carried with them, and their friends, with
whom the Dutch had nothing to doe. But of these matters
more in another place.

It pleased the Lord to visite them this year with an infectious fevoure, of which many fell very sicke, and upward of
20. persons dyed, men and women, besids children, and sundry
of them of their anciente friends which had lived in Holand;
as Thomas Blossome, Richard Masterson, with sundry others,
and in the end (after he had much helped others) Samuell
Fuller, who was their surgeon and phisition, and had been a
great help and comforte unto them; as in his facultie, so otherwise, being a deacon of the church, a man godly, and forward
to doe good, being much missed after his death; and he and
the rest of their brethren much lamented by them, and caused
much sadnes and mourning amongst them; which caused them
to humble them selves, and seeke the Lord; and towards
winter it pleased the Lord the sicknes ceased. This disease
allso swept away many of the Indeans from all the places near
adjoyning; and the spring before, espetially all the month of
May, ther was such a quantitie of a great sorte of flies, like
(for bignes) to wasps, or bumble-bees, which came out of holes

[1] Manhattan.

in the ground, and replenished all the woods, and eate the green-things, and made such a constante yelling noyes, as made all the woods ring of them, and ready to deafe the hearers.[1] They have not by the English been heard or seen before or since. But the Indeans tould them that sicknes would followf and so it did in June, July, August, and the cheefe heat o, sommer.

It pleased the Lord to inable them this year to send home a great quantity of beaver, besids paing all their charges, and debts at home, which good returne did much incourage their freinds in England. They sent in beaver 3366*li*. waight, and much of it coat beaver, which yeeled 20*s*. p^r pound, and some of it above; and of otter-skines [2] 346. sould also at a good prise. And thus much of the affairs of this year.

Anno Dom: 1634.

THIS year Mr. Thomas Prence was chosen Govr.[3]

Mr. Sherleys letters were very breefe in answer of theirs this year. I will forbear to coppy any part therof, only name a head or 2. therin. First, he desirs they will take nothing ill in what he formerly write, professing his good affection towards them as before, etc. 2$^{ly.}$ For Mr. Allertons accounts, he is perswaded they must suffer, and that in no small summes; and that they have cause enough to complaine, but it was now too late. And that he had failed them ther, those here, and him

[1] These were the seventeen-year locusts.

[2] "The skin was sold at 14*s*. and 15. the pound." (Br.)

[3] Thomas Prence came over in the *Fortune* in 1621, about twenty-one years of age. He married in 1624 Patience, daughter of William Brewster, who died in 1634. In 1635 he married Mary, daughter of William Collier, and in 1662 Mercy, widow of Samuel Freeman and daughter of Constant Southworth. He died in 1673. He was governor of Plymouth Colony in 1634 and 1638 and, after the death of William Bradford, from 1657 until his death in 1673. While governor in 1638 he lived on the corner of Spring and High Streets, occupying also an outlying tract of farm land of ten acres including a valley which has long been known as Prence's Bottom. In 1640 he removed to Eastham where he lived for some years. On his return he built and occupied a house on a tract of land at Seaside which he had bought in 1632. He always wrote his name Prence.

selfe in his owne aimes. And that now, having thus left them here, he feared God had or would leave him, and it would not be strang, but a wonder if he fell not into worse things, etc. 3^{ly}. He blesseth God and is thankfull to them for the good returne made this year. This is the effecte of his letters, other things being of more private nature.

I am now to enter upon one of the sadest things that befell them since they came; but before I begine, it will be needfull to premise such parte of their patente as gives them right and priviledge at Kenebeck; as followeth:[1]

The said Counsell hath further given, granted, barganed, sold, infeoffed, alloted, assigned, and sett over, and by these presents doe clearly and absolutly give, grante, bargane, sell, alliene, enffeofe, allote, assigne, and confirme unto the said William Bradford, his heires, associates, and assignes, All that tracte of land or part of New-England in America afforesaid, which lyeth within or betweene, and extendeth it selfe from the utmost limits of Cobiseconte,[2] which adjoyneth to the river of Kenebeck, towards the westerne ocean, and a place called the falls of Nequamkick[3] in America, aforsaid; and the space of 15. English myles on each side of the said river, commonly called Kenebeck River, and all the said river called Kenebeck that lyeth within the said limits and bounds, eastward, westward, northward, and southward, last above mentioned; and all lands, grounds, soyles, rivers, waters, fishing, etc. And by vertue of the authority to us derived by his said late Ma^{tis} Lr̄es patents, to take, apprehend, seise, and make prise of all such persons, their ships and goods, as shall attempte to inhabite or trade with the savage people of that countrie within the severall precincts and limits of his and their severall plantations, etc.

Now it so fell out, that one Hocking, belonging to the plantation of Pascataway, wente with a barke and commodities to trade in that river, and would needs press into their limites; and not only so, but would needs goe up the river above their house, (towards the falls of the river,) and intercept the trade that should come to them. He that was cheefe of the place

---

[1] An extract from the patent from the Council for New England, January 13, 1629/30. See above, pp. 248, 249.

[2] Cobisecontee was where Gardiner, Maine, now stands.

[3] The falls or rapids of Nequamkick lay near the present Winslow, Maine.

forbad them, and prayed him that he would not offer them that
injurie, nor goe aboute to infring their liberties, which had cost
them so dear. But he answered he would goe up and trade
ther in dispite of them, and lye ther as longe as he pleased.
The other tould him he must then be forced to remove him
from thence, or make seasure of him if he could. He bid him
doe his worste, and so wente up, and anchored ther. The
other tooke a boat and some men and went up to him, when
he saw his time, and againe entreated him to departe by what
perswasion he could. But all in vaine: he could gett nothing
of him but ill words. So he considred that now was the season
for trade to come downe, and if he should suffer him to lye,
and take it from them, all ther former charge would be lost,
and they had better throw up all. So, consulting with his men,
(who were willing thertoe,) he resolved to put him from his
anchores, and let him drive downe the river with the streame;
but commanded the men that none should shoote a shote upon
any occasion, except he commanded them. He spoake to him
againe, but all in vaine; then he sente a cuple in a canow to
cutt his cable, the which one of them performes; but Hocking
taks up a pece which he had layed ready, and as the barke
shered by the canow, he shote him close under her side, in the
head, (as I take it,) so he fell downe dead instantly. One of
his fellows (that loved him well) could not hold, but with a
muskett shot Hocking, who fell downe dead and never speake
word. This was the truth of the thing. The rest of the men
carried home the vessell and the sad tidings of these things.
Now the Lord Saye and the Lord Brooks,[1] with some
other great persons, had a hand in this plantation; they
write home to them, as much as they could to exasperate

---

[1] Viscount Saye and Sele and another Puritan lord, Lord Brooke, a cousin
of Sir Fulke Greville, the first Lord Brooke, mentioned in a former foot-note,
are best known in American history as patentees of the Connecticut valley. In
1633 they bought out certain Bristol merchants who were associated with Edward
Hilton in the patent for Cocheco (Dover, New Hampshire), and the incident
which follows is due to their relation to that patent.

them in the matter, leving out all the circomstances, as if
he had been kild without any offenc of his parte, concel-
ing that he had kild another first, and the just occasion
that he had given in offering such wrong; at which their
Lords[ps] were much offended, till they were truly informed
of the mater.

The bruite of this was quickly carried all aboute, (and that
in the worst maner,) and came into the Bay to their neighbours
their. Their owne barke comming home, and bringing a true
relation of the matter, sundry were sadly affected with the
thing, as they had cause. It was not long before they had
occasion to send their vessell into the Bay of the Massachusetts;
but they were so prepossest with this matter, and affected with
the same, as they commited Mr. Alden to prison, who was in
the bark, and had been at Kenebeck, but was no actore in the
bussines, but wente to carie them supply. They dismist the
barke aboute her bussines, but kept him for some time. This
was thought strang here, and they sente Capten Standish to
give them true information, (togeather with their letters,) and
the best satisfaction they could, and to procure Mr. Alden's
release. I shall recite a letter or 2. which will show the passages of these things, as folloeth.

Good Sr:

I have received your lres by Captaine Standish, and am unfainedly
glad of Gods mercie towards you in the recovery of your health, or some
way thertoo. For the bussines you write of, I thought meete to answer a
word or 2. to your selfe, leaving the answer of your Gov[r.] lre to our courte,
to whom the same, together with my selfe is directed. I conceive (till I
hear new matter to the contrary) that your patente may warrente your
resistance of any English from trading at Kenebeck, and that blood of
Hocking, and the partie he slue, will be required at his hands. Yet doe
I with your selfe and others sorrow for their deaths. I thinke likewise
that your generall lres will satisfie our courte, and make them cease
from any further inter medling in the mater. I have upon the same lre
sett Mr. Alden at liberty, and his sureties, and yet, least I should seeme
to neglecte the opinion of our court and the frequente speeches of others
with us, I have bound Captaine Standish to appeare the 3. of June at our

nexte courte, to make affidavid for the coppie of the patente, and to manifest the circumstances of Hockins provocations; both which will tend to the clearing of your innocencie. If any unkindnes hath ben taken from what we have done, let it be further and better considred of, I pray you; and I hope the more you thinke of it, the lesse blame you will impute to us. At least you ought to be just in differencing them, whose opinions concurr with your owne, from others who were opposites; and yet I may truly say, I have spoken with no man in the bussines who taxed you most, but they are such as have many wayes heretofore declared ther good affections towards your plantation. I further referr my selfe to the reporte of Captaine Standish and Mr. Allden; leaving you for this presente to Gods blessing, wishing unto you perfecte recovery of health, and the long continuance of it. I desire to be lovingly remembred to Mr. Prence, your Govr, Mr. Winslow, Mr. Brewster, whom I would see if I knew how. The Lord keepe you all. Amen.

Your very loving freind in our Lord Jesus,

THO: DUDLEY.

New-towne,[1] the 22. of May, 1634.

Another of his about these things as followeth.

Sr: I am right sorrie for the news that Captaine Standish and other of your neigbours and my beloved freinds will bring now to Plimoth, wherin I suffer with you, by reason of my opinion, which differeth from others, who are godly and wise, amongst us here, the reverence of whose judgments causeth me to suspecte myne owne ignorance; yet must I remaine in it untill I be convinced therof. I thought not to have shewed your letter written to me, but to have done my best to have reconciled differences in the best season and maner I could; but Captaine Standish requiring an answer therof publickly in the courte, I was forced to produce it, and that made the breach soe wide as he can tell you. I propounded to the courte, to answer Mr. Prences ʇre, your Govr, but our courte said it required no answer, it selfe being an answer to a former ʇre of ours. I pray you certifie Mr. Prence so much, and others whom it concerneth, that no neglecte or ill manners be imputed to me theraboute. The late ʇres I received from England wrought in me divere[2] fears[3] of some trials

---

[1] *I. e.*, Cambridge, Massachusetts. The name was changed from Newtown to Cambridge in 1638, because of the establishment of Harvard College.

[2] Divers.

[3] "Ther was cause enough of these feares, which arise by the underworking of some enemies to the churches here, by which this Commission following was procured from his Matie." (Br.) See this paper in the appendix, no. II.

which are shortly like to fall upon us; and this unhappie contention betweene you and us, and between you and Pascattaway, will hasten them,
if God with an extraordinarie hand doe not help us.   To reconcile this
for the presente will be very difficulte, but time cooleth distempers, and a
comone danger to us boath approaching, will necessitate our uniting
againe.   I pray you therfore, Sr. set your wisdom and patience a worke,
and exhorte others to the same, that things may not proceede from bad to
worse, so making our contentions like the barrs of a pallace, but that a
way of peace may be kepte open, wherat the God of peace may have
enterance in his owne time.   If you suffer wrong, it shall be your honor
to bear it patiently; but I goe to farr in needles putting you in mind of
these things.   God hath done great things for you, and I desire his blessings may be multiplied upon you more and more.   I will commite no more
to writing, but comending my selfe to your prayers, doe rest,

Your truly loving freind in our Lord Jesus,

Tho: Dudley.

June 4. 1634.

By these things it appars what troubls rise herupon, and
how hard they were to be reconciled; for though they hear
were hartily sorrie for what was fallen out, yet they conceived
they were unjustly injuried, and provoked to what was done;
and that their neigbours (haveing no jurisdiction over them)
did more then was mete, thus to imprison one of theirs, and
bind them to their courte.   But yet being assured of their
Christian love, and perswaded what was done was out of godly
zeale, that religion might not suffer, nor sinne any way covered
or borne with, espetially the guilte of blood, of which all should
be very consciencious in any whom soever, they did indeavore
to appease and satisfie them the best they could; first, by
informing them the truth in all circomstances aboute the matter; 2^{ly}, in being willing to referr the case to any indifferante
and equall hearing and judgmente of the thing hear, and to
answere it els wher when they should be duly called therunto;
and further they craved Mr. Winthrops, and other of the reve^d
magistrats ther, their advice and direction herein.   This did
mollifie their minds, and bring things to a good and comfortable
issue in the end.

For they had this advice given them by Mr. Winthrop, and others concurring with him, that from their courte, they should write to the neigboure plantations, and espetially that of the lords, at Pascataway,[1] and theirs of the Massachusets, to appointe some to give them meeting at some fitt place, to consulte and determine in this matter, so as the parties meeting might have full power to order and bind, etc. And that nothing be done to the infringing or prejudice of the liberties of any place. And for the clearing of conscience, the law of God is that the preist lips must be consulted with, and therfore it was desired that the ministers of every plantation might be presente to give their advice in pointe of conscience. Though this course seemed dangerous to some, yet they were so well assured of the justice of their cause, and the equitie of their freinds, as they put them selves upon it, and appointed a time, of which they gave notice to the severall places a month before hand; viz. Massachusets, Salem, and Pascataway, or any other that they would give notice too, and disired them to produce any evidence they could in the case. The place for meeting was at Boston. But when the day and time came, none apered, but some of the magistrats and ministers of the Massachusets, and their owne. Seeing none of Passcataway of other places came, (haveing been thus desired, and conveniente time given them for that end,) Mr. Winthrop and the rest said they could doe no more then they had done thus to requeste them, the blame must rest on them. So they fell into a fair debating of things them selves; and after all things had been fully opened and discussed, and the opinione of each one demanded, both magistrats, and ministers, though they all could have wished these things had never been, yet they could not but lay the blame and guilt on Hockins owne head; and withall gave them such grave and godly exhortations and advice, as they thought meete, both for the presente and future; which they allso

[1] Meaning the plantation of Lord Saye and Lord Brooke, on the Piscataqua River.

imbraced with love and thankfullnes, promising to indeavor to follow the same. And thus was this matter ended, and ther love and concord renewed; and also Mr. Winthrop and Mr. Dudley write in their behalfes to the Lord Ssay and other gentl-men that were interesed in that plantation, very effectually, with which, togeather with their owne leters, and Mr. Winslows furder declaration of things unto them, they rested well satisfied.

Mr. Winslow was sente by them this year into England, partly to informe and satisfie the Lord Say and others, in the former matter, as also to make answer and their just defence for the same, if any thing should by any be prosecuted against them at Counsell-table, or els wher; but this matter tooke end, without any further trouble, as is before noted. And partly to signifie unto the partners in England, that the terme of their trade with the company here was out, and therfore he was sente to finishe the accounts with them, and to bring them notice how much debtore they should remaine on that accounte, and that they might know what further course would be best to hold. But the issue of these things will appear in the next years passages. They now sente over by him a great returne, which was very acceptable unto them; which was in beaver 3738*li.* waight, (a great part of it, being coat-beaver, sould at 20*s.* p^r pound,) and 234. otter skines;[1] which alltogeather rise to a great sume of money.

This year (in the foreparte of the same) they sente forth a barke to trad at the Dutch-Plantation; and they mette ther with on Captaine Stone, that had lived in Christophers, one of the West-Ende Ilands,[2] and now had been some time in Virginia, and came from thence into these parts. He kept company with the Dutch Gove^r, and, I know not in what drunken fitt, he gott leave of the Govr to ceaise on their barke, when they were ready to come away, and had done their markett, haveing the valew of 500*li.* worth of goods abord her;

---

[1] "And the skin at 14*s.*" (Br.)   [2] St. Christopher, in the West Indies.

having no occasion at all, or any collour of ground for such a thing, but having made the Govr drunck, so as he could scarce speake a right word; and when he urged him hear aboute, he answered him, *Als 't u beleeft.*[1] So he gat abord, (the cheefe of their men and marchant being ashore,) and with some of his owne men, made the rest of theirs waigh anchor, sett sayle, and carry her away towards Virginia. But diverse of the Dutch sea-men, which had bene often at Plimoth, and kindly enter-tayned ther, said one to another, Shall we suffer our freinds to be thus abused, and have their goods carried away, before our faces, whilst our Govr is drunke? They vowed they would never suffer it; and so gott a vessell or 2. and pursued him, and brought him in againe, and delivered them their barke and goods againe.

After wards Stone came into the Massachusets, and they sent and commensed suite against him for this facte; but by mediation of freinds it was taken up, and the suite lett fall. And in the company of some other gentle-men Stone came afterwards to Plimoth, and had freindly and civill entertain-mente amongst them, with the rest; but revenge boyled within his brest, (though concelled,) for some conceived he had a purpose (at one time) to have stabbed the Govr, and put his hand to his dagger for that end, but by Gods providence and the vigilance of some was prevented. He afterward returned to Virginia, in a pinass, with one Captaine Norton and some others; and, I know not for what occasion, they would needs goe up Coonigtecutt River; and how they carried themselves I know not, but the Indeans knoct him in the head, as he lay in his cabine, and had thrown the covering over his face (whether out of fear or desperation is uncertaine); this was his end. They likewise killed all the rest, but Captaine Norton defended him selfe a long time against them all in the cooke-roome, till by accidente the gunpowder tooke fire, which (for readynes) he had sett in an open thing before him, which did

---

[1] That is, "As you please."

so burne, and scald him, and blind his eyes, as he could make
no longer resistance, but was slaine also by them, though they
much comended his vallour.   And having killed the men, they
made a pray of what they had, and chafered away some of
their things to the Dutch that lived their.   But it was not longe
before a quarell fell betweene the Dutch and them, and they
would have cutt of their bark; but they slue the cheef sachem
with the shott of a murderer.[1]

I am now to relate some strang and remarkable passages.
Ther was a company of people lived in the country, up above
in the river of Conigtecut, a great way from their trading house
ther,[2] and were enimise to those Indeans which lived aboute
them, and of whom they stood in some fear (being a stout
people).   About a thousand of them had inclosed them selves
in a forte, which they had strongly palissadoed about.   3. or 4.
Dutch men went up in the begining of winter to live with them,
to gett their trade, and prevente them for bringing it to the
English, or to fall into amitie with them; but at spring to
bring all downe to their place.   But their enterprise failed,
for it pleased God to visite these Indeans with a great sicknes,
and such a mortalitie that of a 1000. above 900. and a halfe of
them dyed, and many of them did rott above ground for want
of buriall, and the Dutch men allmost starved before they
could gett away, for ise and snow.   But about Feb: they
got with much difficultie to their trading house; whom they
kindly releeved, being allmost spente with hunger and could.
Being thus refreshed by them diverce days, they got to
their owne place, and the Dutch were very thankfull for
this kindnes.

This spring, also, those Indeans that lived aboute their
trading house there fell sick of the small poxe, and dyed most
miserably; for a sorer disease cannot befall them; they fear

---

[1] The two paragraphs above were written on the reverse of the folios of the
original manuscript, under this year.   A murderer was a small piece of ordnance.

[2] *I. e.*, Indians living remote from the trading-house of the Plymouth men.

it more then the plague; for usualy they that have this disease
have them in abundance, and for wante of bedding and linning
and other helps, they fall into a lamentable condition, as they
lye on their hard matts, the poxe breaking and mattering, and
runing one into another, their skin cleaving (by reason therof)
to the matts they lye on; when they turne them, a whole side
will flea of at once, (as it were,) and they will be all of a gore
blood, most fearfull to behold; and then being very sore, what
with could and other distempers, they dye like rotten sheep.
The condition of this people was so lamentable, and they fell
downe so generally of this diseas, as they were (in the end)
not able to help on another; no, not to make a fire, nor to
fetch a litle water to drinke, nor any to burie the dead; but
would strivie as long as they could, and when they could procure no other means to make fire, they would burne the woden
trayes and dishes they ate their meate in, and their very bowes
and arrowes; and some would crawle out on all foure to gett
a litle water, and some times dye by the way, and not be able
to gett in againe.   But those of the English house, (though at
first they were afraid of the infection,) yet seeing their woefull
and sadd condition, and hearing their pitifull cries and lamenta-
tions, they had compastion of them, and dayly fetched them
wood and water, and made them fires, gott them victualls
whilst they lived, and buried them when they dyed.   For very
few of them escaped, notwithstanding they did what they
could for them, to the haszard of them selvs.   The cheefe
Sachem him selfe now dyed, and allmost all his freinds and
kinred.   But by the marvelous goodnes and providens of
God not one of the English was so much as sicke, or in the least
measure tainted with this disease, though they dayly did these
offices for them for many weeks togeather.   And this mercie
which they shewed them was kindly taken, and thankfully acknowledged of all the Indeans that knew or heard of the same;
and their m^{rs} here did much comend and reward them for the
same.

Anno Dom: 1635.

MR. WINSLOW was very wellcome to them in England, and the more in regard of the large returne he brought with him, which came all safe to their hands, and was well sould.   And he was borne in hand, (at least he so apprehended,) that all accounts should be cleared before his returne, and all former differences ther aboute well setled.   And so he writ over to them hear, that he hoped to cleare the accounts, and bring them over with him;   and that the accounte of the *White Angele* would be taken of, and all things fairly ended.   But it came to pass that, being occasioned to answer some complaints made against the countrie at Counsell bord, more cheefly concerning their neigbours in the Bay then them selves hear, the which he did to good effecte, and further prosecuting such things as might tend to the good of the whole, as well them selves as others, aboute the wrongs and incroachments that the French and other strangers both had and were like further to doe unto them, if not prevented, he prefered this petition following to their Hon^rs that were deputed Comissioners for the Plantations.

To the right honorable the Lords Comissioners for the Plantations in America.

The humble petition of Edw: Winslow, on the behalfe of the plantations in New-England,

Humbly sheweth unto your Lordships, that wheras your petitioners have planted them selves in New England under his Ma^tis most gratious protection;   now so it is, right Hon^bl, that the French and Dutch doe indeaouer to devide the land betweene them;   for which purpose the French have, on the east side, entered and seased upon one of our houses, and carried away the goods, slew 2. of the men in another place, and tooke the rest prisoners with their goods.   And the Dutch, on the west, have also made entrie upon Conigtecute River, within the limits of his Maj^ts ýrs patent, where they have raised a forte, and threaten to expell your petitioners thence, who are also planted upon the same river, maintaining possession for his Matie to their great charge, and hazard both of lives and goods.

In tender consideration hereof your petitioners humbly pray that your Lo^pps will either procure their peace with those foraine states, oɼ

else to give spetiall warrante unto your petitioners and the English Collonies, to right and defend them selves against all foraigne enimies.   And
your petitioners shall pray, etc.

This petition found good acceptation with most of them,
and Mr. Winslow was heard sundry times by them, and appointed further to attend for an answer from their Lo^{pps}, espetially, having upon conferance with them laid downe a way
how this might be doone without any either charge or trouble
to the state; only by furnishing some of the cheefe of the cuntry
hear with authoritie, who would undertake it at their owne
charge, and in such a way as should be without any publick disturbance.   But this crossed both Sir Ferdinandos Gorges' and
Cap: Masons designe, and the archbishop of Counterberies[1]
by them; for Sr Ferd: Gorges (by the arch-pps favore) was
to have been sent over generall Govr into the countrie, and to
have had means from the state for that end, and was now upon
dispatch and conclude of the bussines.   And the arch-bishops
purposs and intente was, by his means, and some he should
send with him, (to be furnished with Episcopall power,) to
disturbe the peace of the churches here, and to overthrow their
proceedings and further growth, which was the thing he aimed
at.   But it so fell out (by Gods providence) that though he
in the end crost this petition from taking any further effecte
in this kind, yet by this as a cheefe means the plotte and whole
bussines of his and Sr Ferdinandos fell to the ground, and came
to nothing.   When Mr. Winslow should have had his suit
granted, (as indeed upon the pointe it was,) and should have
been confirmed, the arch-bishop put a stop upon it, and Mr.
Winslow, thinking to gett it freed, went to the bord againe;
but the bishop, Sr Ferd: and Captine Masson, had, as it
seemes, procured Morton (of whom mention is made before,

---

[1] The archbishop of Canterbury, William Laud.   Captain John Mason had
been associated with Sir Ferdinando Gorges, as patentees, under the Council for
New England, of the region between the Merrimac and the Kennebec, 1622, and
later had separate patents, 1629 and 1635. for that between the Merrimac and
the Piscataqua (New Hampshire).

and his base carriage) to complaine; to whose complaints Mr. Winslow made answer to the good satisfaction of the borde, who checked Morton and rebuked him sharply, and allso blamed Sr Fer^d Gorges, and Masson, for countenancing him. But the bish: had a further end and use of his presence, for he now begane to question Mr. Winslow of many things; as of teaching in the church publickly, of which Morton accused him, and gave evidence that he had seen and heard him doe it; to which Mr. Winslow answered, that some time (wanting a minster) he did exercise his gifte to help the edification of his breethren, when they wanted better means, which was not often. Then aboute mariage, the which he also confessed, that, haveing been called to place of magistracie, he had sometimes maried some. And further tould their lord^ps that mariage was a civille thinge, and he found no wher in the word of God that it was tyed to ministrie. Again, they were necessitated so to doe, having for a long time togeather at first no minister; besids, it was no ncw-thing, for he had been so maried him selfe in Holand, by the magistrats in their Statthouse. But in the end (to be short), for these things, the bishop, by vemente importunity, gott the bord at last to consente to his comittemente; so he was comited to the Fleete, and lay ther 17. weeks, or ther aboute, before he could gett to be released. And this was the end of this petition, and this bussines; only the others designe was also frustrated hereby, with other things concurring, which was no smalle blessing to the people here.

But the charge fell heavie on them hear, not only in Mr. Winslows expences, (which could not be smale,) but by the hinderance of their bussines both ther and hear, by his personall imploymente. For though this was as much or more for others then for them hear, and by them cheefly he was put on this bussines, (for the plantation knewe nothing of it till they heard of his imprisonmente,) yet the whole charge lay on them.

Now for their owne bussines; whatsoever Mr. Sherleys mind was before, (or Mr. Winslow apprehension of the same,) he now declared him selfe plainly, that he would neither take of the *White-Angell* from the accounte, nor give any further accounte, till he had received more into his hands; only a prety good supply of goods were sent over, but of the most, no note of their prises, or so orderly an invoyce as formerly; which Mr. Winslow said he could not help, because of his restrainte. Only now Mr. Sherley and Mr. Beachamp and Mr. Andrews sent over a letter of atturney under their hands and seals, to recovere what they could of Mr. Allerton for the *Angells* accounte; but sent them neither the bonds, nor covenants, or such other evidence or accounts, as they had aboute these matters. I shall here inserte a few passages out of Mr. Sherleys letters aboute these things.

Your leter of the 22. of July, 1634, by your trustie and our loving friend Mr. Winslow, I have received, and your larg parcell of beaver and otter skines. Blessed be our God, both he and it came safly to us, and we have sould it in tow parcells; the skin at 14*s. li.* and some at 16.; the coate at 20*s.* the pound. The accounts I have not sent you them this year, I will referr you to Mr. Winslow to tell you the reason of it; yet be assured that none of you shall suffer by the not having of them, if God spare me life. And wheras you say the 6. years are expired that the peopl put the trad into your and our hands for, for the discharge of that great debte which Mr. Allerton needlesly and unadvisedly ran you and us into; yet it was promised it should continue till our disbursments and ingagements were satisfied. You conceive it is done; we feele and know other wise, etc. I doubt not but we shall lovingly agree, notwithstanding all that hath been writen, on boath sids, aboute the *Whit-Angell*. We have now sent you a letter of atturney, therby giving you power in our names (and to shadow it the more we say for our uses) to obtaine what may be of Mr. Allerton towards the satisfing of that great charge of the *White Angell.* And sure he hath bound him selfe, (though at present I cannot find it,) but he hath often affirmed, with great protestations, that neither you nor we should lose a peny by him, and I hope you shall find enough to discharg it, so as we shall have no more contesting aboute it. Yet, notwithstanding his unnaturall and unkind dealing with you, in the midest of justice remember mercie, and doe not all you may doe, etc. Set us out of debte, and then let us recone and reason togeither, etc. Mr. Winslow hath undergone an unkind imprisonment, but I am per-

swaded it will turne much to all your good.   I leave him to relate per-
ticuleres, etc.

Your loving freind,

London, Sep: 7. 1635.   JAMES SHERLEY.

This year they sustained an other great loss from the
French.   Monsier de Aulnay[1] coming into the harbore of
Penobscote, and having before gott some of the cheefe that
belonged to the house abord his vessell, by sutlty coming upon
them in their shalop, he gott them to pilote him in; and after
getting the rest into his power, he tooke possession of the
house in the name of the king of France; and partly by
threatening, and other wise, made Mr. Willett (their agente
ther) to approve of the sale of the goods their unto him, of
which he sett the price him selfe in effecte, and made an inventory therof, (yett leaving out sundry things,) but made no
paymente for them; but tould them in convenient time he
would doe it if they came for it.   For the house and fortification, etc. he would not alow, nor accounte any thing, saing that
they which build on another mans ground doe forfite the same.
So thus turning them out of all, (with a great deale of com-
plemente, and many fine words,) he let them have their shalop
and some victualls to bring them home.   Coming home and
relating all the passages, they here were much troubled at it,
and haveing had this house robbed by the French once before,
and lost then above 500*li*. (as is before remembred), and now
to loose house and all, did much move them.   So as they resolved to consulte with their freinds in the Bay, and if they
approved of it, (ther being now many ships ther,) they intended
to hire a ship of force, and seeke to beat out the Frenche, and
recover it againe.   Ther course was well approved on, if them
selves could bear the charge; so they hired a fair ship of above

[1] After the treaty of St. Germain, 1632, the Chevalier de Razilly was appointed by Louis XIII. governor of Acadia.   He appointed Charles de la Tour
his lieutenant for the portion east of the St. Croix, and Charles de Menou, Sieur
d'Aulney-Charnisé, his lieutenant for the part extending thence westward.   Aulney was commissioned by Razilly in 1635 to drive out all English settlers east
of Pemaquid.

300. tune, well fitted with ordnance, and agreed with the m^r (one Girling) to this effect: that he and his company should deliver them the house, (after they had driven out, or surprised the French,) and give them peacable possession therof, and of all such trading comodities as should ther be found; and give the French fair quarter and usage, if they would yeeld. In consideration wherof he was to have 700*li.* of beaver, to be delivered him ther, when he had done the thing; but if he did not accomplish it, he was to loose his labour, and have nothing. With him they also sent their owne bark, and about 20. men, with Captaine Standish, to aide him (if neede weer), and to order things, if the house was regained; and then to pay him the beaver, which they keept abord their owne barke. So they with their bark piloted him thither, and brought him safe into the harbor. But he was so rash and heady as he would take no advice, nor would suffer Captaine Standish to have time to summone them, (who had commission and order so to doe,) neither would doe it him selfe; the which, it was like, if it had been done, and they come to affaire parley, seeing their force, they would have yeelded. Neither would he have patience to bring his ship wher she might doe execution, but begane to shoot at distance like a madd man, and did them no hurte at all; the which when those of the plantation saw, they were much greeved, and went to him and tould him he would doe no good if he did not lay his ship beter to pass (for she might lye within pistoll shott of the house). At last, when he saw his owne folly, he was perswaded, and layed her well, and bestowed a few shott to good purpose. But now, when he was in a way to doe some good, his powder was goone; for though he had . .[1] peece of ordnance, it did now appeare he had but a barrell of powder, and a peece; so he could doe no good, but was faine to draw of againe; by which means the enterprise was made frustrate, and the French incouraged; for all the while that he shot so unadvisedly, they lay close

---

[1] Blank in the original.

under a worke of earth, and let him consume him selfe. He advised with the Captaine how he might be supplyed with powder, for he had not to carie him home; so he tould him he would goe to the next plantation, and doe his indeour to procure him some, and so did; but understanding, by intelligence, that he intended to ceiase on the barke, and surprise the beaver, he sent him the powder, and brought the barke and beaver home. But Girling never assaulted the place more, (seeing him selfe disapoyented,) but went his way; and this was the end of this bussines.

Upon the ill success of this bussines, the Govr and Assistants here by their leters certified their freinds in the Bay, how by this ship they had been abused and disapoynted, and that the French partly had, and were now likly to fortifie them selves more strongly, and likly to become ill neigbours to the English. Upon this they thus writ to them as folloeth:—

Worthy Srs: Upon the reading of your leters, and consideration of the waightines of the cause therin mentioned, the courte hath joyntly expressed their willingnes to assist you with men and munition, for the accomplishing of your desires upon the French. But because here are none of yours that have authority to conclude of any thing herein, nothing can be done by us for the presente. We desire, therfore, that you would with all conveniente speed send some man of trust, furnished with instructions from your selves, to make such agreemente with us about this bussines as may be usefull for you, and equall for us. So in hast we commite you to God, and remaine

Your assured loving freinds,

JOHN HAYNES, Govr.

RI: BELLINGHAM, Dep.

Jo: WINTHROP.

THO: DUDLEY.

Jo: HUMFRAY.

WM: CODDINGTON.

WM: PINCHON.

ATHERTON HOUGHE.

INCREAS NOWELL.

RIC: DUMER.

SIMON BRADSTRETE.

New-towne, Octo^r 9. 1635.

Upon the receite of the above mentioned, they presently deputed 2. of theirs to treate with them, giving them full power to conclude, according to the instructions they gave them, being to this purposs: that if they would afford such assistance as, togeather with their owne, was like to effecte the thing, and allso bear a considerable parte of the charge, they would goe on; if not, they (having lost so much allready) should not be able, but must desiste, and waite further opportunitie as God should give, to help them selves. But this came to nothing, for when it came to the issue, they would be at no charge, but sente them this letter, and referd them more at large to their owne messengers.

Sr: Having, upon the consideration of your letter, with the message you sente, had some serious consultations aboute the great importance of your bussines with the French, we gave our answer to those whom you deputed to conferr with us aboute the viage to Penobscote. We shewed our willingnes to help, but withall we declared our presente condition, and in what state we were, for our abilitie to help; which we for our parts shall be willing to improve, to procure you sufficiente supply of men and munition. But for matter of moneys we have no authority at all to promise, and if we should, we should rather disapoynte you, then incourage you by that help, which we are not able to performe. We likewise thought it fitt to take the help of other Esterne plantations; but those things we leave to your owne wisdomes. And for other things we refer you to your owne committies,[1] who are able to relate all the passages more at large. We salute you, and wish you all good success in the Lord.

Your faithfull and loving friend,

RI: BELLINGHAM, Dep:

In the name of the rest of the Comities.

Boston, Octob' 16. 1635.

This thing did not only thus breake of, but some of their merchants shortly after sent to trad with them, and furnished them both with provissions, and poweder and shott; and so have continued to doe till this day, as they have seen opportunitie for their profite. So as in truth the English them

[1] In the language of the seventeenth century, committee meant a person to whom a thing was committed.

selves have been the cheefest supporters of these French; for besids these, the plantation at Pemaquid (which lyes near unto them) doth not only supply them with what they wante, but gives them continuall intelligence of all things that passes among the English, (espetially some of them,) so as it is no marvell though they still grow, and incroach more and more upon the English, and fill the Indeans with gunes and munishtion, to the great deanger of the English, who lye open and unfortified, living upon husbandrie; and the other closed up in their forts, well fortified, and live upon trade, in good securitie. If these things be not looked too, and remeady provided in time, it may easily be conjectured what they may come toe; but I leave them.

This year, the 14. or 15. of August (being Saturday) was such a mighty storme of wind and raine, as none living in these parts, either English or Indeans, ever saw. Being like (for the time it continued) to those Hauricanes and Tuffons[1] that writers make mention of in the Indeas. It began in the morning, a litle before day, and grue not by degrees, but came with violence in the begining, to the great amasmente of many. It blew downe sundry houses, and uncovered others; diverce vessells were lost at sea, and many more in extreme danger. It caused the sea to swell (to the southward of this place) above 20. foote, right up and downe, and made many of the Indeans to clime into trees for their saftie; it tooke of the borded roofe of a house which belonged to the plantation at Manamet, and floted it to another place, the posts still standing in the ground; and if it had continued long without the shifting of the wind, it is like it would have drouned some parte of the cuntrie. It blew downe many hundered thowsands of trees, turning up the stronger by the roots, and breaking the hiegher pine trees of in the midle, and the tall yonge oaks and walnut trees of good biggnes were wound like a withe, very strang and fearfull to behould. It begane in the southeast,

[1] Hurricanes and typhoons.

and parted toward the south and east, and vered sundry ways; but the greatest force of it here was from the former quarters. It continued not (in the extremitie) above 5. or 6. houers, but the violence begane to abate. The signes and marks of it will remaine this 100. years in these parts wher it was sorest. The moone suffered a great eclips the 2. night after it.

Some of their neighbours in the Bay, hereing of the fame of Conightecute River, had a hankering mind after it, (as was before noted,) and now understanding that the Indeans were swepte away with the late great mortalitie, the fear of whom was an obstacle unto them before, which being now taken away, they begane now to prosecute it with great egernes. The greatest differances fell betweene those of Dorchester plantation and them hear; for they set their minde on that place, which they had not only purchased of the Indeans, but wher they had builte; intending only (if they could not remove them) that they should have but a smale moyety left to the house, as to a single family;[1] whose doings and proceedings were conceived to be very injurious, to attempte not only to intrude them selves into the rights and possessions of others, but in effect to thrust them out of all. Many were the leters and passages that went betweene them hear aboute, which would be to long here to relate.

I shall here first inserte a few lines that was write by their own agente from thence.

Sr: etc. The Masschuset men are coming almost dayly, some by water, and some by land, who are not yet determined wher to setle, though some have a great mind to the place we are upon, and which was last bought. Many of them look at that which this river will not afford, excepte it be at this place which we have, namly, to be a great towne, and have comodious dwellings for many togeather. So as what they will doe

[1] The pronouns require explanation. The meaning is, "between those of Dorchester plantation and those of Plymouth; for the former set their mind on that place, which the Plymouth men had purchased and built on; intending, if they could not remove the Plymouth men, to allow them only a small piece of land around their trading-house, such as would ordinarily be assigned to a single family."

I cannot yet resolve you; for this place ther is none of them say any thing to me, but what I hear from their servants (by whom I perceive their minds). I shall doe what I can to withstand them. I hope they will hear reason; as that we were here first, and entred with much difficulty and danger, both in regard of the Dutch and Indeans, and bought the land, (to your great charge, allready disbursed,) and have since held here a chargable possession, and kept the Dutch from further incroaching, which would els long before this day have possessed all, and kept out all others, etc. I hope these and such like arguments will stoppe them. It was your will we should use their persons and messengers kindly, and so we have done, and doe dayly, to your great charge; for the first company had well nie starved had it not been for this house, for want of victuals; I being forced to supply 12. men for 9. days togeather; and those which came last, I entertained the best we could, helping both them (and the other) with canows, and guids. They gott me to goe with them to the Dutch, to see if I could procure some of them to have quiet setling nere them; but they did peremtorily withstand them. But this later company did not once speak therof, etc. Also I gave their goods house roome according to their ernest request, and Mr. Pinchons [1] letter in their behalfe (which I thought good to send you, here inclosed). And what trouble and charge I shall be further at I know not; for they are comming dayly, and I expecte these back againe from below, whither they are gone to veiw the countrie. All which trouble and charg we under goe for their occasion, may give us just cause (in the judgmente of all wise and understanding men) to hold and keep that we are setled upon. Thus with my duty remembred, etc. I rest

Yours to be comanded

Matianuck,[3] July 6. 1635.   JOHNNATHAN BREWSTER.[2]

Amongst the many agitations that pased betweene them, I shal note a few out of their last letters, and for the present omitte the rest, except upon other occasion I may have fitter opportunity. After their thorrow veiw of the place, they

---

[1] William Pynchon was one of the patentees of the Massachusetts charter and one of the court of assistants in that government. In 1636 he led a body of settlers to Agawam, afterward named Springfield from the name of his birthplace in England. This settlement was at first supposed to be in the jurisdiction of Connecticut, but was afterward found to be in Massachusetts.

[2] Jonathan Brewster, the oldest son of William Brewster, came over in the *Fortune* in 1621, and after living in Duxbury for a time removed to New London, Connecticut.   [3] Matianuck was Windsor, Connecticut.

began to pitch them selves upon their land and near their[1] house; which occasioned much expostulation betweene them. Some of which are such as follow.

Brethren, having latly sent 2. of our body unto you, to agitate and bring to an issue some maters in difference betweene us, about some lands at Conightecutt, unto which you lay challeng; upon which God by his providence cast us, and as we conceive in a faire way of providence tendered it to us, as a meete place to receive our body, now upon removall.

We shall not need to answer all the passages of your larg letter, etc. But wheras you say God in his providence cast you, etc., we tould you before, and (upon this occasion) must now tell you still, that our mind is other wise, and that you cast rather a partiall, if not a covetous eye, upon that which is your neigbours, and not yours; and in so doing, your way could not be faire unto it. Looke that you abuse not Gods providence in such allegations.

Theirs.

Now allbeite we at first judged the place so free that we might with Gods good leave take and use it, without just offence to any man, it being the Lords wast, and for the presente altogeather voyd of inhabitants, that indeede minded the imploymente therof, to the right ends for which land was created, Gen: 1. 28. and for future intentions of any, and uncertaine possibilities of this or that to be done by any, we judging them (in such a case as ours espetialy) not meete to be equalled with presente actions (such as ours was) much less worthy to be prefered before them; and therfore did we make some weake beginings in that good worke, in the place afforesaid.

Ans: Their[2] answer was to this effecte. That if it was the Lords wast, it was them selves[3] that found it so, and not they; and have since bought it of the right oweners, and maintained a chargable possession upon it al this while, as them selves could not but know. And because of present ingagments and other hinderances which lay at presente upon them, must it therfore be lawfull for them to goe and take it from them? It was well known that they[4] are upon a barren place, wher they were by necessitie cast; and neither they nor theirs could

---

[1] The Plymouth men's. Of the three following paragraphs, the first and third are from letters of the Massachusetts authorities, the second from a letter of Plymouth. [2] The Plymouth men's. [3] The Plymouth men. [4] The Plymouth settlers.

longe continue upon the same; and why should they[1] (because they were more ready, and more able at presente) goe and deprive them of that which they had with charg and hazard provided, and intended to remove to, as soone as they could and were able?

They[2] had another passage in their letter; they had rather have to doe with the lords in England, to whom (as they heard it reported) some of them[3] should say that they had rather give up their right to them, (if they must part with it,) then to the church of Dorchester, etc. And that they should be less fearfull to offend the lords, then they were them.

Ans: Their[4] answer was, that what soever they had heard, (more then was true,) yet the case was not so with them that they had need to give away their rights and adventurs, either to the lords, or them; yet, if they might measure their fear of offence by their practise, they had rather (in that poynte) they should deal with the lords, who were beter able to bear it, or help them selves, then they were.

But least I should be teadious, I will forbear other things, and come to the conclusion that was made in the endd. To make any forcible resistance was farr from their thoughts. (they had enough of that about Kenebeck,) and to live in continuall contention with their freinds and brethren would be uncomfortable, and too heavie a burden to bear. Therfore for peace sake (though they conceived they suffered much in this thing) they thought it better to let them have it upon as good termes as they could gett; and so they fell to treaty. The first thing that (because they had made so many and long disputs aboute it) they would have them to grante was, that they had right too it, or ells they would never treat aboute it. The which being acknowledged, and yeelded unto by them, this was the conclusion they came unto in the end after much adoe: that they should retaine their house, and have the 16. parte

---

[1] Those of Massachusetts.   [2] Massachusetts.
[3] Plymouth.   [4] Plymouth's.

of all they had bought of the Indeans; and the other should
have all the rest of the land; leaveing such a moyety to those
of New-towne, as they reserved for them. This 16. part was
to be taken in too places; one towards the house, the other
towards New-townes proporrtion. Also they were to pay
according to proportion, what had been disbursed to the
Indeans for the purchass. Thus was the controversie ended,
but the unkindnes not so soone forgotten. They of New-
towne delt more fairly, desireing only what they could conveniently spare, from a competancie reserved for a plantation,
for them selves; which made them the more carfull to procure
a moyety for them, in this agreement and distribution.

Amongst the other bussinesses that Mr. Winslow had to
doe in England, he had order from the church to provid and
bring over some able and fitt man for to be their minister.
And accordingly he had procured a godly and a worthy man,
one Mr. Glover; but it pleased God when he was prepared for
the viage, he fell sick of a feaver and dyed. Afterwards, when
he was ready to come away, he became acquainted with Mr.
Norton, who was willing to come over, but would not ingage
him selfe to this place, otherwise then he should see occasion
when he came hear; and if he liked better else wher, to repay
the charge laid out for him, (which came to aboute 70*li*.) and
to be at his liberty. He stayed aboute a year with them, after
he came over, and was well liked of them, and much desired by
them; but he was invited to Ipswich, wher were many rich
and able men, and sundry of his aquaintance; so he wente to
them, and is their minister. Aboute half of the charg was repayed, the rest he had for the pains he tooke amongst them.

Anno Dom: 1636.

Mr. Ed: Winslow was chosen Govr this year.

In the former year, because they perceived by Mr. Winslows
later letters that no accounts would be sente, they resolved
to keep the beaver, and send no more, till they had them, or

came to some further agreemente. At least they would forbear
till Mr. Winslow came over, that by more full conferance with
him they might better understand what was meete to be done.
But when he came, though he brought no accounts, yet he
perswaded them to send the beaver, and was confident upon
the receite of that beaver, and his letters, they should have
accounts the nexte year; and though they thought his grounds
but weake, that gave him this hope, and made him so confidente, yet by his importunitie they yeelded, and sente the
same, ther being a ship at the latter end of year, by whom they
sente 1150*li*. waight of beaver, and 200. otter skins, besids
sundrie small furrs, as 55. minks, 2. black foxe skins, etc.
And this year, in the spring, came in a Dutch man, who thought
to have traded at the Dutch-forte; but they would not suffer
him. He, having good store of trading goods, came to this
place, and tendred them to sell; of whom they bought a good
quantitie, they being very good and fitte for their turne, as
Dutch roll, ketles, etc., which goods amounted to the valew
of 500*li*., for the paymente of which they passed bills to Mr.
Sherley in England, having before sente the forementioned
parcell of beaver. And now this year (by another ship) sente
an other good round parcell that might come to his hands, and
be sould before any of these bills should be due. The quantity
of beaver now sent was 1809*li*. waight, and of otters 10. skins,
and shortly after (the same year) was sent by another ship
(Mr. Langrume maister), in beaver 0719*li*. waight, and of otter
skins 199. concerning which Mr. Sherley thus writs.

Your leters I have received, with 8. hoggsheads of beaver by Ed:
Wilkinson, m^r of the *Falcon*. Blessed be God for the safe coming of it.
I have also seen and acceped 3. bills of exchainge, etc. But I must now
acquainte you how the Lords heavie hand is upon this kingdom in many
places, but cheefly in this cittie, with his judgmente of the plague. The
last weeks bill[1] was 1200. and odd, I fear this will be more; and it is much
feared it will be a winter sicknes. By reason wherof it is incredible the
number of people that are gone into the cuntry and left the citie. I am

[1] Bill of mortality

perswaded many more then went out the last sicknes; so as here is no trading, carriors from most places put downe; nor no receiving of any money, though long due. Mr. Hall ows us more then would pay these bills, but he, his wife, and all, are in the cuntrie, 60. miles from London. I write to him, he came up, but could not pay us. I am perswaded if I should offer to sell the beaver at 8*s*. p^r pound, it would not yeeld money; but when the Lord shall please to cease his hand, I hope we shall have better and quicker markets; so it shall lye by. Before I accepted the bills, I acquainted Mr. Beachamp and Mr. Andrews with them, and how ther could be no money made nor received; and that it would be a great discredite to you, which never yet had any turned back, and a shame to us, haveing 1800*li*. of beaver lying by us, and more oweing then the bills come too, etc. But all was nothing; neither of them both will put too their finger to help. I offered to supply my 3. parte, but they gave me their answer they neither would nor could, etc. How ever, your bils shall be satisfied to the parties good contente; but I would not have thought they would have left either you or me at this time, etc. You will and may expect I should write more, and answer your leters, but I am not a day in the weeke at home at towne, but carry my books and all to Clapham;[1] for here is the miserablest time that I thinke hath been known in many ages. I have known 3. great sickneses, but none like this. And that which should be a means to pacifie the Lord, and help us, that is taken away, preaching put downe in many places, not a sermone in Westminster on the saboth, nor in many townes aboute us; the Lord in mercie looke uppon us. In the begining of the year was a great drought, and no raine for many weeks togeather, so as all was burnte up, haye at 5*li*. a load; and now all raine, so as much sommer corne and later haye is spoyled. Thus the Lord sends judgmente after judgmente, and yet we cannot see, nor humble our selves; and therfore may justly fear heavier judgments, unless we speedly repente, and returne unto him, which the Lord give us grace to doe, if it be his blessed will. Thus desiring you to remember us in your prayers, I ever rest

Your loving friend,

Sep^t: 14. 1636. JAMES SHERLEY.

This was all the answer they had from Mr. Sherley, by which Mr. Winslow saw his hops failed him. So they now resoloved to send no more beaver in that way which they had done, till they came to some issue or other aboute these things.

---

[1] Clapham is in Surrey, near London.

But now came over letters from Mr. Andrews and Mr. Beachamp full of complaints, that they marveled that nothing was sent over, by which any of their moneys should be payed in; for it did appear by the accounte sente in An° 1631. that they were each of them out, aboute a leven hundred pounds a peece, and all this while had not received one penie towards the same. But now Mr. Sherley sought to draw more money from them, and was offended because they deneyed him; and blamed them hear very much that all was sent to Mr. Sherley, and nothing to them. They marvelled much at this, for they conceived that much of their moneis had been paid in, and that yearly each of them had received a proportionable quantity out of the larg returnes sent home. For they had sente home since that accounte was received in An° 1631. (in which all and more then all their debts, with that years supply, was charged upon them) these sumes following.

Nov^br 18. An° 1631.	By Mr. Peirce	0400*li*. waight of beaver, and otters 20.	
July 13. An° 1632.	By Mr. Griffin	1348*li*. beaver, and otters .	. 147.
An° 1633.	By Mr. Graves	3366*li*. bever, and otters .	. 346.
An° 1634.	By Mr. Andrews	3738*li*. beaver, and otters .	. 234.
An° 1635.	By Mr. Babb	1150*li*. beaver, and otters .	. 200.
June 24. An° 1636.	By Mr. Willkinson	1809*li*. beaver, and otters .	. 010.
Ibidem.	By Mr. Langrume	0719*li*. beaver, and otters .	. 199.

12150li.[1]   1156.

All these sumes were safly rceived and well sould, as appears by leters. The coat beaver usualy at 20*s*. p^r pound, and some at 24*s*.; the skin at 15. and sometimes 16. I doe not remember any under 14. It may be the last year might be something lower, so also ther were some small furrs that are not recconed in this accounte, and some black beaver at higer rates, to make up the defects. It was conceived that the former parcells of beaver came to litle less then 10000*li*. sterling, and the otter skins would pay all the charge, and they with other furrs make up besids if any thing wanted of the former sume. When the former accounte was passed, all their debts (those of *White-*

---

[1] Not correctly added; the sum should be 12530*li*.

Angelle and *Frendship* included) came but to 4770*li*. And
they could not estimate that all the supplies since sent them,
and bills payed for them, could come to above 2000*li*. so as
they conceived their debts had been payed, with advantage or
intrest. But it may be objected, how comes it that they could
not as well exactly sett downe their receits, as their returnes,
but thus estimate it. I answer, 2. things were the cause of it;
the first and principall was, that the new accountante, which
they in England would needs presse upon them, did wholy
faile them, and could never give them any accounte; but
trusting to his memorie, and lose papers, let things rune into
such confusion, that neither he, nor any with him, could bring
things to rights. But being often called upon to perfecte his
accounts, he desired to have such a time, and such a time of
leasure, and he would doe it. In the intrime he fell into a great
sicknes, and in conclusion it fell out he could make no accounte
at all. His books were after a litle good begining left altogeather unperfect; and his papers, some were lost, and others
so confused, as he knew not what to make of them him selfe,
when they came to be searched and examined. This was not
unknowne to Mr. Sherley; and they came to smarte for it to
purpose, (though it was not their faulte,) both thus in England,
and also here; for they conceived they lost some hundreds of
pounds for goods trusted out in the place, which were lost for
want of clear accounts to call them in. Another reason of this
mischeefe was, that after Mr. Winslow was sente into England
to demand accounts, and to excepte against the *Whit-Angell*,
they never had any price sent with their goods, nor any certaine
invoyce of them; but all things stood in confusion, and they
were faine to guesse at the prises of them.

They write back to Mr. Andrews and Mr. Beachamp, and
tould them they marveled they should write they had sent
nothing home since the last accounts; for they had sente a
great deale; and it might rather be marveled how they could
be able to send so much, besids defraying all charg at home.

and what they had lost by the French, and so much cast away at sea, when Mr. Peirce lost his ship on the coast of Virginia. What they had sente was to them all, and to them selves as well as Mr. Sherley, and if they did not looke after it, it was their owne falts; they must referr them to Mr. Sherley, who had received it, to demand it of him. They allso write to Mr. Sherley to the same purposs, and what the others complaints were.

This year 2. shallops going to Coonigtecutt with goods from the Massachusetts of such as removed theither to plante, were in an easterly storme cast away in coming into this harbore in the night; the boats men were lost, and the goods were driven all alonge the shore, and strowed up and downe at highwater marke. But the Govr caused them to be gathered up, and drawn togeather, and appointed some to take an inventory of them, and others to wash and drie such things as had neede therof; by which means most of the goods were saved, and restored to the owners. Afterwards anotheir boate of theirs (going thither likwise) was cast away near unto Manoanscusett,[1] and such goods as came a shore were preserved for them. Such crosses they mette with in their beginings; which some imputed as a correction from God for their intrution (to the wrong of others) into that place. But I dare not be bould with Gods judgments in this kind.

In the year 1634, the Pequents (a stoute and warlike people), who had made warrs with sundry of their neigbours, and puft up with many victories, grue now at varience with the Narigansets, a great people bordering upon them. These Narigansets held correspondance and termes of freindship with the English of the Massachusetts. Now the Pequents, being conscious of the guilte of Captain-Stones death, whom they knew to be an-English man, as also those that were with him, and

---

[1] Manoanscussett was what was formerly the northern part of Sandwich, Massachusetts, which was for many years known as Scussett. It is now the town of Bourne, between Sandwich and Plymouth.

being fallen out with the Dutch, least they should have over many enemies at once, sought to make freindship with the English of the Massachusetts; and for that end sent both messengers and gifts unto them, as appears by some letters sent from the Gov[r] hither.

Dear and worthy Sr: etc. To let you know somwhat of our affairs, you may understand that the Pequents have sent some of theirs to us, to desire our freindship, and offered much wampum and beaver, etc. The first messengers were dismissed without answer; with the next we had diverce dayes conferance, and taking the advice of some of our ministers, and seeking the Lord in it, we concluded a peace and freindship with them, upon these conditions: that they should deliver up to us those men who were guilty of Stones death, etc. And if we desired to plant in Conightecute, they should give up their right to us, and so we would send to trade with them as our freinds (which was the cheefe thing we aimed at, being now in warr with the Dutch and the rest of their neigbours). To this they readily agreed; and that we should meadiate a peace betweene them and the Narigansetts; for which end they were contente we should give the Narigansets parte of that presente, they would bestow on us (for they stood so much on their honour, as they would not be seen to give any thing of them selves). As for Captein Stone, they tould us ther were but 2. left of those who had any hand in his death; and that they killed him in a just quarell, for (say they) he surprised 2. of our men, and bound them, to make them by force to shew him the way up the river;[1] and he with 2. other coming on shore, 9. Indeans watched him, and when they were a sleepe in the night, they kiled them, to deliver their owne men; and some of them going afterwards to the pinass, it was suddainly blowne up. We are now preparing to send a pinass unto them, etc.

In an other of his, dated the 12. of the first month, he hath this.

Our pinass is latly returned from the Pequents; they put of but litle comoditie, and found them a very false people, so as they mean to have no more to doe with them. I have diverce other things to write unto you, etc.

Yours ever assured,

Jo: Winthrop.

Boston, 12. of the 1. month, 1634.[2]

[1] "Ther is litle trust to be given to their relations in these things." (Br.)

[2] I. e.. March 12, 1634/5.

After these things, and, as I take, this year, John Oldom, (of whom much is spoken before,) being now an inhabitant of the Massachusetts, went with a small vessell, and slenderly mand, a trading into these south parts, and upon a quarell betweene him and the Indeans was cutt of by them (as hath been before noted) at an iland called by the Indeans Munisses, but since by the English Block Iland.[1] This, with the former about the death of Stone, and the baffoyling[2] of the Pequents with the English of the Massachusetts, moved them to set out some to take revenge, and require satisfaction for these wrongs; but it was done so superfitially, and without their acquainting of those of Conightecute and other neighbours with the same, as they did litle good.   But their neigbours had more hurt done, for some of the murderers of Oldome fled to the Pequents, and though the English went to the Pequents, and had some parley with them, yet they did but delude them, and the English returned without doing any thing to purpose, being frustrate of their oppertunitie by the others deceite. After the English were returned, the Pequents tooke their time and oppertunitie to cut of some of the English as they passed in boats, and went on fouling, and assaulted them the next spring at their habytations, as will appear in its place.   I doe but touch these things, because I make no question they will be more fully and distinctly handled by them selves, who had more exacte knowledg of them, and whom they did more properly concerne.[3]

This year Mr. Smith layed downe his place of ministrie, partly by his owne willingnes, as thinking it too heavie a burthen, and partly at the desire, and by the perswasion, of others; and the church sought out for some other, having often been disappointed in their hops and desires heretofore.   And

[1] This island was named after Adrian Block, to whom its discovery has been by many attributed, as occurring in 1614.   There can be little doubt that Verrazano discovered it in 1524 and named it Claudia after the mother of Francis I.   It bears this name on Lock's map of 1582.   See Winsor's *Narrative and Critical History*, III. 40.   [2] Baffling, in the sense of shuffling.

[3] Mason's, Lyon Gardiner's, and Underhill's accounts of the Pequot War all have some claim to be regarded as official.

it pleased the Lord to send them an able and a godly man,[1] and of a meeke and humble spirite, sound in the truth, and every way unreproveable in his life and conversation; whom, after some time of triall, they chose for their teacher, the fruits of whose labours they injoyed many years with much comforte, in peace, and good agreemente.

Anno Dom: 1637.

In the fore parte of this year, the Pequents fell openly upon the English at Conightecute, in the lower parts of the river, and slew sundry of them, (as they were at work in the feilds,) both men and women, to the great terrour of the rest; and wente away in great prid and triumph, with many high threats. They allso assalted a fort at the rivers mouth, though strong and well defended; and though they did not their prevaile, yet it struk them with much fear and astonishmente to see their bould attempts in the face of danger; which made them in all places to stand upon their gard, and to prepare for re- sistance, and ernestly to solissite their freinds and confederats in the Bay of Massachusets to send them speedy aide, for they looked for more forcible assaults. Mr. Vane,[2] being then Gov[r], write from their Generall Courte to them hear, to joyne with them in this warr; to which they were cordially willing, but tooke opportunitie to write to them aboute some former things, as well as presente, considerable hereaboute. The which will best appear in the Gov[r] answer which he returned to the same, which I shall here inserte.

Sr: The Lord having so disposed, as that your letters to our late Gov[r] is fallen to my lott to make answer unto, I could have wished I might have been at more freedome of time and thoughts also, that I might have done it more to your and my owne satisfaction. But what shall be

---

[1] "Mr. John Reinor." (Br.) He graduated at Magdalen College, Cam- bridge. Charles Chauncy was associated with him in the Plymouth ministry from 1638 to 1641. After he left Plymouth in 1654 he was settled in Dover, New Hampshire, where he remained until his death.

[2] Afterward Sir Henry Vane. He was elected governor of Massachusetts in the spring of 1636.

wanting now may be supplyed hereafter. For the matters which from your selfe and counsell were propounded and objected to us, we thought not fitte to make them so publicke as the cognizance of our Generall Courte. But as they have been considered by those of our counsell, this answer we thinke fitt to returne unto you. (1.) Wereas you signifie your willingnes to joyne with us in this warr against the Pequents, though you cannot ingage your selves without the consente of your Generall Courte, we acknowledg your good affection towards us, (which we never had cause to doubt of,) and are willing to attend your full resolution, when it may most seasonably be ripened. (2^{ly}.) Wheras you make this warr to be our peopls, and not to conceirne your selves, otherwise then by consequence, we do in parte consente to you therin; yet we suppose, that, in case of perill, you will not stand upon such terms, as we hope we should not doe towards you; and withall we conceive that you looke at the Pequents, and all other Indeans, as a commone enimie, who, though he may take occasion of the begining of his rage, from some one parte of the English, yet if he prevaile, will surly pursue his advantage, to the rooting out of the whole nation. Therfore when we desired your help, we did it not without respecte to your owne saftie, as ours. (3^{ly}.) Wheras you desire we should be ingaged to aide you, upon all like occasions; we are perswaded you doe not doubte of it; yet as we now deale with you as a free people, and at libertie, so as we cannot draw you into this warr with us, otherwise then as reason may guid and provock you; so we desire we may be at the like freedome, when any occasion may call for help from us. And wheras it is objected to us, that we refused to aide you against the French; we conceive the case was not alicke; yet we cannot wholy excuse our failing in that matter. (4^{ly}.) Weras you objecte that we began the warr without your privitie, and managed it contrary to your advise; the truth is, that our first intentions being only against Block Iland, and the interprice seeming of small difficultie, we did not so much as consider of taking advice, or looking out for aide abroad. And when we had resolved upon the Pequents, we sent presently, or not long after, to you aboute it; but the answer received, it was not seasonable for us to chaing our counsells, excepte we had seen and waighed your grounds, which might have out wayed our owne.

(5^{ly}.) For our peoples trading at Kenebeck, we assure you (to our knowledge) it hath not been by any allowance from us; and what we have provided in this and like cases, at our last Courte, Mr. E. W. can certifie you.

And (6^{ly}); wheras you objecte to us that we should hold trade and correspondancie with the French, your enemise; we answer, you are misinformed, for, besids some letters which hath passed betweene our late

Gov[r 1] and them, to which we were privie, we have neither sente nor incouraged ours to trade with them; only one vessell or tow, for the better conveance of our letters, had licens from our Gov[r] to sayle thither.[2]

Diverce other things have been privatly objected to us, by our worthy freind, wherunto he received some answer; but most of them concerning the apprehention of perticuler discurteseis, or injueries from some perticuler persons amongst us. It concernes us not to give any other answer to them then this; that, if the offenders shall be brought forth in a right way, we shall be ready to doe justice as the case shall require. In the meane time, we desire you to rest assured, that such things are without our privity, and not a litle greeveous to us.

Now for the joyning with us in this warr, which indeed concerns us no other wise then it may your selves, viz.: the releeving of our freinds and Christian breethren, who are now first in the danger; though you may thinke us able to make it good without you, (as, if the Lord please to be with us, we may,) yet 3. things we offer to your consideration, which (we conceive) may have some waight with you. (First) that if we should sinck under this burden, your opportunitie of seasonable help would be lost in 3. respects. 1. You cannot recover us, or secure your selves ther, with 3. times the charge and hazard which now ye may. 2[ly]. The sorrowes which we should lye under (if through your neglect) would much abate of the acceptablenes of your help afterwards. 3[ly]. Those of yours, who are now full of courage and forwardnes, would be much damped, and so less able to undergoe so great a burden. The (2.) thing is this, that it concernes us much to hasten this warr to an end before the end of this sommer, otherwise the newes of it will discourage both your and our freinds from coming to us next year; with what further hazard and losse it may expose us unto, your selves may judge.

The (3.) thing is this, that if the Lord shall please to blesse our en.deaours, so as we end the warr, or put it in a hopefull way without you, it may breed such ill thoughts in our people towards yours, as will be hard to entertaine such opinione of your good will towards us, as were fitt to be nurished among such neigbours and brethren as we are. And what ill consequences may follow, on both sids, wise men may fear, and would rather prevente then hope to redress. So with my harty salutations to you selfe, and all your counsell, and other our good freinds with you, I rest

Yours most assured in the Lord,

Boston, the 20. of the 3. month, 1637.[3]   Jo: WINTHROP.

[1] Vane.

[2] "But by this means they did furnish them, and have still continued to doe." (Br.)   [3] *I. e.*, May 20, 1637.

In the mean time, the Pequents, espetially in the winter before, sought to make peace with the Narigansets, and used very
pernicious arguments to move them therunto: as that the English were stranegers and begane to overspred their countrie, and
would deprive them therof in time, if they were suffered to grow
and increse; and if the Narigansets did assist the English to sub-
due them, they did but make way for their owne overthrow, for
if they were rooted out, the English would soone take occasion to
subjugate them; and if they would harken to them, they should
not neede to fear the strength of the English; for they would not
come to open battle with them, but fire their houses, kill their
katle, and lye in ambush for them as they went abroad upon
their occasions; and all this they might easily doe without any
or litle danger to them selves. The which course being held,
they well saw the English could not long subsiste, but they would
either be starved with hunger, or be forced to forsake the countrie; with many the like things; insomuch that the Narigansets
were once wavering, and were halfe minded to have made peace
with them, and joyned against the English. But againe when
they considered, how much wrong they had received from the
Pequents, and what an oppertunitie they now had by the help
of the English to right them selves, revenge was so sweete unto
them, as it prevailed above all the rest; so as they resolved
to joyne with the English against them, and did. The Court
here agreed forwith to send 50. men at their owne charg; and
with as much speed as posiblie they could, gott them armed,
and had made them ready under sufficiente leaders, and provided a barke to carrie them provisions and tend upon them for
all occasions; but when they were ready to march (with a supply from the Bay) they had word to stay, for the enimy was
as good as vanquished, and their would be no neede.

I shall not take upon me exactly to describe their proceedings in these things, because I expecte it will be fully done by
them selves, who best know the carrage and circumstances of
things; I shall therfore but touch them in generall. From

Connightecute (who were most sencible of the hurt sustained, and the present danger), they sett out a partie of men, and an other partie mett them from the Bay, at the Narigansets, who were to joyne with them. The Narigansets were ernest to be gone before the English were well rested and refreshte, espetially some of them which came last. It should seeme their desire was to come upon the enemie sudenly, and undiscovered. Ther was a barke of this place, newly put in ther, which was come from Conightecutte, who did incourage them to lay hold of the Indeans forwardnes, and to shew as great forwardnes as they, for it would incorage them, and expedition might prove to their great advantage. So they went on, and so ordered their march, as the Indeans brought them to a forte of the enimies (in which most of their cheefe men were) before day. They approached the same with great silence, and surrounded it both with English and Indeans, that they might not breake out; and so assualted them with great courage, shooting amongst them, and entered the forte with all speed; and those that first entered found sharp resistance from the enimie, who both shott at and grapled with them; others rane into their howses, and brought out fire, and sett them on fire, which soone tooke in their matts, and, standing close togeather, with the wind, all was quickly on a flame, and therby more were burnte to death then was otherwise slain; it burnte their bowstrings, and made them unservisable. Those that scaped the fire were slaine with the sword; some hewed to peeces, others rune throw with their rapiers, so as they were quickly dispatchte, and very few escaped. It was conceived they thus destroyed about 400. at this time. It was a fearfull sight to see them thus frying in the fyer, and the streams of blood quenching the same, and horrible was the stinck and sente ther of; but the victory seemed a sweete sacrifice, and they gave the prays therof to God, who had wrought so wonderfuly for them, thus to inclose their enimise in their hands, and give them so speedy a victory over so proud and insulting an enimie. The Narigansett Indeans, all this while, stood round aboute, but aloofe from all danger, and left the whole execution to the English, exept it were the stoping of any that broke away, insulting over their enimies in this their ruine and miserie, when they saw them dancing in the flames, calling them by a word in their owne language, signifing, O brave Pequents! which they used familierly among them selves in their own prayes, in songs of triumph after their victories. After this servis was thus happily accomplished, they marcht to the water side, wher they mett with some of their vesells, by which they had refreshing with victualls and other necessaries. But in their march the rest of the Pequents drew into a body, and acoasted them, thinking to have some advantage against them by reason of a neck of land; but when they saw the English prepare for them, they kept a loofe, so as they neither did hurt, nor could receive any. After their refreshing and repair to geather for further counsell and directions, they resolved to pursue their victory, and follow the warr against the rest, but the Narigansett Indeans most of them forsooke them, and such of them as they had with them for guids, or otherwise, they found them very could and backward in the bussines, ether out of envie, or that they saw the English would make more profite of the victorie then they were willing they should, or els deprive them of such advantage as them selves desired by having them become tributaries unto them, or the like.

For the rest of this bussines, I shall only relate the same as it is in a leter which came from Mr. Winthrop to the Govr hear, as followeth.

Worthy Sr: I received your loving letter, and am much provocked to express my affections towards you, but straitnes of time forbids me; for my desire is to acquainte you with the Lords greate mercies towards us, in our prevailing against his and our enimies; that you may rejoyce and praise his name with us. About 80. of our men, haveing costed along towards the Dutch plantation, (some times by water, but most by land,) mett hear and ther with some Pequents, whom they slew or tooke prisoners. 2. sachems they tooke, and beheaded; and not hearing of Sassacous, (the cheefe sachem,) they gave a prisoner his life, to goe and find him out. He wente and brought them word where he was, but Sassacouse, suspecting him to be a spie, after he was gone, fled away with some 20. more to the Mowakes, so our men missed of him. Yet, deviding them selves, and ranging up and downe, as the providence of God guided them (for the Indeans were all gone, save 3. or 4. and they knew not whither to guide them, or els would not), upon the 13. of this month, they light upon a great company of them, viz. 80. strong men, and 200. women and children, in a small Indean towne, fast by a hideous swampe,[1] which they all slipped into before our men could gett to them. Our captains were not then come togeither, but ther was Mr. Ludlow and Captaine Masson, with some 10. of their men, and Captaine Patrick with some 20. or more of his, who, shooting at the Indeans, Captaine Trask with 50. more came soone in at the noyse. Then they gave order to surround the swampe, it being aboute a mile aboute; but Levetenante Davenporte and some 12. more, not hearing that command, fell into the swampe among the Indeans. The swampe was so thicke with shrub-woode, and so boggie with all, that some of them stuck fast, and received many shott. Levetenant Davenport was dangerously wounded aboute his armehole, and another shott in the head, so as, fainting, they were in great danger to have been taken by the Indeans. But Sargante Rigges, and Jeffery, and 2. or 3. more, rescued them, and slew diverse of the Indeans with their swords. After they were drawne out, the Indeans desired parley, and were offered (by Thomas Stanton, our interpretour) that, if they would come out, and yeeld them selves, they should have their lives, all that had not their hands in the English blood. Wherupon the sachem of the place came forth, and an old man or 2. and their wives and children, and after that some other women and children, and so they spake 2. howers, till it was night. Then Thomas Stanton was sente into them againe, to call them forth; but they said they would selle their lives their, and so shott at him so thicke as, if he had not cried out, and been presently rescued, they had slaine him. Then our men cutt of a place of the swampe with their swords, and cooped the Indeans into so narrow a compass, as they could easier kill them throw the thickets. So they continued all the night, standing aboute 12. foote one from an other, and the Indeans, coming close up to our men, shot their arrows so thicke, as they pierced their hatte brimes, and their sleeves, and stockins, and other parts of their cloaths, yet so miraculously did the Lord preserve them as not one of them was wounded, save those 3. who rashly went into the swampe. When it was nere day, it grue very darke, so as those of them which were left dropt away betweene our men, though

[1] Within the present town of Fairfield, Connecticut.

they stood but 12. or 14. foote assunder; but were presenly discovered, and some killed in the pursute.   Upon searching of the swampe, the next morning, they found 9. slaine, and some they pulled up, whom the Indeans had buried in the mire, so as they doe thinke that, of all this company, not 20. did escape, for they after found some who dyed in their flight of their wounds received.   The prisoners were devided, some to those of the river, and the rest to us.   Of these we send the male children to Bermuda,[1] by Mr. William Peirce, and the women and maid children are disposed aboute in the townes.   Ther have been now slaine and taken, in all, aboute 700.   The rest are dispersed, and the Indeans in all quarters so terrified as all their friends are affraid to receive them.   2. of the sachems of Long Iland came to Mr. Stoughton and tendered them selves to be tributaries under our protection.   And 2. of the Neepnett[2] sachems have been with me to seeke our frendship.   Amonge the prisoners we have the wife and children of Mononotto, a womon of a very modest countenance and behaviour.   It was by her mediation that the 2. English maids were spared from death, and were kindly used by her; so that I have taken charge of her.   One of her first requests was, that the English would not abuse her body, and that her children might not be taken from her.   Those which were wounded were fetched of soone by John Galopp, who came with his shalop in a happie houre, to bring them victuals, and to carrie their wounded men to the pinnass, wher our cheefe surgeon was, with Mr. Willson, being aboute 8. leagues off.   Our people are all in health, (the Lord be praised,) and allthough they had marched in their armes all the day, and had been in fight all the night, yet they professed they found them selves so fresh as they could willingly have gone to such another bussines.

This is the substance of that which I received, though I am forced to omite many considerable circomstances.   So, being in much straitnes of time, (the ships being to departe within this 4. days, and in them the Lord Lee[3] and Mr. Vane,) I hear breake of, and with harty saluts to, etc., I rest

Yours assured,

The 28. of the 5. month, 1637.   Jo: WINTHROP.

The captains reporte we have slaine 13. sachems; but Sassacouse and Monotto are yet living.

[1] "But they were carried to the West-Indeas." (Br.)

[2] Neepnett was in Connecticut.

[3] James, Lord Ley, to whose sister, Lady Margaret Ley, Milton addressed one of his most famous sonnets.   He was the eldest son and heir of the Earl of Marlborough, and came to New England in June, 1637, to see the country. Vane, disappointed at not being re-elected governor, returned to England with him   The date below is July 28, 1637.

That I may make an end of this matter: this Sassacouse (the Pequents cheefe sachem) being fled to the Mowhakes, they cutt of his head, with some other of the cheefe of them, whether to satisfie the English, or rather the Narigansets, (who, as I have since heard, hired them to doe it,) or for their owne advantage, I well know not; but thus this warr tooke end. The rest of the Pequents were wholy driven from their place, and some of them submitted them selves to the Narigansets, and lived under them; others of them betooke themselves to the Monhiggs, under Uncass, their sachem, with the approbation of the English of Conightecutt, under whose protection Uncass lived, and he and his men had been faithful to them in this warr, and done them very good service. But this did so vexe the Narrigansetts, that they had not the whole sweay over them, as they have never ceased plotting and contriving how to bring them under, and because they cannot attaine their ends, because of the English who have protected them, they have sought to raise a generall conspiracie against the English, as will appear in an other place.

They had now letters againe out of England from Mr. Andrews and Mr. Beachamp, that Mr. Sherley neither had nor would pay them any money, or give them any accounte, and so with much discontent desired them hear to send them some, much blaming them still, that they had sent all to Mr. Sherley, and none to them selves. Now, though they might have justly referred them to their former answer, and insisted ther upon, and some wise men counselled them so to doe, yet because they beleeved that they were realy out round sumes of money, (espetialy Mr. Andrews,) and they had some in their hands, they resloved to send them what bever they had.[1] Mr. Sherleys letters were to this purpose: that, as they had left him in the paiment of the former bills, so he had tould them he would leave them in this, and beleeve it, they should find it true. And he was as good as his word, for they could never

---

[1] "But staid it till the next year." (Br.)

gett peney from him, nor bring him to any accounte, though
Mr. Beachamp sued him in the Chancerie. But they all of
them turned their complaints against them here, wher ther
was least cause, and who had suffered most unjustly; first
from Mr. Allerton and them, in being charged with so
much of that which they never had, nor drunke for; and
now in paying all, and more then all (as they conceived),
and yet still thus more demanded, and that with many
heavie charges. They now discharged Mr. Sherley from his
agencie, and forbad him to buy or send over any more
goods for them, and prest him to come to some end about
these things.

Anno Dom: 1638.

THIS year Mr. Thomas Prence was chosen Govr

Amongst other enormities that fell out amongst them, this
year 3. men were (after due triall) executed for robery and
murder which they had committed; their names were these,
Arthur Peach, Thomas Jackson, and Richard Stinnings; ther
was a 4., Daniel Crose, who was also guilty, but he escaped
away, and could not be found. This Arthur Peach was the
cheefe of them, and the ring leader of all the rest. He was a
lustie and a desperate yonge man, and had been one of the
souldiers in the Pequente warr, and had done as good servise
as the most ther, and one of the forwardest in any attempte.
And being now out of means, and loath to worke, and falling
to idle courses and company, he intended to goe to the Dutch
plantation; and had alured these 3., being other mens servants
and apprentices, to goe with him. But another cause ther was
allso of his secret going away in this maner; he was not only
rune into debte, but he had gott a maid with child, (which was
not known till after his death,) a mans servante in the towne,
and fear of punishmente made him gett away. The other 3.
complotting with him, ranne away from their maisters in the
night, and could not be heard of, for they went not the ordinarie

way, but shaped such a course as they thought to avoyd the
pursute of any.   But falling into the way that lyeth betweene
the Bay of Massachusetts and the Narrigansets, and being disposed to rest them selves, struck fire, and took tobaco, a litle
out of the way, by the way side.   At length ther came a
Narigansett Indean by, who had been in the Bay a trading,
and had both cloth and beads aboute him.   (They had meett
him the day before, and he was now returning.)   Peach called
him to drinke tobaco with them, and he came and sate downe
with them.   Peach tould the other he would kill him, and take
what he had from him.   But they were some thing afraid;
but he said, Hang him, rougue, he had killed many of them.
So they let him alone to doe as he would; and when he saw
his time, he tooke a rapier and rane him through the body once
or twise, and tooke from him 5. fathume of wampam, and 3.
coats of cloath, and wente their way, leaving him for dead.
But he scrabled away, when they were gone, and made shift to
gett home,) but dyed within a few days after,) by which means
they were discovered; and by subtilty the Indeans tooke
them.   For they desiring a canow to sett them over a water,
(not thinking their facte had been known,) by the sachems
command they were carried to Aquidnett Iland, and ther
accused of the murder, and were examend and comitted upon
it by the English ther.   The Indeans sent for Mr. Williams,[1]
and made a greeveous complainte; his freinds and kinred
were ready to rise in armes, and provock the rest therunto,
some conceiving they should now find the Pequents words
trew: that the English would fall upon them.   But Mr.
Williams pacified them, and tould them they should see justice
done upon the offenders; and wente to the man, and tooke
Mr. James, a phisition, with him.   The man tould him who
did it, and in what maner it was done; but the phisition found
his wounds mortall, and that he could not live, (as he after
testified upon othe, before the jurie in oppen courte,) and so

[1] Roger Williams, always trusted by the Narragansetts.

he dyed shortly after, as both Mr. Williams, Mr. James, and some Indeans testified in courte. The Gov[rt] in the Bay were aquented with it, but refferrd it hither, because it was done in this jurisdiction;[1] but pressed by all means that justice might be done in it; or els the countrie must rise and see justice done, otherwise it would raise a warr. Yet some of the rude and ignorante sorte murmured that any English should be put to death for the Indeans. So at last they of the iland brought them hither, and being often examened, and the evidence prodused, they all in the end freely confessed in effect all that the Indean accused them of, and that they had done it, in the maner afforesaid; and so, upon the forementioned evidence, were cast by the jurie, and condemned, and executed for the same. And some of the Narigansett Indeans, and of the parties freinds, were presente when it was done, which gave them and all the countrie good satisfaction.[2] But it was a matter of much sadnes to them hear, and was the 2. execution which they had since they came; being both for wilfull murder, as hath bene before related. Thus much of this mater.

They received this year more letters from England full of reneued complaints, on the one side, that they could gett no money nor accounte from Mr. Sherley; and he againe, that he was pressed therto, saying he was to accounte with those hear, and not with them, etc. So, as was before resolved, if nothing came of their last letters, they would now send them what they could, as supposing, when some good parte was payed them, that Mr. Sherley and they would more easily agree aboute the remainder.

So they sent to Mr. Andrews and Mr. Beachamp, by Mr. Joseph Yonge, in the *Mary and Anne*, 1325*li.* waight of beaver, devided betweene them. Mr. Beachamp returned an accounte

---

[1] "And yet afterwards they laid claime to those parts in the controversie about Seacunk." (Br.)

[2] The execution probably took place on the hill between Murdock's Pond and Samoset Street, which was at an early date called Gallows Hill.

of his moyety, that he made 400*li*. starling of it, fraight and all charges paid. But Mr. Andrews, though he had the more and beter parte, yet he made not so much of his, through his owne indiscretion; and yet turned the loss [1] upon them hear, but without cause.

They sent them more by bills and other paimente, which was received and acknowledged by them, in money [2] and the like; which was for katle sould of Mr. Allertons, and the price of a bark sold, which belonged to the stock, and made over to them in money, 434*li*. sterling. The whole sume was 1234*li*. sterling, save what Mr. Andrews lost in the beaver, which was otherwise made good. But yet this did not stay their clamors, as will apeare here after more at large.

It pleased God, in these times, so to blesse the cuntry with such access and confluance of people into it, as it was therby much inriched, and catle of all kinds stood at a high rate for diverce years together. Kine were sould at 20*li*. and some at 25*li*. a peece, yea, some times at 28*li*. A cow-calfe usually at 10*li*. A milch goate at 3*li*. and some at 4*li*. And femall kids at 30*s*. and often at 40*s*. a peece. By which means the anciente planters which had any stock begane to grow in their estats. Corne also wente at a round rate, viz. 6*s*. a bushell. So as other trading begane to be neglected; and the old partners (having now forbidded Mr. Sherley to send them any more goods) broke of their trade at Kenebeck, and, as things stood, would follow it no longer. But some of them, (with other they joyned with,) being loath it should be lost by dis-continuance, agreed with the company for it, and gave them aboute the 6. parte of their gaines for it; with the first fruits of which they builte a house for a prison;[3] and the trade ther hath been since continued, to the great benefite of the place, for some well fore-sawe that these high prises of corne and

---

[1] "Being about 40*li*." (Br.)

[2] "And devided betweene them." (Br.)

[3] This prison was built in Summer Street, where the brook long called Prison Brook crosses the street.

catle would not long continue, and that then the commodities ther raised would be much missed.

This year, aboute the 1. or 2. of June, was a great and fearfull earthquake; it was in this place heard before it was felte. It came with a rumbling noyse, or low murmure, like unto remoate thunder; it came from the norward, and pased southward. As the noyse aproched nerer, they earth begane to shake, and came at length with that violence as caused platters, dishes, and such like things as stoode upon shelves, to clatter and fall downe; yea, persons were afraid of the houses themselves. It so fell oute that at the same time diverse of the cheefe of this towne were mett together at one house, conferring with some of their freinds that were upon their removall from the place, (as if the Lord would herby shew the signes of his displeasure, in their shaking a peeces and re-movalls one from an other.) How ever it was very terrible for the time, and as the men were set talking in the house, some women and others were without the dores, and the earth shooke with that violence as they could not stand without catching hould of the posts and pails that stood next them; but the violence lasted not long. And about halfe an hower, or less, came an other noyse and shaking, but nether so loud nor strong as the former, but quickly passed over; and so it ceased. It was not only on the sea coast, but the Indeans felt it within land; and some ships that were upon the coast were shaken by it. So powerfull is the mighty hand of the Lord, as to make both the earth and sea to shake, and the mountaines to tremble before him, when he pleases; and who can stay his hand? It was observed that the sommers, for divers years togeather after this earthquake, were not so hotte and season-able for the ripning of corne and other fruits as formerly; but more could and moyst, and subjecte to erly and untimly frosts, by which, many times, much Indean corne came not to maturi-tie; but whether this was any cause, I leave it to naturallists to judge.

Anno Dom: 1639. *and Anno Dom:* 1640.

THESE 2. years I joyne togeather, because in them fell not out many things more then the ordinary passages of their commone affaires, which are not needfull to be touched.   Those of this plantation having at sundrie times granted lands for severall townships, and amongst the rest to the inhabitants of Sityate,[1] some wherof issewed from them selves, and allso a large tracte of land was given to their 4. London partners in that place, viz. Mr. Sherley, Mr. Beacham, Mr. Andrews, and Mr. Hatherley.   At Mr. Hatherley's request and choys it was by him taken for him selfe and them in that place; for the other 3. had invested him with power and trust to chose for them.   And this tracte of land extended to their utmoste limets that way, and bordered on their neigbours of the Massachusets, who had some years after seated a towne (called Hingam) on their lands next to these parts.   So as now ther grue great differance betweene these 2. townships, about their bounds, and some meadow grownds that lay betweene them. They of Hingam presumed to alotte parte of them to their people, and measure and stack them out.   The other pulled up their stacks, and threw them.   So it grew to a controversie betweene the 2. goverments, and many letters and passages were betweene them aboute it; and it hunge some 2. years in suspense.   The Courte of Massachusets appointed some to range their line according to the bounds of their patente, and (as they wente to worke) they made it to take in all Sityate, and I know not how much more.   Againe, on the other hand, according to the line of the patente of this place,[2] it would take in Hingame and much more within their bounds.

In the end boath Courts agreed to chose 2. comissioners of each side, and to give them full and absolute power to agree and setle the bounds betwene them; and what they should doe

---

[1] Scituate, Mass.   [2] The Plymouth patent of January 13, 1629/30.

in the case should stand irrevocably.   One meeting they had at
Hingam, but could not conclude; for their comissioners stoode
stiffly on a clawes in their graunte, That from Charles-river,
or any branch or parte therof, they were to extend their limits,
and 3. myles further to the southward; or from the most
southward parte of the Massachusets Bay, and 3. mile further.[1]
But they chose to stand on the former termes, for they had
found a smale river, or brooke rather, that a great way with in
land trended southward, and issued into some part of that river
taken to be Charles-river, and from the most southerly part
of this, and 3. mile more southward of the same, they would
rune a line east to the sea, aboute 20. mile; which will (say
they) take in a part of Plimoth itselfe.   Now it is to be knowne
that though this patente and plantation were much the an-
cienter, yet this inlargemente of the same (in which Sityate
stood) was granted after theirs, and so theirs were first to take
place, before this inlargmente.   Now their answer was, first,
that, however according to their owne plan, they could noway
come upon any part of their ancieante grante.   2[ly]. They
could never prove that to be a parte of Charles-river, for they
knew not which was Charles-river, but as the people of this
place, which came first, imposed such a name upon that river,
upon which, since, Charles-towne is builte (supposing that was
it, which Captaine Smith in his mapp so named).[2]   Now they
that first named it have best reason to know it, and to explaine
which is it.   But they only tooke it to be Charles river, as fare
as it was by them navigated, and that was as farr as a boate
could goe.   But that every runlett or small brooke, that
should, farr within land, come into it, or mixe their stremes
with it, and were by the natives called by other and differente
names from it, should now by them be made Charles-river,

---

[1] The Massachusetts patent defined the southern boundary of that colony
as "three English myles on the south part of the saide river called Charles river,
or of any or every parte thereof," and three south of "the southermost parte of
the said baye called Massachusettes bay."

[2] See page 112.

or parts of it, they saw no reason for it.   And gave instance in
Humber, in Old England, which had the Trente, Ouse, and
many others of lesser note fell into it, and yet were not counted
parts of it; and many smaler rivers and broks fell into the
Trente, and Ouse, and no parts of them, but had nams aparte,
and divisions and nominations of them selves.   Againe, it was
pleaded that they had no east line in their patente, but were
to begine at the sea, and goe west by a line, etc.   At this meeting no conclution was made, but things discussed and well
prepared for an issue.   The next year the same commissioners
had their power continued or renewed, and mett at Sityate,
and concluded the mater, as followeth.

The agreemente of the bounds betwixte Plimoth and Massachusetts.

Wheras ther were tow comissiones granted by the 2. jurisdictions,
the one of Massachsets Govermente, granted unto John Endecott, gent:
and Israell Stoughton, gent: the other of New-Plimoth Govermente, to
William Bradford, Govr, and Edward Winslow, gent: and both these
for the setting out, setling, and determining of the bounds and limitts
of the lands betweene the said jurisdictions, wherby not only this presente
age, but the posteritie to come may live peaceably and quietly in that behalfe.   And for as much as the said comissioners on both sids have full
power so to doe, as appeareth by the records of both jurisdictions; we
therfore, the said comissioners above named, doe hearby with one consente
and agreemente conclude, detirmine, and by these presents declare, that
all the marshes at Conahasett that lye of the one side of the river next to
Hingam, shall belong to the jurisdition of Massachusetts Plantation;
and all the marshes that lye on the other side of the river next to Sityate,
shall be long to the jurisdiction of New-Plimoth; excepting 60. acers of
marsh at the mouth of the river, on Sityate side next to the sea, which we
doe herby agree, conclude, and detirmine shall belong to the jurisdition
of Massachusetts.   And further, we doe hearby agree, determine, and
conclude, that the bounds of the limites betweene both the said jurisditions
are as followeth, viz. from the mouth of the brook that runeth into
Chonahasett marches (which we call by the name of Bound-brooke)
with a stright and directe line to the midle of a great ponde, that lyeth
on the right hand of the uper path, or commone way, that leadeth betweene
Waimoth and Plimoth, close to the path as we goe alonge, which was

formerly named (and still we desire may be caled) Accord pond,[1] lying aboute five or 6. myles from Weimoth southerley; and from thence with a straight line to the souther-most part of Charles-river, and 3. miles southerly, inward into the countrie, according as is expresed in the patente granted by his Matie to the Company of the Massachusetts Plantation.   Provided allways and never the less concluded and determined by mutuall agreemente betweene the said comissioners, that if it fall out that the said line from Accord-pond to the sothermost parte of Charles-river, and 3. myles southerly as is before expresed, straiten or hinder any parte of any plantation begune by the Gove^{rt} of New-Plimoth, or hereafter to be begune within 10. years after the date of these ps^{nts}, that then, notwithstanding the said line, it shall be lawfull for the said Gov^{rt} of New-Plimoth to assume on the northerly side of the said line, wher it shall so intrench as afforesaid, so much land as will make up the quantity of eight miles square, to belong to every shuch plantation begune, or to [be] begune as afforesaid; which we agree, determine, and conclude to appertaine and belong to the said Gov^{rt} of New-Plimoth.   And wheras the said line, from the said brooke which runeth into Choahassett salt-marshes, called by us Bound-brooke, and the pond called Accord-pond, lyeth nere the lands belonging to the tounships of Sityate and Hingam, we doe therfore hereby determine and conclude, that if any devissions allready made and recorded, by either the said townships, doe crose the said line, that then it shall stand, and be of force according to the former intents and purposes of the said townes granting them (the marshes formerly agreed on exepted).   And that no towne in either jurisdiction shall hereafter exceede, but containe them selves within the said lines expressed.   In witnes wherof we, the comissioners of both jurisdictions, doe by these presents indented set our hands and seales the ninth day of the 4. month in 16. year of our soveraine lord, king Charles; and in the year of our Lord, 1640.

WILLIAM BRADFORD, Govr.   JO: ENDECOTT.

ED: WINSLOW.   ISRAELL STOUGHTON.

Wheras the patente[2] was taken in the name of William Bradford, (as in trust,) and rane in these termes: To him,

[1] Accord Pond, three-quarters of a mile long, lies in the towns of Hingham, Rockland and Norwell, and derives its name from a treaty made before 1640 between the Indians and the settlers, the parties meeting in the winter on the frozen pond to make it.

[2] Meaning the patent of January 13, 1629/30, from the Council for New England.

his heires, and associates and assignes; and now the noumber of free-men being much increased, and diverce tounships established and setled in severall quarters of the govermente, as Plimoth, Duxberie, Sityate, Tanton, Sandwich, Yarmouth, Barnstable, Marchfeeld, and not longe after, Seacunke (called afterward, at the desire of the inhabitants, Rehoboth) and Nawsett, it was by the Courte desired that William Bradford should make a surrender of the same into their hands. The which he willingly did, in this maner following.

Wheras William Bradford, and diverce others the first instruments of God in the beginning of this great work of plantation, togeather with such as the allordering hand of God in his providence soone added unto them, have been at very great charges to procure the lands, priviledges, and freedoms from all intanglments, as may appeare by diverse and sundrie deeds, inlargments of grants, purchases, and payments of debts, etc., by reason wherof the title to the day of these presents remaineth in the said William Bradford, his heires, associats, and assignes: now, for the better setling of the estate of the said lands (contained in the grant or pattente), the said William Bradford, and those first instruments termed and called in sondry orders upon publick recorde, The Purchasers, or Old comers; witnes 2. in spetiall, the one bearing date the 3. of March, 1639. the other in Des: the 1. An° 1640. wherunto these presents have spetiall relation and agreemente, and wherby they are distinguished from other the freemen and inhabitants of the said corporation. Be it knowne unto all men, therfore, by these presents, that the said William Bradford, for him selfe, his heires, together with the said purchasers, doe only reserve unto them selves, their heires, and assignes those 3. tractes of land mentioned in the said resolution, order, and agreemente, bearing date the first of Des: 1640. viz. first, from the bounds of Yarmouth, 3. miles to the eastward of Naemschatet,[1] and from sea to sea, crose the neck of land. The 2. of a place called Acoughcouss, which lyeth in the botome of the bay adjoyning to the west-side of Pointe Perill, and 2. myles to the westerne

---

[1] Naemschatet is the same as Naumskachett, referred to in the note on page 220; the reserved tract No. 1, in which it is mentioned, included the present townships of Eastham, Orleans, Brewster and probably Harwich and Chatham. The second reserved tract, in which Acoughcouss, Acushente and Nacata are mentioned, included the modern towns of Acushnet, New Bedford and Dartmouth. The third reserved tract, in which Sowansett and Cawsumsett are mentioned, included Swansea and Rehoboth, Massachusetts, and Barrington, Rhode Island.

side of the said river, to an other place called Acushente river, which entereth at the westerne end of Nacata, and 2. miles to the eastward therof, and to extend 8. myles up into the countrie.   The 3. place, from Sowansett river to Patucket river, (with Cawsumsett neck,) which is the cheefe habitation of the Indeans, and reserved for them to dwell upon,) extending into the land 8. myles through the whole breadth therof.   To-geather with such other small parcells of lands as they or any of them are personally possessed of or intressed in, by vertue of any former titles or grante whatsoever.   And the said William Bradford doth, by the free and full consente, approbation, and agreemente of the said old-planters, or purchasers, together with the liking, approbation, and acceptation of the other parte of the said corporation, surrender into the hands of the whole courte, consisting of the free-men of this corporation of New-Plimoth, all that other right and title, power, authority, priviledges, immu-nities, and freedomes granted in the said letters patents by the said right Honble Counsell for New-England; reserveing his and their personall right of freemen, together with the said old planters afforesaid, excepte the said lands before excepted, declaring the freemen of this corporation, togeather with all such as shal be legally admitted into the same, his associats.   And the said William Bradford, for him, his heiers, and as-signes, doe hereby further promise and grant to doe and performe what-soever further thing or things, acte or actes, which in him lyeth, which shall be needfull and expediente for the better confirming and establishing the said premises, as by counsel lerned in the lawes shall be reasonably advised and devised, when he shall be ther unto required.   In witness wherof, the said William Bradford hath in publick courte surrendered the said letters patents actually into the hands and power of the said courte, binding him selfe, his heires, executors, administrators, and assignes to deliver up whatsoever spetialties are in his hands that doe or may concerne the same.

In these 2. years they had sundry letters out of England to send one over to end the buissines and accounte with Mr. Sherley; who now professed he could not make up his accounts without the help of some from hence, espetialy Mr. Winslows. They had serious thoughts of it, and the most parte of the partners hear thought it best to send; but they had formerly written such bitter and threatening letters as Mr. Winslow was neither willing to goe, nor that any other of the partners should; for he was perswaded, if any of them wente, they

should be arested, and an action of such a summe layed upon
them as they should not procure baele, but must lye in prison,
and then they would bring them to what they liste; or other
wise they might be brought into trouble by the arch-bishops
means, as the times then stood.   But, notwithstanding, they
weer much inclined to send, and Captaine Standish was willing
to goe, but they resolved, seeing they could not all agree in this
thing, and that it was waighty, and the consequence might
prove dangerous, to take Mr. Winthrops advise in the thing,
and the rather, because Mr. Andrews had by many letters
acquaynted him with the differences betweene them, and appoynted him for his assigne to receive his parte of the debte.
(And though they deneyed to pay him any as a debte, till the
controversie was ended, yet they had deposited 110li. in money
in his hands for Mr. Andrews, to pay to him in parte as soone
as he would come to any agreement with the rest.)   But Mr.
Winthrop was of Mr. Winslows minde, and disswaded them
from sending; so they broak of their resolution from sending,
and returned this answer: that the times were dangerous as
things stood with them, for they knew how Mr. Winslow had
suffered formerley, and for a small matter was clapte up in the
Fleete, and it was long before he could gett out, to both his and
their great loss and damage; and times were not better, but
worse, in that respecte.   Yet, that their equall and honest
minds might appeare to all men, they made them this tender:
to refferr the case to some gentle-men and marchants in the Bay
of the Massachusetts, such as they should chuse, and were well
knowne unto them selves, (as they perceived their wer many
of their aquaintance and freinds ther, better knowne to them
then the partners hear,) and let them be informed in the case
by both sids, and have all the evidence that could be prodused,
in writing, or other wise; and they would be bound to stand
to their determination, and make good their award, though
it should cost them all they had in the world.   But this did not
please them, but they were offended at it, without any great

reasone for ought I know, (seeing nether side could give in clear
accountes, the partners here could not, by reason they (to their
smarte) were failed by the accountante they sent them, and
Mr. Sherley pretened he could not allso,) save as they conceived it a disparagmente to yeeld to their inferiours in respecte of the place and other concurring circomstances. So
this came to nothing; and afterward Mr. Sherley write, that
if Mr. Winslow would mett him in France, the Low-Countries,
or Scotland, let the place be knowne, and he come to him ther.
But in regard of the troubles that now begane to arise in our
owne nation, and other reasons, this did not come to any
effecte. That which made them so desirous to bring things to
an end was partly to stope the clamours and aspertions raised
and cast upon them hereaboute; though they conceived them
selves to sustaine the greatest wrong, and had most cause of
complainte; and partly because they feared the fall of catle,
in which most parte of their estats lay. And this was not a
vaine feare; for they fell indeede before they came to a conclusion, and that so souddanly, as a cowe that but a month
before was worth 20*li*., and would so have passed in any
paymente, fell now to 5*li*. and would yeeld no more; and a
goate that wente at 3*li*. or 50*s*. would now yeeld but 8. or 10*s*.
at most. All men feared a fall of catle, but it was thought it
would be by degrees; and not to be from the highest pitch at
once to the lowest, as it did, which was greatly to the damage
of many, and the undoing of some. An other reason was,
they many of them grew aged, (and indeed a rare thing it was
that so many partners should all live together so many years
as these did,) and saw many changes were like to befall; so
as they were loath to leave these intanglments upon their
children and posteritie, who might be driven to remove places,
as they had done; yea, them selves might doe it yet before they
dyed. But this bussines must yet rest; the next year gave
it more ripnes, though it rendred them less able to pay, for
the reasons afforesaid.

Anno Dom: 1641.

MR. SHERLEY being weary of this controversie, and desirous of an end, (as well as them selves,) write to Mr. John Atwode and Mr. William Collier, 2. of the inhabitants of this place, and of his speatiall aquaintance, and desired them to be a means to bring this bussines to an end, by advising and counselling the partners hear, by some way to bring it to a composition, by mutuall agreemente. And he write to them selves allso to that end, as by his letter may apear; so much therof as concernse the same I shall hear relate.

Sr. My love remembered, etc. I have writte so much concerning the ending of accounts betweexte us, as I profess I know not what more to write, etc. If you desire an end, as you seeme to doe, ther is (as I conceive) but 2. waise; that is, to parfecte all accounts, from the first to the last, etc. Now if we find this difficulte, and tedious, haveing not been so stricte and carefull as we should and oughte to have done, as for my owne parte I doe confess I have been somewhat to remisse, and doe verily thinke so are you, etc. I fear you can never make a perfecte accounte of all your pety viages, out, and home too and againe, etc.[1] So then the second way must be, by biding, or compounding; and this way first or last, we must fall upon, etc. If we must warr at law for it, doe not you expecte from me, nether will I from you, but to cleave the heare, and then I dare say the lawyers will be most gainers, etc. Thus let us set to the worke, one way or other, and end, that I may not allways suffer in my name and estate. And you are not free; nay, the gospell suffers by your delaying, and causeth the professors of it to be hardly spoken of, that you, being many, and now able, should combine and joyne togeather to oppress and burden me, etc. Fear not to make a faire and reasonable offer; beleeve me, I will never take any advantage to plead it against you, or to wrong you; or else let Mr. Winslow come over, and let him have such full power and authority as we may ende by compounding; or else, the accounts so well and fully made up, as we may end by reconing. Now, blesed be God, the times be much changed here, I hope to see many of you returne to your native countrie againe, and have such freedome

---

[1] "This was but to pretend advantage, for it could not be done, neither did it need." (Br.)

and libertie as the word of God prescribs. Our bishops were never so near a downfall as now;[1] God hath miraculously confounded them, and turned all their popish and Machavillian plots and projects on their owne heads, etc. Thus you see what is fitt to be done concerning our perticulere greevances. I pray you take it seriously into consideration; let each give way a litle that we may meete, etc. Be you and all yours kindly saluted, etc. So I ever rest,

Your loving friend,
JAMES SHERLEY.

Clapham, May 18. 1641.

Being thus by this leter, and allso by Mr. Atwodes and Mr. Colliers mediation urged to bring things to an end, (and the continuall clamors from the rest,) and by none more urged then by their own desires, they tooke this course (because many scandals had been raised upon them). They apoynted these 2. men before mentioned to meet on a certaine day, and called some other freinds on both sids, and Mr. Free-man, brother in law to Mr. Beachamp, and having drawne up a collection of all the remains of the stock, in what soever it was, as housing, boats, bark, and all implements belonging to the same, as they were used in the time of the trad, were they better or worce, with the remaines of all commodities, as beads, knives, hatchetts, cloth, or any thing els, as well the refuse as the more vendible, with all debts, as well those that were desperate as others more hopefull; and having spent diverce days to bring this to pass, having the helpe of all bookes and papers, which either any of them selves had, or Josias Winslow, who was their accountante; and they found the sume in all to arise (as the things were valued) to aboute 1400li. And they all of them tooke a voluntary but a sollem oath, in the presence one of an other, and of all their frends, the persons abovesaid that were now presente, that this was all that any of them knew of, or could remember; and Josias Winslow did the like for his parte.

---

[1] Strafford had been beheaded on May 12; a bill for the complete abolition of episcopacy was read in the Commons on May 27; the act abolishing the Court of High Commission was signed in July.

But the truth is they wronged them selves much in the valuation, for they reconed some catle as they were taken of Mr. Allerton, as for instance a cowe in the hands of one cost 25*li*. and so she was valued in this accounte; but when she came to be past away in parte of paymente, after the agreemente, she would be accepted but at 4*li*. 15*s*.   Also, being tender of their oaths, they brought in all they knew owing to the stock; but they had not made the like diligente search what the stocke might owe to any, so as many scattering debts fell upon afterwards more then now they knew of.

Upon this they drew certaine articles of agreemente betweene Mr Atwode, on Mr. Sherleys behalfe, and them selves. The effecte is as folloeth.

Articles of agreemente made and concluded upon the 15. *day of October*, 1641. *etc.*

Im°:   Wheras ther was a partnership for diverce years agreed upon betweene James Sherley, John Beacham, and Richard Andrews, of London, marchants, and William Bradford, Edward Winslow, Thomas Prence, Myles Standish, William Brewster, John Aldon, and John Howland, with Isaack Allerton, in a trade of beaver skines and other furrs arising in New-England; the terme of which said partnership being expired, and diverse summes of money in goods adventured into New-England by the said James Sherley, John Beachamp, and Richard Andrews, and many large returnes made from New-England by the said William Bradford, Ed: Winslow, etc.; and differance arising aboute the charge of 2. ships, the one called the *White Angele*, of Bristow, and the other the *Frindship*, of Barnstable, and a viage intended in her, etc.; which said ships and their viages, the said William Bradford, Ed: W. etc. conceive doe not at all appertaine to their accounts of partnership; and weras the accounts of the said partnership are found to be confused, and cannot orderley appeare (through the defaulte of Josias Winslow, the booke keeper); and weras the said W. B. etc. have received all their goods for the said trade from the foresaid James Sherley, and have made most of their returnes to him, by consente of the said John Beachamp and Richard Andrews; and wheras also the said James Sherley hath given power and authoritie to Mr. John Atwode, with the advice and consente of William Collier, of Duxborow, for and on his behalfe, to put such an absolute end to the said partnership, with all and every accounts, reconings, dues, claimes, demands, whatsoever, to the said James Sherley, John Beacham, and Richard Andrews, from the said W. B. etc. for and concerning the said beaver trade, and also the charge the said 2. ships, and their viages made or pretended, whether just or unjuste, from the worlds begining to this presente, as also for the paimente of a purchas of 1800*li.* made by Isaack Allerton, for and on the behalfe of the said W. B., Ed: W., etc., and of the joynt stock, shares, lands, and adventurs, what soever in New-England aforesaid, as apeareth by a deede bearing date the 6. Nov^br. 1627; and also for and from such sume and sumes of money or goods as are received by William Bradford, Tho: Prence, and Myles Standish, for the recovery of dues, by accounts betwexte them, the said James Sherly, John Beachamp, and Richard Andrews, and Isaack Allerton, for the ship caled the *White Angell.* Now the said John Attwode, with advice and counsell of the said William Collier, having had much comunication and spente diverse days in agitation of all the said differances and accounts with the said W. B., E. W., etc; and the said W. B., E. W., etc. have also, with the said book-keeper spente much time in collecting and gathering togeither the remainder of the stock of partnership for the said trade, and what soever hath beene received, or is due by the said attorneyship before expresed, and all, and all manner of goods, debts, and dues therunto belonging, as well those debts that are weake and doubtfull and desperate, as those that are more secure, which in all doe amounte to the sume of 1400*li.* or ther aboute; and for more full satisfaction of the said James Sherley, John Beachamp, and Richard Andrews, the said W. B. and all the rest of the abovesaid partners, togeither with Josias Winslow the booke keeper, have taken a voluntarie oath, that within the said sume of 1400*li.* or theraboute, is contained whatsoever they knew, to the utmost of their rememberance.

In consideration of all which matters and things before expressed, and to the end that a full, absolute, and finall end may be now made, and all suits in law may be avoyded, and love and peace continued, it is therfore agreed and concluded betweene the said John Attwode, with the advice and consent of the said William Colier, for and on the behalfe of the said James Sherley, to and with the said W. B., etc. in maner and forme following: viz. that the said John Attwode shall procure a sufficiente release and discharge, under the hands and seals of the said James Sherley, John Beachamp, and Richard Andrews, to be delivered fayer and unconcealed unto the said William Bradford, etc., at or before the last day of August, next insuing the date hereof, whereby the said William Bradford etc., their heires, executors, and administrators, and everv of them shall be fully and absolutely aquited and discharged of all actions, suits, reconings, accounts, claimes, and demands whatsoever concerning the generall stock of beaver trade, paymente of the said 1800*li.* for the purchass, and all demands, reckonings, and accounts, just or unjuste, concerning the tow ships *White-Angell* and *Frendship* aforesaid, togeather with whatsoever hath been received by the said William Bradford, of the goods or estate of Isaack Allerton, for satisfaction of the accounts of the said ship called the *Whit Angele*, by vertue of a *l*re of attourney to him, Thomas Prence, and Myles Standish, directed from the said James Sherley, John Beachamp, and Richard Andrews, for that purpose as afforesaid.

It is also agreed and concluded upon betweene the said parties to these presents, that the said W. B., E. W., etc. shall now be bound in 2400*li.* for paymente of 1200*li.* in full satisfaction of all demands as afforesaid; to be payed in maner and forme following; that is to say, 400*li.* within 2. months next after the receite of the aforesaid releases and discharges, one hundred and ten pounds wherof is allready in the hands of John Winthrop senior of Boston, Esquire, by the means of Mr. Richard Andrews affore-said, and 80*li.* waight of beaver now deposited into the hands of the said John Attwode, to be both in part of paimente of the said 400*li.* and the other 800*li.* to be payed by 200*li.* p^r annume, to such assignes as shall be appointed, inhabiting either in Plimoth or Massachusetts Bay, in such goods and comodities, and at such rates, as the countrie shall afford at the time of delivery and paymente; and in the mean time the said bond of 2400*li.* to be deposited into the hands of the said John Attwode. And it is agreed upon by and betweene the said parties to these presents, that if the said John Attwode shall not or cannot procure such said releases and discharges as afforesaid from the said James Sherley, John Bachamp, and Richard Andrews, at or before the last day of August next insuing the date hear of, that then the said John Attwode shall, at the said day pre-cisely, redeliver, or cause to be delivered unto the said W. B., E. W., etc. their said bond of 2400*li.* and the said 80*li.* waight of beaver, or the due valew therof, without any fraud or further delay; and for performance of all and singuler the covenants and agreements hearin contained and ex-pressed, which on the one parte and behalfe of the said James Sherley are to be observed and performed, shall become bound in the summe of 2400*li.* to them, the said William Bradford, Edward Winslow, Thomas Prence, Myles Standish, William Brewster, John Allden, and John Howland. And it is lastly agreed upon betweene the said parties, that these presents shall be left in trust, to be kepte for boath parties, in the hands of Mr. John Reanour, teacher of Plimoth. In witnes wherof, all the said parties have hereunto severally sett their hands, the day and year first above writen.

JOHN ATWODE, WILLIAM BRADFORD, EDWARD WINSLOW, etc.
In the presence of EDMOND FREEMAN,
WILLIAM THOMAS,
WILLIAM PADY,
NATHANIELL SOUTHER.

The nexte year this long and tedious bussines came to some issue, as will then appeare, though not to a finall ende with all the parties; but this much for the presente.

I had forgoten to inserte in its place how the church here had invited and sent for Mr. Charles Chansey,[1] a reverend, godly, and very larned man, intending upon triall to chose him pastor of the church hear, for the more comfortable performance of the ministrie with Mr. John Reinor, the teacher of the same. But ther fell out some differance aboute baptising, he holding it ought only to be by diping, and putting the whole body under water, and that sprinkling was unlawfull. The church yeelded that immersion, or dipping, was lawfull, but in this could countrie not so conveniente. But they could not nor durst not yeeld to him in this, that sprinkling (which all the churches of Christ doe for the most parte use at this day) was unlawfull, and an humane invention, as the same was prest; but they were willing to yeeld to him as far as they could, and to the utmost; and were contented to suffer him to practise as he was perswaded; and when he came to minister that ordnance, he might so doe it to any that did desire it in that way, provided he could peacably suffer Mr. Reinor, and such as desired to have theirs otherwise baptised by him, by sprinkling or powering on of water upon them; so as ther might

[1] "Mr. Chancey came to them in the year 1638. and staid till the later part of this year 1641." (Br.) Rev. Charles Chauncy was born in Yardley, England, in 1592, was educated at Westminster School, and took his degree at Cambridge in 1613. He was vicar of Ware from 1627 to 1634, was deprived of his living by Archbishop Laud, and in 1637 came to New England. Settled in Plymouth in 1638, he remained there until 1641, when he was settled in Scituate. In 1654 he was chosen president of Harvard College and continued in office until his death in 1672.

be no disturbance in the church hereaboute. But he said he could not yeeld herunto. Upon which the church procured some other ministers to dispute the pointe with him publikly; as Mr. Ralfe Partrich, of Duxberie, who did it sundrie times, very ablie and sufficently, as allso some other ministers within this govermente. But he was not satisfied; so the church sent to many other churches to crave their help and advise in this mater, and, with his will and consente, sent them his arguments writen under his owne hand. They sente them to the church at Boston in the Bay of Massachusets, to be comunicated with other churches ther. Also they sent the same to the churches of Conightecutt and New-Haven, with sundrie others; and received very able and sufficient answers, as they conceived, from them and their larned ministers, who all concluded against him. But him selfe was not satisfied therwith. Their answers are too large hear to relate. They conceived the church had done what was meete in the thing, so Mr. Chansey, having been the most parte of 3. years here, removed him selfe to Sityate, wher he now remaines a minister to the church ther. Also about these times, now that catle and other things begane greatly to fall from their former rates, and persons begane to fall into more straits, and many being allready gone from them, (as is noted before,) both to Duxberie, Marshfeeld, and other places, and those of the cheefe sorte, as Mr. Winslow, Captaine Standish, Mr. Allden, and many other, and stille some dropping away daly, and some at this time, and many more unsetled, it did greatly weaken the place, and by reason of the straitnes and barrennes of the place, it sett the thoughts of many upon removeall; as will appere more hereafter.

Anno Dom: 1642.

MARVILOUS it may be to see and consider how some kind of wickednes did grow and breake forth here, in a land wher the same was so much witnesed against, and so narrowly looked unto, and severly punished when it was knowne: as in no place more, or so much, that I have known or heard of; insomuch as they have been somewhat censured, even by moderate and good men, for their severitie in punishments. And yet all this could not suppress the breaking out of sundrie notorious sins, (as this year, besids other, gives us too many sad presidents and instances,) espetially drunkennes and unclainnes; not only incontinencie betweene persons unmaried, for which many both men and women have been punished sharply enough, but some maried persons allso. But that which is worse, even sodomie and bugerie, (things fearfull to name,) have broak forth in this land, oftener then once. I say it may justly be marveled at, and cause us to fear and tremble at the consideration of our corrupte natures, which are so hardly bridled, subdued, and mortified; nay, cannot by any other means but the powerfull worke and grace of Gods spirite. But (besids this) one reason may be, that the Divell may carrie a greater spite against the churches of Christ and the gospell hear, by how much the more they indeaour to preserve holynes and puritie amongst them, and strictly punisheth the contrary when it ariseth either in church or comone wealth; that he might cast a blemishe and staine upon them in the eyes of [the] world, who use to be rash in judgmente. I would rather thinke thus, then that Satane hath more power in these heathen lands, as som have thought, then in more Christian nations, espetially over Gods servants in them.

2. An other reason may be, that it may be in this case as it is with waters when their streames are stopped or dammed up, when they gett passage they flow with more violence, and make more noys and disturbance, then when they are suffered to rune quietly in their owne chanels. So wikednes being here more stopped by strict laws, and the same more nerly looked unto, so as it cannot rune in a comone road of liberty as it would, and is inclined, it searches every wher, and at last breaks out wher it getts vente.

3. A third reason may be, hear (as I am verily perswaded)

is not more evills in this kind, nor nothing nere so many by proportion, as in other places; but they are here more discoverd and seen, and made publick by due serch, inquisition, and due punishment; for the churches looke narrowly to their members, and the magistrats over all, more strictly then in other places. Besids, here the people are but few in comparison of other places, which are full and populous, and lye hid, as it were, in a wood or thickett, and many horrible evills by that means are never seen nor knowne; wheras hear, they are, as it were, brought into the light, and set in the plaine feeld, or rather on a hill, made conspicuous to the veiw of all.

But to proceede; ther came a letter from the Govr in the Bay to them here, touching matters of the forementioned nature, which because it may be usefull I shall hear relate it, and the passages ther aboute.

Sr: Having an opportunitie to signifie the desires of our Generall Court in toow things of spetiall importance, I willingly take this occasion to imparte them to you, that you may imparte them to the rest of your magistrats, and also to your Elders, for counsell; and give us your advise in them. The first is concerning heinous offences in point of uncleannes; the perticuler cases, with the circomstances, and the questions ther upon, you have hear inclosed. The 2. thing is concerning the Ilanders at Aquidnett;[1] that seeing the cheefest of them are gone from us, in offences, either to churches, or commone welth, or both; others are dependants on them, and the best sorte are such as close with them in all their rejections of us. Neither is it only in a faction that they are devided from us, but in very deed they rend them selves from all the true churches of Christ, and, many of them, from all the powers of majestracie. We have had some experience hereof by some of their underworkers, or emissaries, who have latly come amongst us, and have made publick defiance against magistracie, ministrie, churches, and church covenants, etc. as antichristian; secretly also sowing the seeds of Familisme,[2] and Anabaptistrie to the infection of some, and danger of others; so that we are not willing to joyne with

---

[1] The settlers on the island of Rhode Island.

[2] The Familists were a sect existing in Holland and England in the sixteenth century, called the Family of Love, because of the love they professed for all human beings, however wicked. They and the Anabaptists were regarded with great horror by the orthodox Puritans.

them in any league or confederacie at all, but rather that you would consider and advise with us how we may avoyd them, and keep ours from
being infected by them.   Another thing I should mention to you, for the
maintenance of the trad of beaver; if ther be not a company to order it in
every jurisdition among the English, which companies should agree in
generall of their way in trade, I supose that the trade will be overthrowne,
and the Indeans will abuse us.   For this cause we have latly put it into
order amongst us, hoping of incouragmente from you (as we have had)
that we may continue the same.   Thus not further to trouble you, I rest,
with my loving remembrance to your selfe, etc.

Your loving friend,
RI: BELLINGHAM.[1]

Boston, 28. (1.) 1642.

The note inclosed follows on the other side.

Worthy and beloved Sr:
Your letter (with the questions inclosed) I have comunicated with our
Assistants, and we have refered the answer of them to such Reve[nd] Elders
as are amongst us, some of whose answers thertoo we have here sent you
inclosed, under their owne hands; from the rest we have not yet received
any.   Our farr distance hath bene the reason of this long delay, as also
that they could not conferr their counsells togeather.

For our selves, (you know our breedings and abillities,) we rather
desire light from your selves, and others, whom God hath better inabled,
then to presume to give our judgments in cases so difficulte and of so high
a nature.   Yet under correction, and submission to better judgments, we
propose this one thing to your prudent considerations.   As it seems to us,
in the case even of wilifull murder, that though a man did smite or wound
an other, with a full pourpose or desire to kill him, (which is murder in a
high degree, before God,) yet if he did not dye, the magistrate was not to
take away the others life.[3]   So by proportion in other grosse and foule
sines, though high attempts and nere approaches to the same be made, and
such as in the sight and account of God may be as ill as the accomplishmente of the foulest acts of that sine, yet we doute whether it may be safe
for the magistrate to proceed to death; we thinke, upon the former grounds,
rather he may not. . . . Yet we confess foulnes of circomstances, and

---

[1] Bellingham had been elected governor of Massachusetts June 2, 1641.
and was governor one year.   The date of this letter may be presumed to be
March 28, 1642.

[2] A leaf is here wanting in the original manuscript, it having been cut out
before Prince's time, as is shown by a note in his handwriting.

[3] "Exod: 21. 22.   Deu: 19. 11.   Num: 35. 16. 18."   (Br.)

frequencie in the same, doth make us remaine in the darke, and desire further light from you, or any, as God shall give.

As for the 2. thing, concerning the Ilanders? we have no conversing with them, nor desire to have, furder then necessitie or humanity may require.

And as for trade? we have as farr as we could ever therin held an orderly course, and have been sory to see the spoyle therof by others, and fear it will hardly be recovered. But in these, or any other things which may concerne the commone good, we shall be willing to advise and concure with you in what we may. Thus with my love remembered to your selfe, and the rest of our worthy friends, your Assistants, I take leave, and rest,

Your loving friend,

W. B.[1]

Plim: 17. 3. month, 1642.

.   .   .   .

But it may be demanded how came it to pass that so many wicked persons and profane people should so quickly come over into this land, and mixe them selves amongst them? seeing it was religious men that begane the work, and they came for religions sake. I confess this may be marveilled at, at least in time to come, when the reasons therof should not be knowne; and the more because here was so many hardships and wants mett withall. I shall therfore indeavor to give some answer hereunto. And first, according to that in the gospell, it is ever to be remembered that wher the Lord begins to sow good seed, ther the envious man will endeavore to sow tares. 2. Men being to come over into a wildernes, in which much labour and servise was to be done aboute building and planting, etc., such as wanted help in that respecte, when they could not have such as they would, were glad to take such as they could; and so, many untoward servants, sundry of them proved, that were thus brought over, both men and women kind; who, when their times were expired, became families of them selves, which gave increase hereunto. 3. An other and a maine reason hearof was, that men, finding so many godly

[1] Here follow clerical opinions, of Reynor, Partridge and Chauncy, which it has been deemed proper to omit, together with a page or two ensuing.

disposed persons willing to come into these parts, some begane
to make a trade of it, to transeport passengers and their goods,
and hired ships for that end; and then, to make up their
fraight and advance their profite, cared not who the persons
were, so they had money to pay them. And by this means
the cuntrie became pestered with many unworthy persons, who,
being come over, crept into one place or other. 4. Againe,
the Lords blesing usually following his people, as well in outward as spirituall things, (though afflictions be mixed withall,)
doe make many to adhear to the people of God, as many followed Christ, for the loaves sake, John 6. 26. and a mixed
multitud came into the willdernes with the people of God out
of Eagipte of old, Exod. 12. 38; so allso ther were sente by
their freinds some under hope that they would be made better;
others that they might be eased of such burthens, and they
kept from shame at home that would necessarily follow their
dissolute courses. And thus, by one means or other, in 20.
years time, it is a question whether the greater part be not
growne the worser.

I am now come to the conclusion of that long and tedious
bussines betweene the partners hear, and them in England,
the which I shall manifest by their owne letters as followeth,
in such parts of them as are pertinente to the same.

Mr. Sherleys to Mr. Attwood.

Mr. Attwood, my approved loving freind: Your letter of the 18. of
October last I have received, wherin I find you have taken a great deall
of paines and care aboute that troublesome bussines betwixte our Plimoth
partners and freinds, and us hear, and have deeply ingaged your selfe, for
which complements and words are no reall satisfaction, etc. For the
agreemente you have made with Mr. Bradford, Mr. Winslow, and the
rest of the partners ther, considering how honestly and justly I am perswaded they have brought in an accounte of the remaining stock, for my
owne parte I am well satisfied, and so I thinke is Mr. Andrewes, and I
supose will be Mr. Beachampe, if most of it might acrew to him, to
whom the least is due, etc. And now for peace sake, and to conclude as
we began, lovingly and freindly, and to pass by all failings of all, the con-

clude is accepted of; I say this agreemente that you have made is condesended unto, and Mr. Andrews hath sent his release to Mr. Winthrop,
with such directions as he conceives fitt; and I have made bould to
trouble you with mine, and we have both sealed in the presence of Mr.
Weld, and Mr. Peeters, and some others, and I have also sente you an
other, for the partners ther, to seale to me; for you must not deliver mine
to them, excepte they seale and deliver one to me; this is fitt and equall,
etc.

Yours to command in what I may or can,

JAMES SHERLEY.

June 14. 1642.

His to the partners as followeth.

Loving freinds,

Mr. Bradford, Mr. Winslow, Mr. Prence, Captaine Standish, Mr.
Brewster, Mr. Alden, and Mr. Howland, give me leave to joyne you all
in one letter, concerning the finall end and conclude of that tedious and
troublsome bussines, and I thinke I may truly say uncomfurtable and un-
profitable to all, etc.   It hath pleased God now to put us upon a way to
sease all suits, and disquieting of our spirites, and to conclude with peace
and love, as we began.   I am contented to yeeld and make good what Mr.
Attwood and you have agreed upon; and for that end have sente to my
loving freind, Mr. Attwood, an absolute and generall release unto you all,
and if ther wante any thing to make it more full, write it your selves, and
it shall be done, provided that all you, either joyntly or severally, seale
the like discharge to me.   And for that end I have drawne one joyntly,
and sent it to Mr. Attwood, with that I have sealed to you.   Mr. Andrews
hath sealed an aquitance also, and sent it to Mr. Winthrop, whith such
directions as he conceived fitt, and, as I hear, hath given his debte, which
he maks 544*li.* unto the gentlemen of the Bay.   Indeed, Mr. Welld, Mr.
Peters, and Mr. Hibbens have taken a great deale of paines with Mr.
Andrews, Mr. Beachamp, and my selfe, to bring us to agree, and to that
end we have had many meetings and spent much time aboute it.   But as
they are very religious and honest gentle-men, yet they had an end that
they drove at and laboured to accomplish (I meane not any private end,
but for the generall good of their patente).   It had been very well you had
sent one over.   Mr. Andrew wished you might have one 3. parte of the
1200*li.* and the Bay 2. thirds; but then we 3. must have agreed togeather,
which were a hard mater now.   But Mr. Weld, Mr. Peters, and Mr.
Hibbens, and I, have agreed, they giving you bond, so to compose with
Mr. Beachamp, as to procure his generall release, and free you from all
trouble and charge that he may put you too; which indeed is nothing, for

I am perswaded Mr. Weld will in time gaine him to give them all that is dew to him, which in some sorte is granted allready; for though his demands be great, yet Mr. Andrewes hath taken some paines in it, and makes it appear to be less then I thinke he will consente to give them for so good an use; so you neede not fear, that for taking bond ther to save you harmles you be safe and well.   Now our accord is, that you must pay to the gentle-men of the Bay 900*li.*; they are to bear all chargs that may any way arise concerning the free and absolute clearing of you from us three. And you to have the other 300*li.* etc.

Upon the receiving of my release from you, I will send you your bonds for the purchass money.   I would have sent them now, but I would have Mr. Beachamp release as well as I, because you are bound to him in them. Now I know if a man be bound to 12. men, if one release, it is as if all released, and my discharge doth cutt them of; wherfore doubte you not but you shall have them, and your commission, or any thing els that is fitt.   Now you know ther is tow years of the purchass money, that I would not owne, for I have formerley certified you that I would but pay 7. years; but now you are discharged of all, etc.

Your loving and kind friend in what I may or can,

June 14. 1642.   JAMES SHERLEY.

The coppy of his release is as followeth.

Wheras diverce questions, differences, and demands have arisen and depended betweene William Bradford, Edward Winslow, Thomas Prence, Mylest Standish, William Brewster, John Allden, and John Howland, gent: now or latly inhabitants or resident at New-Plimoth, in New-England, on the one party, and James Sherley of London, marchante, and others, in th' other parte, for and concerning a stocke and partable trade of beaver and other comodities, and fraighting of ships, as the *White Angell, Frindship,* or others, and the goods of Isaack Allerton which were seazed upon by vertue of a leter of atturney made by the said James Sherley and John Beachamp and Richard Andrews, or any other maters concerning the said trade, either hear in Old-England or ther in New-England or elsewher, all which differences are since by mediation of freinds composed compremissed, and all the said parties agreed.   Now know all men by these presents, that I, the said James Sherley, in performance of the said compremise and agreemente, have remised, released, and quite claimed, and doe by these presents remise, release, and for me, myne heires, executors, and Administrators, and for every of us, for ever quite claime unto the said William Bradford, Edward Winslow, Thomas Prence, Myles

Standish, William Brewster, John Allden, and John Howland, and every of them, their and every of their heires, executors, and administrators, all and all maner of actions, suits, debts, accounts, rekonings, comissions, bonds, bills, specialties, judgments, executions, claimes, challinges, differences, and demands whatsoever, with or against the said William Bradford, Edward Winslow, Thomas Prence, Myles Standish, William Brewster, John Allden, and John Howland, or any of them, ever I had, now have, or in time to come can, shall, or may have, for any mater, cause, or thing whatsoever from the begining of the world untill the day of the date of these presents.   In witnes wherof I have hereunto put my hand and seale, given the second day of June, 1642, and in the eighteenth year of the raigne of our soveraigne lord, king Charles, etc.

JAMES SHERLEY.

Sealed and delivered

  in the presence of THOMAS WELD,

                HUGH PETERS,

                WILLIAM HIBBINS.

                ARTHUR TIRREY, Scr.

                THO: STURGS, his servante.

Mr. Andrews[1] his discharg was to the same effecte; he was by agreemente to have 500*li*. of the money, the which he gave to them in the Bay, who brought his discharge and demanded the money.   And they tooke in his release and paid the money according to agreemente, viz. one third of the 500*li*. they paid downe in hand, and the rest in 4. equall payments, to be paid yearly, for which they gave their bonds.   And wheras 44*li*. was more demanded, they conceived they could take it of with Mr. Andrews, and therfore it was not in the bonde. But Mr. Beachamp would not parte with any of his, but demanded 400*li*. of the partners here, and sent a release to a friend, to deliver it to them upon the receite of the money. But his relese was not perfecte, for he had left out some of the partners names, with some other defects; and besids, the other gave them to understand he had not near so much due.   So no end was made with him till 4. years after; of which in it[s] plase.   And in that regard, that them selves did not agree, I

---

[1] Richard Andrews, it will be remembered, was one of the merchant adventurers, as was also John Beauchamp, mentioned below.

shall inserte some part of Mr. Andrews letter, by which he conceives the partners here were wronged, as followeth. This leter of his was write to Mr. Edmond Freeman,[1] brother in law to Mr. Beachamp.

Mr. Freeman,

My love remembred unto you, etc. I then certified the partners how I found Mr. Beachamp and Mr. Sherley, in their perticuler demands, which was according to mens principles, of getting what they could; allthough the one will not shew any accounte, and the other a very unfaire and unjust one; and both of them discouraged me from sending the partners my accounte, Mr. Beachamp espetially. Their reason, I have cause to conceive, was, that allthough I doe not, nor ever intended to, wrong the partners or the bussines, yet, if I gave no accounte, I might be esteemed as guiltie as they, in some degree at least; and they might seeme to be the more free from taxation in not delivering their accounts, who have both of them charged the accounte with much intrest they have payed forth, and one of them would likwise for much intrest he hath not paid forth, as appeareth by his accounte, etc. And seeing the partners have now made it appear that ther is 1200*li*. remaining due between us all, and that it may appear by my accounte I have not charged the bussines with any intrest, but doe forgive it unto the partners, above 200*li*. if Mr. Sherley and Mr. Beachamp, who have betweene them wronged the bussines so many 100*li*. both in principall and intrest likwise, and have therin wronged me as well and as much as any of the partners; yet if they will not make and deliver faire and true accounts of the same, nor be contente to take what by computation is more then can be justly due to either, that is, to Mr. Beachamp 150*li*. as by Mr. Allertons accounte, and Mr. Sherleys accounte, on oath in chancerie; and though ther might be nothing due to Mr. Sherley, yet he requirs 100*li*. etc. I conceive, seing the partners have delivered on their oaths the summe remaining in their hands, that they may justly detaine the 650*li*. which may remaine in their hands, after I am satisfied, untill Mr. Sherley and Mr. Beachamp will be more fair and just in their ending, etc. And as I intend, if the partners fayrly end with me, in satisfing in parte and ingaging them selves for the rest of my said 544*li*. to returne back for the poore my parte of the land at Sityate, so likwise I intend to relinquish my right and intrest in their dear patente, on which much of our money was laid forth, and also my right and intrest

---

[1] Edmund Freeman came over in the *Abigail* in October, 1635, and settled in Sandwich. Two sons. Edmund and John, married daughters of Governor Prence.

in their cheap purchass, the which may have cost me first and last 350*li*.[1]
But I doubte whether other men have not charged or taken on accounte
what they have disbursed in the like case, which I have not charged,
neither did I conceive any other durst so doe, untill I saw the accounte
of the one and heard the words of the other; the which gives me just cause
to suspecte both their accounts to be unfaire; for it seemeth they consulted
one with another aboute some perticulers therin. Therfore I conceive
the partners ought the rather to require just accounts from each of them
before they parte with any money to either of them. For marchants
understand how to give an acounte; if they mean fairley, they will not
deney to give an accounte, for they keep memorialls to helpe them to give
exacte acounts in all perticulers, and memoriall cannot forget his charge,
if the man will remember. I desire not to wrong Mr. Beachamp or Mr.
Sherley, nor may be silente in such apparente probabilities of their wrong-
ing the partners, and me likwise, either in deneying to deliver or shew any
accounte, or in delivering one very unjuste in some perticulers, and very
suspitious in many more; either of which, being from understanding
marchants, cannot be from weaknes or simplisitie, and therfore the more
unfaire. So comending you and yours, and all the Lord's people, unto
the gratious protection and blessing of the Lord, and rest your loving
friend,

Aprill 7. 1643.

RICHARD ANDREWES.

This leter was write the year after the agreement, as doth
appear; and what his judgmente was herein, the contents doth
manifest, and so I leave it to the equall judgmente of any to
consider, as they see cause.

Only I shall adde what Mr. Sherley furder write in a leter
of his, about the same time, and so leave this bussines. His
is as followeth on the other side.[2]

Loving freinds, Mr. Bradford, Mr. Winslow, Cap: Standish, Mr.
Prence, and the rest of the partners with you; I shall write this generall
leter to you all, hoping it will be a good conclude of a generall, but a costly
and tedious bussines I thinke to all, I am sure to me, etc.

I received from Mr. Winslow a letter of the 28. of Sept: last, and so
much as concernes the generall bussines I shall answer in this, not knowing whether I shall have opportunitie to write perticuler letters, etc. I

[1] "This he means of the first adventures, all which were lost, as hath before
been shown; and what he here writs is probable at least." (Br.)
[2] Of the page of the manuscript.

expected more letters from you all, as some perticuler writs,[1] but it seemeth no fitt opportunity was offered.   And now, though the bussines for the
maine may stand, yet some perticulers is alltered; I say my former agreemente with Mr. Weld and Mr. Peters, before the[y] could conclude or gett
any grante of Mr. Andrews, they sought to have my release; and ther upon
they sealed me a bond for a 110*li*.   So I sente my acquittance, for they
said without mine ther would be no end made (and ther was good reason
for it).   Now they hoped, if they ended with me, to gaine Mr. Andrews
parte, as they did holy, to a pound, (at which I should wonder, but that I
observe some passages,) and they also hoped to have gotten Mr. Beachamp
part, and I did thinke he would have given it them.   But if he did well
understand him selfe, and that acounte, he would give it; for his demands
make a great sound.[2]   But it seemeth he would not parte with it, supposing
it too great a sume, and that he might easily gaine it from you.   Once he
would have given them 40*li*. but now they say he will not doe that, or
rather I suppose they will not take it; for if they doe, and have Mr.
Andrewses, then they must pay me their bond of 110*li*. 3 months hence.
Now it will fall out farr better for you, that they deal not with Mr. Beachamp, and also for me, if you be as kind to me as I have been and will
be to you; and that thus, if you pay Mr. Andrews, or the Bay men, by
his order, 544*li*. which is his full demande; but if looked into, perhaps
might be less.   The man is honest, and in my conscience would not
wittingly doe wronge, yett he may forgett as well as other men; and Mr.
Winslow may call to minde wherin he forgetts; (but some times it is good
to buy peace.)   The gentlemen of the Bay may abate 100*li*. and so both
sids have more right and justice then if they exacte all, etc.   Now if you
send me a 150*li*. then say Mr. Andrews full sume, and this, it is nere 700*li*.
Mr. Beachamp he demands 400*li*. and we all know that, if a man demands
money, he must shew wherfore, and make proofe of his debte; which I
know he can never make good proafe of one hunderd pound dew unto him
as principall money; so till he can, you have good reason to keep the
500*li*. etc.   This I proteste I write not in malice against Mr. Beachamp,
for it is a reall truth.   You may partly see it by Mr. Andrews making up
his accounte, and I think you are all perswaded I can say more then Mr.
Andrews concerning that accounte.   I wish I could make up my owne as
plaine and easily, but because of former discontents, I will be sparing till
I be called; and you may injoye the 500*li*. quietly till he begine; for let
him take his course hear or ther, it shall be all one, I will doe him no

---

[1] Perhaps *write*, for *wrote*.

[2] "This was a misterie to them, for they heard nothing hereof from any
side the last year, till now the conclution was past, and bonds given."   (Br.)

wronge; and if he have not on peney more, he is less loser then either Mr. Andrews or I. This I conceive to be just and honest; the having or not having of his release matters not; let him make such proafe of his debte as you cannot disprove, and according to your first agreemente you will pay it, etc.

Your truly affectioned freind,

JAMES SHERLEY.

London, Aprill 27. 1643.

Anno Dom: 1643.

I AM to begine this year whith that which was a mater of great saddnes and mourning unto them all. Aboute the 18. of Aprill dyed their Reve[d] Elder, and my dear and loving friend, Mr. William Brewster; a man that had done and suffered much for the Lord Jesus and the gospells sake, and had bore his parte in well and woe with this poore persecuted church above 36. years in England, Holand, and in this wildernes, and done the Lord and them faithfull service in his place and calling. And notwithstanding the many troubls and sorrows he passed throw, the Lord upheld him to a great age. He was nere fourskore years of age (if not all out) when he dyed. He had this blesing added by the Lord to all the rest, to dye in his bed, in peace, amongst the mids of his freinds, who mourned and wepte over him, and ministered what help and comforte they could unto him, and he againe recomforted them whilst he could. His sicknes was not long, and till the last day therof he did not wholy keepe his bed. His speech continued till somewhat more then halfe a day, and then failed him; and aboute 9. or 10. a clock that evning he dyed, without any pangs at all. A few howers before, he drew his breath shorte, and some few minuts before his last, he drew his breath long, as a man falen into a sound slepe, without any pangs or gaspings, and so sweetly departed this life unto a better.

I would now demand of any, what he was the worse for any former sufferings? What doe I say, worse? Nay, sure he was the better, and they now added to his honour. *It is a mani-*

fest token (saith the Apostle, 2. Thes: 1. 5, 6, 7.) *of the righ[t]eous judgmente of God that ye may be counted worthy of the kingdome of God, for which ye allso suffer; seing it is a righteous thing with God to recompence tribulation to them that trouble you: and to you who are troubled, rest with us, when the Lord Jesus shall be revealed from heaven, with his mighty angels.* 1. Pet. 4. 14. *If you be reproached for the name of Christ, hapy are ye, for the spirite of glory and of God resteth upon you.* What though he wanted the riches and pleasurs of the world in this life, and pompous monuments at his funurall? yet the memoriall of the just shall be blessed, when the name of the wicked shall rott (with their marble monuments). Pro: 10. 7.

I should say something of his life, if to say a litle were not worse then to be silent. But I cannot wholy forbear, though hapily more may be done hereafter. After he had attained some learning, viz. the knowledg of the Latine tongue, and some insight in the Greeke, and spent some small time at Cambridge, and then being first seasoned with the seeds of grace and vertue, he went to the Courte, and served that religious and godly gentlman, Mr. Davison, diverce years, when he was Secretary of State; who found him so discreete and faithfull as he trusted him above all other that were aboute him, and only imployed him in all matters of greatest trust and secrecie. He esteemed him rather as a sonne then a servante, and for his wisdom and godlines (in private) he would converse with him more like a freind and familier then a maister. He attended his m[r] when he was sente in ambassage by the Queene into the Low-Countries, in the Earle of Leicesters time,[1] as for other waighty affaires of state, so to receive possession of the cautionary townes, and in token and signe therof the keyes of Flushing being delivered to him, in her ma[tis] name, he kepte them some time, and committed them to this his servante, who kept them under his pilow, on

[1] December, 1584–February, 1586. The story is told fully in the first volume of Motley's *History of the United Netherlands.*

which he slepte the first night. And, at his returne, the States[1] honoured him with a gould chaine, and his maister committed it to him, and commanded him to wear it when they arrived in England, as they ridd thorrow the country, till they came to the Courte. He afterwards remained with him till his troubles, that he was put from his place aboute the death of the Queene of Scots;[2] and some good time after, doeing him manie faithfull offices of servise in the time of his troubles. Afterwards he wente and lived in the country, in good esteeme amongst his freinds and the gentle-men of those parts, espetially the godly and religious. He did much good in the countrie wher he lived, in promoting and furthering religion, not only by his practiss and example, and provocking and incouraging of others, but by procuring of good preachers to the places theraboute, and drawing on of others to assiste and help forward in such a worke; he him selfe most comonly deepest in the charge, and some times above his abillitie. And in this state he continued many years, doeing the best good he could, and walking according to the light he saw, till the Lord reveiled further unto him. And in the end, by the tirrany of the bishops against godly preachers and people, in silenceing the one and persecuting the other, he and many more of those times begane to looke further into things, and to see into the unlawfullnes of their callings, and the burthen of many anti-christian corruptions, which both he and they endeavored to cast of; as they allso did, as in the begining of this treatis is to be seene. After they were joyned togither in comunion, he was a spetiall stay and help unto them. They ordinarily mett at his house on the Lords day, (which was a manor of the bishops,)[3] and with great love he enter-

---

[1] *I. e.*, the States General of the United Provinces of the Netherlands.

[2] Mary Queen of Scots was beheaded February 8, 1586/7. The warrant for her execution was placed in the hands of William Davison, as one of Elizabeth's secretaries of state. Elizabeth endeavored to placate the feeling against the execution by asserting that she had ordered Davison not to have the warrant executed without further orders, and sent him to the Tower.

[3] Scrooby Manor House, belonging to the archbishop of York.

tained them when they came, making provission for them to his great charge. He was the cheefe of those that were taken at Boston, and suffered the greatest loss; and of the seven that were kept longst in prison, and after bound over to the assises. Affter he came into Holland he suffered much hardship, after he had spente the most of his means, haveing a great charge, and many children; and, in regard of his former breeding and course of life, not so fitt for many imployments as others were, espetially such as were toylesume and laborious. But yet he ever bore his condition with much cherfullnes and contentation. Towards the later parte of those 12. years spente in Holland, his outward condition was mended, and he lived well and plentifully; for he fell into a way (by reason he had the Latine tongue) to teach many students, who had a disire to lerne the English tongue, to teach them English; and by his method they quickly attained it with great facilitie; for he drew rules to lerne it by, after the Latine maner; and many gentlemen, both Danes and Germans, resorted to him, as they had time from other studies, some of them being great mens sonnes. He also had means to set up printing, (by the help of some freinds,) and so had imploymente inoughg, and by reason of many books which would not be alowed to be printed in England, they might have had more then they could doe.[1] But now removeing into this countrie, all these things were laid aside againe, and a new course of living must be framed unto; in which he was no way unwilling to take his parte, and to bear his burthen with the rest, living many times without bread, or corne, many months together, having many times nothing but fish, and often wanting that also; and drunke nothing but water for many years togeather, yea, till within 5. or 6. years of his death. And yet he lived (by the blessing of God) in health till very old age. And besids that, he would labour with his hands in the feilds as long as he was able; yet when the church had no other minister, he taught twise every

[1] See p. 39, note 1.

Saboth, and that both powerfully and profitably, to the great contentment of the hearers, and their comfortable edification; yea, many were brought to God by his ministrie. He did more in this behalfe in a year, then many that have their hundreds a year doe in all their lives. For his personall abilities, he was qualified above many; he was wise and discreete and well spoken, having a grave and deliberate utterance, of a very cherfull spirite, very sociable and pleasante amongst his freinds, of an humble and modest mind, of a peaceable disposition, under vallewing him self and his owne abilities, and some time over valewing others; inoffencive and innocente in his life and conversation, which gained him the love of those without, as well as those within; yet he would tell them plainely of their faults and evills, both publickly and privatly, but in such a maner as usually was well taken from him. He was tender harted, and compassionate of such as were in miserie, but espetialy of such as had been of good estate and ranke, and were fallen unto want and poverty, either for goodnes and religions sake, or by the injury and oppression of others; he would say, of all men these deserved to be pitied most. And none did more offend and displease him then such as would hautily and proudly carry and lift up themselves, being rise from nothing, and haveing litle els in them to comend them but a few fine cloaths, or a litle riches more then others. In teaching, he was very moving and stirring of affections, also very plaine and distincte in what he taught; by which means he became the more profitable to the hearers. He had a singuler good gift in prayer, both publick and private, in ripping up the hart and conscience before God, in the humble confession of sinne, and begging the mercies of God in Christ for the pardon of the same. He always thought it were better for ministers to pray oftener, and devide their prears, then be longe and tedious in the same (excepte upon sollemne and spetiall occations, as in days of humiliation and the like). His reason was, that the harte and spirits

of all, espetialy the weake, could hardly continue and stand
bente (as it were) so long towards God, as they ought to
doe in that duty, without flagging and falling of. For the
govermente of the church, (which was most proper to his
office,) he was carfull to preserve good order in the same,
and to preserve puritie, both in the doctrine and comunion
of the same; and to supress any errour or contention that
might begine to rise up amongst them; and accordingly
God gave good success to his indeavors herein all his days,
and he saw the fruite of his labours in that behalfe. But I
must breake of, having only thus touched a few, as it were,
heads of things.

I cannot but here take occasion, not only to mention, but
greatly to admire the marvelous providence of God, that notwithstanding the many changes and hardships that these
people wente throwgh, and the many enemies they had and
difficulties they mette with all, that so many of them should
live to very olde age![1] It was not only this reve[d] mans condition, (for one swallow maks no summer, as they say,) but
many more of them did the like, some dying aboute and before
this time, and many still living, who attained to 60. years of
age, and to 65. diverse to 70. and above, and some nere 80.
as he did. It must needs be more than ordinarie, and above
naturall reason, that so it should be; for it is found in experience, that chaing of aeir, famine, or unholsome foode,
much drinking of water, sorrows and troubls, etc., all of them
are enimies to health, causes of many diseaces, consumers of
naturall vigoure and the bodys of men, and shortners of life.
And yet of all these things they had a large parte, and suffered
deeply in the same. They wente from England to Holand,
wher they found both worse air and dyet then that they came
from; from thence (induring a long imprisonmente, as it were,
in the ships at sea) into New-England; and how it hath been

---

[1] Those of the *Mayflower* company who survived the first winter lived an
average of thirty-seven years afterwards.

with them hear hath allready beene showne; and what crosses, troubls, fears, wants, and sorrowes they had been lyable unto, is easie to conjecture; so as in some sorte they may say with the Apostle, 2. Cor: 11. 26, 27. they were *in journeyings often, in perils of waters, in perills of robers, in perills of their owne nation, in perils among the heathen, in perills in the willdernes, in perills in the sea, in perills among false breethern; in wearines and painfullnes, in watching often, in hunger and thirst, in fasting often, in could and nakednes.* What was it then that upheld them? It was Gods vissitation that preserved their spirits. Job. 10. 12. *Thou hast given me life and grace, and thy vissitation hath preserved my spirite.* He that upheld the Apostle upheld them. *They were persecuted, but not forsaken, cast downe, but perished not.* 2. Cor: 4. 9. *As unknowen, and yet knowen; as dying, and behold we live; as chastened, and yett not kiled.* 2. Cor: 6. 9. God, it seems, would have all men to behold and observe such mercies and works of his providence as these are towards his people, that they in like cases might be incouraged to depend upon God in their trials, and also blese his name when they see his goodnes towards others. Man lives not by bread only, Deut: 8. 3. It is not by good and dainty fare, by peace, and rest, and harts ease, in injoying the contentments and good things of this world only, that preserves health and prolongs life. God in such examples would have the world see and behold that he can doe it without them; and if the world will shut ther eyes, and take no notice therof, yet he would have his people to see and consider it. Daniell could be better liking with pulse then others were with the kings dainties. Jaacob, though he wente from one nation to another people, and passed thorow famine, fears, and many afflictions, yet he lived till old age, and dyed sweetly, and rested in the Lord, as infinite others of Gods servants have done, and still shall doe, (through Gods goodnes,) notwith-standing all the malice of their enemies; *when the branch of the wicked shall be cut of before his day,* Job. 15. 32. *and the*

bloody and deceitfull men shall not live out halfe their days.
Psa: 55. 23.

By reason of the plottings of the Narigansets, (ever since the Pequents warr,) the Indeans were drawne into a generall conspiracie against the English in all parts, as was in part discovered the yeare before; and now made more plaine and evidente by many discoveries and free-conffessions of sundrie Indeans (upon severall occasions) from diverse places, concuring in one; with such other concuring circomstances as gave them suffissently to understand the trueth therof, and to thinke of means how to prevente the same, and secure them selves. Which made them enter into this more nere union and confederation following.

Articles of Conffederation betweene the Plantations under the Govermente of Massachusets, the Plantations under the Govermente of New-Plimoth, the Plantations under the Govermente of Conightecute, and the Govermente of New-Haven, with the Plantations in combination therwith.[1]

Wheras we all came into these parts of America with one and the same end and aime, namly, to advance the kingdome of our Lord Jesus Christ, and to injoye the liberties of the Gospell in puritie with peace; and wheras in our setling (by a wise providence of God) we are further disperced upon the sea coasts and rivers then was at first intended, so that we cannot, according to our desires, with conveniencie comunicate in one govermente and jurisdiction; and wheras we live encompassed with people of severall nations and strang languages, which hereafter may prove injurious to us and our posteritie; and for as much as the natives have formerly committed sundrie insolencies and outrages upon severall plantations of the English, and have of late combined them selves against us; and seeing, by reason of those distractions in England (which they have heard of) and by which they know we are hindered from that humble way of seeking advice or reaping those comfurtable fruits of protection which at other times we might well expecte; we therfore doe conceive

[1] On the formation and history of the New England Confederation, see Mr. C. C. Smith's article, "Boston and the Neighboring Jurisdictions," in the first volume of Winsor's *Memorial History of Boston;* and Frothingham's *Rise of the Republic,* chap. II. The records of the meetings of the Confederation are printed in the *Plymouth Colony Records,* vols. IX., X., and in *Colonial Records of Connecticut,* vol. III.

it our bounden duty, without delay, to enter into a presente consociation amongst our selves, for mutuall help and strength in all our future concernments. That as in nation and religion, so in other respects, we be and continue one, according to the tenor and true meaning of the insuing articles. (1) Wherfore it is fully agreed and concluded by and betweene the parties or jurisdictions above named, and they joyntly and severally doe by these presents agree and conclude, that they all be and henceforth be called by the name of The United Colonies of New-England.

2. The said United Collonies, for them selves and their posterities, doe joyntly and severally hereby enter into a firme and perpetuall league of frendship and amitie, for offence and defence, mutuall advice and succore upon all just occasions, both for preserving and propagating the truth of the Gospell, and for their owne mutuall saftie and wellfare.

3. It is further agreed that the plantations which at presente are or hereafter shall be setled with [in] the limites of the Massachusets shall be for ever under the Massachusets, and shall have peculier jurisdiction amonge them selves in all cases, as an intire body. And that Plimoth, Conightecutt, and New-Haven shall each of them have like peculier jurisdition and govermente within their limites and in refference to the plantations which allready are setled, or shall hereafter be erected, or shall setle within their limites, respectively; provided that no other jurisdition shall hereafter be takeen in, as a distincte head or member of this confederation, nor shall any other plantation or jurisdiction in presente being, and not allready in combination or under the jurisdiction of any of these confederats, be received by any of them; nor shall any tow of the confederats joyne in one jurisdiction, without consente of the rest, which consente to be interpreted as is expreseed in the sixte article ensewing.

4. It is by these conffederats agreed, that the charge of all just warrs, whether offencive or defencive, upon what parte or member of this confederation soever they fall, shall, both in men, provissions, and all other disbursments, be borne by all the parts of this confederation, in differente proportions, according to their differente abillities, in maner following: namely, that the comissioners for each jurisdiction, from time to time, as ther shall be occasion, bring a true accounte and number of all their males in every plantation, or any way belonging too or under their severall jurisdictions, of what qualitie or condition soever they be, from 16. years old to 60. being inhabitants ther; and that according to the differente numbers which from time to time shall be found in each jurisdiction upon a true and just accounte, the service of men and all charges of the warr be borne by the pole; each jurisdiction or plantation being

left to their owne just course and custome of rating them selves and people according to their differente estates, with due respects to their qualities and exemptions amongst them selves, though the confederats take no notice of any such priviledg. And that according to their differente charge of each jurisdiction and plantation, the whole advantage of the warr, (if it please God to blesse their indeaours,) whether it be in lands, goods, or persons, shall be proportionably devided amonge the said confederats.

5. It is further agreed, that if these jurisdictions, or any plantation under or in combynacion with them, be invaded by any enemie whomsoever, upon notice and requeste of any 3. magistrats of that jurisdiction so invaded, the rest of the confederats, without any further meeting or expostulation, shall forthwith send ayde to the confederate in danger, but in differente proportion; namely, the Massachusets an hundred men sufficently armed and provided for such a service and journey, and each of the rest forty five so armed and provided, or any lesser number, if less be required according to this proportion. But if such confederate in danger may be supplyed by their nexte confederates, not exeeding the number hereby agreed, they may crave help ther, and seeke no further for the presente; the charge to be borne as in this article is exprest, and at the returne to be victuled and suplyed with powder and shote for their jurney (if ther be need) by that jurisdiction which imployed or sent for them. But none of the jurisdictions to exceede these numbers till, by a meeting of the commissioners for this confederation, a greater aide appear nessessarie. And this proportion to continue till upon knowlege of greater numbers in each jurisdiction, which shall be brought to the nexte meeting, some other proportion be ordered. But in such case of sending men for presente aide, whether before or after such order or alteration, it is agreed that at the meeting of the comissioners for this confederation, the cause of such warr or invasion be duly considered; and if it appeare that the falte lay in the parties so invaded, that then that jurisdiction or plantation make just satisfaction both to the invaders whom they have injured, and beare all the charges of the warr them selves, without requiring any allowance from the rest of the confederats towards the same. And further, that if any jurisdiction see any danger of any invasion approaching, and ther be time for a meeting, that in such a case 3. magistrats of that jurisdiction may summone a meeting, at such conveniente place as them selves shall thinke meete, to consider and provid against the threatened danger, provided when they are mett, they may remove to what place they please; only, whilst any of these foure confederats have but 3 magistrats in their jurisdiction, their requeste, or summons, from any 2. of them shall be accounted of equall force with the

3. mentioned in both the clauses of this article, till ther be an increase of majestrats ther.

6.   It is also agreed that, for the managing and concluding of all affairs propper, and concerning the whole confederation, tow comissioners shall be chosen by and out of each of these 4. jurisdictions; namly, 2. for the Massachusets, 2. for Plimoth, 2. for Conightecutt, and 2. for New-Haven, being all in church fellowship with us, which shall bring full power from their severall Generall Courts respectively to hear, examene, waigh, and detirmine all affairs of warr, or peace, leagues, aids, charges, and numbers of men for warr, divissions of spoyles, and whatsoever is gotten by conquest; receiving of more confederats, or plantations into combination with any of the confederates, and all things of like nature, which are the proper concomitants or consequences of such a confederation, for amitie, offence, and defence; not intermedling with the govermente of any of the jurisdictions, which by the 3. article is preserved entirely to them selves.   But if these 8. comissioners when they meete shall not all agree, yet it concluded that any 6. of the 8. agreeing shall have power to setle and determine the bussines in question.   But if 6. doe not agree, that then such propositions, with their reasons, so farr as they have been debated, be sente, and referred to the 4. Generall Courts, viz. the Massachusets, Plimoth, Conightecutt, and New-haven; and if at all the said Generall Courts the bussines so referred be concluded, then to be prosecuted by the confederats, and all their members.   It was further agreed that these 8. comissioners shall meete once every year, besids extraordinarie meetings, (according to the fifte article,) to consider, treate, and conclude of all affaires belonging to this confederation, which meeting shall ever be the first Thursday in September.   And that the next meeting after the date of these presents, which shall be accounted the second meeting, shall be at Boston in the Massachusets, the 3. at Hartford, the 4. at New-Haven, the 5. at Plimoth, and so in course successively, if in the meane time some midle place be not found out and agreed on, which may be comodious for all the jurisdictions.

7.   It is further agreed, that at each meeting of these 8. comissioners, whether ordinarie, or extraordinary, they all 6. of them agreeing as before, may chuse a presidente out of them selves, whose office and work shall be to take care and directe for order, and a comly carrying on of all proceedings in the present meeting; but he shall be invested with no such power or respecte, as by which he shall hinder the propounding or progrese of any bussines, or any way cast the scailes otherwise then in the precedente article is agreed.

8.   It is also agreed, that the comissioners for this confederation

hereafter at their meetings, whether ordinary or extraordinarie, as they may have comission or opportunitie, doe indeaover to frame and establish agreements and orders in generall cases of a civill nature, wherin all the plantations are interessed, for the preserving of peace amongst them selves, and preventing as much as may be all occasions of warr or difference with others; as aboute the free and speedy passage of justice, in every jurisdiction, to all the confederats equally as to their owne; not receiving those that remove from one plantation to another without due certificate; how all the jurisdictions may carry towards the Indeans, that they neither growe insolente, nor be injured without due satisfaction, least warr breake in upon the confederats through such miscarriages. It is also agreed, that if any servante rune away from his maister into another of these confederated jurisdictions, that in such case, upon the certificate of one magistrate in the jurisdiction out of which the said servante fledd, or upon other due proofe, the said servante shall be delivered, either to his maister, or any other that pursues and brings such certificate or proofe. And that upon the escape of any prisoner whatsoever, or fugitive for any criminall cause, whether breaking prison, or getting from the officer, or otherwise escaping, upon the certificate of 2. magistrats of the jurisdiction out of which the escape is made, that he was a prisoner, or such an offender at the time of the escape, they magistrats, or sume of them of that jurisdiction wher for the presente the said prisoner or fugitive abideth, shall forthwith grante such a warrante as the case will beare, for the apprehending of any such person, and the delivering of him into the hands of the officer, or other person who pursues him. And if ther be help required, for the safe returning of any such offender, then it shall be granted to him that craves the same, he paying the charges therof.

9. And for that the justest warrs may be of dangerous consequence, espetially to the smaler plantations in these United Collonies, it is agreed that neither the Massachusets, Plimoth, Conightecutt, nor New-Haven, nor any member of any of them, shall at any time hear after begine, undertake, or ingage them selves, or this confederation, or any parte therof, in any warr whatsoever, (sundry exegents, with the necessary consequents therof excepted, which are also to be moderated as much as the case will permitte,) without the consente and agreemente of the forementioned 8. comissioners, or at the least 6. of them, as in the sixt article is provided. And that no charge be required of any of they confederats, in case of a defensive warr, till the said comissioners have mett, and approved the justice of the warr, and have agreed upon the summe of money to be levied, which sume is then to be paid by the severall confederats in proportion according to the fourth article.

10. That in extraordinary occasions, when meetings are summoned by three magistrates of any jurisdiction, or 2. as in the 5. article, if any of the comissioners come not, due warning being given or sente, it is agreed that 4. of the comissioners shall have power to directe a warr which cannot be delayed, and to send for due proportions of men out of each jurisdiction, as well as 6. might doe if all mett; but not less then 6. shall determine the justice of the warr, or alow the demands or bills of charges, or cause any levies to be made for the same.

11. It is further agreed, that if any of the confederats shall hereafter breake any of these presente articles, or be any other ways injurious to any one of the other jurisdictions, such breach of agreemente or injurie shall be duly considered and ordered by the comissioners for the other jurisdiction; that both peace and this presente confederation may be intirly preserved without violation.

12. Lastly, this perpetuall confederation, and the severall articles therof being read, and seriously considered, both by the Generall Courte for the Massachusets, and by the comissioners for Plimoth, Conigtecute, and New-Haven, were fully alowed and confirmed by 3. of the forenamed confederats, namly, the Massachusets, Conightecutt, and New-Haven; only the comissioners for Plimoth haveing no commission to conclude, desired respite till they might advise with their Generall Courte; wher upon it was agreed and concluded by the said Courte of the Massachusets, and the comissioners for the other tow confederats, that, if Plimoth consente, then the whole treaty as it stands in these present articls is, and shall continue, firme and stable without alteration. But if Plimoth come not in, yet the other three confederats doe by these presents confeirme the whole confederation, and the articles therof; only in September nexte, when the second meeting of the commissioners is to be at Boston, new consideration may be taken of the 6. article, which concerns number of comissioners for meeting and concluding the affaires of this confederation, to the satisfaction of the Courte of the Massachusets, and the comissioners for the other 2. confederats, but the rest to stand unquestioned. In the testimonie wherof, the Generall Courte of the Massachusets, by ther Secretary, and the comissioners for Conightecutt and New-Haven, have subscribed these presente articles this 19. of the third month, comonly called May, Anno Dom: 1643.

At a meeting of the comissioners for the confederation held at Boston the 7. of Sept: it appearing that the Generall Courte of New-Plimoth, and the severall towneshipes therof, have read and considered and approved these articles of confederation, as appeareth by commission from their Generall Courte bearing date the 29. of August, 1643. to Mr. Edward

Winslow and Mr. William Collier, to ratifie and confirme the same on their behalfes. We, therfore, the Comissioners for the Massachusets, Conightecutt, and New Haven, doe also, for our severall goverments, subscribe unto them.

JOHN WINTHROP, Govr. of the Massachusest.

THO: DUDLEY   THEOPH: EATON.

GEO: FENWICK.   EDWA: HOPKINS.

THOMAS GREGSON.

These were the articles of agreemente in the union and confederation which they now first entered into; and in this their first meeting, held at Boston the day and year abovesaid, amongst other things they had this matter of great consequence to considere on: the Narigansets, after the subduing of the Pequents, thought to have ruled over all the Indeans aboute them; but the English, espetially those of Conightecutt holding correspondencie and frenship with Uncass, sachem of the Monhigg Indeans which lived nere them, (as the Massachusets had done with the Narigansets,) and he had been faithfull to them in the Pequente warr, they were ingaged to supporte him in his just liberties, and were contented that such of the surviving Pequents as had submited to him should remaine with him and quietly under his protection. This did much increase his power and augmente his greatnes, which the Narigansets could not indure to see. But Myantinomo, their cheefe sachem, (an ambitious and politick man,) sought privatly and by trearchery (according to the Indean maner) to make him away, by hiring some to kill him. Sometime they assayed to poyson him; that not takeing, then in the night time to knock him on the head in his house, or secretly to shoot him, and such like attempts. But none of these taking effecte, he[1] made open warr upon him (though it was against the covenants both betweene the English and them, as also betweene them selves, and a plaine breach of the same). He came suddanly upon him with 900. or 1000. men (never denouncing any warr before). The others power at that presente

---

[1] Miantonomi.

was not above halfe so many; but it pleased God to give
Uncass the victory, and he slew many of his men, and wounded
many more; but the cheefe of all was, he tooke Miantinomo
prisoner. And seeing he was a greate man, and the Narigansets a potente people and would seeke revenge, he would doe
nothing in the case without the advise of the English; so he
(by the help and direction of those of Conightecutt) kept him
prisoner till this meeting of the comissioners. The comissioners weighed the cause and passages, as they were clearly
represented and sufficently evidenced betwixte Uncass and
Myantinomo; and the things being duly considered, the comissioners apparently saw that Uncass could not be safe whilst
Miantynomo lived, but, either by secrete trechery or open
force, his life would still be in danger. Wherfore they thought
he might justly put such a false and bloud-thirstie enimie to
death; but in his owne jurisdiction, not in the English plantations. And they advised, in the maner of his death all mercy
and moderation should be showed, contrary to the practise of
the Indeans, who exercise torturs and cruelty. And, Uncass
having hitherto shewed him selfe a freind to the English, and
in this craving their advise, if the Narigansett Indeans or
others shall unjustly assaulte Uncass for this execution, upon
notice and request, the English promise to assiste and protecte
him as farr as they may againste such violence.

   This was the issue of this bussines. The reasons and passages hereof are more at large to be seene in the acts and
records of this meeting of the comissioners.[1] And Uncass fol-
lewd this advise, and accordingly executed him, in a very faire
maner,[2] acording as they advised, with due respecte to his
honour and greatnes. But what followed on the Narigansets
parte will appear hear after.

---

[1] The meeting of September, 1643, their second meeting. See *Plymouth
Colony Records*, IX.

[2] At the place of his capture, the place still called Sachem's Plain, near
Norwich, Connecticut.

Anno Dom: 1644.

MR. EDWARD WINSLOW was chosen Gov[r] this year.

Many having left this place (as is before noted) by reason of the straightnes and barrennes of the same, and their finding of better accommodations elsewher, more sutable to their ends and minds; and sundrie others still upon every occasion desiring their dismissions, the church begane seriously to thinke whether it were not better joyntly to remove to some other place, then to be thus weakened, and as it were insensibly dissolved. Many meetings and much consultation was held hearaboute, and diverse were mens minds and opinions. Some were still for staying togeather in this place, aledging men might hear live, if they would be contente with their condition; and that it was not for wante or necessitie so much that they removed, as for the enriching of them selves. Others were resolute upon removall, and so signified that hear they could not stay; but if the church did not remove, they must; insomuch as many were swayed, rather then ther should be a dissolution, to condescend to a removall, if a fitt place could be found, that might more conveniently and comfortablie receive the whole, with such accession of others as might come to them, for their better strength and subsistence; and some such like cautions and limitations. So as, with the afforesaide provissos, the greater parte consented to a removall to a place called Nawsett, which had been superficially veiwed and the good will of the purchassers (to whom it belonged) obtained, with some addition thertoo from the Courte. But now they begane to see their errour, that they had given away already the best and most commodious places to others, and now wanted them selves; for this place was about 50. myles from hence, and at an outside of the countrie, remote from all society; also, that it would prove so straite, as it would not be competente to receive the whole body, much less be capable of any addition or increase; so as (at least in a shorte time) they should be worse ther then they are now hear.   The which, with sundery other like considerations and inconveniences, made them chaing their resolutions; but such as were before resolved upon removall tooke advantage of this agreemente, and wente on notwithstanding, neither could the rest hinder them, they haveing made some beginning.   And thus was this poore church left, like an anciente mother, growne olde, and forsaken of her children, (though not in their affections,) yett in regarde of their bodily presence and personall helpfullness.   Her anciente members being most of them worne away by death; and these of later time being like children translated into other families, and she like a widow left only to trust in God.   Thus she that had made many rich became her selfe poore.

Some things handled, and pacified by the commissioner[s] this year.

Wheras, by a wise providence of God, tow of the jurisdictions in the westerne parts, viz. Conightecutt and New-haven, have beene latly exercised by sundrie insolencies and outrages from the Indeans; as, first, an Englishman, runing from his m^r out of the Massachusets, was murdered in the woods, in or nere the limites of Conightecute jurisdiction; and aboute 6. weeks after, upon discovery by an Indean, the Indean sagamore in these parts promised to deliver the murderer to the English, bound; and having accordingly brought him within the sight of Uncaway, by their joynte consente, as it is informed, he was ther unbound, and left to shifte for him selfe; wherupon 10. Englishmen forthwith coming to the place, being sente by Mr. Ludlow, at the Indeans desire, to receive the murderer, who seeing him escaped, layed hold of 8. of the Indeans ther presente, amongst whom ther was a sagamore or 2. and kept them in hold 2. days, till 4. sagamors ingaged themselves within one month to deliver the prisoner.   And about a weeke after this agreemente, an Indean came presumtuously and with guile, in the day time, and murtherously assalted an English woman in her house at Stamford, and by 3. wounds, supposed mortall, left her for dead, after he had robbed the house.   By which passages the English were provoked, and called to a due consideration of their owne saftie; and the Indeans generally in those parts arose in an hostile manner, refused to come to the English to carry on treaties of peace, departed from their wigwames, left their corne unweeded, and shewed them selves tumultuously about some of the English plantations, and shott of peeces within hearing of the towne; and some Indeans came to the English and tould them the Indeans would fall upon them. So that most of the English thought it unsafe to travell in those parts by land, and some of the plantations were put upon strong watchs and ward, night and day, and could not attend their private occasions, and yet distrusted their owne strength for their defence. Wherupon Hartford and New-Haven were sent unto for aide, and saw cause both to send into the weaker parts of their owne jurisdiction thus in danger, and New-Haven, for conveniencie of situation, sente aide to Uncaway, though belonging to Conightecutt. Of all which passages they presently acquainted the comissioners in the Bay, and had the allowance and approbation from the Generall Courte ther, with directions neither to hasten warr nor to bear such insolencies too longe. Which courses, though chargable to them selves, yet through Gods blessing they hope fruite is, and will be, sweete and wholsome to all the collonies; the murderers are since delivered to justice, the publick peace preserved for the presente, and probabillitie it may be better secured for the future.

Thus this mischeefe was prevented, and the fear of a warr hereby diverted. But now an other broyle was begune by the Narigansets; though they unjustly had made warr upon Uncass, (as is before declared,) and had, the winter before this, ernestly presed the Gove^r of the Massachusets that they might still make warr upon them to revenge the death of their sagamore, which, being taken prisoner, was by them put to death, (as before was noted,) pretending that they had first received and accepted his ransome, and then put him to death. But the Gove^r refused their presents, and tould them that it was them selves had done the wronge, and broaken the conditions of peace; and he nor the English neither could nor would allow them to make any further warr upon him, but if they did, must assiste him, and oppose them; but if if did appeare, upon good proofe, that he had received a ransome for his life, before he put him to death, when the comissioners mett, they should have a fair hearing, and they would cause Uncass to returne the same. But notwithstanding, at the spring of the year they gathered a great power, and fell upon Uncass, and

slue sundrie of his men, and wounded more, and also had some
loss them selves. Uncass calld for aide from the English;
they tould him what the Narigansets objected, he deney the
same; they tould him it must come to triall, and if he was
inocente, if the Narigansets would not desiste, they would aide
and assiste him. So at this meeting they sent both to Uncass
and the Narrigansets, and required their sagamors to come or
send to the comissioners now mete at Hartford, and they
should have a faire and inpartiall hearing in all their greevances, and would endeavor that all wrongs should be rectified
wher they should be found; and they promised that they
should safly come and returne without any danger or molestation; and sundry the like things, as appears more at large
in the messengers instructions. Upon which the Narigansets sent one sagamore and some other deputies, with
full power to doe in the case as should be meete. Uncass
came in person, accompanyed with some cheefe aboute him.
After the agitation of the bussines, the issue was this. The
comissioners declared to the Narigansett deputies as followeth.

1. That they did not find any proofe of any ransome agreed on.

2. It appeared not that any wampam had been paied as a ransome,
or any parte of a ransome, for Myantinomos life.

3. That if they had in any measure proved their charge against
Uncass, the comissioners would have required him to have made answerable satisfaction.

4. That if hereafter they can make satisfing profe, the English will
consider the same, and proceed accordingly.

5. The comissioners did require that neither them selves nor the
Nyanticks make any warr or injurious assaulte upon Unquass or any of
his company untill they make profe of the ransume charged, and that
due satisfaction be deneyed, unless he first assaulte them.

6. That if they assaulte Uncass, the English are engaged to assist
him.

Hearupon the Narigansette sachim, advising with the other deputies,
ingaged him selfe in the behalfe of the Narigansets and Nyanticks that no
hostile acts should be comitted upon Uncass, or any of his, untill after

the next planting of corne; and that after that, before they begine any warr, they will give 30. days warning to the Gove^r of the Massachusets or Conightecutt.   The comissioners approving of this offer, and taking their ingagmente under their hands, required Uncass, as he expected the continuance of the favour of the English, to observe the same termes of peace with the Narigansets and theirs.

These foregoing conclusions were subscribed by the comissioners, for the severall jurisdictions, the 19. of Sept: 1644.

> Edwa: Hopkins, Presidente.
> Simon Bradstreete.
> Will^M. Hathorne.
> Edw: Winslow.
> John Browne.
> Geor: Fenwick.
> Theoph: Eaton.
> Tho: Gregson.

The forenamed Narigansets deputies did further promise, that if, contrary to this agreemente, any of the Nyantick Pequents should make any assaulte upon Uncass, or any of his, they would deliver them up to the English, to be punished according to their demerits; and that they would not use any means to procure the Mowacks [1] to come against Uncass during this truce.

These were their names subscribed with their marks.

> Weetowish.   Chinñough.
> Pampiamett.   Pummunish.

Anno Dom: 1645.

The comissioners this year were caled to meete togither at Boston, before their ordinarie time; partly in regard of some differances falen betweene the French and the govermente of the Massachusets, about their aiding of Munseire Latore against Munsseire de Aulney,[2] and partly aboute the Indeans, who had broaken the former agreements aboute the peace concluded the last year.   This meeting was held at Boston, the 28. of July.

Besids some underhand assualts made on both sids, the

---

[1] Mohawks.   [2] See p. 318, note 1.

Narigansets gathered a great power, and fell upon Uncass,
and slew many of his men, and wounded more, by reason that
they farr exseeded him in number, and had gott store of
peeces, with which they did him most hurte. And as they did
this withoute the knowledg and consente of the English, (contrary to former agreemente,) so they were resolved to prosecute the same, notwithstanding any thing the English said or
should doe against them. So, being incouraged by ther late
victorie, and promise of assistance from the Mowaks, (being a
strong, warlike, and desperate people,) they had allready devoured Uncass and his, in their hops; and surly they had done
it in deed, if the English had not timly sett in for his aide.
For those of Conightecute sent him 40. men, who were a garison to him, till the comissioners could meete and take further
order.

Being thus mett, they forthwith sente 3. messengers, viz.
Sargent John Davis, Benedicte Arnold,[1] and Francis Smith,
with full and ample instructions, both to the Narigansets and
Uncass; to require them that they should either come in person or send sufficiente men fully instructed to deale in the
bussines; and if they refused or delayed, to let them know
(according to former agreements) that the English are engaged
to assiste against these hostile invasions, and that they have
sente their men to defend Uncass, and to know of the Narigansets whether they will stand to the former peace, or they
will assaulte the English also, that they may provid accord·
ingly.

But the messengers returned, not only with a sleighting,
but a threatening answer from the Narigansets (as will more
appear hereafter). Also they brought a letter from Mr. Roger
Williams, wherin he assures them that the warr would presenly
breake forth, and the whole country would be all of a flame.
And that the sachems of the Narigansets had concluded a
newtrality with the English of Providence and those of Aquid-

---

[1] Benedict Arnold was afterward the governor of Rhode Island.

nett Iland. Wherupon the comissioners, considering the great danger and provocations offered, and the necessitie we should be put unto of making warr with the Narigansetts, and being also carfull, in a matter of so great waight and generall concernmente, to see the way cleared, and to give satisfaction to all the colonies, did thinke fitte to advise with such of the magistrats and elders of the Massachusets as were then at hand, and also with some of the cheefe millitary comanders ther; who being assembled, it was then agreed,—

First, that our ingagmente bound us to aide and defend Uncass. 2. That this ayde could not be intended only to defend him and his forte, or habitation, but (according to the comone acceptation of such covenants, or ingagments, considered with the grounds or occasion therof) so to ayde him as he might be preserved in his liberty and estate. 3^{ly}. That this ayde must be speedy, least he might be swalowed up in the mean time, and so come to late. 4^{ly}. The justice of this warr being cleared to our selves and the rest then presente, it was thought meete that the case should be stated, and the reasons and grounds of the warr declared and published. 5^{ly}. That a day of humilliation should be apoynted, which was the 5. day of the weeke following. 6^{ly}. It was then allso agreed by the comissioners that the whole number of men to be raised in all the colonies should be 300. Wherof from the Massachusets a 190. Plimoth, 40. Conightecute, 40. New-Haven, 30. And considering that Uncass was in present danger, 40. men of this number were forthwith sent from the Massachusets for his sucoure; and it was but neede, for the other 40. from Conightecutt had order to stay but a month, and their time being out, they returned; and the Narigansets, hearing therof, tooke the advantage, and came suddanly upon him, and gave him another blow, to his further loss, and were ready to doe the like againe; but these 40. men being arrived, they returned, and did nothing.

The declaration which they sett forth I shall not transcribe, it being very larg, and put forth in printe,[1] to which I referr those that would see the same, in which all passages are layed open from the first. I shall only note their prowd carriage, and answers to the 3. messengers sent from the comissioners. They received them with scorne and contempte, and tould them they resolved to have no peace without Uncass his head; also they gave them this further answer: that it mattered not who begane the warr, they were resolved to follow it, and that the English should withdraw their garison from Uncass, or they would procure the Mowakes against them; and withall gave them this threatening answer: that they would lay the English catle on heaps, as high as their houses, and that no English-man should sturr out of his dore to pisse, but he should be kild. And wheras they required guids to pass throw their countrie, to deliver their message to Uncass from the comissioners, they deneyed them, but at length (in way of scorne) offered them an old Pequente woman. Besids allso they conceived them selves in danger, for whilst the interpretour was speakeing with them about the answer he should returne, 3. men came and stood behind him with ther hatchets, according to their murderous maner; but one of his fellows gave him notice of it, so they broak of and came away; with sundry such like affrontes, which made those Indeans they carryed with them to rune away for fear, and leave them to goe home as they could.

Thus whilst the comissioners in care of the publick peace sought to quench the fire kindled amongst the Indeans, these children of strife breath out threatenings, provocations, and warr against the English them selves. So that, unless they should dishonour and provoak God, by violating a just ingagmente, and expose the colonies to contempte and danger

[1] *A Declaration of Former Passages and Proceedings betwixt the English and the Narrowgansets, with their confederates, Wherein the grounds and justice of the ensuing warre are opened and cleared,* Published, by order of the commissioners for the united Colonies, At Boston the 11 of the sixth month, 1645, a tract of 7 pages. Its substance is in *Plymouth Colony Records,* IX.

from the barbarians, they cannot but exerciese force, when no other means will prevaile to reduse the Narigansets and their confederats to a more just and sober temper.

So as here upon they went on to hasten the preparations, according to the former agreemente, and sent to Plimoth to send forth their 40. men with all speed, to lye at Seacunke, least any deanger should befalle it, before the rest were ready, it lying next the enemie, and ther to stay till the Massachusetts should joyne with them. Allso Conigtecute and Newhaven forces were to joyne togeather, and march with all speed, and the Indean confederats of those parts with them. All which was done accordingly; and the souldiers of this place were at Seacunk, the place of their rendevouze, 8. or 10. days before the rest were ready; they were well armed all with snaphance peeces,[1] and went under the camand of Captain Standish. Those from other places were led likwise by able comander[s], as Captaine Mason for Conigtecute, etc.; and Majore Gibons[2] was made generall over the whole, with such comissions and instructions as was meete.

Upon the suden dispatch of these souldiears, (the present necessitie requiring it,) the deputies of the Massachusetts Courte (being now assembled immediatly after the setting forth of their 40. men) made a question whether it was legally done, without their comission. It was answered, that howsoever it did properly belong to the authority of the severall jurisdictions (after the warr was agreed upon by the comissioners, and the number of men) to provid the men and means to carry on the warr; yet in this presente case, the proceeding of the comissioners and the comission given was as sufficiente as if it had been done by the Generall Courte.

First, it was a case of such presente and urgente necessitie, as could

---

[1] A snaphance was a firearm discharged by a spring-lock.

[2] Major Edward Gibbons was the commander of the Massachusetts troops, Captain John Mason, who had conducted the Pequot expedition of 1636, of those of Connecticut.

not stay the calling of the Courte or Counsell. 2^ly. In the Articles of Confederation, power is given to the comissioners to consult, order, and determine all affaires of warr, etc. And the word *determine* comprehends all acts of authority belonging therunto.

3^ly. The comissioners are the judges of the necessitie of the expedition.

4^ly. The Generall Courte have made their owne comissioners their sole counsell for these affires.

5^ly. These counsels could not have had their due effecte excepte they had power to proceede in this case, as they have done; which were to make the comissioners power, and the maine end of the confederation, to be frustrate, and that mearly for observing a ceremony.

6^ly. The comissioners haveing sole power to manage the warr for number of men, for time, place, etc., they only know their owne counsells, and *determinations*, and therfore none can grante commission to acte according to these but them selves.

All things being thus in readines, and some of the souldiers gone forth, and the rest ready to march, the comissioners thought it meete before any hostile acte was performed, to cause a presente to be returned, which had been sente to the Gove^r of the Massachusetts from the Narigansett sachems, but not by him received, but layed up to be accepted or refused as they should carry them selves, and observe the covenants. Therfore they violating the same, and standing out thus to a warr, it was againe returned, by 2. messengers and an interpretour. And further to let know that their men already sent to Uncass (and other wher sent forth) have hitherto had express order only to stand upon his and their owne defence, and not to attempte any invasion of the Narigansetts country; and yet if they may have due reperation for what is past, and good securitie for the future, it shall appear they are as desirous of peace, and shall be as tender of the Narigansets blood as ever. If therefore Pessecuss, Innemo, with other sachemes, will (without further delay) come along with you to Boston, the comissioners doe promise and assure them, they shall have free liberty to come, and retourne without molestation or any just greevance from the English. But deputies will not now serve, nor may the preparations in hand be now stayed, or the directions given recalled, till the forementioned sagamors come, and some further order be taken. But if they will have nothing but warr, the Engish are providing, and will proceede accordingly.

Pessecouss, Mixano, and Witowash, 3. principall sachems of the Narigansett Indeans, and Awasequen, deputie for the Nyanticks, with a large traine of men, within a few days after came to Boston.

And to omitte all other circomstances and debats that past betweene them and the comissioners, they came to this conclusion following.

1. It was agreed betwixte the comissioners of the United Collonies, and the forementioned sagamores, and Niantick deputie, that the said Narigansets and Niantick sagamores should pay or cause to be payed at Boston, to the Massachusets comissioners, the full sume of 2000. fathome of good white wampame, or a third parte of black wampampeage, in 4. payments; namely, 500. fathome within 20. days, 500. fathome within 4. months, 500. fathome at or before next planting time, and 500. fathome within 2. years next after the date of these presents; which 2000. fathome the comissioners accepte for satisfaction of former charges expended.

2. The foresaid sagamors and deputie (on the behalfe of the Narigansett and Niantick Indeans) hereby promise and covenante that they upon demand and profe satisfie and restore unto Uncass, the Mohigan sagamore, all such captives, whether men, or women, or children, and all such canowes, as they or any of their men have taken, or as many of their owne canowes in the roome of them, full as good as they were, with full satisfaction for all such corne as they or any of theire men have spoyled or destroyed, of his or his mens, since last planting time; and the English comissioners hereby promise that Uncass shall doe the like.

3. Wheras ther are sundry differences and greevances bewixte Narigansett and Niantick Indeans, and Uncass and his men, (which in Uncass his absence cannot now be detirmined,) it is hearby agreed that Nariganset and Niantick sagamores either come them selves, or send their deputies to the next meeting of the comissioners for the collonies, either at New-Haven in Sept 1646. or sooner (upon conveniente warning, if the said comissioners doe meete sooner), fully instructed to declare and make

due proofe of their injuries, and to submite to the judgmente of the comissioners, in giving or receiving satisfaction; and the said comissioners (not doubting but Uncass will either come him selfe, or send his deputies, in like maner furnished) promising to give a full hearing to both parties with equall justice, without any partiall respects, according to their allegations and profs.

4. The said Narigansett and Niantick sagamors and deputies doe hearby promise and covenante to keep and maintaine a firme and perpetuall peace, both with all the English United Colonies and their successors, and with Uncass, the Monhegen sachem, and his men; with Ossamequine, Pumham, Sokanoke, Cutshamakin, Shoanan, Passaconaway, and all other Indean sagamors, and their companies, who are in freindship with or subjecte to any of the English; hearby ingaging them selves, that they will not at any time hearafter disturbe the peace of the cuntry, by any assaults, hostile attempts, invasions, or other injuries, to any of the Unnited Collonies, or their successors; or to the afforesaid Indeans; either in their persons, buildings, catle, or goods, directly or indirectly; nor will they confederate with any other against them; and if they know of any Indeans or others that conspire or intend hurt against the said English, or any Indeans subjecte to or in freindship with them, they will without delay acquainte and give notice therof to the English commissioners, or some of them.

Or if any questions or differences shall at any time hereafter arise or grow betwext them and Uncass, or any Endeans before mentioned, they will, according to former ingagments (which they hearby confirme and ratifie) first acquainte the English, and crave their judgments and advice therin; and will not attempte or begine any warr, or hostille invasion, till they have liberty and alowance from the comissioners of the United Collonies so to doe.

5. The said Narigansets and Niantick sagamores and deputies doe hearby promise that they will forthwith deliver and restore all such Indean fugitives, or captives which have at any time fled from any of the English, and are now living or abiding amongst them, or give due satisfaction for them to the comissioners for the Massachusets; and further, that they will (without more delays) pay, or cause to be payed, a yearly tribute, a month before harvest, every year after this. at Boston, to the English Colonies, for all such Pequents as live amongst them, according to the former treaty and agreemente, made at Hartford, 1638. namly, one fathome of white wampam for every Pequente man, and halfe a fathume for each Pequente youth, and one hand length for each mal-child. And if Weequashcooke refuse to pay this tribute for any Pequents with him,

the Narigansetts sagamores promise to assiste the English against him
And they further covenante that they will resigne and yeeld up the whole
Pequente cuntrie, and every parte of it, to the English collonies, as due to
them by conquest.

6.   The said Narigansett and Niantick sagamores and deputie doe
hereby promise and covenante that within 14. days they will bring and
deliver to the Massachusetts comissioners on the behalfe of the collonies,
foure of their children, viz. Pessecous his eldest sonn, the sone Tassa-
quanawite brother to Pessecouss, Awashawe his sone, and Ewangsos sone,
a Niantick, to be kepte (as hostages and pledges) by the English, till both
the forementioned 2000. fathome of wampam be payed at the times appoynted, and the differences betweexte themselves and Uncass be heard
and ordered, and till these artickles be under writen at Boston, by Jenemo
and Wipetock.   And further they hereby promise and covenante, that if
at any time hearafter any of the said children shall make escape, or be
conveyed away from the English, before the premisses be fully accomplished,
they will either bring back and deliver to the Massachusett comissioners
the same children, or, if they be not to be founde, such and so many other
children, to be chosen by the comissioners for the United Collonies, or
their assignes, and that within 20. days after demand, and in the mean
time, untill the said 4. children be delivered as hostages, the Narigansett
and Niantick sagamors and deputy doe, freely and of their owne accorde,
leave with the Massachusett comissioners, as pledges for presente securitie,
4. Indeans, namely, Witowash, Pumanise, Jawashoe, Waughwamino,
who allso freely consente, and offer them selves to stay as pledges, till the
said children be brought and delivered as abovesaid.

7.   The comissioners for the United Collonies doe hereby promise and
agree that, at the charge of the United Collonies, the 4. Indeans now left
as pledges shall be provided for, and that the 4. children to be brought and
delivered as hostages shall be kepte and maintained at the same charge;
that they will require Uncass and his men, with all other Indean sagamors
before named, to forbear all acts of hostilitie againste the Narigansetts
and Niantick Indeans for the future.   And further, all the promises being
duly observed and kept by the Narigansett and Niantick Indians and their
company, they will at the end of 2. years restore the said children delivered
as hostiages, and retaine a firme peace with the Narigansets and Nianticke
Indeans and their successours.

8.   It is fully agreed by and betwixte the said parties, that if any
hostile attempte be made while this treaty is in hand, or before notice of
this agreemente (to stay further preparations and directions) can be given,
such attempts and the consequencts therof shall on neither parte be ac-

counted a violation of this treaty, nor a breach of the peace hear made and concluded.

9. The Narigansets and Niantick sagamors and deputie hereby agree and covenante to and with the comissioners of the United Collonies, that henceforth they will neither give, grante, sell, or in any maner alienate, any parte of their countrie, nor any parcell of land therin, either to any of the English or others, without consente or allowance of the commissioners.

10. Lastly, they promise that, if any Pequente or other be found and discovered amongst them who hath in time of peace murdered any of the English, he or they shall be delivered to just punishmente.

In witness wherof the parties above named have interchaingablie subscribed these presents, the day and year above writen.

> JOHN WINTHROP, President.
>
> HERBERT PELHAM.
>
> THO: PRENCE.
>
> JOHN BROWNE.
>
> GEO: FENWICK.
>
> EDWA: HOPKINS.
>
> THEOPH: EATON.
>
> STEVEN GOODYEARE.
>
> PESSECOUSS his mark
>
> MEEKESANO his mark
>
> WITOWASH his mark
>
> AUMSEQUEN his mark the Niantick deputy.
>
> ABDAS his mark
>
> PUMMASH his mark
>
> CUTCHAMAKIN his mark

This treaty and agreemente betwixte the comissioners of the United Collonies and the sagamores and deputy of Narrigansets and Niantick Indeans was made and concluded, Benedicte Arnold being interpretour upon his oath; Sergante Callicate and an Indean, his man, being presente, and Josias and Cutshamakin, tow Indeans aquainted with the English language, assisting therin; who opened and cleared the whole treaty, and every article, to the sagamores and deputie there presente.

And thus was the warr at this time stayed and prevented.

Anno Dom: 1646.

ABOUT the midle of May, this year, came in 3. ships into
this harbor, in warrlike order; they were found to be men of
warr. The captains name was Crumwell, who had taken
sundrie prizes from the Spaniards in the West Indies. He had
a comission from the Earle of Warwick. He had abord his
vessels aboute 80. lustie men, (but very unruly,) who, after
they came ashore, did so distemper them selves with drinke
as they became like madd-men; and though some of them
were punished and imprisoned, yet could they hardly be re-
strained; yet in the ende they became more moderate and
orderly. They continued here aboute a month or 6. weeks,
and then went to the Massachusets; in which time they spente
and scattered a great deale of money among the people, and
yet more sine (I fear) then money, notwithstanding all the
care and watchfullnes that was used towards them, to prevente what might be.

In which time one sadd accidente fell out. A desperate
fellow of the company fell a quarling with some of his company.
His captine commanded him to be quiet and surcease his quar-
elling; but he would not, but reviled his captaine with base
language, and in the end halfe drew his rapier, and intended to
rune at his captien; but he closed with him, and wrasted his
rapier from him, and gave him a boxe on the earr; but he
would not give over, but still assaulted his captaine. Wherupon he tooke the same rapier as it was in the scaberd, and
gave him a blow with the hilts; but it light on his head, and
the smal end of the bar of the rapier hilts peirct his scull, and
he dyed a few days after. But the captaine was cleared by
a counsell of warr. This fellow was so desperate a quareller
as the captaine was faine many times to chaine him under
hatches from hurting his fellows, as the company did testifie;
and this was his end.

This Captaine Thomas Cromuell sett forth another vioage

to the Westindeas, from the Bay of the Massachusets, well maned and victuled; and was out 3. years, and tooke sundry prises, and returned rich unto the Massachusets, and ther dyed the same sommere, having gott a fall from his horse, in which fall he fell on his rapeir hilts, and so brused his body as he shortly after dyed therof, with some other distempers, which brought him into a feavor. Some observed that ther might be somthing of the hand of God herein; that as the forenamed man dyed of the blow he gave him with the rapeir hilts, so his owne death was occationed by a like means.

This year Mr. Edward Winslow went into England, upon this occation: some discontented persons under the govermente of the Massachusets sought to trouble their peace, and disturbe, if not innovate, their govermente, by laying many scandals upon them; and intended to prosecute against them in England, by petitioning and complaining to the Parlemente.[1] Allso Samuell Gorton and his company made complaints against them; so as they made choyse of Mr. Winslow to be their agente, to make their defence, and gave him comission and instructions for that end; in which he so carried him selfe as did well answer their ends, and cleared them from any blame or dishonour, to the shame of their adversaries. But by reason of the great alterations in the State, he was detained longer then was expected; and afterwards fell into other imployments their, so as he hath now bene absente this 4. years, which hath been much to the weakning of this govermente, without whose consente he tooke these imployments upon him.

Anno 1647. And Anno 1648.

[1] The allusion is to the endeavors of William Vassall, Samuel Maverick and Dr. John Child, to secure for members of the Church of England and the Church of Scotland equal civil and ecclesiastical rights in Massachusetts and Plymouth with the members of the Congregational churches.

APPENDIX

No. I.

[Passengers of the *Mayflower*.]

The names of those which came over first, in the year 1620. and were by the blessing of God the first beginers and (in a sort) the foundation of all the Plantations and Colonies in New-England; and their families.

8. Mr. John Carver; Kathrine, his wife; Desire Minter; and 2. man-servants, John Howland, Roger Wilder; William Latham, a boy; and a maid servant, and a child that was put to him, called Jasper More.

6. Mr. William Brewster; Mary, his wife; with 2. sons, whose names were Love and Wrasling; and a boy was put to him called Richard More; and another of his brothers. The rest of his children were left behind, and came over afterwards.

5. Mr. Edward Winslow; Elizabeth, his wife; and 2. men servants, caled Georg Sowle and Elias Story; also a litle girle was put to him, caled Ellen, the sister of Richard More.

2. William Bradford, and Dorothy, his wife; having but one child, a sone, left behind, who came afterward.

6. Mr. Isaack Allerton, and Mary, his wife; with 3. children, Bartholmew, Remember, and Mary; and a servant boy, John Hooke.

2. Mr. Samuell Fuller, and a servant, caled William Butten. His wife was behind, and a child, which came afterwards.

2. John Crakston, and his sone, John Crakston.

2.   Captin Myles Standish, and Rose, his wife.

4.   Mr. Christopher Martin, and his wife, and 2. servants, Salamon Prower and John Langemore.

5.   Mr. William Mullines, and his wife, and 2. children, Joseph and Priscila; and a servant, Robart Carter.

6.   Mr. William White, and Susana, his wife, and one sone, caled Resolved, and one borne a ship-bord, caled Peregriene; and 2. servants, named William Holbeck and Edward Thomson.

8.   Mr. Steven Hopkins, and Elizabeth, his wife, and 2. children, caled Giles, and Constanta, a doughter, both by a former wife; and 2. more by this wife, caled Damaris and Oceanus; the last was borne at sea; and 2. servants, called Edward Doty and Edward Litster.

1.   Mr. Richard Warren; but his wife and children were lefte behind, and came afterwards.

4.   John Billinton, and Elen, his wife; and 2. sones, John and Francis.

4.   Edward Tillie, and Ann, his wife; and 2. children that were their cossens, Henery Samson and Humillity Coper.

3.   John Tillie, and his wife; and Eelizabeth, their doughter.

2.   Francis Cooke, and his sone John. But his wife and other children came afterwards.

2.   Thomas Rogers, and Joseph, his sone. His other children came afterwards.

3.[1]   Thomas Tinker, and his wife, and a sone.

2.   John Rigdale, and Alice, his wife.

3.   James Chilton, and his wife, and Mary, their dougter. They had an other doughter, that was maried, came afterward.

3.   Edward Fuller, and his wife, and Samuell, their sonne.

3.   John Turner, and 2. sones. He had a doughter came some years after to Salem, wher she is now living.

[1] Written 2 by error in the manuscript.

3. Francis Eaton, and Sarah, his wife, and Samuell, their sone, a yong child.

10. Moyses Fletcher, John Goodman, Thomas Williams, Digerie Preist, Edmond Margeson, Peter Browne, Richard Britterige, Richard Clarke, Richard Gardenar, Gilbart Winslow.

1. John Alden was hired for a cooper, at South-Hampton, wher the ship victuled; and being a hopfull yong man, was much desired, but left to his owne liking to go or stay when he came here; but he stayed, and maryed here.

2. John Allerton and Thomas Enlish were both hired, the later to goe m^r of a shalop here, and the other was reputed as one of the company, but was to go back (being a seaman) for the help of others behind. But they both dyed here, before the shipe returned.

2. There were allso other 2. seamen hired to stay a year here in the country, William Trevore, and one Ely. But when their time was out, they both returned.

These, being aboute a hundred sowls,[1] came over in this first ship; and began this worke, which God of his goodnes hath hithertoo blesed; let his holy name have the praise.

And seeing it hath pleased him to give me to see 30. years compleated since these beginings; and that the great works of his providence are to be observed, I have thought it not unworthy my paines to take a veiw of the decreasings and increasings of these persons, and such changs as hath pased over them and theirs, in this thirty years. It may be of some use to such as come after; but, however, I shall rest in my owne benefite.

I will therfore take them in order as they lye.

Mr. Carver and his wife dyed the first year; he in the spring, she in the sommer; also, his man Roger and the litle

[1] The actual number arriving was 102.

boy Jasper dyed before either of them, of the commone infection.   Desire Minter returned to her freinds, and proved not very well, and dyed in England.   His servant boy Latham, after more then 20. years stay in the country, went into England, and from thence to the Bahamy Ilands in the West Indies, and ther, with some others, was starved for want of food.   His maid servant maried, and dyed a year or tow after, here in this place.

His servant, John Howland, maried the doughter of John Tillie, Elizabeth, and they are both now living, and have 10. children, now all living; and their eldest daughter hath 4. children.   And ther 2. daughter, 1. all living; and other of their children mariagable.   So 15. are come of them.

15.

Mr. Brewster lived to very old age; about 80. years he was when he dyed, having lived some 23. or 24. years here in the countrie; and though his wife dyed long before, yet she dyed aged.   His sone Wrastle dyed a yonge man unmaried; his sone Love lived till this year 1650. and dyed, and left 4. children, now living.   His doughters which came over after him are dead, but have left sundry children alive; his eldst sone is still liveing, and hath 9. or 10. children; one maried, who hath a child or 2.

4.

2.

Richard More his brother dyed the first winter; but he is maried, and hath 4. or 5. children, all living.

4.

Mr. Ed: Winslow his wife dyed the first winter; and he maried with the widow of Mr. White, and hath 2. children living by her marigable, besids sundry that are dead.

2.

One of his servants dyed, as also the litle girle, soone after the ships arivall.   But his man, Georg Sowle, is still living, and hath 8. children.

8.

William Bradford his wife dyed soone after their arivall; and he maried againe; and hath 4. children, 3. wherof are maried.

4.

Mr. Allerton his wife dyed with the first, and his servant, John Hooke. His sone Bartle is maried in England but I know not how many children he hath.   His doughter Remember is maried at Salem, and hath 3. or 4. children living.   And his doughter Mary is maried here, and hath 4.

8. children.   Him selfe maried againe with the doughter of Mr. Brewster, and hath one sone living by her, but she is long since dead.   And he is maried againe, and hath left this place long agoe.   So I account his increase to be 8. besids his sons in England.

Mr. Fuller his servant dyed at sea; and after his wife

2. came over, he had tow children by her, which are living and growne up to years; but he dyed some 15 years agoe.

John Crakston dyed in the first mortality; and about some 5. or 6. years after, his sone dyed; having lost him selfe in the wodes, his feet became frosen, which put him into a feavor, of which he dyed.

[1] Captain Standish his wife dyed in the first sicknes,

4. and he maried againe, and hath 4. sones liveing, and some are dead.

Mr. Martin, he and all his, dyed in the first infection not long after the arivall.

Mr. Molines, and his wife, his sone, and his servant, dyed the first winter.   Only his dougter Priscila survied,

15. and maried with John Alden, who are both living, and have 11. children.   And their eldest daughter is maried, and hath five children.

Mr. White and his 2. servants dyed soone after ther landing.   His wife maried with Mr. Winslow (as is be-

7. fore noted).   His 2. sons are maried, and Resolved hath 5. children, Perigrine tow, all living.   So their increase are 7.

Mr. Hopkins and his wife are now both dead, but they lived above 20. years in this place, and had one sone and

5. 4. doughters borne here.   Ther sone became a seaman, and

[1] "Who dyed 3. of Octob. 1655."   (Br.)

dyed at Barbadoes; one daughter dyed here, and 2. are maried; one of them hath 2. children; and one is yet to mary. So their increase which still survive are 5. But

4. his sone Giles is maried, and hath 4. children.

12. His doughter Constanta is also maried, and hath 12. children, all of them living, and one of them maried.

Mr. Richard Warren lived some 4. or 5. years, and had his wife come over to him, by whom he had 2. sons

4. before dyed; and one of them is maryed, and hath 2. children. So his increase is 4. But he had 5. doughters more came over with his wife, who are all maried, and living, and have many children.

John Billinton, after he had bene here 10. yers, was

8. executed for killing a man; and his eldest sone dyed before him; but his 2. sone is alive, and maried, and hath 8. children.

Edward Tillie and his wife both dyed soon after their

7. arivall; and the girle Humility, their cousen, was sent for into England, and dyed ther. But the youth Henery Samson is still liveing, and is maried, and hath 7. children.

John Tillie and his wife both dyed a litle after they came ashore; and their daughter Elizabeth maried with John Howland, and hath issue as is before noted.

Francis Cooke is still living, a very olde man, and hath seene his childrens children have children; after his wife

8. came over, (with other of his children,) he hath 3. still living by her, all maried, and have 5. children; so their encrease is 8. And his sone John, which came over with

4. him, is maried, and hath 4. chilldren living.

Thomas Rogers dyed in the first sicknes, but his sone

6. Joseph is still living, and is maried, and hath 6. children. The rest of Thomas Rogers [children] came over, and are maried, and have many children.

Thomas Tinker and his wife and sone all dyed in the first sicknes.

And so did John Rigdale and his wife.

James Chilton and his wife also dyed in the first infec-
10. tion. But their daughter Mary is still living, and hath 9.
children; and one daughter is maried, and hath a child;
so their increase is 10.

Edward Fuller and his wife dyed soon after they came
4. ashore; but their sone Samuell is living, and maried, and
hath 4. children or more.

John Turner and his 2. sones all dyed in the first
siknes. But he hath a daugter still living at Salem, well
maried, and approved of.

Francis Eaton his first wife dyed in the generall
siknes; and he maried againe, and his 2. wife dyed, and
he maried the 3. and had by her 3. children. One of
4. them is maried, and hath a child; the other are living,
but one of them is an ideote. He dyed about 16. years
agoe. His sone Samuell, who came over a sucking child,
1. is allso maried, and hath a child.

Moyses Fletcher, Thomas Williams, Digerie Preist,
John Goodman, Edmond Margeson, Richard Britteridge,
Richard Clarke. All these dyed sone after their arivall,
in the generall sicknes that befell. But Digerie Preist
had his wife and children sent hither afterwards, she
being Mr. Allertons sister. But the rest left no posteritie
here.

Richard Gardinar became a seaman, and died in England, or at sea.

Gilbert Winslow, after diverse years aboad here, returned into England, and dyed ther.

Peter Browne maried twise. By his first wife he had
6. 2. children, who are living, and both of them maried, and
the one of them hath 2. children; by his second wife he
had 2 more. He dyed about 16. years since.

Thomas English and John Allerton dyed in the generall
siknes.

John Alden maried with Priscila, Mr. Mollines his doughter, and had issue by her as is before related.

Edward Doty and Edward Litster, the servants of Mr. Hopkins. Litster, after he was at liberty, went to Virginia, and ther dyed. But Edward Doty by a second wife hath 7. children, and both he and they are living.

Of these 100. persons which came first over in this first ship together, the greater halfe dyed in the generall mortality; and most of them in 2. or three monthes time. And for those which survied, though some were ancient and past procreation, and others left the place and cuntrie, yet of those few remaining are sprunge up above 160. persons, in this 30. years, and are now living in this presente year, 1650. besids many of their children which are dead, and come not within this account.

And of the old stock (of one and other) ther are yet living this present year, 1650. nere 30. persons. Let the Lord have the praise, who is the High Preserver of men.

[1] Twelfe persons liveing of the old stock this present yeare, 1679.

Two persons liveing that came over in the first shipe 1620, this present yeare, 1690. Resolved White and Mary Chusman [Cushman], the daughter of Mr. Allerton.

And John Cooke, the son of Frances Cooke, that came in the first ship, is still liveing this present yeare, 1694; and Mary Cushman is still living, this present year, 1698.

[1] The following memoranda are in a later hand.

No. II.

[Commission for Regulating Plantations.][1]

Charles by the grace of God king of England, Scotland, France, and Ireland, Defender of the Faith, etc.

To the most Reve[d] father in Christ, our wellbeloved and faithfull counsellour, William, by devine providence Archbishop of Counterbery, of all England Primate and Metropolitan; Thomas Lord Coventry, Keeper of our Great Seale of England; the most Reverente father in Christ our wellbeloved and most faithful Counselour, Richard, by devine providence Archbishop of Yorke, Primate and Metropolitan; our wellbeloved and most faithfull coussens and Counselours, Richard, Earle of Portland, our High Treasurer of England; Henery, Earle of Manchester, Keeper of our Privie Seale; Thomas, Earle of Arundalle and Surry, Earle Marshall of England; Edward, Earle of Dorsett, Chamberline of our most dear consorte, the Queene; and our beloved and faithfull Counselours, Francis Lord Cottington, Counseler, and Undertreasurour of our Eschequour; Sr: Thomas Edmonds, knight, Treasourer of our houshould; Sr: Henery Vane, Knight, controuler of the same houshould; Sr: John Cooke, Knight, one of our Privie Secretaries; and Francis Windebanck, Knight, another of our Privie Secretaries,

Wheras very many of our subjects, and of our late fathers of beloved memory, our sovereigne lord James, late king of England, by means of licence royall, not only with desire of inlarging the teritories of our empire, but cheefly out of a pious

---

[1] See page 307, note 3. This document was written on the reverse of folio 201 *et seqq.* of the original manuscript, and for the sake of convenience is transferred to this place.

and religious affection, and desire of propagating the gospell
of our Lord Jesus Christ, with great industrie and expences
have caused to be planted large Collonies of the English nation,
in diverse parts of the world alltogether unmanured, and voyd
of inhabitants, or occupied of the barbarous people that have
no knowledg of divine worship.   We being willing to provid a
remedy for the tranquillity and quietnes of those people, and
being very confidente of your faith and wisdom, justice and
providente circomspection, have constituted you the aforesaid
Archbishop of Counterburie, Lord Keeper of the Great Seale
of England, the Archbishop of Yorke, etc. and any 5. or more,
of you, our Comissioners; and to you, and any 5. or more of
you, we doe give and commite power for the govermente and
saftie of the said collonies, drawen, or which, out of the English
nation into those parts hereafter, shall be drawne, to make
lawes, constitutions, and ordinances, pertaining ether to the
publick state of these collonies, or the private profite of them;
and concerning the lands, goods, debts, and succession in those
parts, and how they shall demaine them selves, towards foraigne
princes, and their people, or how they shall bear them selves
towards us, and our subjects, as well in any foraine parts
whatsoever, or on the seas in those parts, or in their returne
sayling home; or which may pertaine to the clergie govermente, or to the cure of soules, among the people ther living,
and exercising trad in those parts; by designing out congruente
porcions arising in tithes, oblations, and other things ther,
according to your sound discretions, in politicall and civill
causes; and by haveing the advise of 2. or 3. bishops, for the
setling, making, and ordering of the bussines, for the de-
signeing of necessary ecclesiasticall, and clargie porcions, which
you shall cause to be called, and taken to you.   And to make
provission against the violation of those laws, constitutions,
and ordinances, by imposing penealties and mulcts, imprisonmente if ther be cause, and that the quality of the
offence doe require it, by deprivation of member, or life, to be

inflicted. With power allso (our assente being had) to remove, and displace the governours or rulers of those collonies, for causes which to you shall seeme lawfull, and others in their stead to constitute; and require an accounte of their rule and govermente, and whom you shall finde culpable, either by deprivation from their place, or by imposition of a mulcte upon the goods of them in those parts to be levied, or banishmente from those provinces in which they have been gove or otherwise to cashier according to the quantity of the offence. And to constitute judges, and magistrats politicall and civill, for civill causes and under the power and forme, which to you 5. or more of you shall seeme expediente. And judges and magistrats and dignities, to causes Ecclesiasticall, and under the power and forme which to you 5. or more of you, with the bishops vicegerents (provided by the Archbishop of Counterbure for the time being), shall seeme expediente; and to ordaine courts, pretoriane and tribunall, as well ecclesiasticall, as civill, of judgmentes; to detirmine of the formes and maner of procceedings in the same; and of appealing from them in matters and causes as well criminall, as civill, personall, reale, and mixte, and to their seats of justice, what may be equall and well ordered, and what crimes, faults, or exessess, of contracts or injuries ought to belonge to the Ecclesiasticall courte, and what to the civill courte, and seate of justice.

Provided never the less, that the laws, ordinances, and constitutions of this kinde, shall not be put in execution, before our assent be had therunto in writing under our signet, signed at least, and this assente being had, and the same publikly proclaimed in the provinces in which they are to be executed, we will and command that those lawes, ordinances, and constitutions more fully to obtaine strength and be observed shall be inviolably of all men whom they shall concerne.

Notwithstanding it shall be for you, or any 5. or more of you, (as is afforsaid,) allthough those lawes, constitutions, and ordinances shalbe proclaimed with our royall assente, to

chainge, revocke, and abrogate them, and other new ones, in
forme afforsaid, from time to time frame and make as afforesaid; and to new evills arissing, or new dangers, to apply new
remedyes as is fitting, so often as to you it shall seeme expediente. Furthermore you shall understand that we have
constituted you, and every 5. or more of you, the afforesaid
Archbishop of Counterburie, Thomas Lord Coventrie, Keeper
of the Great Seale of England, Richard, Bishop of Yorke,
Richard, Earle of Portland, Henery, Earle of Manchester,
Thomas, Earle of Arundale and Surry, Edward, Earell of
Dorsett, Francis Lord Cottinton, Sr Thomas Edwards [Ed-
monds], knighte, Sr Henry Vane, knight, Sr Francis Winde-
banke, knight, our comissioners to hear, and determine, according to your sound discretions, all maner of complaints
either against those collonies, or their rulers, or govenours,
at the instance of the parties greeved, or at their accusation
brought concerning injuries from hence, or from thence, betweene them, and their members to be moved, and to call
the parties before you; and to the parties or to their procura-
tors, from hence, or from thence being heard the full comple-
mente of justice to be exhibted. Giving unto you, or any 5.
or more of you power, that if you shall find any of the collonies
afforesaid, or any of the cheefe rulers upon the jurisdictions of
others by unjust possession, or usurpation, or one against
another making greevance, or in rebelion against us, or with-
drawing from our alegance, or our comandments, not obeying,
consultation first with us in that case had, to cause those
colonies, or the rulers of them, for the causes afforesaid, or for
other just causes, either to returne to England, or to comand
them to other places designed, even as according to your sounde
discretions it shall seeme to stand with equitie, and justice,
or necessitie. Moreover, we doe give unto you, and any 5.
or more of you, power and spetiall command over all the
charters, leters patents, and rescripts royall, of the regions,
provinces, ilands, or lands in foraigne parts, granted for

raising colonies, to cause them to be brought before you, and the same being received, if any thing surrepticiously or unduly have been obtained, or that by the same priviledges, liberties, and prerogatives hurtfull to us, or to our crowne, or to foraigne princes, have been prejudicially suffered, or granted; the same being better made knowne unto you 5. or more of you, to command them according to the laws and customs of England to be revoked, and to doe such other things, which to the profite and safgard of the afforesaid collonies, and of our subjects residente in the same, shall be necessary. And therfore we doe command you that aboute the premisses at days and times, which for these things you shall make provission, that you be diligente in attendance, as it becometh you; giving in precepte also, and firmly injoyning, we doe give command to all and singuler cheefe rulers of provinces into which the colonies afforesaid have been drawne, or shall be drawne, and concerning the colonies themselves, and concerning others, that have been interest therein, that they give atendance upon you, and be observante and obediente unto your warrants in those affaires, as often as, and even as in our name they shall be required, at their perill. In testimoney wherof, we have caused these our letters to be made pattente. Wittnes our selfe at Westminster the 28. day of Aprill, in the tenth year of our Raigne.

By write from the privie seale,

WILLIES.

Anno Dom: 1634.

INDEX

Abbot, George, Archbishop of Canterbury, 51, 51 n.

Abdas, 403.

Abigail, ship, 372 n.

Adams, C. F., *Three Episodes of Massachusetts History*, 110 n.

Admiralty, High Court of, 156 n.

Adventurers, partners of the Pilgrims, 10; offer to assist the Pilgrims, 65; agreements and articles between the Pilgrims and, 65–78, 158; disagreement of, with the Pilgrims, 77, 80–82; arrangements made by, for the voyage, 78; correspondence between the Pilgrims and, 81–82, 133–134, 149–150, 154–155, 167–169, 189–190, 202–203; the Pilgrims agree to the conditions of, 123; colonists make a settlement with, 129 n.; dissensions among, 131, 132–134, 166–168; oppose sending to America the Leyden company of Pilgrims, 132; buy out Weston, 132–133; failure of, to assist the colonists, 137, 149; answer to the letter of, 156 n.; Pilgrims' answers to the complaints of, 170–172; Leyden company of Pilgrims deserted by, 173, 174; dissolution of, 201, 203; colonists deserted by, 201; reasons of, for deserting the colonists, 201; conditions laid down by, for again assisting the colonists, 202; *see also* Sherley, Andrews, Beauchamp, Hatherley.

Ainsworth, Rev. Henry, 38 n.; 60 n.

Alden, John, 98 n., 409, 411, 414; undertakes the debt of the colony, 227–229, 227 n.; imprisonment, 306; agreement of, with Sherley, 359–362; leaves Plymouth, 363; settles with Sherley, 371.

Alden, Robert, 215 n.

Allerton, Bartholomew, 253 n., 407, 411.

Allerton, Isaac, 204, 407, 410; letter of, 71, 71 n.; is appointed assistant to the governor, 116; answer of, to the adventurers, 156 n.; is sent to England to arrange with the adventurers, 212–213, 223; makes a new agreement with the adventurers, 213–216; undertakes the debt of the colony, 227–229, 227 n.; mission of, respecting the debt of the colony, 228; authorizes agents in London, 231–232; conduct of, as agent, 233–234; double-dealing of, 243, 251–252, 253–254, 255–257–258, 263, 264–270, 273–280; is sent to England as agent for the colonists, 244, 258; Sherley's commendation of, 249–250; designs of, 250; brings Morton over from England, 250-251; marriage, 253, 253 n.; discharge of, 270, 272; commission of, 273, 274; accounts of, 280–281, 282, 294, 296, 297, 298, 303; bad conduct of, 283–284; appropriates funds belonging to the colonists, 290–291; fails to fulfil his obligations, 292; suit against, 292–293.

Allerton, John, 9, 409.

Allerton, Mary, 253 n., 407, 411.

Allerton, Remember, 253 n., 407, 411.

Alltham, Emanuel, 215 n.

America, reasons for and against, as a home for the Pilgrims, 46–49.

American Historical Review, 18, 156 n., 164 n., 169 n.

Ames, Dr. Azel, *The May-Flower and her Log*, 19 n., 215 n.

Amsterdam, 77; the Pilgrims reach, 7; religious refugees settle at, 32; Pilgrims at, 38.

Anabaptism, 365.

Andrews, Richard, 215 n., 233, 273; endorses the note of the colonists, 129 n.; undertakes the debt of the colony, 227–229, 227 n., 230; becomes a partner with the colonists, 245, 246, 254; double-dealings of, 279–280; letter of attorney of, 317; refuses to settle bills, 329; complaints of, 330,

420

241-243; arrival of members from Leyden in, 246-247, 248; division of, into counties, 249 n.; enters into business with Ashley, 256-257; fishing industry undertaken by, 258; instructions of, to Allerton, 258-259; executions in, 270, 344-346; expansion of, 294, 353, 363, 390; exceptions of, to Allerton's accounts, 295; establishes a plantation on Connecticut River, 301-302; measures adopted by, concerning Hocking's murder, 308-310; trading-house of, at Penobscot, 318-320; efforts of, against the French, 320-321; agreement with Massachusetts, concerning the Connecticut River Colony, 326-327; complaints of, against Sherley, 343-344; growing prosperity of, 347; boundary dispute between Massachusetts and, 349-354; longevity of the men in, 380, 380 n.; enters into the New England Confederation, 382-388; complaints against, 405; business relations, see Adventurers, also Sherley, Andrews, Beauchamp, Hatherley; *Records of*, 79 n., 98 n., 217 n., 382 n., 389 n., 398 n.

Pocahontas, 59 n.
Pocock, John, 214, 215 n.
Point Care, 95.
Pokanoket Indians, 112, 113.
Polyander, Johannes, 39 n., 42 n., 43.
Pond Village, 99.
Portland, Earl of, 415, 416, 418.
Portsmouth, 164 n., 241 n.
Port Royal, destruction of, 50 n.
Pory, John, letter of, 140; official positions of, 140 n.
Poynton, Daniel, 215 n.
Prence, Thomas, 98 n.; governor of the colony, 14, 303-313, 344-349; undertakes the debt of the colony, 227-229, 227 n.; biographical sketch of, 303 n.; agreement of, with Sherley, 359-362; settles with Sherley, 371; signs the Indian treaty, 403.
Priest, Degory, 409, 413; occupation in Leyden, 39 n.
Prince, Rev. Thomas, 15, 16, 58 n., 68 n., 71 n., 74 n.; *Chronological History of New England*, 16.
Prince Society, 112 n.; *Gorges*, 158 n.

Privy Council, order of, concerning New England, 289-290.
Providence Plantations, 249 n.
Prower, Solomon, 408.
Pummunish, 394, 401, 402, 403.
Purchas, Samuel, *Pilgrimes*, 113, 113 n.
Puritans, religious belief of, 3; name of, applied to the non-conformists, 27.
Pynchon, William, 320; letter of, 324; official positions, 324 n.

Quarles, William, 215 n.

Rasières, Isaac de, Plymouth described by, 138 n.; letters of, 223-225, 234 n.
Rassdall, Mr., 237.
Razilly, Chevalier de, 318 n.
Rehoboth, 353.
Reinholds, captain of the *Speedwell*, 75, 75 n.
Reinor, John, 335, 335 n., 362, 367 n.
Relation or Journal of the Beginning and Proceedings of the English Plantation settled at Plymouth in New England, theories concerning, 11-13; editions,14.
Revell, John, 215 n.
Reynolds, Mr., 135.
Rhode Island, controversy between Massachusetts and, 249 n.; religion in, 365-367.
Rigdale, Alice, 408, 413.
Rigdale, John, 408, 413.
Riggs, Sergeant, 341.
Robinson, John, 32, 60, 72, 154 n., 167 n. 180; reaches Amsterdam, 7; contribution to "Mourt's *Relation*", 11; arrives in Holland, 38; pastor of the church in Leyden, 40; death, 41 n., 43, 208-209; religious views of, 42 n.; disputes of, with Polyander, 43; Sandys's letter to, 52-53; the Seven Articles signed by, 53, 53 n.; answer of, to Sandys's letter, 54-55; letter of, to Wolstenholme, 56-57; conference of, with Weston, 65; letter of, concerning the preparations for removal, 68-70; letters of, to the Pilgrims, 83-86; Cushman's accusation against, 90-91; farewell discourse of, concerning new light, 117 n.; letter of, concerning the treatment of the Indians, 172-173; conditions upon which the adventurers will assist, 202; memorial tablet to, 209 n.